GEORG SIMMEL AND GER

G000124486

The significance of the German philoso
Georg Simmel (1858–1918), is only now bei
tual historians. Through penetrating readi
taken as a series of reflections on the es
modern civilisation, Efraim Podoksik places his ideas within the
context of intellectual life in Germany, and especially Berlin, under
the Kaiserreich. Modernity, characterised by the growing differentiation and fragmentation of culture and society, was a fundamental
issue during Simmel's life, underpinning central intellectual debates
in Imperial Germany. Simmel's thought is depicted here as an
attempt at transforming the complexity of these debates into a coherent worldview that can serve as an effective guide to understanding
their main parameters. Paying particular attention to the genealogy
and usage of the concepts of *Bildung*, culture and civilisation in
Germany, this study offers contextual analyses of Simmel's philosophies of culture, society, art, religion and the feminine, as well as his
interpretations of Dante, Kant, Nietzsche, Schopenhauer, Goethe
and Rembrandt.

EFRAIM PODOKSIK is Associate Professor of Political Science at the
Hebrew University of Jerusalem where he specialises in modern intel-
lectual history, focusing on German and British thinkers. He is the
author of *In Defence of Modernity: Vision and Philosophy in Michael
Oakeshott* (2003) and editor of *Doing Humanities in Nineteenth-Century
Germany* (2019) and *The Cambridge Companion to Oakeshott* (2012).
His articles have appeared in numerous journals, including the *Journal
of the History of Ideas, Modern Intellectual History* and *New German
Critique.*

IDEAS IN CONTEXT

Edited by DAVID ARMITAGE, RICHARD BOURKE and JENNIFER PITTS

The books in this series will discuss the emergence of intellectual traditions and of related new disciplines. The procedures, aims and vocabularies that were generated will be set in the context of the alternatives available within the contemporary frameworks of ideas and institutions. Through detailed studies of the evolution of such traditions, and their modification by different audiences, it is hoped that a new picture will form of the development of ideas in their concrete contexts. By this means, artificial distinctions between the history of philosophy, of the various sciences, of society and politics, and of literature may be seen to dissolve.

The series is published with the support of the Exxon Foundation.

A full list of titles in the series can be found at: www.cambridge.org/IdeasContext

GEORG SIMMEL AND GERMAN CULTURE

Unity, Variety and Modern Discontents

EFRAIM PODOKSIK

Hebrew University of Jerusalem

CAMBRIDGE
UNIVERSITY PRESS

Shaftesbury Road, Cambridge CB2 8EA, United Kingdom

One Liberty Plaza, 20th Floor, New York, NY 10006, USA

477 Williamstown Road, Port Melbourne, VIC 3207, Australia

314–321, 3rd Floor, Plot 3, Splendor Forum, Jasola District Centre, New Delhi – 110025, India

103 Penang Road, #05–06/07, Visioncrest Commercial, Singapore 238467

Cambridge University Press is part of Cambridge University Press & Assessment, a department of the University of Cambridge.

We share the University's mission to contribute to society through the pursuit of education, learning and research at the highest international levels of excellence.

www.cambridge.org
Information on this title: www.cambridge.org/9781108964975

DOI: 10.1017/9781108990783

First published 2021
First paperback edition 2023

A catalogue record for this publication is available from the British Library

Library of Congress Cataloging-in-Publication data
NAMES: Podoksik, Efraim, author.
TITLE: Georg Simmel and German culture : unity, variety and modern discontents / Efraim Podoksik.
DESCRIPTION: Cambridge ; New York, NY : Cambridge University Press, 2021. | Series: Ideas in context | Includes bibliographical references and index.
IDENTIFIERS: LCCN 2021000584 (print) | LCCN 2021000585 (ebook) | ISBN 9781108845748 (hardback) | ISBN 9781108964975 (paperback) | ISBN 9781108990783 (ebook)
SUBJECTS: LCSH: Simmel, Georg, 1858–1918. | Sociologists – Germany – Biography. | Sociology – Philosophy – History. | Germany – Civilization. | Germany – Intellectual life – 19th century.
CLASSIFICATION: LCC HM479.S55 P63 2021 (print) | LCC HM479.S55 (ebook) | DDC 301.092 [B]–dc23
LC record available at https://lccn.loc.gov/2021000584
LC ebook record available at https://lccn.loc.gov/2021000585

ISBN   978-1-108-84574-8   Hardback
ISBN   978-1-108-96497-5   Paperback

Contents

Acknowledgements	*page* vi
Note on Translations and References	viii
	Introduction	1
1	*Bildung, Kultur,* Crisis	16
2	Unity in Variety	90
3	Unity versus Variety	145
4	Unity above Variety	214
	Conclusion	293
Bibliography	296
Index	329

Acknowledgements

It took many years for my interest in and subsequent research into Georg Simmel and his thoughts to crystallise into the argument which I now present to the reader. I owe special gratitude to the institutions whose support allowed me to complete this work: the Alexander von Humboldt Foundation, the German Academic Exchange Service (DAAD), the German-Israeli Foundation, the Center for Austrian Studies (European Forum at the Hebrew University) and the Israel Science Foundation (grant no. 220/05).

I also thank my academic hosts in Germany and Austria – Anne Eusterschulte, Hajo Funke, Martin Geyer, Eckhart Hellmuth, Hans Joas, Martin Kusch and Erhard Stölting – whose kind support was essential for the success of this enterprise.

Over the course of all these years I was very lucky to meet and communicate with many people – friends and colleagues – with whom I discussed the progress of my research and from whose advice, criticism and assistance I greatly benefited. I would like to mention in particular Heinrich Adolf, Matthieu Amat, Christian Dambӧck, Gregor Fitzi, Uta Gerhardt, Willfried Geßner, Friedrich Wilhelm Graf, Steven Grosby, Austin Harrington, Gerald Hartung, Horst Jürgen Helle, Joseph Imorde, Matthew Jefferies, Melissa Lane, Donald Levine, Klaus Lichtblau, Georg Lohmann, Iain McDaniel, Ingo Meyer, Andrea Mina, Yoel Mitrani, Douglas Moggach, Amos Morris-Reich, Guy Oakes, João Proença, Otthein Rammstedt, Yoel Regev, Olivier Remaud, Melanie Riedel, Harry Ritter, Ritchie Robertson, Cécile Rol, Daniel Rosenberg, Martin Ruehl, Daniel Schwartz, Johannes Steizinger and Hotam Yotam.

I am also grateful to Daniel Lehmann and Sharon Oranski for polishing the manuscript's language. Finally, my thoughts are always with my friend Mustafa Özmen, a person of great fortitude and humanity, who remembers the time when studying Simmel was just an idea in my mind.

***

Parts of chapter two are revised versions of my two previously published articles: 'Society as the Mode of Redemption: The Individual in Georg Simmel's Early Sociological Writings', *Intellectual History Review* 25(4), 2015, pp. 413–431 (the author thanks the journal's editors for the permission), and 'Neo-Kantianism and Georg Simmel's Interpretation of Kant', *Modern Intellectual History* 13(3), 2016, pp. 597–622 (reprinted with the permission of Cambridge University Press).

Note on Translations and References

All of Simmel's writings have been published in *Georg Simmel Gesamtausgabe*, twenty-four volumes, edited by O. Rammstedt (Frankfurt am Main: Suhrkamp, 1989–2015), hereafter cited as GSG. In the present book, all citations have been rendered in English. Where available, I used an existing English translation. In these cases, the reference is to the text in English, while the corresponding location in GSG is given in square brackets. Where no English translation exists, or where I disagreed with the existing translation, the translation is my own, and the reference is directly to GSG. To prevent confusion, all references to GSG are made according to the formula: GSG, volume number, page numbers, without using 'ibid'.

When other German sources are rendered in accordance with an existing English translation, the reference is to that translation. When the reference is directly to the German text, the translation is my own.

I wish to express my gratitude to Sharon Oranski and Einat Ohana for editing and polishing my translations.

Introduction

Why Simmel?

One hundred years have passed since the death of Georg Simmel (1858–1918), one of the most fascinating minds of the Second German Empire (*Kaiserreich*). Simmel's intellectual brilliance and productivity have never been in doubt, and they are themselves sufficient grounds for writing about him. Indeed, there is no shortage of studies that grapple with various aspects of his thought. Simmel scholarship has recently received fresh impetus with the collection of all his available texts in the monumental twenty-four-volume edition of the *Gesamtausgabe* coordinated and edited by Otthein Rammstedt.

Despite this growing interest, intellectual historians have been slow in appreciating Simmel's significance. The most important studies about him and his work so far were produced by scholars whose primary focus lies in other disciplines, such as social and cultural sciences and philosophy. Many of these works have made important contributions to our knowledge of the historical Simmel and his various contexts. However, the underlying motif and focus of the greater part of them are the question of Simmel's significance for the present day. He is mainly read and studied because it is believed, and often with good reason, that his insights are very helpful for solving our own metaphysical, social and cultural problems. The question of what Simmel meant for his own time, and his relation to it, draws considerably less attention.

I believe this state of affairs is partly the consequence of the stereotypical perception of Simmel as a maverick within his own intellectual setting. This perception is often presented in a favourable light. As a recent study suggests, 'certain figures in the history of thought seem to derive their significance from their marginality'.[1] Yet when an object of study is

---

[1] Elizabeth S. Goodstein, *Georg Simmel and the Disciplinary Imaginary* (Stanford: Stanford University Press, 2017), p. 1.

described in this manner, justification of interest in him or her often, even if not always, acquires an unhistorical air. For if someone's ideas were truly 'marginal', then studying them is not likely to shed much light on the *Zeitgeist* of the epoch in which that person lived. Studying an allegedly marginal thinker often serves a double purpose: to reproach the past for its negligence and to employ that thinker's thoughts in the service of the present and future.

This book, however, presents a very different perspective. It presumes that Simmel, far from being a maverick, was a central intellectual figure for the historical moment in which he lived, and it is precisely this status that makes him a worthy object of historical attention. For studying a major thinker historically helps us not only to understand the train of his thought but also – and even more importantly – to partake of the spiritual atmosphere of the age and culture in which he operated, from which he absorbed his key questions and to which he contributed. With specific regard to Simmel, two things are important. First, he was a mind who reflected and synthesised in a profound and encompassing manner the major intellectual currents of German high culture in the nineteenth and early twentieth centuries. Second, this reflection was not mere mirroring. Rather, Simmel creatively produced out of a very complex and sometimes chaotic tradition a highly idiosyncratic and at the same time elegant and relatively accessible synthesis that displayed a style of thinking and set of questions which translated the totality of this tradition perhaps better than anything produced by his contemporaries.

This assessment of Simmel is based on two arguments. One is brief and the other is very long. The brief argument appeals to a number of well-known biographical facts from which one unfortunately does not always draw correct inferences. These facts relate to Simmel's cultural role during his lifetime. Educated at the University of Berlin, Simmel quickly became part of the city's cultural elite, socialised on different occasions with almost every person of talent and significance, and even rose to the position of cultural authority, as in the case of the reception of Stefan George's early work. As for the professional realm, he became a highly popular lecturer of philosophy at his alma mater. It is true that for a long time Simmel failed to earn full professional recognition from the academic establishment, as only very late in life – in 1914 – was he awarded a full professorship and this at the University of Strasbourg which was relatively unimportant at that time. This and the many other obstacles he faced in his career are indeed important facts when examining his biography or the social dynamics within the German academia of his time. However, with regard to the historical significance and impact of his ideas, the more important fact by far is this: For almost thirty years he taught numerous and very well attended classes in philosophy at one of the most prestigious German universities[2] and this had implications that spread well beyond the walls of that specific university. It was common at that time for German students to change their home university from time to time in order to attend courses by different teachers and in different settings. Given the prestige of the discipline of philosophy and of the University of Berlin, as well as the high enrolment numbers in Simmel's classes, it is safe to assume that many of the most brilliant and philosophically inclined young minds of Germany at that time happened to attend Simmel's lectures at one point or another. Indeed, some of them gave accounts of their experience of being taught by Simmel.

Another fact should be added here: From the early 1900s onwards, Simmel's books and essays quickly grew in popularity and were widely read by the educated public. Moreover, in the last decade of his life, Simmel all but reached the status of spiritual guru for a specific segment of young students. As Kurt Gassen recalled:

> For us, Simmel's students in Berlin, it was . . . an irreplaceable loss when in spring 1914 he left the city after being active at the University of Berlin for almost 30 years in order to move to Strasbourg . . . Rarely perhaps has such a farewell ceremony been organised for a university teacher which was so deeply felt inside as for Simmel on that spring day when he spoke to us for the last time on a rostrum decorated with roses. At that moment, each of us became harrowingly aware that this was not merely a change of lecturer and another would now talk about the same factually endorsed problems. Rather, something ended for us for which there was no substitute and we now had to try and see whether we were capable of continuing to think and work in his spirit without his presence. Only this explains the ardent suspense and enthusiasm with which we anticipated and took possession of Simmel's every new book.[3]

It is no accident that in 1920, when Heinrich Rickert launched his critique against the new and fashionable trend of life-philosophy, he mentioned Simmel together with Wilhelm Dilthey and Friedrich Nietzsche as one of its leading proponents.[4]

---

[2] Simmel's first lecture on the ethical teaching of Kant was delivered in the summer semester of 1885. See Kurt Gassen and Michael Landmann (eds.), *Buch des Dankes an Georg Simmel* (Berlin: Duncker & Humblot, 1958), p. 345.

[3] Kurt Gassen, 'Erinnerungen an Simmel', in Gassen and Landmann (eds.), *Buch des Dankes*, p. 302.

[4] Cf. Heinrich Rickert, *Die Philosophie des Lebens: Darstellung und Kritik der philosophischen Modeströmungen unserer Zeit* (Tübingen: J. C. B. Mohr, 1920), p. 28.

That was the brief argument on behalf of my claim. The long one is embedded in my book as a whole. For the book's aim is indeed to reveal the extent to which Simmel's thought was integrated within the intellectual discourses of his time, occasionally pushing them to their limits and taking them to hitherto unexplored territories. My central task is therefore to identify those cultural and discursive patterns of the German intellectual tradition that were absorbed and transformed by Simmel in the course of his constructive dialogue with his contemporaries. Even if this study is not about Simmel's reception but rather about Simmel itself and, therefore, does not touch on the long-term impact of his ideas, the knowledgeable and inquiring reader will nonetheless easily spot those moments that testify to Simmel's legacy for the leading minds of the following generations.

This impact could have been even broader and more explicit but for a historical contingency: the German intellectual elite's loss of confidence in its own tradition following Germany's defeat in 1918, as many of the major figures broke with the cultural spirit of the *Kaiserreich* and succumbed to shallow radical fashions of different stripes. It is partly because of this loss of nerve by the intellectual mainstream that Simmel, who in many respects embodied the cultural yearnings of the *Kaiserreich* age, later began to be anachronistically treated as a maverick. One can only wonder what his intellectual legacy would have been had the country emerged victorious from the war. The defeat – and subsequent rise of National Socialism – had a distorting effect on our perception of the intellectual world of the Wilhelmine period. One of the tasks of the intellectual historian is, however, to treat the age under investigation as open-ended and to ignore what one knows about the future still to come.

This approach by no means dismisses the significance of reading Simmel through the lens of present concerns. However, it suggests that before doing this, one would be well-advised to take a step back and look carefully into the figure of the historical Simmel in the context of the German social and philosophical thought of his time. A contextually informed under-standing of Simmel as a thinker is indeed a prerequisite for answering the question of what in his thought remains relevant for us today.

Why Simmel as a German?

Exploring the German intellectual context will enable us to understand Simmel better. However, the opposite is also true. If I am correct in my suggestion that Simmel was among the most important thinkers of his time, then understanding his thought properly is crucial for a better understanding of the 'German mind' in general. I see Simmel as a thinker who performed the synthetic work of organising the various and disparate currents and ideas before him in a more or less coherent structure of mutually related conceptual distinctions and philosophical problems. He filtered the incessant stream of chaotic cultural and intellectual activity into patterns that can be outlined, schematised and analysed. He took the most fundamental concerns of the German educated classes of his time (or at least of their Protestant segment), their ways of perceiving the spiritual and social reality among and around them, and elevated them to a very sophisticated degree of reflection.

Simmel was exceptionally suited to this role because he was an academic philosopher who also spoke and appealed to a broader audience. In Germany, to be a philosopher had for a long time entailed much more than just being a philosopher. Philosophy in modern Germany was a major cultural marker. Philosophy and its emerging canon formed the core of national cultural identity. Philosophical literacy came to be considered a necessary component of general cultivation, and philosophical habits of mind penetrated other fields of culture, such as poetic expression.

It is true that by the end of the nineteenth century widespread concern had grown that the ongoing professionalisation of the academic world threatened to narrow the horizons of philosophy, potentially leading to it losing in significance for broad cultivation. Nevertheless, despite these worries, respect for philosophy still remained high and its presence in cultural pursuits of all kinds still visible. Yet this was a contingent situation. Philosophy was not necessarily born to play such a role. Moreover, it was quite unlikely for it to acquire such stature, given the degree of mental refinement and complexity required for good philosophical thinking. Indeed, if one looks at other contemporary societies, one finds that the role of principal cultural marker was played by cultural fields of other kinds. In France and Russia, for example, literature was by far more important; Italy assigned prominence to theatre and opera, while in Britain classical antiquity and moral philosophy seemed to be the primary path to cultivation. In Germany, however, philosophy and metaphysics emerged, together with music, as the main criteria of sophisticated cultivation. As a result, German general culture of the time was imbued with allusions to philosophers, their famous texts and their argumentation, which was emulated, if not in content, then at least in its formal patterns, such as dialectics – hence the propensity of German cultural discourse of the time to abstractness or, more precisely, to the constant combination of the immediately given and the metaphysical. For when the philosophical frame of mind governs every cultural sphere, from the minutest interaction to the highest achievements of artistic life, there can be no distance between everyday experience and the most refined philosophical abstraction. When Johann Gottlieb Fichte described the German language as peculiarly suitable for the pursuit of philosophy, due to the fact that its abstractions are derived from and based on the concreteness of the linguistic stems signifying empirical images in everyday language, he was simply expressing in the form of a theoretical argument what was intuitively familiar to German cultural self-understanding.[5]

In the early twentieth century, it was Simmel who most faithfully maintained philosophy's role as a cultural marker. In a situation in which a gap had begun to emerge between philosophy and culture in general, he was the custodian of the long-established alliance between the two. Simmel was, of course, an academic expert in philosophy by training. He interpreted the philosophical thought of others and took part in philosophical activities himself. As a young man, he displayed pride in philosophical professionalism, asserting that only 'once philosophy is recognised as a specialist science, which in its immanent course concerns in the first instance only the specialists, will it be able to navigate away from the anarchy that dominated and still dominates its output towards paths that are clear and set in their own existence'.[6] For a long time, historians of philosophy underestimated his philosophical importance,[7] yet more recent studies have remedied this omission to some degree, revealing the breadth of Simmel's philosophical contributions. These ranged from an unjustly forgotten early treatise on ethics entitled *Introduction to Moral Sciences* (1892/1893), to the dialectical architectonics of his *Philosophy of Money* (1900) and a popular exposition of the main philosophical dichotomies in his *Main Problems of Philosophy* (1910), to his final masterpiece *The View of Life* (1918), which produced an original synthesis of life-philosophy, Schopenhauerianism and neo-Kantianism.[8]

---

[5] Johann Gottlieb Fichte, *Addresses to the German Nation*, trans. G. Moore (Cambridge: Cambridge University Press, 2008), pp. 37–49.

[6] 'Eine neue Popularisirung Kants' [1883], GSG 1, p. 181.

[7] There is an exception here: Simmel's reception in France. From the very beginning, Simmel's commentators in France acknowledged him as a philosopher of the first order, and the most comprehensive and penetrating studies of Simmel as a philosopher thus far were written in French. See A. Mamelet, *Le relativisme philosophique chez Georg Simmel* (Paris: Félix Aclan, 1914); François Léger, *La Pensée de Georg Simmel: Contribution à l'histoire des idées en Allemagne au début du XXe siècle* (Paris: Kime, 1989); Matthieu Amat, *Le relationisme philosophique de Georg Simmel: Une idée de la culture* (Paris: Honoré Champion, 2018).

[8] On Simmel's philosophy of life in the philosophical context, see Gregor Fitzi, *Soziale Erfahrung und Lebensphilosophie: Georg Simmels Beziehung zu Henri Bergson* (Constance: UVK, 2002); Olli Pyyhtinen,

However, Simmel was not just a philosopher in the professional sense, and he very soon abandoned the scholarly snobbery expressed in the above quotation. He was also a philosopher in a much broader sense, employing his formidable dialectical abilities to reflect, often at the highest level of abstraction, on the burning issues of modern culture in general and of modern German culture in particular. In other words, he was a philosopher not only by profession but also by cultivation.

Simmel as a professional philosopher can be an important object of study for philosophers and historians of philosophy, but Simmel as a philosopher by cultivation is of especial interest to the intellectual historian, who is generally less concerned with the technical achievements and failures of a philosophical argument and whose main task is to understand the intellectual aspirations of a certain age through the prism of the innermost thoughts of its major thinkers. The philosophical brilliance of such minds simply serves here as a vehicle for re-enacting in the most condensed and coherent form the often incoherent hopes and demands, yearnings and doubts, thoughts and imaginations of manifold writers and thinkers of a more conventional or mediocre sort. Simmel the philosopher in this sense was just a translator and a voice for those thoughts and yearnings. He was an articulate witness to the principal questions and dilemmas that troubled the Germans of his – and of preceding – times.

In this respect a few words should be said regarding the issue of Simmel's Jewishness, a topic which has been treated extensively by prominent commentators such as Klaus Christian Köhnke and Amos Morris-Reich.[9] My approach is, to put it briefly, that Simmel was culturally and linguistically German, confessionally Protestant (up to his last years) and ethnically Jewish. This means that his Jewish identity had little if any role in his philosophical and cultural pursuits – he had no interest whatsoever in the Jewish cultural heritage and the Jewish religion, and he turned a cold shoulder to the Zionist aspirations. His writings on religiosity, for example, drew almost exclusively on the standard cultural Protestant discourse of the time. Jews occasionally figure as examples in his sociological publications, but not very often and certainly not with any more emphasis than other peoples and ethnic groups. To some prominent Jewish philosophers and sociologists Simmel felt close, for example, his teacher Moritz Lazarus and

---

'Life, Death and Individuation: Simmel on the Problem of Life Itself', *Theory, Culture & Society* 29(7–8), 2012, pp. 78–100.

[9] Cf. Klaus Christian Köhnke, 'Georg Simmel als Jude', *Simmel Newsletter* 5(1), 1995, pp. 53–72; Amos Morris-Reich, 'Georg Simmel's Logic of the Future: "The Stranger", Zionism, and "Bounded Contingency"', *Theory, Culture & Society* 36(5), 2019, pp. 71–94.

his younger colleague Martin Buber. For these intellectuals, as for many others, Jewishness constituted an important part of their identity as thinkers. But not for Simmel.

Yet, while being indifferent to Jewishness culturally, Simmel was aware of himself as being Jewish ethnically and as being perceived as such. He socialised within a Jewish bourgeois milieu and was not shy about acknowledging his Jewish 'look' or poking fun at Jewish themes. Anti-Semites in turn disliked what they considered to be the peculiarly Jewish traits of his mind. Towards the end of his life Simmel gave voice to bitterness about anti-Semitic prejudice which, he believed, placed obstacles in the way of his academic career.[10]

This distinction between the two levels of identity – cultural and ethnic – has implications for Simmel research. Simmel as a Jew is indeed a fitting subject for any historical study that either puts a central emphasis on Simmel's personality and professional biography or treats him in the context of examining the role of Jews in the intellectual life of the German *Kaiserreich*.

This subject can also give rise to some ambitious philosophical interpretations. Indeed Jewish philosophical features were occasionally attributed to Simmel's ideas. Thus just after his death, legal and social theorist Elias Hurwicz referred to his 'dialectical' style as the most important mark of his being a 'Jewish thinker'.[11] And since then a number of studies have been published that examine Simmel's thought through the lens of Jewish philosophy or Jewish themes.[12] As long as these studies remain on the level of philosophical extrapolation, such interpretations are valid and fruitful. For an intellectual historian, however, they are too far-reaching. With a few exceptions, there is not much in Simmel's texts that can be positively attributed to any specifically Jewish concerns or cultural patterns. And it would be methodologically wrong to assume a priori that all aspects of the author's life experience are necessarily related to his ideas. One should always allow that ideas may develop autonomously from identity and that they are often determined by a logic of their own, and all the more so in refined thinkers.

---

[10] E.g., his letter to Heinrich Rickert, 13 December 1915, GSG 23, p. 578.
[11] Elias Hurwicz, 'Georg Simmel als jüdischer Denker', *Neue jüdische Monatshefte* 3, 1918/1919, pp. 196–198.
[12] E.g., Hans Liebeschütz, *Von Georg Simmel zu Franz Rosenzweig: Studien zum Jüdischen Denken im deutschen Kulturbereich* (Tübingen: J. C. B. Mohr, 1970), pp. 103–141; Amos Morris-Reich, 'The Beautiful Jew Is a Moneylender: Money and Individuality in Simmel's Rehabilitation of the "Jew"', *Theory, Culture & Society* 20(4), 2003, pp. 127–142; idem, 'Three Paradigms of "The Negative Jew": Identity from Simmel to Žižek', *Jewish Social Studies* 10(2), 2004, pp. 179–214.

As I see it, then, the proper cultural and intellectual context for analysing Simmel's thought is those ideas, images and cultural patterns which apparently exercised the greatest and most lasting impact on his own. And as my study will try to show, these were unmistakably the sets of ideas and convictions that constituted the mainstream German cultural and philosophical canon.

How to Understand Simmel?

The historical study of Simmel must be contextual and aim at the maximum degree of coherence in interpretation. As for the former, only a contextual study will allow us to understand both the recurring motifs in Simmel's thought and their adequacy for the dilemmas of his age. One should, however, be clear from the outset about the kind of contextual perspective one wishes to adopt. Scholars and theorists in the last decades have correctly stressed the futility of attempts to write intellectual history as a story of a series of influences between specific authors. Yet since leading studies in the field of intellectual history focused on periods such as early modernity, in which the scope of the relevant material, however wide it may have been, still allowed for a more or less comprehensive account of intertextual networks, this important methodological observation has often remained somewhat blurred in practice. By contrast, when one comes to the study of more recent times, such comprehensiveness is out of the question, given the sheer number of authors, texts and readers, the growing fragmentation of discursive communities, and the acceleration and intensification of reading practices.

It is occasionally possible to identify specific texts or personalities that directly influenced Simmel. Many such influences have already been discovered, and the present study will add its own share of findings. Nevertheless, focusing merely on connections between individual texts and personalities can hardly be adequate. Simmel lived and was active at a time when extensive reading of diverse texts became a cultural habit. He was himself an avid reader who became familiar with almost every publication of importance, ranging from periodicals to scholarly monographs. Besides, he had an ecumenical mind which aimed to do justice to the entirety of the intellectual life of his time. For this reason, it is more important to identify not the specific textual fragments which may or may not have borne direct influence on his thought but instead the set of relevant discourses, or patterns of thinking, in relation to which his ideas can be made intelligible.[13] The role of the intellectual historian here is, broadly speaking, that of a translator rather than a biographer or philosopher. It is to make the thinker's texts readable, or at least less puzzling or misleading, by elucidating the specific languages he spoke to present-day readers for whom those languages are at best comprehended imperfectly. What I therefore strive to do is to identify the set of intellectual languages that are relevant for understanding Simmel's own thought and vice versa, to better understand those languages by studying Simmel as one of their most interesting and influential practitioners.

As for the question of coherence, it is related to contextualism understood as the examination of intellectual languages because no language, being to a certain extent a system, can entirely lack in inner coherence. Therefore, the historical study of Simmel, supported by contextual analysis of the relevant intellectual languages, must aim at revealing the scope of inner coherence that can be assigned to his thought as it evolved while practising those languages.

There is a stereotype that Simmel was a fragmentary thinker who failed to develop a coherent philosophical worldview of his own. This reading, voiced already during Simmel's lifetime and further propagated by the younger generation of critics with fratricidal inclinations, is often accepted at face value by modern-day commentators. To take just one recent example, a study of Simmel's thought from the standpoint of his aesthetics begins with the assertion that Simmel's writings do not form a whole and that he was a heterogeneous thinker whose contradictions cannot be brought to a common ground.[14] This assertion is an important correction to the superficial attempts to derive a formal unity from Simmel's thought by either subsuming his writings under one master idea, such as interaction, life or culture, or by reducing them to one master field, so that they are presented as aspects of a grand sociological, culturological or metaphysical theory. A danger of this focus on heterogeneity is, however, that it may end in a one-sided understanding of Simmel's thought as a whole or even lead to a distorted view of the particular field under investigation. For none of Simmel's works or notions are self-contained and self-explanatory. They

---

[13] I am influenced here by the methodological outlook espoused by J. G. A. Pocock in 'Languages and Their Implications: The Transformation of the Study of Political Thought', in *Politics, Language & Time: Essays on Political Thought and History* (Chicago: University of Chicago Press, 1989), pp. 3–41. Cf. my own exposition of this approach in Efraim Podoksik, 'How Is Modern Intellectual History Possible?', *European Political Science* 9(3), 2010, pp. 304–315.

[14] Ingo Meyer, *Georg Simmels Ästhetik: Autonomiepostulat und soziologische Referenz* (Weilerswist: Velbrück, 2017), p. 11.

always presuppose something else that informs and explains them. What this is remains a matter of interpretation. But that certain fundamental presuppositions which inform Simmel's writings in all their manifoldness do exist is a notion often suggested by Simmel himself. Indeed, in almost all his writings he is obsessed with the problem of unity: unity in thought and unity in the world. It is impossible to ignore this passion for unity.

To be sure, this passion is accompanied by a recognition of the condition of diversity that allegedly exists in modern thought and modern life and which complicates the task of attaining inner coherence. One may well come to the conclusion that Simmel's striving for unity resulted in failure. At least, one can confidently argue that Simmel's drive for unity ended with a question mark. As the story narrated in this book will demonstrate, his philosophical endeavours emerged from an acute sense of cultural conflict, reflecting deep anxieties that characterised the German mind in the early twentieth century. Each time Simmel appeared to have arrived at a creative solution supposed to reconcile these conflicts by means of an ever more encompassing worldview, the insufficiency of the solution immediately made itself felt, forcing him to explore new possibilities. This incessant quest culminated in the deep inner conflict between the ideals of Goethe-like universal cultivation and quasi-mystical absolute decisionism in the writings of his final years.

But there is hardly any important thinker whose thought was not torn by fundamental conflicts of one kind or another. Indeed, it is these very conflicts that usually provide the fuel for the philosophical drive for unity. To what extent this is true for Simmel remains to be seen. In any case, judgement on whether and to what degree his ideas were coherent cannot be pronounced on the basis of a merely partial familiarity with his works. A careful examination of his corpus in toto is required. This sort of study is rarely undertaken, given the tremendous amount of labour it demands. Simmel was an intense thinker, a prolific writer and often a careless compiler of his own works. Each of these features augments the difficulty of interpreting him. The sheer volume of his writings, as well as the breadth of topics he dealt with, seriously complicates the task of bringing them into some kind of encompassing worldview. Moreover, he often put his thoughts in writing before they fully ripened and harmonised with other aspects of his thinking. What is more, on many occasions, he borrowed parts of his earlier texts and inserted them into later revisions of the same texts, only half-adjusting them to the changes that had meanwhile taken place in his views. This requires the interpreter to be attentive to the different chronological layers of the same work, for only by distinguishing between those layers can one hope to determine which aspects of a certain text are more 'representative' of Simmel's thinking in a particular period. As for intensity, Simmel did not make any concessions to his audience. Reading him requires an unusual degree of concentration, for his argument is rarely linear or schematic. Rather, it is reminiscent of a labyrinth where a single moment of inattention may cause the whole argument to appear nonsensical, as the text simply begins to look like a series of conflicting statements. Consider, for example, the 250-page monograph *Goethe* (1913), which I regard as one of Simmel's most important works. As will be argued later, its argument is quite coherent. Yet it is at the same time so dense and full of unexpected turns that sometimes one must read dozens of pages before being able to grasp Simmel's specific approach to a particular question.[15]

A similar degree of intellectual intensity apparently characterised Simmel's manner of lecturing, as is reported by many of his students. We are told that an entire lecture often consisted of no more than one long and very complex argument. One had to listen very carefully in order to be able to follow Simmel as he manoeuvred towards his destination, which in retrospect seemed to be the only one possible. Here is one such report:

> In lectures . . . he wanted to deliver not results but processes. By placing the previously found result at the beginning in a dull and ponderous manner, he set only a fugue theme. The attraction of his interpretations lay in the theme's exposition and stretto. For when Simmel lectured, he explored like a consummate dentist. With the finest tweezers sharpened by himself, he penetrated the hole of things, seizing the nerve at the root with utmost care and slowly pulling it out. Now we students could throng round the table in order to look at the delicate object curled around the silver tweezers.[16]

The side effect of this intensity of thinking was the formation of the opinion that Simmel's thought was fragmentary, an opinion held by those who were unwilling to follow him all the way throughout his thinking process.

These are, then, the features that often deterred interpreters from attempting a comprehensive interpretation of Simmel's thought. Yet it is

---

[15] This work may be compared to a publication by another author – *Experience and Poetry* by Wilhelm Dilthey – which contains a long chapter on Goethe (Wilhelm Dilthey, *Das Erlebnis und die Dichtung* [Leipzig: B. G. Teubner, 1916]). Dilthey was considered one of the leading philosophical minds of the time, and his take on many philosophical issues resembled Simmel's. He was, however, a much more readable author, despite being less coherent or perhaps even because he was less coherent. In his writing about Goethe, his philosophical abstractions are often interrupted by illustrations in the form of long, easily digestible quotations from Goethe's works or with snippets of biographical information. Rarely is the reader kept in philosophical suspense for long.

[16] Emil Ludwig, 'Erinnerungen an Simmel', in Gassen and Landmann (eds.), *Buch des Dankes*, p. 156.

precisely these features that make forming such interpretations an especially valuable task. As I just said above, Simmel's writings are not self-
explanatory. It is rarely possible to understand what he wanted to say in
a particular piece of writing without juxtaposing it with both the entirety of
his oeuvre and the intellectual context on which he drew. The complexity
of Simmel's thought requires a certain general view regarding its main
parameters. Of course, no single interpretation of this kind can claim to be
the only correct way of understanding him. Some sort of interpretative
paradigm is, however, essential if one wishes to attain a satisfactory understanding of his mind.

The Book's Structure

The purpose of this book is to offer an outline of one such paradigmatic
reading.[17] Briefly, its starting point is as follows. Simmel's thought can be
seen as a series of engagements with a fundamental problem of his time: the
alleged tension between the ideal of personal and social harmony and the
condition of growing differentiation.

The contextual setting for this problem is outlined in the book's first
chapter. As I argue there, at the turn of the nineteenth and twentieth
centuries the question of the tension between harmony (unity) and differentiation, while salient in the cultural life of all Western societies, acquired
particular significance for German intellectuals. It was they who developed
the conceptual apparatus to deal with what they perceived as the ultimate
problem of modernity. For them, modernity was characterised first and
foremost by the condition of differentiation or even fragmentation. Their
main fear was that this condition was incompatible with the innate human
striving for integrity and harmony, resulting in the estrangement of individuals from the differentiated world.[18]

Simmel was among the most important contributors to this debate. His
attitude to the problem changed as his thought evolved, but over the course
of his entire life he approached it with more or less the same set of
conceptual tools. The most important of these was the notion of the

---

[17] My interpretation of Simmel is especially influenced by the following studies: Rudolph
H. Weingartner, *Experience and Culture: The Philosophy of Georg Simmel* (Middletown, CO:
Wesleyan University Press, 1962); Willfried Geßner, *Der Schatz im Acker: Georg Simmels
Philosophie der Kultur* (Weilerswist: Velbrück Wissenschaft, 2003); Amat, *Le relationisme philoso-
phique de Georg Simmel.*
[18] Cf. Arthur Mitzman, *Sociology and Estrangement: Three Sociologists in Imperial Germany* (New York:
Alfred A. Knopf, 1973).

conflict between unity and variety. This conflict is the focus of the three other chapters of my book. In them I discuss Simmel's continued attempts to solve the discontents of modern culture by examining various possibilities for the reconciliation of unity and variety.

The three chapters explore three different periods in Simmel's intellectual life and are divided into sections, each dealing with a particular subject or field then prominent in his thought. His approach towards each such subject is treated contextually and against the background of his thought as a whole. Taken by themselves, none of those sections confirm the correctness of my general interpretation of Simmel. But together, I hope, they produce robust evidence in favour of it. What emerges from their juxtaposition is that Simmel's thought across various themes was, on the whole, consistent and that there existed a certain logic in the evolution of his thinking from one period to the next.

A fully comprehensive study would have to examine every aspect of Simmel's thought in this manner. That, however, would demand a multivolume project. The present book does not aim at such comprehensiveness. Its task is more modest: to present Simmel's ideas across a relatively broad sample of themes without aiming at an exhaustive account of his thought. This sample will nevertheless be sufficiently diverse to bestow on my interpretation a prima facie plausibility.

My choice of themes is also related to the current state of Simmel scholarship. I have chosen subjects which, despite their centrality for Simmel, have remained under-researched in scholarly literature. These are, for example, Simmel's engagements with great cultural figures of the past: Kant, Goethe and Rembrandt. It is in fact in his writings on these figures that Simmel outlined in the most explicit manner his strategy for overcoming the disunity that allegedly threatened the modern world. Conversely, I pay less attention to the better-known aspects of Simmel's thought, such as sociology,[19] the philosophy of

---

[19] Recent literature on Simmel's social thought in English includes Olli Pyythinen, *Simmel and 'the Social'* (London: Palgrave Macmillan, 2010); Henry Schermer and David Jary, *Form and Dialectic in Georg Simmel's Sociology: A New Interpretation* (New York: Palgrave Macmillan, 2013); Olli Pyythinen and Thomas Kemple (eds.), *The Anthem Companion to Georg Simmel* (London: Anthem Press, 2016); Goodstein, *Georg Simmel and the Disciplinary Imaginary*; Gregor Fitzi, *The Challenge of Modernity: Simmel's Sociological Theory* (London: Routledge, 2019). For earlier studies in English, see especially the works of David Frisby, such as *Sociological Impressionism: A Reassessment of Georg Simmel's Social Theory* (London: Routledge, 1992) and *Simmel and Since: Essays on Georg Simmel's Social Theory* (London: Routledge, 1992). For German-language literature, see especially Heinz-Jürgen Dahme, *Soziologie als exakte Wissenschaft: Georg Simmels Ansatz und seine Bedeutung in der gegenwärtigen Soziologie* (Stuttgart: Ferdinand Enke, 1981) and Hartmann Tyrell, Otthein Rammstedt and Ingo Meyer (eds.), *Georg Simmels große 'Soziologie': Eine kritische Sichtung nach hundert Jahren* (Bielefeld: transcript, 2011).

money[20] or even metaphysics. These are no less or no more important in the general scheme of things than the subjects on which I have chosen to focus. However, the availability of high-quality research regarding these subjects exempts me from discussing them in detail. Some other subjects, such as history, have been omitted because I have already dealt with them elsewhere.[21] Suffice to note that, in my view, the logic of Simmel's ideas in those fields corresponds to my general interpretative scheme.

[20] The most lucid account of Simmel's philosophy of money in English is Gianfranco Poggi, *Money and the Modern Mind: Georg Simmel's Philosophy of Money* (Berkeley: University of California Press, 1993). See also Guy Oakes, 'Metaphysik des Geldes: Die *Philosophie des Geldes* als Philosophie', in W. Geßner and R. Kramme (eds.), *Aspekte der Geldkultur: Neue Beiträge zu Georg Simmels Philosophie des Geldes* (Magdeburg: Scriptum, 2002), pp. 63–76; Otthein Rammstedt (ed.), *Georg Simmels* Philosophie des Geldes (Frankfurt am Main: Suhrkamp, 2003); Alois Hartmann, *Sinn und Wert des Geldes in der Philosophie von Georg Simmel und Adam (von) Müller: Untersuchungen zur anthropologisch sinn- und werttheoretischen und soziopolitisch-kulturellen Bedeutung des Geldes in der Lebenswelt und der Staatskunst* (Berlin: WiKu, 2002); Annika Schlitte, *Die Macht des Geldes und die Symbolik der Kultur: Georg Simmels* Philosophie des Geldes (Munich: Wilhelm Funk, 2012); Arthur Bueno, 'Economic Pathologies of Life', in G. Fitzi (ed.), *The Routledge International Handbook of Simmel Studies* (London: Routledge, 2021), pp. 336–349.

[21] See, for example, my interpretation of the evolution of Simmel's philosophy of history in Efraim Podoksik, 'Georg Simmel: Three Forms of Individualism and Historical Understanding', *New German Critique* 109(1), 2010, pp. 119–145.

CHAPTER I

Bildung, Kultur, Crisis

In *Introduction to Moral Sciences* (1892/1893), Simmel made an observation about a certain feature of human personality. The self, he wrote, can 'split [*spalten*] itself, so to speak, into different parts'. The consequence of this ability to split ourselves is that 'we can face ourselves objectively, so that we observe and judge ourselves as we would observe and judge others'.[1] This explains, for example, the ability to feel at conflict with one's own duty or conscience. Such an inner conflict happens when those elements of our personality that belong to the category of duty split from the other elements of our personality and begin to fight against them.[2]

This treatise on ethics was one of Simmel's earliest works, and later he admitted to have been unsatisfied with many aspects of it.[3] Yet this particular observation about the nature of the human personality remained valid for him throughout his entire life, and he repeated it almost word for word in other works. Thus, in *Religion* (1906), he mentioned the ability of man 'to dismantle [*zerlegen*] himself into different parts and to feel any such part of himself as his real self which clashes with other parts and competes for the determination of his actions'.[4] Exactly the same phrase is repeated in *Fundamental Problems of Sociology* (1917),[5] and similar ideas can be found in many other writings. Specific formulations of the idea sometimes varied, but its basic point remained unchanged: human personality tends to split itself into different parts, and out of this split, the conflict between a part and the whole emerges.

This conflict is reinforced by the basic structure of human society. As Simmel noted in his *Sociology* (1908), society demands that the individual

---

[1] *Einleitung in die Moralwissenschaft: Eine Kritik der ethischen Grundbegriffe*, GSG 3, p. 180.
[2] See GSG 4, p. 355.   [3] GSG 3, p. 9.
[4] *Die Religion*, GSG 10, p. 86. A slightly different translation can be found in 'Religion', trans. H. J. Helle, in *Essays on Religion* (New Haven: Yale University Press, 1997), p. 182.
[5] 'Fundamental Problems of Sociology: Individual and Society', trans. K. H. Wolff, in Kurt H. Wolff (ed.), *The Sociology of Georg Simmel* (New York: The Free Press, 1950), p. 58. [GSG 16, p. 122.]

take upon himself a certain role, that he choose a vocation (*Beruf*). This demand presupposes the existence of harmony between the general social structure and personal qualities. It suggests that 'for every personality there exists a position and a function in society to which he is called [*berufen*] and which he must seek and find'.[6] However, this presupposition is problematic. Personality is never fully determined by one's professional qualities and social position, for every element of society is a priori 'not only a societal part but, in addition, something else'.[7] We know 'of a bureaucrat that he is not only a bureaucrat, of the businessman that he is not only a businessman, of the officer that he is not only an officer. This extrasocial nature ... gives a certain nuance to the picture formed by all who meet him. It intermixes his social picture with non-social imponderables'.[8]

This lack of complete harmony between personality and its social function leads to an inner tension, which becomes especially salient in advanced civilisations. There, social spheres and functions are greatly differentiated, and no individual belongs exclusively to one such sphere. In the ancient world, some measure of functional differentiation can also be found,[9] yet there it existed in an undeveloped form. Simmel often spoke about the naivety of undifferentiated ancient societies and about the inner harmony of the Greeks.[10] By contrast, in the modern world, as described in *Philosophy of Money* (1900), personality often fails to achieve even a relative unity. Such unity is supposed to develop out of the interaction and connection between various qualities of character. Yet, taken separately, each such quality exists by itself, bearing 'an objective character'.[11] In the conditions of the modern money economy, the objective character of each particular quality achieves pre-eminence over the personality as a whole. Individuals then begin to matter only as bearers of their specific objective functions, for example, as moneylenders or workers, and the personality is thereby almost completely destroyed.

The same happens in the modern aesthetic experience as well. The modern mind is inclined 'to uproot life's elements from primordial

---

[6] 'How Is Society Possible?', trans. K. H. Wolff, in Kurt H. Wolff (ed.), *Essays on Sociology, Philosophy and Aesthetics* (New York: Harper & Row, 1959), p. 354. [GSG 11, p. 60.]

[7] Ibid., p. 345. [GSG 11, p. 51.]   [8] Ibid., p. 346. [GSG 11, p. 51.]

[9] Ibid., p. 354. [GSG 11, p. 60.]

[10] See, for example, 'Bemerkungen zu socialethischen Problemen' [1888], GSG 2, p. 29; *Einleitung in die Moralwissenschaft*, GSG 3, p. 383; 'The Problem of Style' [1908], trans. M. Ritter, in D. Frisby and M. Featherstone (eds.), *Simmel on Culture: Selected Writings* (London: Sage, 1997), p. 216. [GSG 8, p. 383.]

[11] *The Philosophy of Money*, trans. T. Bottomore and D. Frisby (London: Routledge, 2004), p. 296. [GSG 6, p. 393.]

unity, to individualise and to differentiate, and to bring to consciousness of themselves, in order to draw them back again into a new unity'.[12] Sometimes, a great artist, such as the sculptor Auguste Rodin, succeeds in achieving this new unity. Very often, however, we are left with 'a characteristically modern sense of fracture [*Zerrissenheit*], of bare specialisation of individual contents of existence'.[13]

This inner conflict is the fundamental predicament of modern culture in general. In 1918, Simmel argued that modern people had lived without any common idea for at least several decades.[14] This was not always the case. In earlier periods, unifying ideas did indeed exist:

> The Middle Ages . . . had the idea of the Christian Church; the Renaissance had the restoration of secular nature as a value which did not need to be legitimised by transcendental forces; the eighteenth-century Enlightenment lived by the idea of universal human happiness through the rule of reason, and the great age of German idealism suffused science with artistic imagination, and aspired to give art a foundation of cosmic breadth by means of scientific knowledge. But today, if one were to ask educated people [*die Menschen der gebildeten Schichten*] what idea actually governs their lives, most of them would give a specialised answer relating to their occupation [*Beruf*]. One would not hear much of any cultural idea governing them as whole men and guiding all their specialised activities.[15]

Throughout his entire life, therefore, Simmel was concerned with what he once described as the 'mysterious relationship between our unified wholeness and our individual energies and perfections'[16] and with the nature and consequences of the conflict that this relationship provokes, especially in the condition of modernity. This concern is present both in his early and later works: it can be found in his reflections on economy, psychology and society as well as in his writings on art, religion and ethics. This constancy is quite impressive, especially if we take into account the fact that Simmel was often perceived as a fragmented thinker and unsystematic philosopher. What is the meaning of the perpetual recurrence of

---

[12] 'Auguste Rodin: Part I', in Austin Harrington (ed.), *Georg Simmel: Essays on Art and Aesthetics* (Chicago: University of Chicago Press, 2020), p. 306. ['Rodins Plastik und die Geistesrichtung der Gegenwart', GSG 7, p. 98.]

[13] Ibid. [GSG 7, p. 98.]

[14] 'The Conflict of Modern Culture', trans. D. E. Jenkinson, in Frisby and Featherstone (eds.), *Simmel on Culture*, pp. 75–90.

[15] Ibid., p. 80. [GSG 16, p. 190.]

[16] 'The Concept and Tragedy of Culture', trans. M. Ritter and D. Frisby, in ibid., p. 65. [GSG 12, p. 209.]

this theme in Simmel's writings? What significance did it possess for him and for his time? What lay behind his concerns?

1.1   The crisis of fragmentation

Simmel was in fact not alone in his concern about the conflict between personality as a whole and one of its specific determinations. The regularity with which this theme appeared in his writings matched the regularity with which it was articulated by the leading minds in Imperial Germany.[17]

The subject itself was not new. The problem of the relation of unity to variety had long been present in German culture. Yet, from the 1870s onwards, a new mood regarding this question can be discerned. Any mention of the conflict between whole and part was accompanied by a feeling of acute uneasiness and a sense of growing urgency. Friedrich Nietzsche was one of the first authors to express such a mood.

In 1874, three years after the foundation of the Second Empire, Nietzsche, by then professor of classical philology at the University of Basel, recalled that in his youth he had been obsessed with the idea of finding a philosopher to whose teaching he could devote himself.[18] The first and main thing such a philosopher would have to teach him was how to respond to two very different maxims of the time. One maxim demanded that a teacher concentrate on developing the entire potential of the pupil in the direction of the one side that appears to be his strongest. The contrary maxim demanded the development of all the pupil's abilities into a harmonious whole. Nietzsche was searching for a philosopher who would show him a way of reconciling these two maxims and forming a true unity out of them, which would then make him a Cellini, a Renaissance man. Finding such a philosopher was not an easy task, and this difficulty was a sign of the misfortune of the moderns in comparison to the ancients: the Greeks and Romans.

In Nietzsche's view, the modern tension between demands for universality, on the one hand, and for the concentration of power, on the other,

---

[17] This issue did not remain unnoticed by intellectual historians (see, e.g. Fritz K. Ringer, *The Decline of the German Mandarins: The German Academic Community, 1890–1933* [Hanover: Wesleyan University Press, 1990], pp. 256–258; or Herbert Schnädelbach, *Philosophy in Germany 1831–1933*, trans. E. Matthews [Cambridge: Cambridge University Press, 1984], pp. 27–32). Yet it is rarely isolated from other forms of critique of modernity and brought into the spotlight. This is unfortunate since the frequency with which this particular issue appeared in various contexts during the entire period of the *Kaiserreich* may indicate that something important was felt to be at stake here. The issue evidently deserves closer attention.

[18] Friedrich Nietzsche, *Untimely Meditations*, trans. R. J. Hollingdale (Cambridge: Cambridge University Press, 1997), pp. 130–131.

presented a question of almost existential significance. I shall refer later to one of the solutions he suggested. Meanwhile, however, it is important to pay attention to the question itself and to the earnestness with which it was displayed. Nietzsche could hardly be satisfied with the pragmatic attitude adopted by his older colleague in Basel, Jacob Burckhardt, who once said that a scholar should be a specialist in one field and a dilettante in all others.[19] To Nietzsche, the path of the Swiss historian was out of the question. Moderation was never his strong side.

Nietzsche was perhaps the most radical but not the only thinker concerned with this question. Just a few years later, another young professor, Wilhelm Windelband of the University of Freiburg, announced his own reflections on the same subject. Windelband, the future leader of the Southwest neo-Kantian School, was a thinker of quite a different mould than Nietzsche. However, in his talk at the meeting of the Freiburg Academic Society in November 1878, he sounded very much like Nietzsche.[20] The topic of his presentation was the fate of Friedrich Hölderlin (whom Nietzsche also admired). This great poet was overcome by madness. This should not be seen merely as Hölderlin's personal tragedy. Rather, his madness reflects the tragedy of modern Germany or even of the entire modern world: the tragedy of the clash between ancient harmony and modern division. German phil-osophy and poetry took upon themselves the task of accomplishing a fusion between the two, although only two men really succeeded in this: Hegel and Goethe. Unlike them, Hölderlin felt that ancient Greece and fragmented modernity stood in the sharpest possible opposition to each other and that no reconciliation between the two was in sight. His ideal of Greece made him launch a bitter and at times unjust critique of the 'ugliness, disruption (*Zerrissenheit*), one-sidedness and inner absent-mindedness (*Zerfahrenheit*) of the modern, and especially German, life'.[21]

These features of modern life were not accidental. Their appearance became inevitable due to a profound difference between antiquity and the modern age:

> The ancient world was still so simple that the individual was in the position to embrace through his interests the whole extent of the common cultural life. Science and art, state and religion still stood in such a close and intimate relation to each other, that, taken all together, they formed only a harmonious

[19] Jacob Burckhardt, *Weltgeschichtliche Betrachtungen* (Hamburg: Heinrich Ellermann, 1948), p. 45.
[20] An essay based on this presentation was published as Wilhelm Windelband, 'Ueber Friedrich Hölderlin und sein Geschick', in *Präludien* (Freiburg: J. C. B. Mohr, 1884), pp. 146–175.
[21] Ibid., pp. 155–156.

unity. The scope of what belonged to it was still so small that the individual was able to combine the full enjoyment of general culture [*Bildung*] with the complete devotion to his particular occupation [*Beruf*].[22]

Things are different today. The scope of every professional activity has increased so much that it is now impossible for any individual to master the totality of things. In this situation of growing differentiation, it becomes difficult to see things in their connections with each other. We have lost 'that fortunate identity between the personal and general culture [*Bildung*]'.[23] Therefore, today one would look in vain for a human being (*einen Mensch*); at most, one would find professionals (*Leute des Berufs*).[24] Citizens of Athens, Renaissance men, and even German thinkers and poets of Hölderlin's age, all received universal education (*Bildung*). Nowadays, even a genius cannot acquire the same. Culture has become so wide and specialised that it cannot be encompassed by a single individual.[25]

The solution, however, cannot be found in a compromise between the imperative of universality and that of a specific vocation. Windelband disliked dilettantism, which he regarded as a superficial familiarity with what lies beyond one's professional interests. Not unlike Nietzsche, who despised cultural philistines, he regarded dilettantism as even more problematic than narrow professionalism.[26] Dilettantes consider it to be their right to judge what they in fact do not comprehend. Modern parliamentarism, with its sophists daring to criticise experienced officials and statesmen of genius, is a good example of dilettantism.[27] What is more, if the choice is between professionals and dilettantes, one must support professionals who know their subject matter in all its details rather than intellectual impostors with an allegedly wider outlook. Windelband yearned for an ultimate synthesis between harmonious culture and dedicated professionalism but not for a half-baked compromise between them.

Windelband spoke in the year in which Bismarck initiated his conservative shift.[28] Leading parliamentarians from the left wing of the National Liberal party, such as Eduard Lasker, refused to support this policy. Lasker, who earlier had successfully challenged corrupt officials,[29] now became the favourite target of the chancellor's rhetorical attacks and as such might have fitted Windelband's portrait of a dilettantish parliamentarian who

---

[22] Ibid., p. 167.   [23] Ibid.   [24] Ibid., p. 168.   [25] Ibid., p. 170.   [26] Ibid., pp. 171–172.
[27] Ibid., p. 172.
[28] See on this, for example, Heinrich August Winkler, *Germany: The Long Road West*, vol. 1: *1789–1933* (Oxford: Oxford University Press, 2006), pp. 213–223.
[29] Volker Ullrich, *Die nervöse Großmacht: Aufstieg und Untergang des deutschen Kaiserreichs 1871–1918* (Frankfurt am Main: Fischer, 2007), p. 41.

castigates great statesmen and their advisers. It is thus even more telling that Lasker's diagnosis of the problem, which he called the problem of 'half-education' (*Halbbildung*), was very similar to that of Windelband.[30] Lasker attributed this 'half-education' to the increasing complexity of advancing civilisation. In a complex environment, one is pressed to familiarise oneself with a greater amount of material. This pressure, in turn, creates the temptation to get to know things superficially, and 'this is the reason of why the advance of civilisation is accompanied by an increase in half-education'.[31] Moderns are in danger of losing their creative abilities and becoming epigones. Thus, for example, although modern art is superior in its variety and psychological profundity to its ancient counterparts, and especially Greek art, the latter remains unmatched in its simple beauty.

Lasker was not a nostalgic foe of modernity. A left-leaning liberal, he considered attempts to reverse the path of progress not only wrong but also impossible. In his opinion, the problem of half-education was characteristic of the transitional stage in the development of civilisation, which would eventually lead to the emergence of a new form of synthetic knowledge.[32] Yet, at the same time, he was by no means a blind optimist. He admitted that this development also entailed loss, and he took modern discontent seriously, fearing that with the progress of humankind, an individual who would not adapt to the new condition might 'disperse oneself' (*sich zerstreuen*).[33]

A great part of Windelband's analysis was therefore shared by Lasker, a progressive liberal of Jewish descent. It was also shared by another parliamentarian, historian Heinrich von Treitschke. Unlike Lasker, Treitschke had been a right-wing liberal who turned into a moderate conservative and anti-Semite. Yet, regarding the condition of modern culture, Lasker and Treitschke thought alike, even using the same forms of expression to describe the situation (such as the notion of dispersion: *Zerstreutheit*). In 1883, for example, Treitschke argued: '[T]he greatest danger threatening modern culture [*Bildung*] was already recognised by Goethe in the beginning of the new century. It lies in an endless dispersion of our inward life.'[34]

This threat especially preoccupied those thinkers who were trained in the humanities: historian Treitschke, jurist Lasker, philosopher Windelband

[30] Eduard Lasker, 'Ueber Halbbildung' [1878], in *Wege und Ziele der Culturentwickelung* (Leipzig: Brockhaus, 1881), pp. 141–205.

[31] Ibid., p. 156.   [32] Ibid., pp. 188–189.   [33] Ibid., p. 167.

[34] Heinrich von Treitschke, 'Einige Bemerkungen über unser Gymnasialwesen', *Preußische Jahrbücher* 51(2), 1883, pp. 160–161.

and philologist Nietzsche. Yet it was not ignored by natural scientists, such as gynaecologist Alfred Hegar, another professor from Freiburg. In 1882, Hegar spoke on the danger of unabated specialism in the natural sciences. He criticised those scientists who tend to narrow the scope of their research. It is very doubtful, he argued, that a scientist, by concentrating on one small thing, can discover in it the Archimedean point which would allow him to turn the world upside down. Rather, the chances are that such a scientist would just damage his eyes by overburdening himself with knowledge of unimportant details in his own field. To the lofty debate about the destiny of culture Hegar contributed his own perspective as a physician, by complaining about 'the deterioration of our noblest sense-organ, eyes, which gradually became a national calamity'.[35]

A few years later (1890), poet and critic Julius Langbehn opened his anonymously published book *Rembrandt as Educator* with a reproach of German eyes. He reminded his readers that 'Goethe ... could not stand people with eyeglasses; yet today Germany is full of actual and spiritual wearers of glasses'.[36] Medical problems aside, it was disease in the metaphorical sense that troubled Langbehn. The embodiment of this disease was the German professor. In general, Langbehn perceived the problem of modernity in terms of the opposition between art and science. He despised the latter, arguing that true science must admit the superiority of art. Without such recognition, science would degenerate into specialism. This indeed happened to modern science: one of its major sins is that it 'revels in particulars'.[37] Thereby, it becomes 'spiritless' because 'spirit is precisely the connection of all parts with the whole and of the whole with all its parts'.[38] Specialisation destroys creative individualities, for only a complete person can really be creative.[39] A specialist, on the contrary, is devoid of this ability. He 'has given away his soul. One is even allowed to say that the devil is a specialist, just as God is surely a universalist'.[40]

Langbehn's book became a bestseller, and dozens of editions appeared over the course of just one year.[41] Its success may have turned out to be the starting point in the process of the reorientation of the European mind away from rationalism and naïve positivism.[42] Yet, as we have seen, the

[35] Alfred Hegar, *Spezialismus und allgemeine Bildung* (Freiburg: J. C. B. Mohr, 1882), p. 29.
[36] [Julius Langbehn], *Rembrandt als Erzieher: Von einem Deutschen* (Leipzig: C. L. Hirschfeld, 1890), p. 1.
[37] Ibid., p. 56.   [38] Ibid.   [39] Ibid., p. 57.   [40] Ibid., p. 66.
[41] On Langbehn, see Fritz Stern, *The Politics of Cultural Despair: A Study in the Rise of the Germanic Ideology* (Berkeley: University of California Press, 1989), pp. 95–180.
[42] H. Stuart Hughes, *Consciousness and Society: The Reorientation of European Social Thought 1890–1930* (New York: Alfred A. Knopff, 1961), pp. 43–45.

specific debate on the tension between totality and particularity did not start with Langbehn. Nor did it become the exclusive reserve of the disenchanted cultural critics of the fin-de-siècle decade. Certainly, the bitterest complaints about specialisation came from the ranks of dissenting intellectuals. However, the mainstream cultural establishment was affected by this mood too. And if a decade earlier prominent intellectuals such as Treitschke found it necessary to address this issue, luminaries of no lesser stature spoke about it in the 1890s.

Thus, in 1895, Theodor Mommsen, renowned historian of Roman antiquity, spoke on the predicament of the contemporary scientist, whose condition he compared with that of the great synthetic minds of the past. Addressing his audience on Leibniz Day, Mommsen presented Leibniz as an example of such a synthetic mind. Leibniz was equally a mathematician, physicist, philosopher and historian, thus acquiring the right to apply to himself the notion of predestined harmony: 'The great mystery of individuality, the unity of heterogeneous powers, probably never so perfectly realised itself inwardly and had such a strong effect outwardly, as in this great man of a not very shining era of our national history.'[43] Today, unfortunately, no one can become a Leibniz, due to the advancement of science and its specialisation. Scientific progress is accompanied by failure in self-realisation: 'certainly, science paces forward irresistibly and powerfully; yet an individual worker looks ever more negligible and small vis-à-vis this rising gigantic construction.'[44]

The 'grand enterprise of science' had its most enthusiastic supporter in the figure of liberal theologian Adolf Harnack.[45] Harnack, director of the Royal Library in Berlin and founder and president of the Kaiser Wilhelm Society, was the very embodiment of the German scholarly establishment of the Wilhelmine era. However, in his pessimistic moments, he could sound very harsh with regard to modern scientific activity. In his history of the Prussian Academy of Sciences (1900), for example, Harnack claimed that modern scientists had become epigones.[46] In each previous era of significant advancement in scientific knowledge, such as the age of Plato, the Renaissance or Germany at the beginning of the nineteenth century,

---

[43] Theodor Mommsen, 'Das Verhältnis der Wissenschaft zum Staat' [1895], in *Reden und Aufsätze* (Berlin: Weidmannsche Buchhandlung, 1905), p. 196.

[44] Ibid.

[45] Adolf Harnack, 'Vom Großbetrieb der Wissenschaft' [1905], in *Aus Wissenschaft und Leben* I (Gießen: Alfred Töpelmann, 1911), p. 13.

[46] 'Epigone' is a favourite catchword in this genre of cultural self-criticism. See Martin Doerry, *Übergangsmenschen: Die Mentalität der Wilhelminer und die Krise des Kaiserreichs* (Weinheim: Juventa, 1986), pp. 30–31.

science, apart from providing a glance at the external world, also endeavoured to determine our inner life. Leibniz, the first head of the academy and a universal thinker and organiser, was a scientist of this kind. By contrast, modern science 'did not become a guide of life in the loftiest meaning'.[47] The reason for this is no secret: modern science is characterised by the norm of objectivity and the division of labour. It 'devoted itself to the "routine one-sidedness" of work; yet it paid dearly with loss of life'.[48]

The heavy price that professionalisation exacts from intellectual life continued to preoccupy German thinkers during the following two decades, which happened to be the final decades of the Second Empire. The complaint was voiced, for example, by Adolph Wagner, a conservative economist and a leading 'socialist of the chair'. The contemporary age, he argued, was too estranged from the days of Goethe, Schiller, Kant and the Romantics. Those men had lived aesthetically and ethically in the highest world of thought. Today, however, the increasing division of labour and the enormous competition it brought 'made us into better experts, but *not* into more profound and spiritual men'.[49] This worry was shared by the educationalist Eduard Spranger who warned against the excesses of specialism, which adopts the form of anarchic positivism: 'an endless differentiation means decay [*Zerfall*].'[50] And the high priest of 'life-philosophy', Nobel Prize winner Rudolf Eucken, analysed the same problem in more general terms, finding its roots in the contemporary shortage of inward culture. In the condition of modernity, the progress of work goes hand in hand with a growing fragmentation in all fields of activity. Fragmentation prevents us from building ourselves into complete and inward human beings.[51] This lack of unity is found everywhere. Chaos rules in religion, philosophy, education, art, literature and morals. In the past, Germans excelled both in labour and in pure inward culture. Not anymore. Work culture has split from inward culture, and the latter can be regained only if we start seeing humans as humans and not solely as bearers of specific professions.[52]

---

[47] Adolf Harnack, *Geschichte der Königlich Preussischen Akademie der Wissenschaften zu Berlin*, vol. 1 (Berlin: Reichsdruckerei, 1900), p. 980.
[48] Ibid. For criticism of specialisation in the universities see also Adolf Langguth, *Die Bilanz der akademischen Bildung* (Berlin: Carl Heymann, 1901).
[49] *Die Verhandlungen des achtzehnten Evangelisch-sozialen Kongresses* (Göttingen: Vandenhoeck & Ruprecht, 1907), p. 48.
[50] Eduard Spranger, *Wandlungen im Wesen der Universität seit 100 Jahren* (Leipzig: Ernst Wiegandt, 1913), p. 24.
[51] Rudolf Eucken, *Zur Sammlung der Geister* (Leipzig: Quelle & Meyer, 1913), p. 5.
[52] Ibid., especially pp. 14, 33, 95.

Some disaffected intellectuals, such as philosopher of history Kurt Breysig, cherished the dream of finding harmonious personalities among the nobility, who could provide some kind of aristocratic leadership. Yet Breysig came to recognise that the upper classes too were affected by this modern middle-class disease: the mechanisation of soul, that is, the 'monotony, disjointment [*Zerspaltenheit*], obsequiousness, feebleness, dullness, emptiness of what should be our most free possession – our very Self'.[53] This divided mechanical existence is the mark of a professional (*Berufsmensch*), who 'sees no disgrace, but only honour and fame in the fact that he knows about nothing else in the world except his own profession [*Beruf*]'.[54]

The problem of leadership in the condition of fragmentation not only troubled disenchanted 'reactionaries', such as Breysig, but also occupied 'progressives', such as economist and sociologist Alfred Weber, who composed an article on the problem of the absence of intellectual leaders in Germany.[55] Unlike Breysig, Weber did not possess any aristocratic longings. On the contrary, he argued that a new and better leadership could appear only as a result of the democratic process. Yet his diagnosis of the situation was not very different from that of Breysig. Contemporary Germany, in his view, lacked true intellectual leaders. This shortage did not always exist. Once upon a time, Germany had its Fichte, Hegel or Humboldt, and even in the years of Bismarck one could find figures such as Nietzsche, Marr, Lassalle or Treitschke. Yet by then the decline was already underway, as gradually the feeling of the whole was lost. Even great personalities, such as Schopenhauer and Nietzsche, spoke already 'to fragments of our life, and no longer to the whole'.[56] Nowadays the situation is even worse. Today's intellectuals have turned themselves into experts, each dealing with their own specific question. The spirits who are still looking for totality are lonely people. No longer listened to by the nation, they are its hidden prophets.[57]

Weber published this article in October 1918, one month before the end of the First World War and one month after Simmel's death. Yet the same article could just as easily have been written and published a few decades earlier. It is amazing to discover how little changed in the discourse

---

[53] Kurt Breysig, *Von Gegenwart und von Zukunft des deutschen Menschen* (Berlin: Georg Bondi, 1912), p. 186.

[54] Ibid., p. 188.

[55] Alfred Weber, 'Die Bedeutung der geistigen Führer in Deutschland', *Die neue Rundschau* 29(10), 1918, pp. 1249–1268.

[56] Ibid., p. 1250.   [57] Ibid., p. 1251.

concerning this particular question during the entire period of Simmel's adult life. Over the course of all those years, Germany's leading minds were obsessed with the problem of the tension between whole and part, between unity and particularity, between harmonious cultivation and professionalisation. Differing from each other in their backgrounds, interests and political views, they showed a remarkable measure of agreement and consistency both in the diagnosis of the problem and in the idiomatic patterns employed to describe it. Over more than four decades, one could hear complaints from all sides about the same fragmentation of spiritual life, be compared unfavourably with the same heroes of the past (such as Leibniz, Goethe or Hegel) and read verbs and nouns with the same prefix *zer-*, signifying the tearing of something asunder: *Zerrissenheit* (disruption), *sich zerstreuen* (disperse oneself), *Zerfall* (decay), *zerbrechen* (break to pieces) and so forth.

Furthermore, this discourse represented a specifically German form of cultural criticism. For although cultural discontent (as the counterpart to optimistic faith in progress) was in those years a pan-European phenomenon, only in Germany were the ills of modernity so often deduced from the tension between whole and part.

German writers were aware of this peculiarity. In 1880, the British journal *Contemporary Review* published an essay written by cultural critic Karl Hillebrand.[58] There, Hillebrand acquainted his readers with the debate on 'half-education' that was emerging in Germany, noting that half-education was often attributed to the extension of knowledge that 'renders it impossible for anyone to attain such a general acquaintance with the whole intellectual life of our age as, *e.g.*, a Leonardo possessed of that of his day, or Goethe and the Humboldts in a period nearer to our own'.[59] We are already familiar with this discourse. But one detail is worth noticing. The essay was not originally written for the *Contemporary Review*. It was in fact a translation of an article published a year earlier in the German journal *Deutsche Rundschau*.[60] In the original text the sentence I just quoted was absent. It was probably inserted specifically for the Anglophone reader. This suggests that the British and international public was not very familiar with this kind of discourse and

---

[58] Karl Hillebrand, 'On Half-Culture in Germany: Its Causes and Remedies', *Contemporary Review* 38, 1880, pp. 199–220.

[59] Ibid., p. 199.

[60] Karl Hillebrand, 'Halbbildung und Gymnasialreform: Ein Appell an die Unzufriedenen', *Deutsche Rundschau* 18, 1879, pp. 422–451. 'On Half-Culture in Germany' was in fact the second part of this article. The first part was published under the title 'On the Sources of German Discontent' in *Contemporary Review* 38, 1880, pp. 40–54.

needed further explanation. The situation remained basically the same almost four decades later, when Alfred Weber suggested that his French and English contemporaries were neither bothered like the Germans by the problem of growing specialisation and fragmentation nor were they even used to this sort of talk.[61]

Hillebrand and Weber were right. Consider Britain, for example. Although nineteenth-century Britain had its own share of cultural critics, such as Coleridge, Carlyle, Arnold or Ruskin, to name a few, their worries differed in many respects from those of their German peers. Matthew Arnold's *Culture and Anarchy* (1867–1869), a work clearly indebted to continental influences, perhaps comes closest to what was seen in Germany in those days. Arnold drew dichotomies between the notions of 'culture', 'Hellenism' and 'establishment' on the one hand and those of 'anarchy', 'Hebraism' and 'sectarianism' on the other. Hebraism was attributed to non-conformist liberals, whom Arnold attacked for their fanatical narrow-mindedness in the pursuit of liberal reforms. This narrow-mindedness, in his view, was inimical to the true culture of 'sweetness and light'.

So far, the basic dichotomy seems parallel to that which we have seen. Culture can be understood here as the embodiment of a complete and harmonious existence and be contrasted with the fragmentariness and apartness of anarchical sectarianism. Yet what was lacking in Arnold's book was the sense that this dichotomy might signify a profound and almost insolvable inner conflict. While unhappy about the effects of philistinism, Arnold did not suggest that the contradiction between the universality of culture and the narrow-mindedness of anarchy was an inevitable tragic feature of modern civilisation. He perceived the problem as specifically British and American, pointing to the influence of radical Puritanism as its source. Arnold described culture as 'a pursuit of our total perfection by means of getting to know, on all the matters which most concern us, the best which has been thought and said in the world'.[62] Such a definition almost certainly implied a denial of tragedy. For if perfection, or culture, was just knowledge of the best achievements of civilisation, and only in the most important matters, then nothing made it a priori impossible for anyone to acquaint oneself with these achievements and thus become a person of culture. The feeling of despair could appear only when

[61] Weber, 'Die Bedeutung der geistigen Führer in Deutschland', pp. 1254–1255.
[62] Matthew Arnold, *Culture and Anarchy: An Essay in Political and Social Criticism*, in *Culture and Anarchy and Other Writings* (Cambridge: Cambridge University Press, 1993), p. 190.

the ideal itself was perceived as impossible to reach, for example, when perfection meant the totality of knowledge in which every part was connected to the whole and vice versa.

Yet even when the ideal was formulated in this latter way, the response to it could, in fact, not be a sense of crisis but an acceptance of our imperfect condition. In 1914, the Green Moral Philosophy Prize at Oxford was awarded to an essay on the conception of personality written by a young fellow of New College, Arthur George Heath. Strongly influenced by German philosophy, Heath argued that the ideal of self-realisation had been torn in two opposite directions. One direction was that of breadth, the other was that of depth. These ideals are contradictory: 'Everyone would recommend whole-heartedly a great range of interests and pursuits if it were possible to do justice to them all: because this soon becomes impossible we turn to the other extreme and urge men to find their true selves in concentration, even in apparent narrowness.'[63] Yet Heath did not consider this dilemma to be intrinsically tragic. He argued that the solution to it would consist in just disposing of the false idea of perfection and accepting the inescapable finitude of our selves.

Thus the question of the split between human personality as a whole and one of its parts did not torment British thinkers that much. Even less did it affect the intellectual atmosphere in the United States, a country more immune to expressions of cultural discontent. To many European observers of the time, this immunity could be explained by what they perceived as a lack of high culture in America.[64] When taken literally, this common stereotype was an exaggeration. Culture-oriented education did indeed exist in nineteenth-century America, as its colleges offered a classical humanistic education, and the notion of harmonious self-formation became popular among American philosophers and was advocated, for example, by the St. Louis Hegelians.[65] Nevertheless, it is true that this sort of education did not benefit from the same degree of social prestige it acquired in Europe.[66] This is why the expansion and professionalisation of American universities, which took place towards the end of the nineteenth

---

[63] Arthur George Heath, *The Moral and Social Significance of the Conception of Personality* (Oxford: Clarendon Press, 1921), p. 66.

[64] On anti-Americanism in Germany see, for example, Dan Diner, *America in the Eyes of the Germans: An Essay on Anti-Americanism* (Princeton: Markus Wiener Publishers, 1996).

[65] On Hegelian influences in America in the nineteenth century see James A. Good, *A Search for Unity in Diversity: The 'Permanent Hegelian Deposit' in the Philosophy of John Dewey* (London: Lexington Books, 2006), pp. 55–95.

[66] It is on this account that Arnold considered America to be a country without establishment (*Culture and Anarchy*, pp. 197–201).

century, proceeded very quickly and relatively smoothly.[67] This development was not accompanied by vocal complaints from the 'cultural elite'.
On the contrary, in the realm of ideas, the continentally minded Hegelian
philosophical tradition lost ground and was virtually forgotten by 1910.[68]

Occasionally, however, the conflict between general culture and professional activity was approached in terms more reminiscent of Germany, for
example by John Dewey, who had once come under the spell of Hegelian
philosophy and retained many Hegelian influences even after developing
his own version of pragmatism.[69] Dewey admitted that the division of
labour characteristic of modern society might have a pernicious effect on
the modern personality by narrowing its horizons. The division of labour
'is reduced to a mechanical routine unless workers see the technical,
intellectual, and social relationships involved in what they do, and engage
in their work because of the motivation furnished by such perceptions'.
Dewey criticised 'the tendency to reduce such things as efficiency of
activity and scientific management to purely technical externals', for in
this case intelligence is 'narrowed to the factors concerned with technical
production and marketing of goods'. According to him, 'the failure to take
into account the significant social factors means . . . an absence of mind,
and a corresponding distortion of emotional life'.[70]

This worry, however, did not shake Dewey's faith in modern society. He
did not consider the gap between personality and technical efficiency to be
inevitable.[71] Subscribing to a sort of monistic optimism, Dewey believed that
modernity itself provided the solution for the problem it created. The
solution was democratic mobility. 'It is a commonplace', he argued, 'that
an alert and expanding mental life depends upon an enlarging range of
contact with the physical environment. But the principle applies even more
significantly to the field where we are apt to ignore it – the sphere of social
contacts'.[72] Therefore, in order to overcome the narrowness of specialisation

---

[67] See Harry Liebersohn, 'The American Academic Community before the First World War:
A Comparison with the German "Bildungsbürgertum"', in Werner Conze and Jürgen Kocka
(eds.), *Bildungsbürgertum im 19. Jahrhundert,* vol. 1: *Bildungssystem und Professionalisierung in
internationalen Vergleichen* (Stuttgart: Klett-Cotta, 1985), pp. 163–185.

[68] Good, *A Search for Unity in Diversity,* p. xx.

[69] On the parallels between Simmel and Dewey, see Heike Koenig, 'Enabling the Individual: Simmel,
Dewey and "The Need for a Philosophy of Education"', *Simmel Studies* 23(1), 2019, pp. 109–146.

[70] John Dewey, *Democracy and Education* [1916] (New York: The Free Press, 1944), p. 85.

[71] Dewey believed the gap between these two spheres to be the distinctive property of the German
mind, being a legacy of the Kantian dualism of inner freedom and outward necessity. See
John Dewey, *German Philosophy and Politics* (New York: Henry Holt and Company, 1915), pp.
28–30.

[72] Dewey, *Democracy and Education,* p. 86.

one should 'bring peoples and classes into closer and more perceptible connection with one another'.[73] Modern democratic society, 'which is full of channels for the distribution of a change occurring anywhere, must see to it that its members are educated to personal initiative and adaptability'.[74] For Dewey, therefore, finding the solution to the problem was possible and, in a certain sense, inevitable. It would consist of connecting every individual to the present world of physical and social diversity.

Let me now return to Europe and cast a glance at a final example: France. France's cultural connections with Germany were naturally the closest of the three countries considered here. Many French thinkers came under the influence of one variety or another of German philosophy. What is more, the prestige of the German higher education system was such that, after the defeat of 1870, it was even claimed that the real winners of the war were the German universities and that it was incumbent upon the French to learn from those institutions.[75]

The sources of the cultural discontent of many French intellectuals can also be traced to Germany. Nevertheless, the form this discontent took in France was different. Indeed, one often heard about fear, anxiety or *ennui* (boredom).[76] Yet the tension between totality and particularity was less on the agenda. There was no fatigue of specialisation in the air, partly because the French universities of the time were less specialised than the German ones. Emphasis on general culture was the predominant attitude, as 'the French idealised the professor as a man of broad culture and encyclopaedic knowledge rather than as a narrow specialist . . . He was a *savant*, steeped in the ancient and classic culture that was to be passed on via his students to the next generation'.[77]

This situation actually caused some thinkers to call for the adoption of the level of professionalisation that existed in Germany. Indeed, by learning from the Germans how to be scientific professionals, French academics also learned the pattern of thought which questioned the value of professionalism. Sociologist Émile Durkheim was one such academic. During the 1880s, he visited German universities and, despite his later protestations to the contrary, the impact of German ideas on his thinking was

---

[73] Ibid.   [74] Ibid., p. 88.
[75] Theodore Zeldin, *France 1848–1945*, vol. 2: *Intellect, Taste and Anxiety* (Oxford: Clarendon Press, 1977), p. 320.
[76] Ibid., pp. 823–875. For a detailed survey of French cultural pessimism in the nineteenth century, see Koenraad W. Swart, *The Sense of Decadence in Nineteenth-Century France* (The Hague: Martin Nijhoff, 1964).
[77] Robert Gilpin, *France in the Age of the Scientific State* (Princeton: Princeton University Press, 1968), p. 97.

significant. He was influenced, among others, by psychologist Wilhelm Wundt, sociologist Albert Schäffle and economist Adolph Wagner.[78] In *The Division of Labour in Society* (1893), the book 'whose dependence on these German sources is palpable on every page',[79] Durkheim asked: 'Does not division of labour, by rendering each one of us an incomplete being, not entail some curtailment of the individual personality?'[80]

The question is already familiar to us; less so is the answer, which was an unambiguous and unapologetic 'no'. Durkheim asked: 'Why should more dignity attach to being complete and mediocre than in leading a more specialised kind of life but one more intense . . . ?'[81] Furthermore, he argued that the so-called harmonious life of ancient society was merely an illusion. The fact that activities in the ancient world were less specialised does not mean that each member of society was a more complete and more harmonious individual. In truth, he was less of an individual. His activities were of course more complete, yet they were not his own: 'It is society, it is the race, which act in and through him; he is only the intermediary through which they are realised.'[82] Therefore, the modern individual, by being a professional, does not lose anything in comparison with a member of ancient society. On the contrary, he gains in individuality because, however more one-sided his actions may look, they are *his* actions reflecting *his* personality.

Thus Durkheim's familiarity with the discourse under consideration did not compel him to arrive at the standard conclusions. Nor did his standpoint turn him into an intellectual pariah. On the contrary, his confidence in modern society reflected the combative and confident mood of many figures among the intellectual elite of the French Third Republic, whose belief in progress and bourgeois republicanism constituted an essential part of their value system.

The same cannot be said about the mainstream intellectual elite of Imperial Germany. This does not mean that a position similar to that of Durkheim was never articulated. In Germany too one would occasionally hear voices praising modern specialisation and refusing to see it as the cause of the alleged destruction of inner harmony. Thus, in 1890, Max von Pettenkofer, an epidemiologist and the president of the Royal Bavarian

---

[78] See Robert Alun Jones, *The Development of Durkheim's Social Realism* (Cambridge: Cambridge University Press, 1999), pp. 172–231.
[79] Ibid., p. 231.
[80] Émile Durkheim, *The Division of Labour in Society* [1893], trans. W. D. Halls (New York: The Free Press, 1997), p. 334.
[81] Ibid.   [82] Ibid., p. 336.

Academy of Sciences, addressed the academy with the following defence of the scientific enterprise:

> Many people think that sciences, which had nothing in common with each other at the moment of their emergence, would have to move away centrifugally from each other even farther as a result of their further development. But the case is precisely the opposite, for the trees of knowledge do not grow into the sky either. Rather, the taller they grow, the wider they stretch out their arms, intertwining their branches even more with each other.[83]

Fourteen years later, sociologist Franz Oppenheimer also came out with a similar defence of modern science, arguing that the much-lamented quality of specialism would in the end lead back to universal culture (*Bildung*).[84]

Yet these two examples are the exceptions that confirm the rule. The Bavarian doctor, more than seventy when he delivered his speech, belonged to an older and perhaps more naive generation of scholars, whereas the Jewish liberal socialist was too marginal a figure. Neither spoke for an emerging consensus, the true representatives of which were mandarins such as Mommsen and Harnack. This consensus was not that of radical cultural pessimism. Mommsen and Harnack, as well as many other of their contemporaries, trusted the society in which they lived, happily pursued their intellectual activities and believed themselves to have achieved a great degree of self-cultivation. Yet, at the same time, the complaint about the dispersion of the harmonious personality as a result of the requirement to concentrate on one's duty was a major element of this consensus. This question was considered extremely important, and it was not expected that the solution to the problem would be found easily. Hope and optimism were indeed present, but they were accompanied by a growing nervousness. The most salient symbol of this nervousness was the recurring theme of the tension between *Bildung* and *Beruf*.

1.2 *Bildung, Beruf*

The conflict between *Bildung* (self-cultivation) and *Beruf* (vocation)[85] was considered a grave problem by the leading minds of Imperial Germany.

---

[83] Max v. Pettenkofer, *Rerum cognoscere causas* (Munich: K. B. Akademie der Wissenschaften, 1890), p. 7.

[84] Franz Oppenheimer, 'Werdende Wissenschaften', *Neue Rundschau* 15, 1904, p. 828.

[85] This pair of terms – '*Bildung*' and '*Beruf*' – is perhaps the most convenient heuristic device to refer to the conflict between whole and part. It was already in use in the nineteenth century. We encountered it, for example, in Windelband's essay. Later, Friedrich Paulsen, in his analysis of the

But how did this particular problem happen to acquire such great importance? How did it come about that this pair of two very common words
produced so much anxiety?

The tension between the appeal of general culture and that of
a specialised vocation is a widespread feature of modern differentiated
society. Almost every young man and woman growing up in such
a society needs, at some point, to make up their mind about the proper
balance between the two. It is unlikely, however, that nowadays many
people would come to regard this specific dilemma as the measure of all
things. In other words, it is easy to grasp why this issue can be perceived as
a problem. It is less clear why anyone should regard it as *the* problem of
modernity. Yet in Imperial Germany it was often perceived as *the* question.

One way to approach this issue would be to look for the 'social causes' of
this phenomenon. For example, one could examine the structural dynamic
within the educated middle classes, focusing on the status anxiety caused by
the growing differentiation of professions within that social group.[86] This
approach, however, has its limits. It can explain quite well why the group
develops a certain set of sentiments. Yet it is not as good at explaining why
those sentiments are channelled towards particular patterns of thought and
speech. Activities of the mind are autonomous and cannot be reduced to
merely the social positions of those who perform them. Patterns of thought
and speech relate to what is heard and read, and what is heard and read is often
independent of one's own social identity and activities. One may absorb ways
of thinking from texts written in different contexts and for different types of
audience. Such texts can leave their imprint on their readers' minds and thus
modify their understanding of themselves and their environment. Had those
readers read other texts, their self-understanding would have acquired
a different form.

---

essence of education ('Das moderne Bildungswesen', in W. Lexis et al., *Die allgemeinen Grundlagen
der Kultur der Gegenwart* [Berlin: B.G. Teubner, 1906], pp. 54–86), argued that education (*Bildung*)
consists of two elements. One is personal self-formation, or self-cultivation (*persönliche Bildung*), the
purpose of which is the well-being of the individual. The other is training for a profession (*Beruf*),
through which the individual becomes a member of a society (ibid., pp. 55–56). Over the course of
the twentieth century, this pair was often evoked by scholars to signify the problem depicted here.
See, for example, Theodor Litt, *Berufsbildung und Allgemeinbildung* (Wiesbaden: Eberhard
Brockhaus, 1947), p. 8; Herwig Blankertz, *Bildung im Zeitalter der großen Industrie: Pädagogik,
Schule und Berufsbildung im 19. Jahrhundert* (Hannover: Hermann Schroedel, 1969), p. 28;
Clemens Menze, *Die philosophische Idee der Universität und ihre Krise im Zeitalter der
Wissenschaften* (Krefeld: Scherpe, 1975), p. 20.

[86] See Claudia Huerkamp, 'Die preußisch-deutsche Ärzeschaft als Teil des Bildungsbürgertums:
Wandel in Lage und Selbstverständnis vom ausgehenden 18. Jahrhundert bis zum Kaiserreich', in
Conze and Kocka (eds.), *Bildungsbürgertum im 19. Jahrhundert*, vol. 1, p. 387.

In order therefore to understand the importance of the *Bildung / Beruf* dichotomy, one needs to grasp the full scope of its possible meanings and be aware of the connotations it may have evoked in the minds of cultivated Germans of the time, connotations embedded in a long intellectual tradition: the tradition of self-cultivation (*Bildung*).[87] The discussion will be inevitably concise, as I will focus only on those aspects of this tradition which directly relate to the question under consideration, skipping over other issues.

In the first half of the twentieth century, the tradition of *Bildung* became increasingly self-reflective. Numerous studies on its origin, development and significance were published.[88] Generally speaking, traditions tend to become self-reflective when their highest achievements are already behind them. Very often self-reflection is a sign of both past greatness and current crisis. A feeling of crisis certainly existed in the 1900s, and it intensified during the First World War and the Weimar Republic. In this atmosphere, there were many who regarded the tradition as no longer relevant. In 1931, Hans Freyer pronounced his verdict: 'the problem of *Bildung* is not topical.'[89]

But when did awareness of the crisis first appear? According to Karl Löwith, the discordance started sometime in the middle of the nineteenth century, when the great synthetic work of Goethe and Hegel was particularised by their followers.[90] At first glance, this interpretation may seem

---

[87] For a general overview of the concept of *Bildung*, see Ernst Lichtenstein, *Zur Entwicklung des Bildungsbegriffs von Meister Eckhart bis Hegel* (Heidelberg: Quelle & Mayer, 1966); idem, 'Bildung', in J. Ritter (ed.), *Historisches Wörterbuch der Philosophie* (Basel: Schwabe & Co., 1971), vol. 1, pp. 921–937; Aleida Assmann, *Arbeit am nationalen Gedächtnis: Eine kurze Geschichte der deutschen Bildungsidee* (Frankfurt am Main: Campus, 1993); Georg Bollenbeck, *Bildung und Kultur: Glanz und Elend eines deutschen Deutungsmusters* (Frankfurt am Main: Insel, 1994); W. H. Bruford, *Culture and Society in Classical Weimar 1775–1806* (Cambridge: University Press, 1962); idem., *The German Tradition of Self-Cultivation: Bildung from Humboldt to Thomas Mann* (London: Cambridge University Press, 1975); David Sorkin, 'Wilhelm von Humboldt: The Theory and Practice of Self-Formation (*Bildung*), 1791–1810', *Journal of the History of Ideas* 44(1), 1983, pp. 55–73; Raymond Geuss, '*Kultur, Bildung, Geist*', *History & Theory* 35(2), 1996, pp. 151–164.

[88] See, for example, Hans Weil, *Die Entstehung des deutschen Bildungsprinzips* (Bonn: Friedrich Cohen, 1930); Ilse Schaarschmidt, *Der Bedeutungswandel der Worte 'bilden' und 'Bildung' in der Literatur-Epoche von Gottsched bis Herder* (Elbing: Seiffert, 1931); E. L. Stahl, *Die religiöse und die humanitätsphilosophische Bildungsidee und die Entstehung des deutschen Bildungsromans im 18. Jahrhundert* (Bern: Paul Haupt, 1934); Irmgard Taylor, *Kultur, Aufklärung, Bildung, Humanität und verwandte Begriffe bei Herder* (Gießen: von Münchow, 1938).

[89] Hans Freyer, 'Zur Bildungskrise der Gegenwart', *Die Erziehung* 6(10/11), 1931, p. 597.

[90] Karl Löwith, *From Hegel to Nietzsche: The Revolution in Nineteenth-Century Thought*, trans. D. E. Green (New York: Columbia University Press, 1964), especially pp. 235–305. See also Blankertz, *Bildung im Zeitalter der großen Industrie*, p. 46. Blankertz argues that the antithesis of general and professional education was the dominant pedagogic antithesis of the nineteenth century.

problematic. For even at the time of Hegel and Goethe, known as the *Blütezeit*, the problem was already well known. Goethe's Wilhelm Meister, for example, complained to his friend that it was difficult for a burgher to acquire proper cultivation. In the burgher's manner of existence there can be no harmonious interplay of qualities, 'because in order to make himself useful in one direction, he has to disregard everything else'.[91] The same problem tormented Friedrich Schiller, who claimed that the moderns lacked the natural humanity of the Greeks. With the moderns, 'the various faculties appear as separate in practice as they are distinguished by the psychologist in theory', so that whole classes develop just 'one part of their potentialities, while of the rest, as in stunted growths, only vestigial traces remain'.[92] As Theodor Litt noted, the complaints of the German classics about fragmentation were surprisingly similar to those of later generations, even though the classics' condition was child's play in comparison to the more recent radical one-sidedness.[93]

Yet the difference between the two ages seems to have been more than one of degree. Löwith was right when he suggested that something had gone wrong along the way. It is true that the classics complained about modern fragmentation. Coming mostly from the ranks of the middle class, they rebelled against the narrow-mindedness of their environment. Renouncing the careers of salesmen or craftsmen, they found escape in poetry, philosophy, theatre, scholarship or some kind of unorthodox religious devotion. Yet it seems that there was one crucial difference between them and the thinkers of later generations. The *Blütezeit* generation was, on the whole, forward-looking. It was convinced that self-cultivation was possible even in the conditions of modernity and determined to pursue it.

Strategies of self-cultivation might differ. For example, one could attempt to reach harmonious perfection through a fusion with the world in its variety. Some of Goethe's writings can be read this way. Thus the young Wilhelm Meister rejects the path intended for him by his family – the

---

[91] See J. W. von Goethe, *Wilhelm Meister's Apprenticeship*, trans. E. A. Blackall, in *Goethe's Collected Works*, vol. 9 (New York: Suhrkamp Publishers, 1989), p. 175. One can also mention the influence of Rousseau's dilemma of 'man' and 'citizen' on German thinkers. See Löwith, *From Hegel to Nietzsche*, pp. 236–240; Richard Velkley, 'The Tension in the Beautiful: On Culture and Civilization in Rousseau and German Philosophy', in C. Orwin and N. Tarcov (eds.), *The Legacy of Rousseau* (Chicago: University of Chicago Press, 1997), pp. 65–86.

[92] Friedrich Schiller, *On the Aesthetic Education of Man*, trans. E. M. Wilkinson and L. A. Willoughby (Oxford: Clarendon Press, 1967), p. 33.

[93] Theodor Litt, *Das Bildungsideal der deutschen Klassik und die moderne Arbeitswelt* (Bonn: Bundeszentrale für Heimatdienst, 1958), pp. 33–36.

occupation of merchant – and embarks upon a journey of self-discovery. In the beginning, this journey is driven by his dream of becoming an actor. This obsession, however, does not lead him to escapism. On the contrary, the variety of the situations and of the kinds of human intercourse in which he engages allows him to actually acquaint himself with the world. And although in the end his dream about the theatre turns out to be an illusion, his adventure teaches him how to reconnect with the world and find his place in it. In *Wilhelm Meisters Wanderjahre* (1821–1829), we learn that Wilhelm chooses to dedicate himself to the vocation of surgeon.[94] This moment in Goethe's work can be interpreted as a break with the tradition of *Bildung*. Yet the opposite interpretation is equally possible. Wilhelm's choice of profession can be seen not as a departure from *Bildung* in favour of *Beruf* but as a successful absorption of the latter into the former. Thus Max Wundt argued (1913) that Wilhelm's choice of a specific vocation did not mean that the idea of totality was forgotten. On the contrary, in this specific activity Wilhelm found a way to reconcile the diversity of life with the singularity of his inward personality.[95] Such an interpretation helped, of course, to sustain Goethe's image as the very embodiment of the *Bildung* ideal.

Friedrich Schleiermacher's *Monologen* (1800) represented an alternative strategy of self-cultivation. Harmony of personality was achieved here not through fusion with the world but through liberation from it. The text carried a very strong flavour of German pietism and of a mystic's yearning for the life of a recluse. For Schleiermacher, true individuality was a unique point situated beyond the world. Worldly activity hampers individuality, even if it is artistic activity, for it distracts the mind from itself and directs its attention towards the object of its work. Schleiermacher defended himself against those 'who would have every one become a virtuoso and expert in some field of knowledge'. It is useless to hope, he said, that 'I should ever seriously devote myself to one thing'.[96] Worldly activities are always fragmentary, and concentration on any such activity will prevent the personality from absorbing other aspects of existence and thereby will render its individuality less complete. Schleiermacher's description of the process through which the variety of the world was united with the singularity of the personality thus differed from that of Goethe. In

---

[94] J. W. von Goethe, *Wilhelm Meister's Journeyman Years or The Renunciants*, trans. K. Winston, in *Goethe's Collected Works*, vol. 10 (New York: Suhrkamp Publishers, 1989), ch. III.3, pp. 321–329.

[95] Max Wundt, *Goethes Wilhelm Meister und die Entwicklung des modernen Lebensideals* (Berlin: Walter de Gruyter, 1932 [1913]), pp. 471–472.

[96] Friedrich Schleiermacher, *Soliloquies*, trans. H. L. Friess (Chicago: The Open Court Publishing Company, 1957), pp. 39–40.

Goethe, personality fused with the world, while in Schleiermacher the world abolished itself by becoming absorbed into individuality.

Yet, these differences notwithstanding, there was something important that Goethe's and Schleiermacher's ideals possessed in common. They both required integration between the diversity of the world and the singularity of the personality in order to produce an accomplished individuality. Moreover, both Goethe and Schleiermacher seemed to believe that such integration was possible. Goethe's optimism is unsurprising. Over the course of his entire life, he remained, to a great extent, a man of the Enlightenment. Schleiermacher's optimism is more unexpected given his quasi-mystical rejection of the world as well as his perfectionism – for him, a fully unique individuality had to reflect the totality of the world and at the same time remain untainted by it. And yet, even though Schleiermacher admitted that he had not reached perfection in some particulars, he nevertheless was sure that on the whole he succeeded in reaching the blissful condition of harmonious individuality. He expressed this conviction with great zeal, in a manner reminiscent of conversion stories:

> With proud joy I still recall the time, when I discovered humanity and knew that henceforth I should never lose it ... I can affirm that since then I have never forsaken my true self ... In quiet tranquillity, in utter simplicity I preserve with me an uninterrupted consciousness of humanity's entire essence.[97]

Not all the literary figures of that generation were as self-celebratory as Schleiermacher. Yet most of them shared his fundamental belief in the possibility of self-cultivation. Hölderlin (if one accepts Windelband's interpretation of him) was an exception.

Nevertheless, Windelband's analysis reveals something important. It shows that by the time he lectured on Hölderlin, the mood had changed. Just a few decades after Goethe and Schleiermacher, the initial naivety seems to have dissipated. More and more thinkers began to question the feasibility of the ideal of self-cultivation. Although the ideal and the ways of its expression remained more or less the same, attitudes towards it became more pessimistic. How did so (relatively) fast a change come about? In order to answer this question, one should take a closer and more analytical look at the components that make up the ideal of *Bildung.*

---

[97] Ibid., pp. 28–29.

Bildung can be translated simply as education. However, the word can also refer to a specific kind of education: education through self-formation towards the condition of harmonious personality. This is the neo-humanistic vision of *Bildung.* The term 'neo-humanism' (*Neuhumanismus*) was coined by Friedrich Paulsen in 1885.[98] The logic behind Paulsen's terminology is clear. The neo-humanistic movement in Germany was perceived as being parallel to the humanistic movement of the Renaissance age.[99]

The Renaissance was often related to the ideal of the formation of the universal man who achieves excellence in respect of human nature as such and not in respect of any specific social function. 'The ideal now being held out for imitation is that of the so-called "Renaissance man," the man who aims at nothing less than universal excellence. He is no longer allowed to think of himself as a specialist either in the arts of government or scholarship or war'.[100] Of course, this ideal was not necessarily shared, let alone explicitly and unambiguously articulated, by all humanists.[101] Nevertheless, the specific image of the Renaissance man is important because it underlies a common perception of the Renaissance in the nineteenth century. The image of the many-sided, and even all-sided, man was painted by Burckhardt and exercised a powerful effect on the imagination of his contemporaries.[102]

---

[98] Friedrich Paulsen, *Geschichte des gelehrten Unterrichts: Auf den deutschen Schulen und Universitäten vom Ausgang des Mittelalters bis zur Gegenwart* (Leipzig: Veit, 1885). The term *Humanismus* was first used by Friedrich Immanuel Niethammer (*Der Streit des Philanthropinismus und Humanismus in der Theorie des Erziehungs-Unterrichts unsrer Zeit* [Jena: Friedrich Frommann, 1808]), not historically but normatively. Niethammer did not deal with the revival of antiquity in the late mediaeval period. Rather, he articulated his own views about what pedagogy ought to be. He defended an anti-utilitarian approach to education which had the study of classical languages as its basis. Later, during the 1830s and 1840s, the words 'humanists' and 'humanism' began to be used with regard to the Renaissance period (e.g., Karl Hagen, *Der Geist der Reformation und seine Gegensätze*, vol. 1 [Erlangen: Palm, 1841], pp. 37–39, 79–81). The pioneering study of Georg Voigt (*Die Wiederbelebung des classischen Alterthums*, oder das erste Jahrhundert des Humanismus [Berlin: G. Reimer, 1859]) finally established this meaning of 'humanism'. On the history of the word '*Humanismus*', see Erich Heyfelder, 'Die Ausdrücke "Renaissance" und "Humanismus"', *Deutsche Literaturzeitung* 34, 6 September 1913, pp. 2245–2250.

[99] This interest received the name *Renaissancismus*. See, for example, Martin A. Ruehl, *The Italian Renaissance in the German Historical Imagination, 1860–1930* (Cambridge: Cambridge University Press, 2015).

[100] Quentin Skinner, *The Foundations of Modern Political Thought*, vol. 1: *The Renaissance* (Cambridge: Cambridge University Press, 1978), p. 91.

[101] In fact, the Renaissance image espoused by Burckhardt and his adepts downplayed the role of humanist learning in the formation of the Renaissance individuality. See Ruehl, *The Italian Renaissance in the German Historical Imagination*, pp. 8–10.

[102] 'No acute and practiced eye might be able to trace, step by step, the increase in the number of complete men during the fifteenth century. Whether they had before them as a conscious object the harmonious development of their spiritual and material existence is hard to say; but several of them attained it, so far as is consistent with the imperfection of all that is earthly.' Jacob Burckhardt, *The*

The idea of the universal man and the rejection of usefulness could thus be seen as features belonging to both humanism and neo-humanism.

Furthermore, the idea of the universal man was connected with a certain kind of theology. For example, many humanists believed that all-sided cultivation fulfilled the essence of man as a creature moulded in the image of God. Since they perceived God first and foremost as the creator of every being, to be in God's image meant to imitate the divine quality of creativity and thereby earn honour and fame, analogous to the honour and fame due to God.[103] In other words, man was called to engage in his own harmonious creation so that the plenitude of his qualities could reflect the whole variety of the world.

Alternatively, the origins of the neo-humanistic ideal of harmonious personality can be traced back to theological elements in the early modern philosophy of nature.[104] This tradition differed in some respects from humanism, yet its quasi-pantheistic image of nature and divinity could also lead to the view that man's purpose lies in his inner development towards becoming a reflection of the totality of nature.

The idea of inner organic self-development thus carried heavy theological baggage. At the same time, towards the eighteenth century, it began to adopt more secular forms. Herder, for example, applied his views of harmonious unity to secular totalities such as peoples or cultures.[105] In Hegel, God was replaced by the absolute spirit (*Geist*) that undergoes the process of its own *Bildung*.[106] And Goethe's own version of natural philosophy can also be seen as an expression of the urge for a quasi-pantheistic universality.[107]

To summarise, when the ideal of *Bildung* was evoked in a humanistic context, it was understood to be aiming at the formation of a universal

---

Civilization of the Renaissance in Italy, trans. S. G. C. Middlemore (New York: Albert & Charles Boni, 1935), p. 147.

[103] 'It is a remarkable measure of the extent to which men were by this time felt to possess God-like qualities that the humanists express this sense of what is due to a *vir virtutis* in precisely the same language later used in the Authorised Version of the Bible to describe what is due to God: in each case what is said to be owed to such unsurpassable excellence is the tribute of honour, glory and praise'. Skinner, *The Foundations of Modern Political Thought*, vol. I, p. 99.

[104] On the 'organologic' philosophy of nature, see Günther Dohmen, *Bildung und Schule: Die Entstehung des deutschen Bildungsbegriffs und die Entwicklung seines Verhältnisses zur Schule*, vol. I: *Der religiöse und der organologische Bildungsbegriff* (Weinheim: Julius Beltz, 1964), pp. 68–78.

[105] See Frederick M. Barnard, *Herder's Social and Political Thought: From Enlightenment to Nationalism* (Oxford: Clarendon Press, 1965), pp. 54–87.

[106] G. W. F. Hegel, *Phenomenology of Spirit* [1807], trans. A. V. Miller (Oxford: Oxford University Press, 1977).

[107] On Goethe's natural philosophy, see, for example, Wolfgang Yourgrau, 'Reflections on the Natural Philosophy of Goethe', *Philosophy* 26(96), 1951, pp. 69–84.

harmonious personality, which was supposed to reflect the totality of the world. This ideal was best expressed in Wilhelm von Humboldt's dictum that the true end of man was 'the highest and most harmonious development of his powers to a complete and consistent whole'.[108]

Inner harmonious cultivation constitutes, therefore, a basic component of the neo-humanistic ideal of *Bildung*, and very often the entire ideal is reduced to this component. Yet the ideal is more complex. It is characterised by a certain duality, which must not be overlooked if one wants to understand the peculiarities of neo-humanism and the problems it faced.

Hans Weil argued that the notion of *Bildung* originated in two different principles. One, which postulates the harmonious development of abilities, has been outlined. Now we should turn to the other principle: *Bildung* as making oneself into an image (*Bildung als Zum-Bilde-Machen*).[109] This very expression already points to the moment that distinguishes between the two principles. Whereas the first principle emphasises inner growth, the second principle postulates an external standard, an objective criterion or an image, towards which the process of formation should be directed and by which it will be judged.

The roots of this second element go back to several waves of German religious enthusiasm, such as mediaeval mysticism, the Lutheran Reformation and pietism.[110] The very word '*Bildung*' (formed from the word '*Bild*', 'image') originated in German mediaeval mysticism, represented, for example, by Meister Eckhart, a Dominican theologian of the late thirteenth and early fourteenth centuries. Mystics yearned to form themselves into the image of God or to immerse their souls in God. Yet the God in whose image the soul was created and whose image it was called to imitate was different from God the creator of the world in all its diversity. Meister Eckhart and other German mystics were strongly influenced by neo-Platonic teachings,[111] and their God was the transcendental One who stands above and beyond the world.

As such, the development of all the potentialities of human nature was less relevant to their worldview. The way towards God lay not in embracing the world but in retreating from it. The soul had to be liberated from

---

[108] Wilhelm von Humboldt, *The Limits of State Action*, trans. J. W. Burrow (Indianapolis: Liberty Fund, 1993), p. 10.

[109] Weil, *Die Entstehung des deutschen Bildungsprinzips*, pp. 10–83. A somewhat similar idea of the dual origin of *Bildung* (in mystical teachings on the one hand and the 'organologic' philosophy of nature on the other) can be found in Dohmen, *Bildung und Schule*, vol. 1.

[110] On the religious origins of *Bildung*, see Hans Schilling, *Bildung als Gottesbildlichkeit* (Freiburg: Lambertus, 1961).

[111] Dohmen, *Bildung und Schule*, vol. 1, p. 56.

the fetters of matter so that it could restore its essential purity and reunite with God, from whom it emanated.[112] Hence, the emphasis lay on inward spiritual activity rather than on improving the world.[113]

Furthermore, to retreat also meant to abandon the variety of the world and cultivate instead the singularity of the soul. This was also a way to imitate God. The imitation here was not of the all-encompassing totality of the Creator but rather of the singularity of the One. Making oneself into an image meant turning oneself into one specific form or finding a single point or condition which would open the gates to a blissful fusion with God. The whole mystical process of elevation was therefore the process of concentration through which this or that particular form, or image, could be attained.

Finally, *Bildung* thus understood was also a process of self-annulment.[114] The vanity of independence had to be renounced on the way to union with God. The whole process here was essentially passive, however much effort was invested in mystical elevation. For every activity was performed as an act of obedience rather than of self-affirmation. The form to be attained was determined not by free choice but by God's command. The ultimate source of the so-called inwardness of this mystical *Bildung* was therefore not the inner self but an extraneous object to which the soul was driven. *Bildung* in this sense could be described as a process of devotion to a single, indivisible, extraneous, other-worldly object.

Subsequent religious movements were not as other-worldly as mediaeval mysticism. Pietism, for example, preached the value of good work. While objecting to the rationalism of Enlightenment philosophy, it also contributed to the development of the educational practice of the Enlightenment (*Aufklärung*), with its emphasis on teaching useful skills.[115] Yet the fundamental vision of pietism with regard to *Bildung* was similar to that of mediaeval mysticism. Although pietism placed strong emphasis on the conscientious performance of social duty, this emphasis was driven by a similar sentiment: simple-minded inward devotion to a single extraneous object. For inwardness does not necessarily exclude the notion of work. It only signifies the other-worldly source of the command to engage in work.

Now, if this is what the second aspect of *Bildung* means, then it has a synonym in the German language: the word '*Beruf*'. Like '*Bildung*', '*Beruf*' is, today, a common German word. In everyday language it signifies

---

[112] Ibid., p. 51.   [113] On the idea of inwardness in Eckhart, see ibid., pp. 42–43.   [114] Ibid., p. 51.
[115] On the more worldly attitude to vocation in pietism, see, for example, Anthony J. LaVopa, *Grace, Talent, and Merit: Poor Students, Clerical Careers, and Professional Ideology in Eighteenth-Century Germany* (Cambridge: Cambridge University Press, 1988), p. 143.

'profession'. Yet, again like *Bildung*, it possesses theological and philosophical connotations. These connotations played an important role at two moments at least. First, the word *'Beruf'* had a clear theological meaning when it initially entered the mediaeval German language. Second, this meaning received much attention at the beginning of the twentieth century when Max Weber published his study on the ethics of Protestantism.[116]

The theological roots of the word go back to the New Testament. *'Beruf'* is a noun derived from the verb *'rufen'* (to call), the translation for the Latin verb *'voco'*. It was used specifically in respect of Jesus, who was said to have been called by God to carry out the mission of humankind's salvation. *Beruf* thus came to be understood as a specific sacral mission which was distinguished from other secular activities. This mission passed from Jesus to the chosen order: ecclesiastics, and especially monks. This order was called on to set itself apart from the world in order to serve God. By contrast, the work of laymen was not regarded as *Beruf*. No special calling was attached to secular occupations.[117] Gradually, however, the usage of *Beruf* was expanded. Broader usage of the word can already be found in some texts by scholastics and German mystics.[118] This tendency was further reinforced by Luther, who argued that each Christian was, in a certain sense, 'called' by God. Luther thereby equated spiritual with worldly occupations.[119] As a result of this expansion of meaning, *Beruf* could now refer to 'occupation' in general. Yet even in this broad sense, the notion that conscientious performance of one's work possessed some sacral significance was often preserved.

Thus both *Bildung* (in its second meaning) and *Beruf* refer to the ethics of vocation, that is, to a whole-hearted devotion to an extraneous object. One could therefore call this second aspect of the *Bildung* ideal '*Bildung-as-Beruf*', in contrast to the first aspect which could be called '*Bildung-as-Cultivation*'. It is important to emphasise here that my intention is neither to delineate a comprehensive etymology of these terms nor to write a history of their usage in German culture. Rather, I employ them heuristically to signify two principles of *Bildung*, under whatever name they may appear in various texts. These two words – *Bildung* and *Beruf* – are very suitable because the range of their connotations corresponds almost precisely to the range of connotations of the two principles of *Bildung*.

---

[116] Max Weber, *The Protestant Ethics and the Spirit of Capitalism* [1904–1905], trans. T. Parsons (New York: Charles Scribner's Sons, 1958), pp. 79, 204–206.

[117] On the history of the term *'Beruf'*, see Karl Holl, 'Die Geschichte des Worts Beruf', in *Gesammelte Aufsätze zur Kirchengeschichte*, vol. 3: *Der Westen* (Tübingen: J.C.B. Mohr, 1928), pp. 189–219.

[118] Ibid., pp. 201, 204–208.   [119] Ibid., p. 217.

In the eighteenth century, the principle of *Bildung*-as-*Beruf*, like that of *Bildung*-as-Cultivation, was significantly secularised. The story of Shaftesbury's reception in Germany is a good example of this. The third Earl of Shaftesbury (1671–1713) was an English philosopher and writer who became very influential in Germany in the middle of the eighteenth century.[120] Shaftesbury was a religious thinker, yet his thought contributed to an aesthetic reinterpretation of the idea of *Bildung*. The neo-Platonic notion of 'inner form', into which one was called to develop oneself, was a major term in Shaftesbury's philosophy. This notion had a strong aesthetic flavour, as for Shaftesbury the way to virtue passed through good taste. A key characteristic of good taste was its disinterestedness.[121] As a result, the terms 'inner', 'form' and 'disinterestedness' became related to each other in the German discourse on *Bildung*, given especially that 'inner form' was translated into German as '*Bildung*'. The emphasis in this discourse was on inward 'disinterested' formation in accordance with a certain ideal, although this formation was now understood less as a return to God and more as a fulfilment of the aesthetic imperative. This aesthetic imperative, however, took from God the quality of being transcendental. Situated by Winckelmann and others in the bygone past of Greece, it became purely ideal and almost unachievable.[122]

All this resembles, of course, the notion of *Bildung*-as-*Beruf*, only that here it is secularised through aesthetics. Yet secularisation did not take away the sublime character of this principle, at least insofar as neo-humanism was concerned. Neo-humanists did not believe that every occupation could lead to a state of pure, single-minded, disinterested devotion. They tended to dismiss the value of 'useful' middle-class occupations. At the same time, neo-humanists did not abandon the ethics of *Beruf* altogether. Even if many of them rejected the career paths prepared for them by their fathers, they did not renounce the ideal of *Beruf* itself or however else this ethics of quasi-mystical devotion might be called. They

---

[120] On Shaftesbury's reception in Germany, see Rebekka Horlacher, '*Bildung* – A Construction of a History of Philosophy of Education', *Studies in Philosophy and Education* 23(5/6), 2004, pp. 409–426. See also Christian Friedrich Weiser, *Shaftesbury und das deutsche Geistesleben* (Leipzig: B. G. Teubner, 1916).

[121] Here starts a long tradition within the German philosophy of aesthetics which emphasises disinterestedness as the principal feature of true aesthetic experience. On the notion of disinterestedness in Shaftesbury and Kant, see Dabney Townsend, 'From Shaftesbury to Kant: The Development of the Concept of Aesthetic Experience', in P. Kivy (ed.), *Essays on the History of Aesthetics* (Rochester: University of Rochester Press, 1992), pp. 205–223.

[122] On Shaftesbury's influence on Winckelmann, see Horlacher, '*Bildung*', pp. 418–419.

abandoned their 'lowly' occupations precisely in order to fulfil their true calling.

God no longer served as the only object towards which one might be called to form oneself. Such an object might now be described as *Geist* or truth or any other thing which embodied a single transcendental point of reference. Yet it still demanded a complete inward obedience, exercised through some kind of exclusive activity, such as science or art. This is what stands behind Nietzsche's claim that the activity of the modern scientist is the ultimate expression of Christian asceticism, despite the fact that, at first glance, the scientist appears to be an atheist who tries to overcome the dogmas of Christianity.[123] Science is not merely work; it is a calling.

And this is also the reason why, in the period of the emergence of German neo-humanism, one does not usually observe that feeling of despair provoked by the conflict between occupation and *Bildung*. The occupation that opposed itself to *Bildung* was not *Beruf* and abandoning it in favour of true self-cultivation did not entail any loss.

To summarise, the second aspect of the *Bildung* ideal signifies a single-minded devotion to a transcendental object. God is imitated here not by virtue of his pantheistic essence but by virtue of his singularity and uniqueness. The imitation is attained by concentrating one's own powers on a single task or cause.

It appears then that the neo-humanistic ideal of *Bildung* was not based exclusively on the notion of harmonious self-cultivation. Rather, this ideal should be seen as a more or less successful synthesis between *Bildung*-as-Cultivation and *Bildung*-as-*Beruf*. To a certain extent, this is a post factum interpretation. Not all neo-humanists were aware of the tension, or even difference, between *Bildung*-as-Cultivation and *Bildung*-as-*Beruf*. However, the most perceptive of them were and it would not be a gross exaggeration to suggest that the aspiration to establish the possibility of unity between the two principles was the fundamental drive behind much of the activity of the neo-humanistic thinkers. This drive found its most refined intellectual expression in the philosophy of German Idealism and left its most important institutional legacy in the model of the neo-humanistic university.[124]

---

[123] Friedrich Nietzsche, *On the Genealogy of Morality*, trans. C. Diethe (Cambridge: Cambridge University Press, 1994), pp. 115–120.

[124] On the impact of German Idealism in the nineteenth century, see Nicholas Boyle, 'General Introduction: The Eighteenth and Nineteenth Centuries' in Nicholas Boyle and Liz Disley (eds.), *The Impact of Idealism: The Legacy of Post-Kantian German Thought*, vol. I: *Philosophy and Natural Sciences*, ed. by Karl Ameriks (Cambridge: Cambridge University Press, 2013), pp. 13–21.

Roughly speaking, the cultural, even if not philosophical, importance of German thought of that time lay in its attempt to develop a synthesis of the singular and the universal. I have already hinted at this, by mentioning Goethe's and Schleiermacher's attempts to combine the diversity of the world with the singularity of personality.[125] I would now like to introduce two other thinkers: Humboldt and Hegel. Apparently more self-reflective than others, they were better aware of the tension implicit in the ideal of *Bildung*. Nevertheless, they believed that the grand synthesis of *Bildung* was still possible.

Wilhelm von Humboldt, reformer of the Prussian system of education, believed that the perfect personality had to be both unique and universal. But how could these two features go together? Humboldt found a likely answer in Leibniz.[126] As I have already mentioned, many an anxious fin-de-siècle intellectual considered Leibniz to be one of those giants of the past who had been able to perform the great task of forming themselves into harmonious personalities. Indeed, the problem of unity in diversity was one of Leibniz's major concerns. His description of the best possible world as that which combines the maximum unity (in respect of laws) with the maximum diversity (in respect of phenomena)[127] was just the opening salvo in the long quest of German philosophy for the proverbial grail where unity and diversity would fuse into a blissful union. One particular aspect of Leibniz's philosophy had an especially significant impact on Humboldt as well as on other *Bildung* intellectuals.[128] This was Leibniz's theory of monads.

According to Leibniz, the world consists of simple indivisible particles – monads, which are 'the true atoms of nature'.[129] These monads must be 'different from each other'.[130] That is, each of them possesses the quality of uniqueness. At the same time, each monad embodies in itself the

---

[125] The difference between the two now appears in new light. A prima facie interpretation would be that Goethe inclines more towards vocation, whereas Schleiermacher inclines towards self-cultivation. Yet now the opposite seems to be the case. If *Beruf* is understood as devotion to the singularity of other-worldliness, it is Schleiermacher, brought up within the pietistic tradition, who tends to put a stronger emphasis on *Beruf*, rather than Goethe, with his rejection of the 'beautiful soul' and his emphasis on the variety of this-worldliness.

[126] Lichtenstein, *Zur Entwicklung des Bildungsbegriffs von Meister Eckhart bis Hegel*, p. 21.

[127] On the combination of variety and simplicity in Leibniz, see, for example, David Blumenfeld, 'Perfection and Happiness in the Best Possible World', in N. Jolley (ed.), *The Cambridge Companion to Leibniz* (Cambridge: Cambridge University Press, 1995), pp. 383–393.

[128] For example, Christoph Martin Wieland. See Schaarschmidt, *Der Bedeutungswandel der Worte 'bilden' und 'Bildung' in der Literatur-Epoche von Gottsched bis Herder*, pp. 33–34.

[129] Gottfried Wilhelm Leibniz, 'Monadology [1714]', in *Philosophical Writings*, trans. M. Morris (London: J. M. Dent, 1934), § 3, p. 3.

[130] Ibid., § 9, p. 4.

knowledge of everything: 'each created monad represents the whole universe.'[131] Yet the monads' representations are always confused, as every monad relates to the same totality from its own unique position in the universe. In other words, 'each individual substance . . . expresses the whole universe from a certain point of view'.[132]

Each individual mind is a monad and therefore possesses the twofold quality of monads: the uniqueness of a point of view and the universality inherent in its comprehensive representation of the world. Monadology can therefore explain not only how an individual human being *can* combine uniqueness with universality but also why he or she *must* do so. This was the philosophical fundament on which Humboldt built his neo-humanistic vision.[133] Spranger interpreted Humboldt's ideal of *Bildung* as aiming towards 'totality', which is understood as the third and final aspect in a person's development towards humanity. The first two aspects are individuality (signifying uniqueness but also one-sidedness) and universality (signifying the personality's immersion into many-sided reality). Totality is the form of personality achieved when its individuality aspect is united with its universality aspect.[134] This idea, according to Spranger, represents an aesthetic conception of humanity.[135]

This approach presented a possible strategy to perform the grand synthesis of *Bildung*. Its Leibnizian foundations, however, had become quite backward.[136] The new philosophical game in town was German post-Kantian Idealism, which provided a more dynamic and historically minded view of the universe in general and of human personality in particular. The most famous and philosophically most outstanding representative of this trend was Hegel.[137] The question of synthesis captured a central place in his

---

[131] Ibid., § 62, p. 14.

[132] Gottfried Wilhelm Leibniz, 'Correspondence with Arnauld [1686]', in *Philosophical Writings*, p. 64.

[133] On the connection between Leibniz's monadology and the ideal of *Bildung*, see also Karl Ernst Nipkow, '"Ganzheitliche Bildung" zwischen dem Ich und dem anderen: Eine anthropologisch-ethische und bildungsphilosophische Skizze', in V. Drehsen (ed.), *Der 'ganze' Mensch: Perspektiven lebensgeschichtlicher Individualität* (Berlin: Walter de Gruyter, 1997), pp. 415–417.

[134] Eduard Spranger, *Wilhelm von Humboldt und die Humanitätsidee* (Berlin: Reuther & Reichard, 1909), pp. 13–14. In the Weimar period, the same terminology was also used by the Brockhaus Encyclopaedia with regard to Pestalozzi. See Ringer, *The Decline of the German Mandarins*, p. 86.

[135] To seek reconciliation between the unique and the universal in the realm of the beautiful was not an uncommon step for German thinkers. This was Schiller's solution for modern fragmentation. He in turn saw himself as a follower of the third critique of Kant (Schiller, *On the Aesthetic Education of Man*, pp. 3–5). For Leibniz, the greatest possible diversity within the greatest possible unity accounted not only for the moral perfection of the existing world but also for its perfect beauty (Blumenfeld, 'Perfection and Happiness in the Best Possible World', p. 395).

[136] Lichtenstein, *Zur Entwicklung des Bildungsbegriffs von Meister Eckhart bis Hegel*, p. 21.

[137] On the significance of the neo-humanist ideal of *Bildung* for Hegel, see, for example, Terry Pinkard, *Hegel: A Biography* (Cambridge: Cambridge University Press, 2000), pp. 172, 282–285, 304–307, 321, 369–370.

philosophy. One need only reflect on his dialectic of identity and difference[138] or on his analysis of the interaction between whole and parts.[139] Without embarking on an in-depth examination of his philosophy, I will bring one example from his vocabulary.

Hegel was very careful in his choice of words, considering philosophy to be intimately connected with language.[140] And his language reflected and reinforced the cultural imagination of his age in its quest for the synthesis of the singular and the universal. The word 'concrete' is a key component of Hegel's language. In its common meaning, it refers to something specific, individual and particular, often implying a close proximity to empirical reality as it is. The opposite of 'concrete' is 'abstract', understood as something too general and disconnected from reality. As is well known, Hegel turned the meaning of 'concrete' upside down. When he claimed that *concept* (*Begriff* in the Hegelian sense) is concrete,[141] he did not mean that it can be found in specific particulars of a phenomenon. Rather, he wanted to say precisely the opposite: that the 'concrete' can be found in the totality of all determinations of reality. 'Concrete' for Hegel means the whole. For example, the 'concrete' truth is the all-sided truth. 'Abstract', by contrast, is something partial, one-sided and consequently false. Therefore, it is the word 'abstract' which is more likely to refer to something 'specific' and 'particular'. This swap of meaning is not arbitrary. It preserves a connection with the everyday usage, without which this new meaning would become void.[142] As in the common usage, 'abstract' still retains the connotation of something vague and distant from reality, whereas 'concrete' is understood as genuine reality. It is just that genuine reality is attained through grasping the totality of its determinations and not through concentrating on a specific aspect of reality or adopting a one-sided perspective.

Moreover, linguistically speaking, when one reads Hegel, one is incapable of entirely disposing of the whole set of common connotations of the word 'concrete', which include the sense of singularity. And Hegel's intention had to be precisely this: when one sees the word 'concrete', one

---

[138] G. W. F. Hegel, *Hegel's Science of Logic*, 2 vols., trans. W. H. Johnston and L. G. Struthers (London: Georg Allen & Unwin, 1929), vol. 2, pp. 35–70.

[139] G. W. F. Hegel, *Hegel's Logic* (Part I of the Encyclopaedia of the Philosophical Sciences [1830]), trans. W. Wallace (Oxford: Clarendon Press, 1975), § 136.

[140] Charles Taylor, *Hegel and Modern Society* (Cambridge: Cambridge University Press, 1979), pp. 17–18, 164.

[141] Hegel, *Hegel's Logic*, § 164.

[142] On this point, see W. T. Stage, *The Philosophy of Hegel: A Systematic Exposition* (New York: Dover Publications, 1955), pp. 104–105.

can think simultaneously in terms of everyday language and Hegelian philosophy. 'Concrete' is both singularity and universality. This combination is made even clearer in Hegel's notion of the 'concrete universal'.[143] What other expression could serve as a better metaphor for the entire project of German Idealism: to provide the metaphysical grounds for the vision of unity in variety, of individuality in totality, of uniqueness in universality?

The passage from the realm of human personality to that of the metaphysical foundations of the world was not an idiosyncratic feature of Hegel's thought. Rather, Hegel, like Humboldt with his Leibnizian worldview, exemplified an important characteristic of the German *Bildung* discourse in general: its overwhelming tendency to draw parallels between man and universe and to endow the question of *Bildung* with cosmic significance. *Bildung* is not something that happens only within the individual mind. A similar process of *Bildung* takes place in the universe as a whole. Man and universe are, so to speak, microcosm and macrocosm.[144] The intellectual life of cultivated Germans was prone to the constant fluctuation between the mundane and the metaphysical, the practical and the philosophical, the human and the divine. This was an important aspect of the cultural heritage of those men and women and therefore of their self-understanding. The dilemmas of personality were, for them, also the dilemmas of the world.

Sometimes, this style of thinking even left its imprints on foreign soil. Consider the American historian of ideas Arthur Lovejoy, author of *The Great Chain of Being*.[145] Lovejoy argued that since its inception (in Plato), European thought was characterised by the irresolvable tension between other-worldliness and this-worldliness, between the transcendental God who stands apart from the illusory reality of this world and the immanent God who encompasses the whole variety of created beings. If this story looks similar to ours, that is no accident. Having been strongly influenced by German philosophy,[146] Lovejoy simply brought its major theme to the awareness of the non-suspecting Anglophone reader. Taken by itself, Lovejoy's thesis and methodology can be reproached for not being

---

[143] On the concrete universal see ibid., pp. 229–230.

[144] Cf. the use of these terms in relation to *Bildung* in Max Scheler, *Bildung und Wissen* [1925] (Frankfurt am Main: G. Schulte-Blumke, 1947), pp. 6–7.

[145] Arthur O. Lovejoy, *The Great Chain of Being: A Study in the History of Ideas* (Cambridge, MA: Harvard University Press, 1936).

[146] For Lovejoy, German philosophy was the endpoint of European philosophical development. His book ends with an analysis of German philosophy at the beginning of the nineteenth century. See ibid., pp. 288–333.

historical enough.[147] However, when his book is examined in its own context, it can be perceived as yet another example of the use of the *Bildung / Beruf* dichotomy at the highest level of abstraction.

Somewhat anachronistically, Lovejoy argued that the synthesis finally came apart at the beginning of the nineteenth century, thereby attributing to that earlier age the feeling of crisis that characterised his own time. The age of neo-humanism and Romanticism was not overburdened with a sense of failure. Synthesis could still be perceived as feasible. As we have seen, Humboldt and Hegel offered strategies for overcoming the tension between two kingdoms within the empire of *Bildung*: the kingdom of singular vocation and the kingdom of harmonious cultivation. These two kingdoms pushed relentlessly in opposite directions. Nevertheless, it was believed for a while that if these two opposite ideals were faithfully pursued to their respective states of perfection, they would in the end turn out to be one and the same. Yet once this certainty or hope was lost, the decline and fall of the ideal seemed inevitable. What remains to be explained, however, is how it came about that this loss of intellectual confidence happened so quickly.

The neo-humanistic ideal of *Bildung* aimed at a synthesis of two different principles: *Bildung*-as-Cultivation and *Bildung*-as-*Beruf*. Both components possessed religious roots, yet both entered neo-humanism in a somewhat secularised form. This secularisation, however, potentially created significant problems, especially for *Bildung*-as-*Beruf*. Harmonious cultivation, at least in principle, implies certainty about the final goal. There is only one total harmony of the world, be its meaning God, Nature or something else. This is, however, not the case with vocation, because there is a variety of single points of devotion. How can one be sure about which point to choose? Devotion to a single point understood as God is easy to justify. God as a point is superior to all other possible points. But if God disappears from the picture, defending devotion to a specific point at the expense of all others becomes more difficult. One has to be convinced that a particular specific point paves the way to the totality of the world. For example, in order to be fully devoted to art, one needs to believe that the artist is a genius who belongs to the transcendental realm. And the same is true of science.

The basic question is therefore whether specific vocational activities of mind can retain their connection with the whole and thereby preserve their

---

[147] See, for example, Skinner's criticism of Lovejoy's methodology in Quentin Skinner, 'Meaning and Understanding in the History of Ideas', in *Visions of Politics*, vol. 1: *Regarding Method* (Cambridge: Cambridge University Press, 2002), pp. 62, 83–85.

meaningfulness. Neo-humanists believed this was possible. However, very soon doubts began to creep in, leading to the shift towards cultural pessimism that took place somewhere around the 1870s. Prior to this, discussions on the subject were relatively calm. For example, in 1850, when classical philologist August Boeckh spoke about intellectual specialisation, he argued that, despite its dangers, a certain degree of specialisation was necessary and did not contradict the principle of the unity of scholarly activity. The duty of scholars, he claimed, was 'to feel themselves as members of one great republic of letters, in which separate associations restrain themselves just like single states within a federation of peoples'.[148] Science, which he understood as a cooperative enterprise of the entire community of scholars in the pursuit of the totality of knowledge, was not a meaningless activity inimical to the harmony of personality. Likewise, in 1868, historian Heinrich von Sybel described university faculties as trees growing from the same root.[149] Although he was aware of the increasing differentiation between faculties, he believed that a basic unity still existed.

However, by that time the initial neo-humanistic enthusiasm had already begun to dissipate. I will illustrate this process with two examples from the realm of intellectual history: the story of the change in philosophical fashion, on the one hand, and in the character of the universities, on the other. Both are, of course, important for understanding the background and outlook of Simmel: a philosopher by conviction and a university academic by profession.

As for philosophical fashion, the conventional story runs as follows. The late eighteenth and early nineteenth centuries were the age that saw the flourishing of German philosophy. Philosophical life was dominated by Idealism with its persistent quest for developing grand philosophical systems, which were supposed to lead towards total, or absolute, knowledge. Initially, this project was regarded as plausible. Hegel, for example, believed that he had discovered the true philosophy and managed to implant this conviction in the hearts of many of his students. The 1820s and 1830s were the period of Hegelian domination of German philosophical life. Yet this domination proved to be short-lived. Soon after Hegel's death, cracks appeared between several groups of his followers, and not

---

[148] August Boeckh, 'Von der Philologie, besonders der klassischen in Beziehung zur morgenländischen, zum Unterricht und zur Gegenwart' [1850], in *Gesammelte kleine Schriften II: Reden gehalten auf der Universität und in der Akademie der Wissenschaften zu Berlin* (Leipzig: B. G. Teubner, 1859), p. 191.

[149] Heinrich von Sybel, 'Die deutschen und die auswärtigen Universitäten' [1868], in *Die deutschen Universitäten, ihre Leistungen und Bedürfnisse* (Bonn: Max Cohen & Sohn, 1874), pp. 19–20.

much later the entire Hegelian approach lost its appeal among the educated classes. The breakdown of the Hegelian system signified the end of attempts at system building. The Hegelian system was the last grand system. It was followed by a growing interest in positivism, materialism and the natural sciences. Yet from the end of the 1860s one can observe a renewed interest in philosophical Idealism, exemplified by the increasing influence of the multi-faceted movement known as 'neo-Kantianism'.[150]

This story is indeed a stereotype, and some of its particulars are in need of revision. One could claim, for example, that neo-Kantianism, as a specific movement within German academic philosophy, was born much earlier.[151] Nevertheless, the story is valuable because, by showing us how the philosophical transformation was perceived by a broader public, it reveals the cultural impact of this transformation. What we learn here is that, in the course of the nineteenth century, the general atmosphere turned increasingly sceptical towards the ideal of grasping the total truth and that neo-Kantianism was regarded as the most symptomatic among various responses to this growing scepticism. Neo-Kantians seem to have gone further than others in adjusting their vision of philosophy to the new situation of uncertainty. This is especially true of the Southwest neo-Kantian School, represented by Wilhelm Windelband and Heinrich Rickert.

Towards the end of his life, Windelband summarised his vision of the neo-Kantian project in his article 'Philosophy of Culture and Transcendental Idealism'.[152] He argued that Kant's transcendental idealism, which attempted to delineate the limits of possible knowledge, was akin to the project of the contemporary philosophy of culture. The great discovery of Kant was that human reason was not a passive instrument of perception. Rather, our knowledge and understanding are always conditioned by our own creative activity. And since what we create can be called 'culture', human understanding as a whole can be regarded as cultural activity.

The crucial point for Windelband was that cultural phenomena, created by our minds, do not compose a unified whole. Culture contains a great

---

[150] See, for example, John Passmore, *A Hundred Years of Philosophy* (London: Penguin Books, 1994), pp. 48–49.

[151] Klaus Christian Köhnke, *The Rise of Neo-Kantianism: German Academic Philosophy between Idealism and Positivism* (Cambridge: Cambridge University Press, 1991). See also Frederick C. Beiser, *The Genesis of Neo-Kantianism 1796–1880* (Oxford: Oxford University Press, 2014).

[152] Wilhelm Windelband, 'Kulturphilosophie und transzendentaler Idealismus', *Logos* I, 1910/1911, pp. 186–196.

variety of forms which cannot be subsumed under any unified system of categories. Windelband attributed this view to Kant, who distinguished between three different spheres – science, ethics and aesthetics – assigning to each of them its own set of postulates.

Windelband did not go so far as to claim that unity did not exist in principle. He believed in the existence of some transcendental unity of spirit behind cultural activities. Yet this unity could not be reached in practice. It can only be postulated. Culture was accessible only through its specific spheres separated from each other by their particular categories. The only consolation was the awareness that each such fragment of culture was a part of the transcendental whole.

Rickert elaborated on a similar idea in his book *Kant as a Philosopher of Modern Culture.*[153] He claimed that European mediaeval culture was characterised by a synthesis of three traditions: the Greek tradition of rational knowledge, the Roman tradition of practical (or political) activity and the Christian tradition of irrational belief. The modern age brought this synthesis to dissolution. In modern cultural consciousness, each of these three elements began to fight for independence. Science for science's sake became the principal criterion of the theoretical man; the state for the state's sake that of the political man; and God for God's sake that of the religious man.[154] Rickert argued that Kant was the first thinker who diagnosed this plurality and recognised the autonomy of each sphere of value. Consequently, Kant turned philosophy into critique, the task of which was to elucidate the categories of each particular sphere.

At the same time, like Windelband, Rickert did not perceive radical plurality as the ultimate ideal. He considered Kantian philosophy to be the first step on the way towards the creation of a new synthesis, which would restore some kind of unity but also reconcile it with a greater distinctiveness of spheres, thereby avoiding the fallacy of the pre-modern unity. This was, however, a task for the future. In the meantime, philosophy had to focus on delineating proper limits for each sphere of value.

Rickert's and Windelband's views can be summarised as follows. Both believed that modern culture was characterised by a plurality of spheres of value. Both regarded Kant's thought, first and foremost, as a response to this plurality. From Kant they learned that, in different spheres of culture, our mind creates different systems of postulates. They regarded Kant's alleged conceptualisation of the distinction between the spheres of the true,

---

[153] Heinrich Rickert, *Kant als Philosoph der modernen Kultur* (Tübingen: J. C. B. Mohr, 1924).
[154] Ibid., p. 110.

good and beautiful as the main achievement of his philosophy. Although neither was prepared to renounce the ideal of unity in principle, both gave up the quest for totality de facto and were prepared to focus on fragments – Windelband by attributing unity to some transcendental realm and Rickert by postponing it until some indeterminate future.

This neo-Kantian vision had a significant impact on the consciousness of the educated classes in Germany. In other countries, the philosophical atmosphere was somewhat different. Let us take, for example, Britain. Precisely in the period in which philosophical system building went out of fashion in Germany and neo-Kantianism rose in prominence, Britain became acquainted with Hegelianism. It was popularised there by the philosophical movement known as British Idealism, which became the leading philosophical school towards the end of the nineteenth century. The most prominent thinkers of this movement, such as Bradley and Bosanquet, believed that the search for totality of experience constituted the essence of philosophy.[155] Fragmentation was thus a less burning problem for them than it was for their German colleagues.

Neo-Kantianism was a symptom of the disillusionment with the neo-humanistic project. And a similar development took place with regard to the ideal of the university. Neo-humanists hoped that universities, reformed according to their principles, would provide the institutional framework for the pursuit of *Bildung*. The foundation of the University of Berlin in 1810 by Wilhelm von Humboldt and his colleagues was a major step in this direction, and it was followed by important reforms in the entire university system in Prussia and other German states. Although the image of this reformed system as the perfect embodiment of the neo-humanistic ideology has been shown to be exaggerated, there is no doubt that the impact of neo-humanism in this sphere was significant.[156]

Neo-humanists set two purposes for the university: to educate youth according to the ideal of self-cultivation (as the continuation of classical education in *Gymnasien*) and encourage the disinterested search for knowledge and truth. Or, more precisely, this was one and the same purpose. For only through the disinterested quest for truth could one really hope to

---

[155] On Absolute Idealism, see Passmore, *A Hundred Years of Philosophy*, pp. 48–71, 85–90.
[156] On the emergence of modern German universities and on the role of the *Bildung* ideology in this process, see Charles E. McClelland, *State, Society, and University in Germany 1700–1914* (Cambridge: Cambridge University Press, 1980), pp. 101–149; T. A. Howard, *Protestant Theology and the Making of the Modern German University* (Oxford: Oxford University Press, 2006), pp. 45–211.

reach true self-cultivation. In order to fulfil this purpose, German universities were to be based on the combination of teaching and research.

Yet it was not long before these two ideals – the ideal of harmonious cultivation and that of the uncompromising pursuit of truth – began to be perceived as conflicting. Research very quickly came to dominate the entire experience of academic life and even penetrated *Gymnasien*, as university graduates, who took up positions as school teachers, tended to focus on transmitting current scholarly knowledge to their pupils rather than on the formation of their character. Driven by what has been called the 'research imperative' or '*Wissenschaft* ideology', German universities became the best schools of professional research in the world.[157] This happened, however, at the expense of the ideal of harmonious education.

The story of the development of classical philology in German universities, as described by Anthony Grafton, is a good example of this process.[158] Since the ideal of *Bildung* was intimately connected with the veneration of ancient culture, classical philology came to be regarded as the crown discipline of the neo-humanistic university. Knowledge of classical languages and texts was considered indispensable for the development of thinking skills, moral qualities and the sense of beauty. At the same time, classical philology was expected to become a legitimate science. It therefore had to develop an objective scientific research method. A scholar was supposed to be able to evaluate classical texts critically. For example, it was not the beauty of Homer's texts that was supposed to concern the scholar, but their authenticity. Were they written by one or several persons; which versions of the text are more genuine; was the manuscript corrupted and when? A researcher advanced knowledge by discovering errors in the existing manuscripts. Thus, ironically, scholars came to be more interested in errors than in the texts themselves. The aesthetic and educational value of those texts did not play a role in the scientific process. Consequently, as Grafton writes, 'Humboldtian ideals of research came to contradict equally Humboldtian ideals of *Bildung*'.[159]

Yet one can add here that these ideals of research were in fact based on the second principle of *Bildung*. Humboldt himself was not an adept of the research imperative. It is reported that he disliked professors.[160] Yet his

[157] R. Steven Turner, 'The Prussian Universities and the Concept of Research', *Internationales Archiv für Sozialgeschichte der deutschen Literatur* 5, 1980, pp. 68–93. See also Joseph Ben-David, *The Scientist's Role in Society* (Chicago: University of Chicago Press, 1984), pp. 108–138.
[158] Anthony Grafton, 'Polyhistor into *Philolog*: Notes on the Transformation of German Classical Scholarship, 1780–1850', *History of Universities* 3, 1983, pp. 159–192.
[159] Ibid., p. 169.
[160] Leonore O'Boyle, 'Learning for Its Own Sake: The German University as Nineteenth-Century Model', *Comparative Studies in Society and History* 25(1), 1983, p. 11.

ideal of *Bildung* included the disinterested pursuit of truth, and this principle was prone to evolve into the research imperative that disconnected itself from the notion of harmonious cultivation and demanded total devotion to a particular field of knowledge. The ethics of specialisation was less a result of some external impact than it was an expression of the inner contradiction within the *Bildung* ideal itself.

Again, the situation was different elsewhere. In Britain, for example, the elite universities were obviously less 'modern', if judged by the German standards. They were quite backward in research, concentrating rather on the formation of character. It was even argued that due to this 'backwardness' they looked more like *Bildung* institutions than their German counterparts.[161] 'Oxford of the past', wrote its graduate Matthew Arnold, 'has many faults; and she has heavily paid for them in defeat, in isolation, in want of hold upon the modern world. Yet we in Oxford ... have not failed to seize one truth, – the truth that beauty and sweetness are essential characters of a complete human perfection'.[162]

Arnold was referring to the Oxford of the 1840s. By that time, the research imperative had already fully entrenched itself in the ethos of German universities. It took some time, however, before the tension between research and education erupted. The 1870s again appear to have been the defining point. This decade was characterised by a rapid expansion of the universities and a sharp increase in student enrolment in Imperial Germany.[163] Yet the sense of discontent seems to have been caused less by this increase than by changes in the character of university life which preceded the 1870s. The most important of these changes was the introduction of the seminar method of teaching. The seminar, which began 'as a means of circumventing the too universalistic approach of the general lecture ... ended in dominating the university curriculum and taking away much of the vaunted German sense of the "unity of science"'.[164] Towards the 1870s, a new generation of scholars was educated for whom the seminar was basically the only framework of learning. Once such a generation appeared, it was only a matter of time before at least some of its members would turn against the ethos of specialisation. Nietzsche was one of the first academics to voice his protest, and his critique would eventually become powerful precisely because he was so intimately familiar

---

[161] On the very different ethos in British universities of that period, see ibid., pp. 13–17.
[162] Arnold, *Culture and Anarchy*, pp. 72–73.
[163] On the expansion of the universities, see McClelland, *State, Society, and University in Germany*, pp. 239–287.
[164] Ibid., p. 180.

with the condition he detested. When he compared science to a vampire that 'consumes its creatures',[165] he knew what he was talking about.

Thus in the two spheres in which the contribution of the German mind to nineteenth-century European culture was most significant – modern Idealist philosophy and the modern university – a parallel development took place. Both German Idealism and the neo-humanistic model of the university were based on the yearning for the synthesis of totality and singularity, of harmonious many-sidedness and pure devotion. Both were the products of the *Bildung* ideology. Yet neither succeeded in maintaining this synthesis. The two constituent elements of *Bildung* – the whole and the part – moved away from each other. The part (*Beruf*) no longer recognised itself as a part. It rebelled against the whole (*Bildung*), claiming to be its equal rival. The hope of unity was lost.

This loss of inner unity is what made the *Bildung* /*Beruf* conflict so problematic. The situation was grave not because of the alleged impossibility of reconciling the ideal of gentlemanly cultivation with the requirement of work in an industrial society. As a response to this dilemma, an attitude of resignation, in which resentment against modernity is accompanied by inner confidence, would suffice. The tension between universal culture and technical skills would be perceived as a general social problem but not as a personal problem of those individuals who were fully determined to cultivate themselves. In other words, one would get just another version of Schiller's or Schleiermacher's critique of certain features of modernity.

Here, however, the conflict appeared to be internal. The *Beruf* which threatened *Bildung* was not the external work. It was the true inner *Beruf* of devotion to an object. This *Beruf* was a necessary ingredient of *Bildung*. Yet it turned out to be unwilling or even incapable of leading towards *Bildung*. Once, in the very distant past of Greece, Aristotle suggested that a good craftsman could not be a properly cultivated person, but now it appeared that the same predicament haunted good artists and even good philosophers. As Simmel would have said, this condition was not sorrowful (which it would have been in the case of an external conflict) but tragic, for it was a symptom of a profound inner contradiction of the modern era.

Now, the duality of singularity and universality was not the exclusive property of the German tradition of self-cultivation. Traces of this duality can be found in other humanistic traditions as well, even if in Germany it

---

[165] Friedrich Nietzsche, *On the Future of Our Educational Institutions*, trans. M. W. Grenke (South Bend: St. Augustine's Press, 2004), p. 39.

appeared in its most radical form. Consider, for example, the *Oration* of Pico della Mirandola, which numbers among the key texts of Italian humanism.[166] The *Oration* presents man as an active collaborator with God, called on to complete the process of his own creation. The text asserts the potential universality of human nature and thereby promulgates the idea of harmonious self-formation. Yet, at the same time, the ultimate goal of human formation is shown to be emancipation from the world and complete fusion with God. In Pico, this-worldliness is accompanied by other-worldliness. One could therefore say that his *Oration* is a *Bildung* text par excellence.

Nor did the danger of the tension between harmonious cultivation and devoted vocation remain unrecognised by other cultural traditions. The answer to this tension was usually some form of compromise between the two principles. Consider the Scottish Enlightenment. This intellectual movement presided over a relatively smooth and rapid process of the replacement of traditional humanistic values with those of commercial society.[167] It is true that drawing a comprehensive analogy between the Scottish and German cases would be a problematic undertaking, for the two traditions are not entirely comparable. For example, one will not find in Germany the Aristotelian political elements which were characteristic of the Scottish humanistic tradition. Nevertheless, in respect of the question of individual cultivation, the Scottish example can be instructive. Most Scottish thinkers appeared to believe that modern commercial man could be educated to develop at least an appearance of humanity, even if in a diluted and less demanding form. The Scottish Enlightenment introduced the idea that *manners* would become a gentlemanly quality of the modern age. Manners – those mirrors of virtue – would endow a decent worker with habits of honesty and self-respect and enable cultivated conversation about sciences and arts.[168] Thus a professional person, while focusing on his own vocation, would also develop life skills in a polite society, thereby turning himself into a civilised person.

This kind of approach was not entirely absent in Germany. A similar ethos characterised *Aufklärung*, quite unsurprisingly, since Scottish ideas

[166] Giovanni Pico della Mirandola, *Oration on the Dignity of Man*, trans. A. R. Caponigri (Washington: Regnery Publishing, 1956).
[167] On the Scottish Enlightenment, see Nicholas Phillipson, 'The Scottish Enlightenment', in R. Porter and M. Teich (eds.), *The Enlightenment in National Context* (Cambridge: Cambridge University Press, 1981), pp. 19–40.
[168] On the language of manners in early modern political thought, see J. G. A. Pocock, 'Virtues, Rights, and Manners: A Model for Historians of Political Thought', in *Virtue, Commerce, and History: Essays on Political Thought and History, Chiefly in the Eighteenth Century* (Cambridge: Cambridge University Press, 1985), pp. 37–50.

significantly influenced German thinkers of the end of the eighteenth century, including many early neo-humanists who partly followed in the *Aufklärung* tradition.[169] Yet, on the whole, the legacy of this way of thinking turned out to be relatively limited, as *Aufklärung* was later outmanoeuvred by neo-humanism, which sharpened its perfectionist rhetoric as it approached the status of cultural hegemony. One can assume that if the rhetoric of compromise prevailed and the two principles of *Bildung* were allowed to enter German cultural consciousness in a condition of relative imperfection, a solid synthesis could result from their mixture. They were, however, pushed towards their respective points of perfection, and this could only end in tearing the whole edifice apart.

The attitude of perfection might have originated in a specific mode of the Lutheran vision of vocation. Richard Douglas argued that the discourse on vocation as such was present not only in Protestantism. The value of vocation was also recognised by humanists. Although humanists criticised the life of business and assigned a higher status to the life of letters, they regarded the latter as a vocational activity too. Their ideal of humanity did not reside in abstract universality. 'The universal genius may indeed have existed as a real figure admired in Renaissance society, but he rarely appears as an abstract ideal in Renaissance theory. The humanists seem to have admired the man in a single *gran ingegno* far more than the *uomo universale*'.[170]

The difference between the languages of Protestantism and humanism lies rather in their divergent interpretations of the meaning of vocation. The humanists' criterion for the choice of a career was whether it was consistent with the aptitudes and inclinations of the individual. In other words, one's duty was to develop one's talents in accordance with one's own nature. By contrast, the Protestant, especially Lutheran, idea of vocation[171] emphasised the external criterion of choice. As man was called to his particular station by God, his duty was to obey this calling, regardless of whether it corresponded to his own inclinations and desires or not. Or, one might say, human imperfection was not taken into consideration here.

---

[169] On the influence of Scottish thought in Germany, see Fania Oz-Salzberger, *Translating the Enlightenment: Scottish Civic Discourse in Eighteenth-Century Germany* (Oxford: Clarendon Press, 1995).

[170] Richard M. Douglas, 'Talent and Vocation in Humanist and Protestant Thought', in T. K. Rabb and J. E. Seigel (eds.), *Action and Conviction in Early Modern Europe* (Princeton: Princeton University Press, 1969), p. 280.

[171] According to Douglas (ibid., pp. 295–298), the original Calvinist idea of vocation, which was similar to that of Luther, proved to be transient and was replaced by the Puritan conception, which was more favourable to the emphasis on one's own inclinations.

Furthermore, the imperative of perfection could be attributed to the neo-humanistic fascination with Greece. Swiss scholar Walter Rüegg argued that the major fault of neo-humanism was its preference for Greek rather than Latin culture.[172] Rüegg considered this preference to be an inherent feature of German cultural consciousness and presented the example of Theodor Mommsen's disdain for Cicero, who was the major inspiration for Italian humanists. Cicero's personality, according to Rüegg, was unsystematic and ironic.[173] Its unity was achieved by means of a flexible and playful linguistic excellence, which is the only excellence that does not postulate the imperative of transcendental perfection: 'language is the only kind of objectification of an individual that reflects the wholeness of his person as he engages physically and mentally with others.'[174]

Neo-humanism, however, moved in the opposite direction – to Greece, where it learned to base the ideal of harmony not on man in all his imperfection but on some absolute criterion. The role of language and communication was de-emphasised: 'in neo-humanism ... the decisive standards of education [*Bildung*] and valuation are moved away from the linguistic form into absolute categories.'[175] This observation led Rüegg to suggest that neo-humanism may not have been a humanism at all, for 'its interest is directed not towards language that is shaped via person, but towards objective qualities, facts and functions'.[176]

This criticism was onto something. The neo-humanistic ideal of Greece was perfectionist. Moreover, since it constituted a major aspect of the *Bildung* tradition, it was marked by *Bildung*'s typical duality: It looked for perfection both in singularity and in wholeness. For while it postulated the perfect harmony of human personality, this perfect harmony demanded the attainment of perfect form in its singularity (as opposed to the variety of matter). Thus, placed in the distant past of a very different civilisation, the Greek ideal became an unachievable standard, an absolute point of reference.[177] An aesthetic myth took upon itself the features of an other-worldly divinity.

[172] Walter Rüegg, *Cicero und der Humanismus: Formale Untersuchungen über Petrarcha und Erasmus* (Zurich: Rhein, 1946). A decade earlier, a similar position was adopted by Eliza M. Butler in her very hostile critique of German culture. See E. M. Butler, *The Tyranny of Greece over Germany* (Boston: Beacon Press, 1955). On Butler's view of Germany, see Sandra J. Peacock, 'Struggling with the Daimon: Eliza M. Butler on Germany and Germans', *History of European Ideas* 32(1), 2006, pp. 99–115.

[173] Rüegg, *Cicero und der Humanismus*, p. xiii.   [174] Ibid., pp. xvi–xvii.   [175] Ibid., p. xii.
[176] Ibid., p. xvii.

[177] Here can be found the difference between the German attitude to Greece and the French attitude to Rome. France considered Latin culture not as a distant ideal but as its own heritage. See Fritz

At the same time, there was much exaggeration in Rüegg's claims, put forward around the end of the Second World War. The dichotomy between Cicero's humane Latin values and suffocating Greek objectivity is certainly a caricature. Latin culture did have a share in the German neo-humanistic ideal, and even Cicero himself was not completely forgotten, as one can learn from the calls for his revival made in the German educational debates of the 1900s.[178] Moreover, Greece could mean different things to different people. At the dawn of neo-humanism, Greece symbolised for Schiller the free play of imagination,[179] just as, much later, Hannah Arendt would present it as an arena of the free play of action.[180] Arendt herself argued that at least one major German cultural figure – Lessing – distrusted metaphysical absoluteness and gave priority to language and communication.[181] These qualities are similar to those which Rüegg attributed to Cicero.

Another attempt at the reformulation of the *Bildung* tradition according to less radical lines was made by philosopher Hans-Georg Gadamer. In Gadamer's description, *Bildung* presupposed the notions of restraint and self-limitation. Gadamer found traces of these notions in the ideas of Hegel and physicist Hermann von Helmholtz. For Hegel, 'to give oneself to the universality of a profession is at the same time "to know how to limit oneself – i.e., to make one's profession wholly one's concern"'.[182] For Helmholtz (1821–1894), *Bildung* meant the capacity for self-limitation and for an intuitive understanding of what is appropriate in the vocation of a scientist. Another word for this capacity is 'tact'.[183] For Gadamer, tact, or the feeling of propriety, was a necessary precondition of aesthetical understanding or historical understanding. He attributed tact to German human studies in general, attempting thereby to establish what one may call 'a non-perfectionist tradition of *Bildung*' or 'a tradition based on tact'. For tact is usually the opposite of perfectionism.

Yet Gadamer's interpretation was biased too. Where Rüegg saw too much perfectionism, Gadamer saw too little. His (as well as Arendt's)

K. Ringer, *Fields of Knowledge: French Academic Culture in Comparative Perspective, 1890–1920* (Cambridge: Cambridge University Press, 1992), p. 144.

[178] See Ute Preuße, *Humanismus und Gesellschaft: Zur Geschichte des altsprachlichen Unterrichts in Deutschland von 1890 bis 1933* (Frankfurt am Main: Peter Lang, 1988), pp. 70–79.

[179] Cf. Schiller, *On the Aesthetic Education of Man*, pp. 107–109.

[180] Hannah Arendt, *The Human Condition* [1958] (Chicago: University of Chicago Press, 1998), pp. 22–28.

[181] Hannah Arendt, 'On Humanity in Dark Times: Thoughts about Lessing' [1959], in *Men in Dark Times* (New York: Harcourt, Brace & World, 1968), pp. 3–31.

[182] Hans-Georg Gadamer, *Truth and Method* [1960], trans. J. Weinsheimer and D. G. Marshall (New York: Crossroad, 1989), p. 13.

[183] Ibid., p. 15.

discovery of somewhat forgotten aspects of the *Bildung* tradition was made in the 1950s, in the aftermath of the shattering experience of the Nazi period. The atmosphere of complete loss of cultural confidence was a fitting moment to say goodbye to the language of perfection. Yet in the years with which I am concerned, the perfectionist rhetoric was at its peak. Paradoxically, it not only remained undisturbed but even intensified as a result of the awareness of *Bildung*'s inner tension. Just as the demands of life were pushing towards compromises in practice, the rhetoric of *Bildung* became more and more uncompromising. The custodians of 'true culture' were on their guard, trying to prevent a complacent philistinism from turning itself into the leading cultural trend. Their fear that compromise meant philistinism, or betrayal of style, was a self-fulfilling prophecy. The culture of compromise remained timid and apologetic. It produced its David Strausses but not its Nietzsches. It did not develop an aristocratic carelessness about what others thought about it, and thus it gradually lost its attractiveness.

Now, if to give up perfectionism was not an option, only three strategies for addressing the crisis remained. One – the most obvious and least interesting – consisted of creating a new form of synthesis.[184] The synthesis would usually involve some kind of dialectic, for (Gadamer's interpretation of Hegel notwithstanding) dialectic is the ultimate device that, on the one hand, enables the combination of two opposite principles and, on the other hand, keeps perfectionism intact because every notion there is pushed to the point of its perfection.

The two remaining strategies were adopted by thinkers who became convinced of the impossibility of maintaining the *Bildung* ideal as a synthesis of two rival perfectionist principles. Unwilling to give up perfection, those thinkers chose to do away with duality. *Supersint seria, pereat cultura.*[185] In other words, they either emphasised *Bildung* (in the narrow sense of self-cultivation) at the expense of *Beruf* or *Beruf* at the expense of *Bildung*. These two strategies are more interesting, for they

---

[184] See, for example, Scheler, *Bildung und Wissen*. Synthesis as a goal underlay new ideas about pedagogical reform, however novel these ideas might appear from a practical point of view. See Aloys Fischer, 'Berufsbildung und Allgemeinbildung', *Zeitschrift für pädagogische Psychologie und experimentelle Pädagogik* 12(3), 1911, pp. 165–175; Georg Kerschensteiner, *Grundfragen der Schulorganisation* (Leipzig: B. G. Teubner, 1912). For a later, post-war discourse on synthesis, see Ringer, *The Decline of the German Mandarins*, pp. 384–403. For an even later search for synthesis in the philosophy of *gnosis* see Yotam Hotam, 'Gnosis and Modernity: A Postwar German Intellectual Debate on Secularisation, Religion and "Overcoming" the Past', *Totalitarian Movements and Political Religions* 8(3), 2007, pp. 591–608.

[185] Let earnestness survive, even if *Bildung* must perish.

introduce an essentially new element into the story of *Bildung*. For the first time, the idea of cutting the Gordian knot of *Bildung* became influential.

Nietzsche exemplifies the strategy of reducing *Bildung* to its narrow element of self-cultivation. Quite early in his life, he came to believe that the grand synthesis between the cultivation of personality and the scholarly vocation was untenable. As he argued in his lectures *On the Future of Our Educational Institutions*, delivered in 1872, 'the scientific human being and the educated human being belong to two different spheres, which here and there touch in *one* individual, but never fall together with one another'.[186] Hating the idea of compromise intensely, Nietzsche advocated retreat from the ever more specialised modern culture. He called for establishing institutions of learning for a small elite that would become a new aristocracy of spirit, untainted by the ills of differentiated modernity. Similar educational proposals, though in a more cautious form, were put forward by Hillebrand and Treitschke.[187]

Towards the close of the Imperial era, this tendency began to form itself into what would be later known as the 'Third Humanism'. Its main proponent was the classicist Werner Jaeger, whose programme consisted in reducing classical education to a reverent study of the Greek canon. As Jaeger argued in 1914:

> Our age possesses no integrated culture of a kind with which antiquity, middle ages, and even the eighteenth century was still familiar . . . This fact is given, and we must ensure that in the condition of fragmentation (*Zersplitterung*) the continuity of spiritual life is maintained and that the most pure, unadulterated and authentic elements within this motley historical multitude of forces preserve their pedagogic effect.[188]

In other words, in order to build a proper system of education, one has to reject central aspects of fragmentary modernity and develop a well-chosen classical canon which would be conducive to harmonious cultivation.

---

[186] Nietzsche, *On the Future of Our Educational Institutions*, p. 51.

[187] Both Hillebrand and Treitschke proposed establishing education towards *Bildung* (without *Beruf*) at least in elite institutions. Hillebrand argued that the leading classes still needed humanistic education in order to perform their social role. He advocated the reduction of material taught in elite schools – *Gymnasien*. Culture, he argued, 'demands a wise restriction' (Hillebrand, 'On Half-Culture in Germany', p. 200). Treitschke was a less radical critic. A proud professional scholar, he admitted the necessity of a certain degree of specialisation in the universities ('Einige Bemerkungen über unser Gymnasialwesen', pp. 164–165). Yet with regard to secondary education, he closely followed Hillebrand's suggestions, arguing that the education in *Gymnasien* should be based on classical languages and mathematics ('Einige Bemerkungen über unser Gymnasialwesen', pp. 168–169, 179).

[188] Werner Jaeger, 'Philologie und Historie' [1914], in *Humanistische Reden und Vorträge* (Berlin: Walter de Gruyter, 1937), p. 16.

What Nietzsche or Jaeger proposed should not be interpreted as a call for happy gentlemanly resignation. No one could really ignore the feeling that *Beruf* was an integral part of the grand *Bildung*. The rejection of *Beruf* was therefore a sacrifice. It demanded heroic self-abnegation. Nietzsche seemed to admit that a purified disciplined self-formation, which he advocated, could be attained only through a kind of asceticism.[189] For Nietzsche, the non-ascetic option simply no longer existed. The only available choice was between the asceticism of fresh air and that of the resentful priest. To use my terminology, one can say that the former led to *Bildung*-as-Cultivation, whereas the latter belonged to *Bildung*-as-*Beruf* (for, as we have already seen, the professional scientist who is fully committed to his vocation is nothing more than a new embodiment of the ascetic Christian). Nietzsche wanted to escape the *Beruf* logic of the ascetic priest, even though the question of whether he really succeeded in this undertaking remains open.

There existed, however, an opposite solution. It was based not on the rejection of fragmentation but on its acceptance without compromise. This solution was equally heroic and ascetic, although the asceticism it postulated was not the humanistic asceticism of fresh air but the vocational asceticism of devotion to a cause. This was Max Weber's solution.[190]

In many respects, Weber was close to the Southwest neo-Kantians, especially with regard to the idea that the plurality of value spheres was an inescapable feature of modernity.[191] He believed that the modern person had no choice but to accept this plurality and devote himself to one of its fragments. As he wrote in 1905, 'the Puritan *wanted* to be a man of vocation [*Berufsmensch*]; we *must* be such a man'.[192]

Weber admitted that narrow professionalism might lead to the loss of meaning. Yet this danger was to be combated only from within the ethics of *Beruf*. In opposition to the mechanical specialisation of the philistine, Weber posited the ideal of service to a professional cause.[193] In this service, at least some elements of meaning could be preserved. Yet it still remained a vocation: *Beruf*.

---

[189] See, for example, his description of the philosopher's asceticism. Nietzsche, *On the Genealogy of Morality*, pp. 76–80.

[190] On Weber's departure from the tradition of *Bildung*, see Fritz K. Ringer, *Max Weber: An Intellectual Biography* (Princeton: Princeton University Press, 2004), pp. 225–230.

[191] Max Weber, 'Religious Dimensions of the World and Their Directions' [1915], in *Essays in Sociology*, trans. H. H. Gerth and C. Wright Mills (London: Routledge, 1991), pp. 323–359.

[192] Max Weber, *Die protestantische Ethik und der Geist des Kapitalismus* [1904–1905] (Tübingen: J. C. B. Mohr, 1934), p. 203. Parson's translation of this phrase is not literal.

[193] See Georg Stauth and Bryan S. Turner, 'Nietzsche in Weber oder die Geburt des modernen Genius' im professionellen Menschen', *Zeitschrift für Soziologie* 15(2), 1986, p. 92.

This view was seconded by some philosophers and sociologists of the younger generation. Thus Helmuth Plessner spoke about the impossibility of maintaining theoretical unity between modern sciences.[194] The only framework in which modern research could fruitfully proceed was that in which various disciplines possessed full independence and coexisted by means of a 'republican-democratic constitution'.[195]

The story of the clash between the advocates of *Bildung* and those of *Beruf* cannot be reduced to the dichotomy between reactionaries and progressives. Advocacy of *Beruf* crossed political lines. Thus the idea that modern industrial society was characterised by technique and cold rationalisation, and that in such a society *Bildung* was outdated, was advanced by Hans Freyer, a proponent of 'the revolution from the right'.[196] It is then simplistic to attribute the origins of the German *Sonderweg* to the alleged weakness of the principle of *Beruf.* Rather, the outright rejection of the value of self-cultivation and the fascination with industrial ethics were in themselves expressions of that spirit of perfectionism which led the ideal of *Bildung* into trouble in the first place.[197] The conceptualisation of the ethics of modern fabric by German adepts of *Beruf* was itself a *Sonderweg* in reverse, rather than a faithful account of the values which maintain modern Western society.

1.3   Simmel and *Kultur*

Having completed this excurse, we can now return to Simmel and attempt to locate him within this context. From what has already been said, one can clearly conclude that Simmel's dilemmas were in many respects those of a typical educated German of his time. As a German intellectual of the Second Empire, he regarded the problem of the inner tension of *Bildung* as a very important issue.[198] He spent much effort in analysing the conflict

---

[194] On Plessner's sociology of modern science, see Schnädelbach, *Philosophy in Germany*, pp. 68–71.

[195] Helmuth Pleßner, 'Zur Soziologie der modernen Forschung und ihrer Organisation in der deutschen Universität', in Max Scheler (ed.), *Versuche zu einer Soziologie des Wissens* (Munich: Duncker & Humblot, 1924), p. 424.

[196] Hans Freyer, *Revolution von rechts* (Jena: Eugen Diederichs, 1931). Freyer may have later modified his political views but not his advocacy of modern technique. See Hans Freyer, *Über das Dominantwerden technischer Kategorien in der Lebenswelt der industriellen Gesellschaft* (Mainz: Akademie der Wissenschaften und der Literatur, 1960).

[197] It is amazing that the stereotype of the West as a mechanism was shared not only by 'reactionaries' but also by 'progressives' such as Weber, who could see in the modern English political system nothing but a machine ('Politics as a Vocation' [1919], in *Essays in Sociology*, p. 107 [77–128]). The difference between them was that 'progressives' recommended implementing this caricature in Germany as well.

[198] On Simmel and *Bildung*, see Fabio D'Andrea, 'Simmel: Bildung as the Form of Subjectivity', *Simmel Studies* 23(1), 2019, pp. 43–66.

between vocation and cultivation, between singularity and universality, between variety and unity, and he did this with a high degree of sophistication.

I have already quoted Simmel's references to these dualisms in the context of the microcosm of human personality. Yet, for him, just as for many other intellectuals of his time, these dilemmas also reflected the fundamental dualism inherent in the macrocosm of the universe. In 'The Personality of God' (1911), for example, he went as far as to attribute the same dualism to our perception of God. That is, in order to perceive God, one must presuppose, on the one hand, a duality between God and the world. God is extraneous to the believer. Without this separation, God can be perceived as neither powerful nor loved. In other words, in order to worship God, one should perceive him as an object. On the other hand, however, God cannot be removed from his creations. If he is really all-powerful, nothing can be extraneous to him. All aspects of reality must be merely reflections of God, which leads us to the pantheistic view. But again, the dialectical process 'cannot end there ... because indispensable religious values are based on the notion that God and the world or God and man are juxtaposed and distinct'.[199]

Thus God must be both the pantheistic essence of the world and a singular object of devotion removed from the world. Precisely the same articulation of the dichotomy between this-worldliness and other-worldliness will later appear in Lovejoy. He presents this dichotomy as the basic dilemma of European philosophy and culture. Lovejoy's final verdict is that the combination between this-worldliness and other-worldliness was a failure. The American historian of ideas observed *Bildung* from outside. But the German philosopher Simmel could still believe in 1911 that the concept of the personality of God was capable of encompassing dualisms. He argued that the notion of personality contains 'duality and contradiction between the individual element and the unified whole'[200] that signifies 'the centre and the periphery, the unified whole and its parts and this unique relationship between them'.[201]

Now, if applied to human personality, this twofold conception turns out to be just another formulation of the notion of *Bildung*, in which the emphasis on the apartness, or uniqueness, of every individual is combined with the idea of the individual's universality. Yet Simmel was more than just another thinker who upheld the ideal synthesis of *Bildung*. A mere

---

[199] 'The Personality of God', trans. H. J. Helle, in *Essays on Religion*, p. 55. [GSG 12, p. 300.]
[200] Ibid., p. 56. [GSG 12, p. 301.]   [201] Ibid., p. 57. [GSG 12, p. 301.]

synthesis of *Bildung* and *Beruf* would not encompass the Wilhelmine intellectual atmosphere in its entirety because it would ignore the more radical strategies, which called for a departure from the grand *Bildung* and which by then had already been formulated and voiced.

Rather, the singularity of Simmel was that he combined all three aforementioned strategies: the strategy of cultivation, that of vocation (devotion) and that of yet another attempt at a perfectionist synthesis of cultivation and vocation. Simmel wanted to comprehend the crisis of *Bildung* in its totality. He attempted to belong to both its extremes. He was both Nietzsche and Weber, Jaeger and Plessner, modernist and trad-itionalist, a custodian of the official cultural canon and a connoisseur of the counter-culture of his time, a university mandarin and an academic mav-erick, a proponent of both self-cultivation and professionalisation. By developing his thought out of the manifold and diverse aspects of German intellectual life, he became the figure in whom this life in its entirety acquired a very high, and possibly maximal, degree of coherence.

The term that embodied for Simmel the three possibilities all at once and that enabled him to develop an encompassing image of the entire problematics was '*Kultur*'. This word was of crucial significance for Simmel and his age. Therefore, before embarking on a detailed analysis of Simmel's thought, one should make a final contextual detour in order to examine the meaning of *Kultur* in its intellectual setting as well as its relation to the notion of *Bildung*.

In Simmel's time, it was expected, in Germany and elsewhere, for a well-educated person to be a person of culture. However, this understanding became increasingly challenged. By the turn of the century, culture was perceived as constantly fragmenting and causing fragmentation to those who were trying to attain it. The scope of its growth outweighed the personal capacity to absorb it. Culture multiplied into cultures, and the ideal of synthesis receded more and more into an uncertain distant future. Whereas the ideal of culture in the singular came to signify a yearning for a more or less comprehensive harmony, the same ideal taken in the plural led to the notion of a growing differentiation between various cultural spheres or even to an incompatibility or conflict between them.[202] The idea of *Kultur* was torn between the ideal of cultivation and the variety of *Berufe*.

---

[202] Cf. Rüdiger vom Bruch, 'Einleitung: Kulturbegriff, Kulturkritik und Kulturwissenschaften um 1900', in Rüdiger vom Bruch, Friedrich Wilhelm Graf and Gangolf Hübinger (eds.), *Kultur und Kulturwissenschaften um 1900: Krise der Moderne und Glaube an die Wissenschaft* (Stuttgart: Franz Steiner, 1989), p. 19.

This was an almost inevitable predicament of triumph. For *Kultur* was taken by then as a ubiquitous and rarely questioned value. Introduced into the German language by Samuel Pufendorf, the word already acquired prominence towards the late eighteenth century. While its salience diminished in the mid-nineteenth century, as it was by and large substituted by *Geist* as a result of the widespread influence of Hegelian terminology, it conquered the public imagination again towards the late nineteenth century.[203] It almost attained the status of a regulative idea or at least a consensual value criterion by which other societal values were to be judged.

As is often the case with master ideals, the range of possible meanings and connotations of *Kultur* was very broad,[204] which provided infinite possibilities for decontestation with regard to determining the specific meaning of this ideal while excluding alternatives. On the most general level, *Kultur* in all its meanings seemed to include a component of contrast with nature, roughness and uncultivated existence. It was taken to be the exclusive property of human beings, since only humans were capable of raising themselves above the level of meaningless physical survival on the way to the sphere of spirit and consciousness: 'to possess culture is clearly a human prerogative'.[205]

Within this common denominator, however, a great number of different and even contradictory specifications were possible. Hubertus Busche has aptly summarised the varieties of the classical meaning of the German *Kultur* under four main groupings. The first two refer to culture in respect of an individual. Thus *Kultur* can be understood either as the process of personal cultivation, especially the cultivation of the spirit or soul (the famous *cultura animi*), or it can refer to the outcome of this process of cultivation: attainment of the state of cultured personality. The third meaning refers to culture in respect of societies, signifying the totality of institutions, habits and beliefs that characterise the life of a given society in a certain period. Finally, *Kultur* can refer to the products of cultural activity: cultural artefacts and values of exceptional significance.[206]

---

[203] On the relative absence of *Kultur* in the period before 1870 and its substitution by *Geist*, see Geuss, 'Kultur, Bildung, Geist'.

[204] On *Bildung* and *Kultur* as *Deutungsmuster* (pattern of interpretation), see Bollenbeck, *Bildung und Kultur*, pp. 18, 24–27.

[205] Bruford, *Culture and Society in Classical Weimar*, p. 7.

[206] Hubertus Busche, '"Kultur": Ein Wort, viele Begriffe', in H. Busche, et al. (eds.), *Kultur – Interdisziplinäre Zugänge* (Wiesbaden: Springer, 2018), pp. 5–24. An older, in some respects similar and in other respects different, fourfold division can be found in Bruford, *Culture and Society in Classical Weimar*, pp. 3–7.

Remarkably, Busche suggested that Simmel's concept of culture incorporated all four components, as he formulated Simmel's main question in
the following way: '*What opportunities remain for the individual in our
culture₃ characterised by advancing mechanisation and a monetary economy,
which produces an inherently dynamic and expansive subdomain of culture₄, to
bring his own nature to a state of total perfection (culture₂) by cultivating mind
and personality (culture₁)?*'[207] Simmel's outlook thus appears in this reading
the most synoptic and at the same time most coherent expression of the
German concept of *Kultur*.

This book happily acquiesces to the spirit of Busche's assessment, as its
purpose is to present Simmel as the most articulate and versatile user of his
own intellectual tradition. Nonetheless, my reading of Simmel's approach to
Kultur – however broad – is somewhat more restrictive. Of the four meanings
enumerated above, there is at least one which was less relevant to him: the view
of culture as the totality of social institutions, habits and beliefs, which can also
be called the anthropological meaning of culture. In the Anglophone world,
this view was first introduced in 1871 by E. B. Tylor, who considered culture
and civilisation as referring to the same concept which, 'taken in its wide
ethnographic sense, is that complex whole which includes knowledge, belief,
art, morals, law, custom, and any other capabilities and habits acquired by
man as a member of society'.[208] However, its origins go back to a German
author: Gustav Klemm and his *General Cultural History of Mankind* (1843).[209]

This usage was highly relevant for the specialised scholarly discourse in
Germany already in Simmel's time. However, the general public discourse
was still dominated by the usage of *Kultur* that pertained to individuals or
to cultural artefacts and that was strongly related to the image of a high
level of civilisational development. Culture was something singular and,
even when it was taken in the plural, it referred to the plurality of cultural
spheres, such as art, science etc., rather than the plurality of national and
ethnic cultures. Culture was in this sense the domain of every developed
individual, and even the patriotic appeal of German professors 'To the
Cultural World' (1914) presupposed culture as a universal value and spoke
about the German people as *Kulturvolk* in this civilisational sense.

---

[207] Hubertus Busche, 'Georg Simmels "Tragödie der Kultur": 90 Jahre danach', *JABLIS: Jahrbuch für
europäische Prozesse* 3, 2004, p. 217.
[208] Edward B. Tylor, *Primitive Culture*, 2 vols. (London: John Murray, 1871), vol. 1, p. 1.
[209] Gustav Klemm, *Allgemeine Cultur-Geschichte der Menschheit* (Leipzig: B. G. Teubner, 1843). See
A. L. Kroeber and Clyde Kluckhohn, *Culture: A Critical Review of Concepts and Definitions*
(New York: Vintage Books, 1952), pp. 44–46. On Tylor's definition, see also Torsten Botz-
Bornstein, 'What Is the Difference between Culture and Civilization? Two Hundred Years of
Confusion', *Comparative Civilizations Review* 66, 2012, pp. 11–13.

Simmel too spoke in his analysis of culture not as an anthropologist or sociologist but as a cultivated mandarin addressing a cultivated audience. Therefore, the range of meanings of 'culture' in his writings corresponded to the range of meanings common in the public debates of his time. Only on a few occasions did he speak about cultures in the anthropological sense. Even then, however, the focus of the word 'culture' was on the pursuit of human cultivation. Thus in *Kant and Goethe* (1906) he mentioned the (apparently high classical) *Kultur* that preceded the rise of Christianity, while referring to less refined forms of culture as half-cultures (*Halbkulturen*).[210] And in *Schopenhauer and Nietzsche* (1907) he spoke about 'all higher culture of our kind'.[211]

On the whole, however, this usage appears in Simmel only incidentally. When Simmel focused his attention specifically on the meaning of culture, he usually considered it as signifying a universal human condition that belongs either to the inner world of an individual or to his cultural production in the world at large and only rarely as signifying the peculiarity of habits, beliefs and institutions in a particular society.

To understand more precisely the specifically Simmelian range of the meanings of *Kultur*, one can juxtapose this word with two semantically related terms: '*Bildung*' and '*Zivilisation*'. Research on the history of the word '*Kultur*' often mentions each of them in a pair with '*Kultur*', either as a partner or as an opponent. Consider *Bildung*:[212] it can be translated both as education and as the accomplished culture of an educated individual. In this latter sense, *Bildung* and *Kultur* can be synonymous. On the other hand, when the product of the cultural formation is separated from the individual, *Kultur* departs from *Bildung*. In this sense, '"culture" means the result, in the individual, of the process of civilisation'.[213] '*Kultur*' can thus also be synonymous with the term '*Zivilisation*'; but it can also stand in sharp contrast to it.

In fact, it is possible to think about *Bildung* and *Zivilisation* as the opposite extremes of the same scale that rarely, if ever, overlap, whereas *Kultur* fills the entire space between. *Bildung* by and large refers to the personal sphere, the inner development of an individual. *Zivilisation*, by contrast, generally refers to the outward products of that development.

---

[210] GSG 10, p. 121. The English rendering of this sentence is not precise: 'Kant and Goethe: On the History of the Modern *Weltanschauung*', trans. J. Bleicher, *Theory, Culture & Society* 24(6), 2007, pp. 163–164.

[211] *Schopenhauer und Nietzsche: Ein Vortragszyklus*, GSG 10, p. 176.

[212] Cf. Bollenbeck, *Bildung und Kultur*.

[213] Bruford, *Culture and Society in Classical Weimar*, p. 4.

And *Kultur*, like the queen in chess, can make any move, sometimes choosing to come closer to the extreme of *Bildung* and sometimes coming closer to the extreme of *Zivilisation*.

Up until the last third of the nineteenth century, the latter meaning, where culture becomes synonymous with civilisation, both signifying the social or material aspects of human life, was probably more widespread in the German language than the idea of a contrast between the two, and even afterwards it remained quite common. This was, for example, the approach of Heymann Steinthal in his *Allgemeine Ethik* (1885).[214] Interestingly, when culture and civilisation were thus conflated, the idealistic connotations of the word '*Kultur*' tended to impart to civilisation a less mechanistic meaning. Thus Steinthal argued that 'culture in itself is always moral', and therefore 'language, writing, post, telegraphy and railways are moral institutions, regardless of how much lies are uttered and how many thieves use the railroad'.[215] Similarly, in 1906 a volume was published that celebrated the German spirit in all its spheres of achievement – artistic and technical – under the general heading of *Kultur*.[216] Culture in general was defined as 'the elevation of man over the state of nature through the development [*Ausbildung*] and activation of his spiritual and moral powers'.[217] Moreover, the conflation of culture and civilisation did not have to take a celebratory tone. Outbursts against modernity and technical progress could also regard the two terms as synonymous. The young Richard Wagner, for example, put culture and civilisation together in his 'Art and Revolution' (1849), claiming that they were two sisters who waged war against living human nature. Culture, he argued, employs the human mind merely as 'steampower for its machinery'.[218]

Towards the later nineteenth century, however, culture began to be perceived as contrasting with civilisation, and the pair thus turned into a stark antithesis.[219] The same Wagner who spoke about culture in disparaging terms in the late 1840s worked hard to establish this contrast in his later writings. Thus, in 'Religion and Art' (1880) he assigned to civilisation

---

[214] H. Steinthal, *Allgemeine Ethik* (Berlin: Georg Reimer, 1885), § 115, pp. 168–170. See Simmel's review of this book in GSG 1, pp. 192–210.

[215] Steinthal, *Allgemeine Ethik*, p. 169.

[216] Wilhelm Lexis et al., *Die allgemeinen Grundlagen der Kultur der Gegenwart*.

[217] Wilhelm Lexis, 'Das Wesen der Kultur', in Lexis et al., *Die allgemeinen Grundlagen der Kultur der Gegenwart*, p. 1.

[218] Richard Wagner, 'Art and Revolution' [1849], in *Richard Wagner's Prose Works*, vol. 1, trans. W. A. Ellis (London: Kegan Paul, Trench, Trübner & Co., 1895), p. 54.

[219] Michael Pflaum, 'Die Kultur-Zivilisations-Antithese im Deutschen', in Johann Knobloch, et al. (eds.), *Kultur und Zivilisation* (Munich: Max Hueber, 1967), pp. 307–327.

a negative meaning, while praising 'mental and moral culture [*geistigen und sittlichen Kultur*]', the true basis of which had to be Schopenhauer's philosophy.[220] This was echoed by many other authors. Ferdinand Tönnies, for example, argued (1887) that civilisation belongs to the modern *Gesellschaft*, protected by the legal apparatus of the state, whereas culture is better protected by the arrangements and ways of life of *Gemeinschaft*.[221] Likewise, Ferdinand Avenarius suggested (1901) that 'the *preserving* and *easing* of life are the ultimate intentions of civilisation, whereas the *heightening* and *ennobling* of life are engendered by culture'.[222]

The view of culture as distinct from civilisation naturally positioned it closer to the sphere of meaning of *Bildung*. Interestingly, when Wagner's 'Religion and Art' was translated, the English word 'culture' came to indicate both *Kultur* and *Bildung*, as, for example, in the phrase where Wagner spoke about the imperative of following 'with the utmost diligence, and to its farthest bifurcation, each path whereon man's mental culture [*geistige Bildung*] may lead to the establishment of true morality'.[223] Avenarius similarly argued that the two words mean basically the same thing:

> Goethe sometimes uses the words *Bildung* and *Kultur* in the same sense. Indeed, both mean that a soul material, whether man or time, is transformed into a work of art and that the character and value of life are increasingly heightened not by the undirected rushing forth of powers but by their harmonisation. And both signify a self-contained development which is subject to the laws of becoming.[224]

Indeed, *Kultur* in its role as a synonym of inner *Bildung* was as old as, if not older than, *Kultur* as signifying civilisation. Already in 1793, Fichte defined *Cultur* as the 'exercise of all powers towards the purpose of complete freedom, complete independence from everything which is not ourselves, our pure self'.[225] This connection of culture with inwardness naturally drew on the contrast with civilisation. Kant, for example, described (1784) the contrast between genuine morality belonging to culture and the outward conduct of a civilised person, arguing that

---

[220] Richard Wagner, 'Religion and Art' [1880], in *Richard Wagner's Prose Works*, vol. 6, trans. W. A. Ellis (London: Kegan Paul, Trench, Trübner & Co., 1897), p. 257.

[221] Ferdinand Tönnies, *Community and Civil Society*, trans. J. Harris and M. Hollis (Cambridge: Cambridge University Press, 2001), p. 249.

[222] Ferdinand Avenarius, 'Kultur und Zivilisation', *Kunstwart* 14(2), 1901, p. 81.

[223] Wagner, 'Religion and Art', p. 262.   [224] Avenarius, 'Kultur und Zivilisation', pp. 82–83.

[225] Johann Gottlieb Fichte, *Beitrag zur Berechtigung der Urtheile des Publicums über die französische Revolution* [1793] (Berlin: Contumax, 2014), p. 37.

'while the idea of morality is indeed present in culture, an application of this idea which only extends to the semblances of morality, as in love of honour and outward propriety, amounts merely to civilisation [*Civilisirung*]'.[226] Although here, unlike in the century of industrial revolution, civilisation did not signify the material technique, it signified a technique nonetheless: the outward aspect of human behaviour. Thirty years later (1815–1816), Johann Heinrich Pestalozzi posited the same contrast, writing in one of his drafts of the 'perfection and universality of every step made by *Cultur*', while distinguishing it from the 'inhibition, standstill and one-sidedness of each developmental step that springs from *Civilisation*'.[227] Culture alluded here to the ideal of unity, whereas civilisation signified fragmentation that results from the division of labour.

This contrast was often related to the motif of German national pride. *Kultur* was taken to be the specific characteristic of German-ness which made it superior to those societies that possessed mere 'civilisation'. And if in Kant's times the civilised other was represented by France, in the course of the nineteenth century it was America that began to be perceived as the principal embodiment of civilisation in its vulgar sense. Historian Karl Lamprecht, for example, wrote, with reference to the Germans who visited the United States in the mid-nineteenth century, that 'the Germans could have helped in culture (spiritual and artistic development) and much less in the field of scientific education, of civilisation. However, America was not yet ready for culture'.[228]

This contrast between culture and civilisation was, however, not the only discourse game in town. In the same years, the opposite usage of the same words developed as well. Here, culture was concerned 'with the technological-economic activities or the "material sphere"; but civilisation, with spiritual ennoblement or enriching'.[229] This meaning was outlined by philosopher and sociologist Paul Barth, who attributed it to figures such as Wilhelm von Humboldt, Albert Schäffle and Julius Lippert.[230]

---

[226] Immanuel Kant, 'Idea for a Universal History with a Cosmopolitan Purpose', in *Political Writings*, trans. H. B. Nisbet (Cambridge: Cambridge University Press, 1991), p. 49.

[227] Johann Heinrich Pestalozzi, 'An die Unschuld, den Ernst und den Edelmuth meines Zeitalters und meines Vaterlandes: Aufzeichnungen zu einer zweiten Auflage' [1815–1816], in *Sämtliche Werke* (Zurich: Orell Füssli, 1978), vol. 24B, p. 7.

[228] Karl Lamprecht, *Americana: Reiseeindrücke, Betrachtungen, Geschichtliche Gesamtansicht* (Freiburg im Breisgau: Hermann Heyfelder, 1906), p. 31. On the German perception of America and growing anti-Americanism, see Diner, *America in the Eyes of the Germans*.

[229] Kroeber and Kluckhohn, *Culture*, p. 288.

[230] Paul Barth, *Die Philosophie der Geschichte als Soziologie* (Leipzig: O. R. Reisland, 1897), pp. 144, 253–254; see Kroeber and Kluckhohn, *Culture*, pp. 25–27.

A. L. Kroeber and Clyde Kluckhohn have suggested that 'the number of writers who made culture the material or technological aspect is about as great as the number of those who called that same aspect civilisation'.[231] Nevertheless, the sheer number of usages may be misleading. From the point of view of an intellectual history that wishes to re-enact the general spiritual tendencies of a certain age, the decisive point should be the salience of one usage or another in the cultural imagination. And it can be safely said that in terms of the general *cultural* effect, the usage that attributed to culture a meaning close to *Bildung* was, in the early twentieth century, more significant than the materialistic one suggested by Lippert and Barth.

Now, beyond the two usages of *Kultur* – spiritual inwardness or material outwardness – there existed a third possibility that superseded them both. As Kroeber and Kluckhohn suggested, 'probably still a greater number of Germans than both the foregoing together used culture in the inclusive sense'.[232] The 'inclusive sense' means that, placed on a scale between spirit (*Bildung*) and matter (*Zivilisation*), culture rarely came to exclusively indicate either of them. Rather, it constantly fluctuated between the inward (*Bildung*) and the outward (*Zivilisation*), and even those authors who emphasised one tendency over the other never fully freed the definition of culture from the other tendency's influences. In many instances, *Kultur* was consciously employed to signify the higher middle (or 'third') between the two extremes.

Consider, for example, the approach of educationist Otto Willmann, who distinguished between civilisation and culture in the following way. Both humanise men by raising them beyond the state of nature. Civilisation, however, focuses on forming social conditions, signifying the institutional forms of social life, such as customs and laws that bind humans together. Culture, by contrast, signifies human work, activity and creativity, the production of goods of all kinds. Both words refer to external characteristics, and each has its counterpart in human subjectivity: Civilisation is the external form of inner *Gesittung*, and culture is the external form of *Bildung*.[233] Willmann's notion of *Gesittung* as the inner foundation of civilisation was somewhat idiosyncratic and did not have much impact.[234] What was, however, more indicative of the general usage

---

[231] Kroeber and Kluckhohn, *Culture*, pp. 29–30.   [232] Ibid., p. 30.

[233] Otto Willmann, *Didaktik als Bildungslehre: nach ihren Beziehungen zur Socialforschung und zur Geschichte der Bildung*, vol. 1 (Braunschweig: Friedrich Vieweg und Sohn, 1882), pp. 101–103.

[234] *Gesittung* can also be translated as 'civilisation' or 'good manners'.

was the meaning he attributed to culture. It was supposed to signify those spheres of human activity that were generally perceived as more related to individual personality than to socially oriented civilisation: human activity and creativity. This positioned culture closer to personal *Bildung*, although it still referred to the sphere of the external products of cultivation.

With the intensification of the debates about culture, it became even more common to present *Kultur* more explicitly as a 'third' category. In this sense, *Kultur*, taken neither as exclusively the cultivation of the self nor as exclusively the totality of the outward productions of the human spirit, signified the synthetic unity by means of which the self was realised in the world, whereas nature (or matter) was spiritualised. In this sense, culture could be taken as the crowning stage of human development. As one author suggested, 'the cultivation [*Bearbeitung*] of the whole nature by man and the formation [*Ausbildung*] of his moral, intellectual and technical faculties and skills' should be distinguished from civilisation, which is essentially 'the overcoming of barbarism, which precedes a more accomplished cultural development [*Kulturentwicklung*] or forms its lowest level'.[235]

Like the two previous meanings – *Kultur* as civilisation and *Kultur* as *Bildung* – this one too was as old as classical German culture. It was already intimated by Friedrich Schiller. Although Schiller did not use the term 'culture' in this respect, he formulated a triadic scheme in which the dichotomy between savagery and civilisation (which he termed 'barbarism') was to be supplanted by a triadic form in which the middle part (the aesthetic feeling) was a necessary stage in the progression from savagery to civilisation.

In the subsequent turnaround of this motif, the middle element of the triad tended to indicate the highest stage, which was supposed to resolve the discontents of civilisation. For example, in 1903, young philosopher Leopold Ziegler, later one of the leading thinkers of the conservative revolution, presented culture as the crowning stage in the dialectical triad of nature-civilisation-culture. His argument and definition of culture mixed fashionable Schopenhauerianism with influences from the broad tradition of German Idealism, and its main lines were as follows. Nature is the stage of rough instinctive life which must be overcome by civilisation, which is the conscious pursuit of happiness through a reflective setting of practical goals. Subsequently, however, civilisation is overcome by culture,

---

[235] Wilhelm Münch, 'Kulturfortschritt und Gegenwart', in *Zum deutschen Kultur- und Bildungsleben* (Berlin: Weidmannsche Buchhandlung, 1912), p. 30.

so that 'the ideal here would be a maximum of culture with a minimum of civilisation'.[236] Culture is a return to nature on a higher stage, informed by the achievements of civilisation. It is a return to the unconscious aspect of nature, which is now brought into the moral sphere of conscious individuals; it is the divination of human beings through their immersion in the universal natural unconscious. Culture is thus conceived as 'the growing recognition and realisation of the one and only absolute spirit'.[237] It is 'the totality of all the relationships of humans towards the objectively existing and eternally unconscious world spirit that attains the consciousness of its own will in man, signifying in its course the process of self-liberation of the unconscious divine essence in human *consciousness* and *existence*'.[238] In a quite Feuerbachian vein, Ziegler argued that the aims of culture (like those of religion) are 'the realisation of the idea of the God-man'.[239] Culture, for him, was therefore the stage at which nature (that is, the spiritual universe) attains perfection by coming into consciousness via human will.[240]

What is interesting here for our purposes is the positioning of culture as the higher, ideal 'third' or synthesis. Thus, as Ziegler claimed, quoting from Schiller's *On the Aesthetic Education of Man*, '"transforming the work of compulsion into a work of free choice and elevating physical necessity into moral necessity" – *this is the realisation of culture*',[241] or '*the essence of culture is the history of the motives that human consciousness devises to justify its work*'.[242]

Now, consider Alfred Weber, who was very much Ziegler's opposite: an economist and sociologist with the left-liberal leanings characteristic of the *Kathedersozialisten* of the Schmoller circle. Weber, too, appeared to understand culture as a kind of 'ideal third'. In his opening speech at the Second Congress of German sociologists (1912), he delineated the dialectical contrast between civilisation and culture. The civilisational process, according to Weber, is the continuation of biological evolution on the level of intellect that serves the purpose of biological survival by incessantly expanding human power over nature. Culture, by contrast, is a phenomenon of a higher and different order, whose ideal task is not the continuation of life but the sphere that stands above life. Even though culture is possible only in the context of natural existence supported by the civilising process, its

---

[236] Leopold Ziegler, *Das Wesen der Kultur* (Leipzig: E. R. Weiss, 1903), p. 176. On culture versus civilisation, see ibid., pp. 172–191.

[237] Ibid., p. 139.   [238] Ibid., p. 138.   [239] Ibid., p. 139.   [240] Ibid., p. 126.

[241] Ibid., p. 15. Cf. Schiller, *On the Aesthetic Education of Man*, p. 11.

[242] Ziegler, *Das Wesen der Kultur*, p. 15.

autonomous value lies in the fact of its dealing, as it were, with the superfluous by-products of this process. By building on the inner energies of life, culture secures the '*continuous existence* of life's *superfluous*', thus producing what is supra- or non-purposive.[243] Culture is embedded in feeling rather than in the intellect, representing the non-intellectual synthesis between personality and the world. The dialectical triad suggested by Ziegler was not spelled out by Weber, but he did assume something similar, as culture is conceived here as resolving on a higher level the contradiction between the natural spirit and artificial refinement.[244]

This positioning of culture as an all-encompassing ideal finally brings us to Simmel, who himself was an active participant in the discourse on the essence of culture and who too – like Ziegler or Weber – conceived culture as the crowning ideal of the civilising process. At the same time, what made his writings peculiar and significant was that, far from assigning to culture an exclusive, if even elevated, meaning, Simmel tried to incorporate into his understanding of culture the whole variety of its meanings. Here, too, he played the role of the unifier of the main tenets of his intellectual world.

Thus Simmel's writings contain the entire spectrum of possible usages of culture, while offering a definition meant to constitute a philosophical synthesis of these usages. Some of his texts treat culture as bordering on civilisation. For example, he described the cultural process in terms of 'a heightened consciousness, sophistication and purposefulness in the art of living [*Lebenstechnik*]';[245] mentioned 'the technical progress that characterises the objective culture of our time';[246] referred to 'the goods of higher culture';[247] or spoke about 'the path of culture – at least of technical culture, in the outer as well as in the spiritual sense'.[248] When culture was thus understood by him as synonymous with civilisation, it could occasionally also be the target of civilisation criticism, as, for example, in a passage where he spoke of the condition in which 'the individual is pressed into a one-sided mould of exclusive, specialised activity, and all

---

[243] Alfred Weber, 'Der soziologische Kulturbegriff', in *Verhandlungen des Zweiten Deutschen Soziologentages* (Tübingen: J. C. B. Mohr, 1913), p. 12.

[244] Similar implications can be derived from his later essay: Alfred Weber, 'Prinzipielles zur Kultursoziologie: Gesellschaftsprozess, Zivilisationsprozess und Kulturbewegung', *Archiv für Sozialwissenschaft und Sozialpolitik* 47, 1920, pp. 1–49. On Alfred Weber's approach to culture, see Colin Loader, *Alfred Weber and the Crisis of Culture, 1890–1933* (New York: Palgrave Macmillan, 2012).

[245] 'A Review of *Social Medicine*' [1897], trans. J. Casparis and A. C. Higgins, *Social Forces* 47(3), 1969, p. 332. [GSG 1, p. 382.]

[246] '[Über:] *Karl Joël*, Professor in Basel: *Philosophenwege*. Ausblicke und Rückblicke. Berlin, Heyfelder, 1901' [27 April 1901], GSG 17, p. 328.

[247] 'Socialismus und Pessimismus' [1900], GSG 5, p. 554.   [248] *Kant*, GSG 9, p. 118.

the energies he possesses that are not thus employable are stunted in their growth: such is the flaw of all very complex cultures'.[249]

On other occasions, Simmel used the notion of culture as referring to the ideal of inward *Bildung*, for example, in a passage where he criticised misguided attempts at self-cultivation: '[T]hese people employ one of those easy self-deceptions whereby their own culture, which would find egoism shocking, retains a subjectivity despite its lofty sentiments and seeks shamelessly to cloak its own pleasures with objective justifications,'[250] or in the following passage where he dealt with 'philosophical culture', which, as he argued,

> does not in fact consist in the knowledge of metaphysical systems or the confession of faith in individual theories, but rather in a consistent intellectual attitude towards all existence, in an intellectual motion towards the stratum in which, in the broadest variety of profundities and connected to the broadest variety of actualities, all possible currents of philosophy run.[251]

Yet the true essence of culture for Simmel lay not in either of these two meanings taken separately but in their continuous interaction. Culture, properly speaking, is the third realm, which emerges when personal cultivation is challenged and enriched by the world of extraneous values and objects it itself produces. In other words, Simmel saw culture as the ideal that abolishes the split between the inward and outward, although, in contrast to thinkers such as Ziegler or Weber, he did not remove the exclusively inward or outward from the concept of culture, seeing an exclusive emphasis on either as merely an unavoidable problem in the course of the cultural process.

To emphasise the peculiarity of Simmel's position, let us juxtapose it with the aforementioned text of Alfred Weber. In fact, Weber's words in 1912 can be interpreted as a critique of Simmel, notwithstanding the respect that each of them had for the other. It was Simmel who insisted that Weber be invited to deliver the public lecture at the Sociological Congress despite the reservations of some of the other organisers, as Weber's general topic seemed to be irrelevant to the 'professional' subject of the event: the question of nationalities.[252] Yet in his talk, Weber, without naming

---

[249] 'Religion', p. 189. [GSG 10, p. 93.]
[250] 'The Alpine Journey', trans. S. Whimster, in Frisby and Featherstone (eds.), *Simmel on Culture*, p. 220. [GSG 5, p. 92.]
[251] '"Introduction" to *Philosophical Culture*', trans. M. Ritter and D. Frisby, in Frisby and Featherstone (eds.), *Simmel on Culture*, p. 35. [GSG 14, pp. 165–166.]
[252] See, for example, Simmel's letter to the board of the German Sociological Congress [*Vorstand der DGS*], 10 June 1912, GSG 23, pp. 69–70.

Simmel explicitly, rejected Simmel's thesis, according to which the condition of culture was tragic, since it was torn from within by the discrepancy between its inward and outward aspects. Weber mentioned the common notion of the 'tragedy of the cultural process',[253] in the course of which the objects of one's cultural activity allegedly place themselves in opposition to one's existence, claim autonomy for themselves and thus enslave their creator. However, he claimed that this view involved terminological confusion. Most of what was regarded as the objective side of culture belonged to a completely different sphere: that of the *civilising* process, whereas the logic of culture was completely different, and the pressures of civilisation did not relate to and therefore did not hamper cultural needs. The contemporary world was characterised not by the tragedy of culture but by its opposite, and in fact in those days, according to Weber, one could feel that this was 'a moment that heightens the cultural will and certainly the cultural feeling'.[254]

Simmel apparently took some notice of these points. Thus Weber's notion of the superfluous turned in Simmel into the concept of 'more-than-life': the sphere of autonomous cultural spheres that stand above life.[255] Yet he was not prepared to adopt the semantic distinction between the two phenomena – culture and civilisation – that were intertwined in social reality. By referring to them by the same term, Simmel was simply pointing to this interconnectedness which could not be disentangled by analytical division. He likewise would not accept placing culture in the sphere of 'feeling', which was supposed to prevail over the 'intellect' relegated to the world of externalities.

In fact, Simmel rarely spoke in the terminology of either *Bildung* or civilisation. For these were, for him, just two sides of the same complex and tragic phenomenon: culture. Thus, when he mentioned the external element of culture, he noticed that 'linguistic usage dismisses [it] as mere civilisation'[256], but for Simmel this external element was merely the objective side of culture. What he in fact spoke about was the split between culture in its objective aspect and culture in its subjective aspect, or to use his own words, objective culture and subjective culture.[257] Culture as such emerges when the two keep apace of each other.

[253] Weber, 'Der soziologische Kulturbegriff', p. 17.   [254] Ibid., p. 18.
[255] *The View of Life: Four Metaphysical Essays with Journal Aphorisms*, trans. J. A. Y. Andrews and D. N. Levine (Chicago: University of Chicago Press, 2010), pp. 13–17. [GSG 16, pp. 229–235.]
[256] 'The Concept and Tragedy of Culture', p. 57. [GSG 12, p. 197.]
[257] Karl-Siegbert Rehberg, 'Kultur, subjektive und objektive', in H. P. Müller and T. Reitz (eds.), *Simmel-Handbuch: Begriffe, Hauptwerke, Aktualität* (Frankfurt am Main: Suhrkamp, 2018), pp. 328–334.

Culture, understood as the coordination of subjective culture and objective culture, depends on a number of conditions. First, it implies conscious cultivation, the application of intelligence for the purpose of directing the development of the qualities embedded in the innate nature of the object of cultivation. Thus it is the nature of a tree to bear fruit, and an application of intelligence on the part of the gardener is cultivation because it merely maximises this natural potential. By contrast, when a table is made out of that tree, this cannot be considered a process of cultivation because it is not the innate nature of the tree to be cut into pieces of wood.

Second, the process of inward cultivation requires constant engagement with the extraneous world: '[C]ulture implies also that such human development involves *something external to man.*'[258] External objects are thus part of culture too – not by themselves, but only in respect of their service to the cultivation of the individual. They are 'only the raw material for the process of civilisation [*Kultivierungsprozeß*], like wood and metal, plants and electricity'.[259]

Third, only a human being, properly speaking, can undergo such a process of intelligent cultivation of innate characteristics through engagement with the extraneous world, for 'he is the only being known to us with an inherent a priori demand for perfection'.[260] A human being is thus the only creature who can possess culture, for a human is the only creature who can perform the twofold step: de-subjectivising one's own values and products in order to reintroduce them afterwards into one's own personality. Culture is a dialectical process, and only a human being is capable of dialectics. As Simmel defined it, 'culture is the path from the closed unity through the developed diversity (*Vielheit*) to the developed unity'.[261]

Culture is thus a harmonious unity forming itself by means of dynamic interaction between the inward and outward. This means that, on the one hand, the extraneous world is endowed with cultural meaning only when it is related to our personalities. Therefore, the cultural value of cultural objects is not objective. Autonomous cultural spheres, exemplified by works of art or scientific research, 'may be imperfect and insignificant in the objective, technical perspective of their specific province, but may, for all that, offer precisely what our life [*Sein*] needs for the harmony of its

---

[258] 'On the Essence of Culture', trans. D. E. Jenkinson, in Frisby and Featherstone (eds.), *Simmel on Culture*, p. 42. [GSG 8, pp. 367–368.]
[259] *The Philosophy of Money*, p. 447. [GSG 6, p. 618.]
[260] 'On the Essence of Culture', p. 42. [GSG 8, p. 366.]
[261] 'The Concept and Tragedy of Culture', p. 56. [GSG 12, p. 196.]

parts, for its mysterious unity over and above all specific needs and energies'.[262] At least, the extraneous world cannot be despiritualised if it is to contain cultural value: '[T]he subjective spirit (*Geist*) must abandon its subjectivity but not its intellectuality (*Geistigkeit*) in order to experience that relationship to the object through which it becomes cultivated.'[263]

On the other hand, one cannot be a cultivated person if one stays, so to speak, in a state of pure inwardness, that is, if one's spiritual energies do not engage with the world. If 'the development of the subjective soul does not involve any objective artefact as a means and stage of its progress back to itself, then even if values of the highest order are created . . . it is not by way of culture in our specific sense'.[264] It is for this reason, for example, that 'highly introverted individuals, to whom it is abhorrent that the soul should seek self-perfection indirectly via anything external to itself, can feel hatred for culture'.[265]

This does not mean that the balance between the two sides in Simmel's definition of culture lies precisely in the centre. On the whole, it appears that in the dialectic of culture, it is the side of personality which is the beginning and the end of the dialectical process. For Simmel, the decisive aspect of cultivation is that of the cultivation of the subject.[266] Subjective culture is 'the only thing that gives the former [objective culture] any real value'.[267] Cultural policy should therefore be aligned with this consideration: '[T]he great eras that did have a cultural policy . . . always concentrated on the subjective factor: the *education* of the *individual*.'[268]

In other words, culture does require interaction with the external, but the decisive criterion for it is the return to the individual. It is this moment in Simmel's understanding of culture which made his critics perceive it as too individualistic and aestheticist. Ernst Cassirer, for example, suggested that Simmel did not take notice of the intersubjective processual character of cultural activity and that he focused too much on transporting the finished content of culture into the souls of individuals, whereas the essential in culture is not producing finished cultural products but inspiring the cultural activity of the receivers.[269] Simmel, according to Cassirer,

---

[262] 'On the Essence of Culture', p. 43. [GSG 8, p. 369.]
[263] 'The Concept and Tragedy of Culture', p. 58. [GSG 12, p. 199.]
[264] 'On the Essence of Culture', p. 43. [GSG 8, p. 368.]   [265] Ibid. [GSG 8, p. 368.]
[266] Ibid., p. 45. [GSG 8, p. 372.]
[267] 'The Future of Our Culture', trans. D. E. Jenkinson, in Frisby and Featherstone (eds.), *Simmel on Culture*, p. 102. [GSG 17, p. 83.]
[268] Ibid., p. 102. [GSG 17, p. 82.]
[269] Ernst Cassirer, *The Logic of the Cultural Science*, trans. S. G. Lofts (New Haven: Yale University Press, 2000), pp. 110–111.

did not fully realise the importance of the mediating symbols in the cultural process and was too obsessed with the ideal of the unity of the individual soul. Cassirer considered this to be the attitude of a mystic.[270]

This criticism was somewhat exaggerated. As will be shown, in his last years Simmel did move towards an appreciation of the mystical attitude to life. Yet his principal writings on culture, discussed by Cassirer, did not go that far.[271] Besides, in many respects Simmel's philosophy of culture did deal with the independent value of cultural mediating symbols. What was, however, true in Cassirer's criticism was that when it came to the philosophical ideal of culture, Simmel put the harmonious individual personality at the centre.

It is this striving for harmony and individuality which propelled Simmel towards the sense of tragedy or despair. For the two-sided essence of culture, divided into the subjective and the objective, inevitably implied discrepancy or even inner conflict. These two aspects tend to drift apart from one another and rarely, if ever, coexist in perfect harmony. In one of his last texts on the subject, Simmel listed three ways in which subjective and objective culture may lose sight of one another. It often happens that 'mere means are regarded as ultimate ends' or 'that objective culture is developing to an extent and at a pace that leaves subjective culture … further and further behind' or that 'the separate branches of culture are evolving in different directions towards mutual estrangement'.[272]

Busche has called these three suggestions 'the thesis of growing independence' (*Verselbständigungsthese*), that is, the situation in which the means become autonomous from the ends to which they were supposed to lead; 'the thesis of growing disproportion' (*Disproportionierungsthese*), that is, the situation in which the growth of objective culture outpaces that of subjective culture; and 'the thesis of growing dissociation' (*Dissoziationsthese*), that is, the situation in which separate cultural fields such as art, economy, science or religion drift apart from each other.[273]

---

[270] Ibid., p. 107. On Simmel's impact on Cassirer's thought, see Willfried Geßner, 'Geld als symbolische Form: Simmel, Cassirer, und die Objektivität der Kultur', *Simmel Newsletter* 6(1), 1996, pp. 1–30; John Michael Krois, 'Ten Theses on Cassirer's Late Reception of Simmel's Thought', *Simmel Newsletter* 6(1), 1996, pp. 73–78. On Cassirer's criticism of Simmel's notion of the tragedy of culture, see Willfried Geßner, 'Tragödie oder Schauspiel? Cassirers Kritik an Simmels Kulturkritik', *Simmel Newsletter* 6(1), 1996, pp. 57–72.

[271] See also Amat's criticisms of Cassirer's reception, in Matthieu Amat, *Le relationisme philosophique de Georg Simmel: Une idée de la culture* (Paris: Honoré Champion, 2018), pp. 217–218.

[272] 'The Crisis of Culture', trans. D. E. Jenkinson, in Frisby and Featherstone (eds.), *Simmel on Culture*, p. 100. [GSG 16, p. 51.]

[273] Hubertus Busche, 'Was ist Kultur? Zweiter Teil: Die dramatisierende Verknüpfung verschiedener Kulturbegriffe in Georg Simmels "Tragödie der Kultur"', *Dialektik: Zeitschrift für Kuturphilosophie* (2), 2000, pp. 6–7.

It can be also shown, however, that these three different ways of drifting apart are based on the same fundamental condition, of which they are just three different forms. For what fundamentally distinguishes between subjective and objective culture is that the former is grounded in unity and the latter in variety. The notion of inward culture postulates the idea of unity and harmony. Nietzsche provided perhaps the most succinct expression of this ideal of culture, arguing that 'culture is, above all, unity of artistic style in all the expressions of the life of a people'.[274] However, culture as a conglomerate of cultural values and items is first and foremost the world of variety. And the more mature a certain culture is, the more differentiated its products become, so that the task of integrating them into a stylistic whole becomes ever more difficult. As a friend of Simmel, philosopher Karl Joël, once argued, 'the problem to be solved by culture – the sum of everything great – is that of seeking the synthesis of all syntheses: the most intimate unity out of extreme differentiation'.[275]

To use the terms set forth at the beginning of the present chapter, *Kultur* as unified cultivation is inevitably challenged by the varieties of cultural vocations. This challenge can take the form of the predominance of means over ends, of the disproportional growth of objective culture at the expense of subjective culture or of the incommensurability of various cultural spheres.

It is easy to see how the last of the three challenges is related to the fundamental conflict between unity and variety. For here the variety of autonomous cultural spheres comes into conflict with the ideal of culture as a harmonising unity. In his course on the philosophy of culture (1906/1907), Simmel suggested that culture was a value of secondary order reconciling between values of the first order: 'it is the single value of higher potency through which all other primary valuations are transformed.'[276] And in 'The Concept and Tragedy of Culture', he stressed that the refinement of particular personal interests does not by itself contribute to the individual's cultural development: '[I]t is not all these, with their individual perfections, which make a person cultivated, but only their significance for or their development of the individual's indefinable personal unity.'[277] What is more, since it is not certain that such a reconciliation of values can be

---

[274] Nietzsche, *Untimely Meditations*, p. 5; cf. ibid., p. 79.

[275] Karl Joël, 'Das Zeitalter der Ethik. II: Das Herz der Wissenschaft', *Neue Deutsche Rundschau* 6(1), 1895, p. 474.

[276] 'Philosophie der Kultur' [Winter-Semester 1906/07, by Hermann Schmalenbach], GSG 21, p. 557.

[277] 'The Concept and Tragedy of Culture', p. 56. [GSG 12, p. 196.]

achieved under the master value of culture, this variety of cultural spheres constitutes a grave problem for the ideal of culture.

The thesis of the growing disproportion between the extent of objective culture and that of subjective culture is, however, also related to the conflict between variety and unity. For vastly growing objective culture produces a multiplicity of objects that must be reabsorbed back into the personality. Personality at its core is singular; it is unity thrown into the world of individuations. This discrepancy between unity and individuations, apart from the sheer difficulty or even impossibility of encompassing the entirety of the world's individuations, is also a serious problem.

Finally, less obviously at first glance but no less decisively, the thesis of the growing independence of means vis-à-vis ends also implies a conflict between unity and variety. For regardless of whether there is a unity of ends in the world (something that Simmel appeared to deny[278]), the very fact of the independence of means presupposes a plurality of pursuits. As each means becomes an end in itself, it detaches itself from the fundamental goal of the personality and forms an independent teleological chain, distinct from other such chains.

In other words, from whatever angle one looks at the problem of the discrepancy between subjective culture and objective culture, one arrives at the problem of the conflict between unity and variety, in which the subjective side presupposes a unified essence, whereas the objective side presupposes a universe consisting of individuations.

The general issue of the conflict between unity and variety was an ever-present motif in Simmel's writings, regardless of the specific terms he might use to conceptualise the diverse forms this conflict took. Thus on some occasions he used the term 'variety' (*Vielheit*) or synonymous words, and on other occasions he spoke in terms of dualism or duality. There was no consistency in his usage. However, he was consistent throughout in seeing unity versus *dis*unity of whatever kind (whether the disunity of two or of many) as the fundamental problem of life, and he dedicated many of his writings to seeking and elucidating solutions to this problem.

Simmel's central theme was thus the problem of culture. Its essence was, in his terminology, the tension between objective and subjective culture, and the underlying grounds of this tension was the discrepancy between unity and disunity. This motif remained constant throughout his life. At the same time, the way Simmel approached this problem underwent significant evolution. It is the evolution of his thought in this principal

---

[278] *Einleitung in die Moralwissenschaft,* GSG 4, pp. 284–402.

aspect – the discrepancy between unity and disunity – that needs to be examined in order to make sense of the meaning of Simmel's intellectual development as a whole. This examination will constitute the core of the rest of this book. Beforehand, however, I wish to draw a general outline of this evolution in respect of his writings specifically on culture.

Simmel's texts that deal with the notion of culture can be divided into three different clusters. The first belongs to the period of the publication of *Philosophy of Money* (1900). It is there and in related texts that Simmel formulated his distinction between personal (subjective) and objective culture.[279] The second cluster includes essays written a decade later, towards the publication of the volume *Philosophical Culture* (1911). These are 'On the Essence of Culture' (1908), 'The Future of Our Culture' (1909) and 'The Concept and Tragedy of Culture' (1911). Their main motif is the notion of tragedy embedded in the conflict between the ideal of unified culture and culture's inner contradictions.[280] The third cluster contains Simmel's writings composed during the war years, the most important of which are 'The Crisis of Culture' (1916), 'The Change in Cultural Forms' (1916) and 'The Conflict in Modern Culture' (1918).[281]

The crucial point to note is that each of these clusters marks, as it were, the ending of a certain period in Simmel's thought. Thus the first cluster belongs to the years in which Simmel began to distance himself from Kant, Spencerian sociology and pragmatism, whose influence had marked his early period, and move towards a certain combination of neo-Kantianism, Nietzscheanism and aestheticism. The second cluster belongs to the time when Simmel despaired of that combination and began to adopt the philosophical apparatus of life-philosophy. And the third cluster belongs to his final years, completing the third – life-philosophy – period.

Each of these clusters treats the subject of culture differently. Thus the 'young Simmel', that is, the Simmel of the period ending with the publication of *Philosophy of Money*, posited the problem of culture mainly in a socio-economic setting, in which the unity of personal culture was threatened by objectification and estrangement. The cause of this estrangement was the growing division of labour in society.

---

[279] *The Philosophy of Money*, ch. 6, especially part II, pp. 446–460 [GSG 6, pp. 591–616]; 'Persönliche und sachliche Kultur' [1900], GSG 5, pp. 560–582.
[280] 'On the Essence of Culture'; 'The Future of Our Culture'; 'The Concept and Tragedy of Culture'. [GSG 8, pp. 363–373; 17, pp. 80–83; 12, pp. 194–223.]
[281] 'The Crisis of Culture'; 'The Change in Cultural Forms', trans. M. Ritter and D. Frisby, in Frisby and Featherstone (eds.), *Simmel on Culture*, pp. 103–107; 'The Conflict of Modern Culture'. [GSG 13, pp. 190–201; 13, pp. 217–223; 16, pp. 181–207.]

At that time, Simmel did not yet speak a pessimistic language.[282] Thus, pointing in *Philosophy of Money* to the problematic chasm emerging as a result of the extensive growth of reified culture that leaves subjectivity far behind, he nevertheless maintained a careful balance between the advantages and shortcomings of modernity. He described the problem not as a tragedy but as a series of challenging questions, such as whether, in respect of the individual, 'the objective, historically given elements' are 'an autonomous power within his own mental life, so that they and the specific core of his personality develop independently of each other', or whether 'is the soul, so to speak, master in its own house, or is there at least a harmony with regard to standards [*Höhe*], meaning and rhythm established between its innermost life and what it has to absorb into that life as impersonal contents'.[283]

These questions did not exclude the possibility – either on the individual or on the social level – that the two sides could find a point of equilibrium. For example, the advanced degree of specialisation on the side of production could be seen as balanced by the broadening that took place on the side of consumption, so that 'even the most intellectually and occupationally specialised people today read the newspaper and thereby indulge in a more extensive mental consumption than was possible a hundred years ago, for even the most versatile and widely interested person'.[284] The split between the subjective and objective sides of culture was therefore described as a challenge which could be addressed with solutions of various degrees of comprehensiveness.

Simmel's attitude to this problematic changed, however, in the texts of the second cluster. In his 1909 essay 'Future of Our Culture', the loaded term 'tragedy' appeared for the first time, when he referred to 'the tragic discrepancy between objective culture, with its unlimited capacity for growth, and subjective culture, which can grow only slowly'.[285] In this text, Simmel still dealt with the issue of the quantitative growth of objective culture and the gap between personality and things. However, very soon this gap acquired a broader meaning in his writings. The estrangement of cultural objects, Simmel argued, as well as the issue arising out of the division of labour, was 'a very radical case of a quite general human spiritual fate'. For 'the great majority of products of our intellectual

---

[282] Cf. Willfried Geßner, *Der Schatz im Acker: Georg Simmels Philosophie der Kultur* (Weilerswist: Velbrück Wissenschaft, 2003), p. 180.

[283] *The Philosophy of Money*, p. 467. [GSG 6, pp. 649–650.]

[284] Ibid., p. 455. [GSG 6, pp. 618–619.]

[285] 'The Future of Our Culture', p. 102. [GSG 17, p. 83.] Cf. Geßner, *Der Schatz im Acker*, p. 171.

creation contain a certain portion of significance which we did not our-selves create'.[286] The problem of culture thus turned out to be not an accidental feature of the mode of the modern system of production but an endemic feature of the cultural process as such. Moreover, the tension embedded in culture became itself internalised. The conflict was now not only between the soul and things but between the subjective and objective sides of the spirit itself. If the earlier Simmel had occasionally described the two sides of culture in terms of 'personal' and '*sachlich*', these words disappeared in his writings of the middle period, as the problem turned out to run much deeper than mere reification. It was the tension between the soul's yearning for the harmony of its components and the autonomy of its particular values: 'there is no cultural value that would merely be a cultural value; rather, in order to acquire this significance, each must also be a value on an objective scale.'[287]

In other words, the problem of culture is that as 'a value of values' it comes into an unavoidable conflict with particular values. This is not an incidental historical misfortune resulting from the accumulation of cul-tural goods. It is an essential moment that signifies the split within the soul itself. This split is by definition tragic, for the essence of the tragic, unlike that of the simply sad (*trauriges*), is that 'the annihilating forces aimed against an entity stem from the deepest layers of this very entity'.[288]

Now, if one looks at the third cluster of Simmel's writings on culture, one can note that the notion of tragedy is replaced in them by the notions of conflict and crisis. To the extent that one considers this to be a substantive rather than terminological change, two lines of interpretation are possible. On the one hand, there are commentators who claim that Simmel moderated his earlier cultural pessimism and began to see the crisis of culture as simply a temporary stage to be overcome after newer and more appropriate cultural forms emerge.[289] It is, however, also possible to inter-pret this terminological change in an opposite light, as an intensification of the feeling of despair. This interpretation would consider Simmel to be moving towards a rejection of the ideal of culture as such. As Simmel argued in 'The Conflict of the Modern Culture' (1918), the essential problem of culture was not the inadequacy of one form or another but the failure of form in general to satisfy the modern feeling of life. He spoke there about the 'repudiation of the principle of form' that characterised the

---

[286] 'The Concept and Tragedy of Culture', p. 69. [GSG 12, p. 215.]
[287] Ibid., p. 62. [GSG 12, p. 204.]   [288] Ibid., p. 72. [GSG 12, p. 219.]
[289] Cf. Heinrich Adolf, 'Kultur ohne Tragik: Cassirers Entschärfung von Simmels tragischer Konzeption von Kultur', *Dialektik* (2), 2003, pp. 75–103.

contemporary spiritual life[290] and suggested 'that of all the periods of history in which this chronic conflict has become acute and affected the entirety of life [*Existenz*], no period has revealed as clearly as our own that this is its fundamental dilemma [*Grundmotiv*]'.[291]

Simmel also grew more sceptical as to whether harmony and unity formed out of variety should be considered a mark of cultural perfection. In 'The Change in Cultural Forms' (1916), referring to philosophical dualisms, such as that of soul and body, he argued that 'neither duality nor unity adequately expresses their relationship and that thus we still possess no conceptual formulation at all for all this relationship'.[292] The whole project of reaching unity out of diversity appears here to have been put in doubt.

These differences in the way Simmel spoke about culture in his different periods – insignificant as they may appear at first glance – actually point to the most fundamental aspect of his intellectual transformation. The three aforementioned approaches to the problem of culture point to three very different answers which Simmel offered to what he regarded as the central problem of the modern age: the problem of reconciling unity with variety after the primordial unity had been lost forever. As he once said, 'only a period so marked by analysis as the modern age could see in synthesis the most profound aspect, the one and all of the formal relationship between spirit and world – whereas there is in fact an original and pre-differentiated unity of the two'.[293]

The three answers can be summarised as follows. The first considers the contradictions of culture as presenting us with a complicated but solvable task. The resulting solution would be to envisage the specifically modern unity that emerges out of modern differentiation. This was the spirit of Simmel's writings leading to the *Philosophy of Money*. The second answer regards the very possibility of such reconciliation between unity and variety with scepticism. Instead, it comes up with a tentative solution of retreating into inwardness and cherishing one's own harmony at the expense of the encompassing reconciliation with the variety of the world. The third answer appears to be two-edged: either some kind of revolutionary unity can be achieved that transcends the very division into unity and variety or the entire quest for unity reaches an impasse and should simply be abandoned. The third answer is simultaneously victory and despair.

[290] 'The Conflict of Modern Culture', p. 85. [GSG 16, p. 198.]
[291] Ibid., p. 90. [GSG 16, p. 206.]
[292] 'The Change in Cultural Forms', p. 106. [GSG 13, p. 222.]
[293] 'The Concept and Tragedy of Culture', p. 63. [GSG 12, p. 206.]

These three answers are correspondingly reflected in the three clusters of Simmel's writings on culture. Each cluster intimates Simmel's approach to unity and variety in the period of thought it concludes. Thus Simmel's writings on culture around 1900 sum up his optimistic belief in the possibility of harmonising contradictions that he espoused during the 1880s and 1890s. His writings of 1909–1911 synopsise his middle period with its scepticism towards the very possibility of forming an overall synthesis. Finally, his later essays conclude the third period in which Simmel was torn between hope for a unity of a higher order that encompasses contradictions without abolishing them and radical despair towards this possibility.

In other words, Simmel's writings on culture can be seen as a synopsis of his entire thought or at least as signposts that faithfully reflect the vector of his intellectual development. The task now will be to decipher these signposts by examining in detail Simmel's approaches to modernity and the conflict between unity and variety in his different periods and across a variety of intellectual fields with which he dealt in his writings.

CHAPTER 2

Unity in Variety

Simmel, like many of his contemporaries, believed that the modern age was facing a crucial problem: the growing tension between the reality of complex multiplicity that underlay the material and spiritual life of progressing societies and the imperative of personal and social harmony which was still adhered to as the main cultural ideal. This complex multiplicity could be conceived in different ways and signified by different words. For example, it could be presented as the condition of chaotic coexistence of disparate elements, that is, as variety, diversity or fragmentation that undermines unity, or it could be referred to as the condition of irreconcilable dichotomy between two elements, in which case it could be described in terms of the conflict between dualism and monism. The common discourse did not define any strict conceptual demarcation between these formulas, and Simmel too used them interchangeably. However, their general motif is quite obvious: the motif of tension between unity and variety, however else this tension might be called.

Throughout Simmel's entire intellectual career, the question of reconciling 'unity and variety' in the condition of modernity was his principal preoccupation and he toyed with a great number of strategies and solutions. All of these can be reduced to three main models. They were outlined by Simmel himself in one of his last publications: a monograph study on Rembrandt (1916). There he presented the alternatives, according to which 'the unity of manifold elements [*Mannigfaltigkeiten*] either lies beyond them – as something higher and more abstract – or remains in the sphere of manifoldness, assembling itself piece by piece out of its elements'.[1] To these two he added a third possibility, expressed through the notion of 'life'. Life, according to Simmel,

> cannot be expressed in terms of any of these formulas, for it is an absolute continuity in which there is no assembly of fragments or parts. Life,

---

[1] *Rembrandt: Ein kunstphilosophischer Versuch*, GSG 15, p. 314. My translation removes the error in the existing English translation, in *Rembrandt: An Essay in the Philosophy of Art*, trans. A. Scott and H. Staubmann (New York: Routledge, 2005), p. 6.

moreover, is a unity, but one that at any moment expresses itself as a whole in distinct forms … Each moment of life is the whole life whose steady stream – which is exactly its unique form – has its reality only at the crest of the wave in which it respectively rises.[2]

When formulated in such a succinct way, almost as an afterthought, this distinction is not immediately clear to the reader. Yet on further reflection one finds that it summarises very well the landmarks of Simmel's intellectual evolution. For if one adopts the traditional division of his life into three periods, one can notice that each period is dominated by a different strategy regarding the solution of the problem of unity and variety. The earliest period is dominated by the idea that unity 'remains in the sphere of manifoldness, assembling itself piece by piece out of its elements'. Here I will call this 'unity in variety'. The middle period is marked by the idea of unity conceived as 'something higher and more abstract' than variety. I will call this 'unity versus variety'. Finally, in his later period Simmel gravitates towards the idea of unity as 'absolute continuity in which there is no assembly of fragments or parts'. I will call this 'unity above variety' or 'unity transcending variety'.

It is the purpose of this and the following chapters to explain in detail the meaning of these three possibilities and reveal the manner in which they emerge, develop and crystallise in Simmel's writings. The story starts with the classical quest for 'unity in variety'.

2.1   Dante, the Alps, Moltke

In 1884, Simmel published the first of his studies about great cultural figures of the past: an essay on Dante.[3] Written, one could assume, under the influence of art historian Herman Grimm,[4] one of Simmel's favourite teachers during his studies at the University of Berlin, it was

---

[2] Ibid.
[3] 'Dantes Psychologie', GSG 1, pp. 91–177. The essay was published in the *Zeitschrift für Völkerpsychologie und Sprachwissenschaft*, which was edited by Moritz Lazarus (one of Simmel's teachers in Berlin) and Heymann Steinthal, and it reflects both aspects of his education. On the one hand, it can be seen as an example of what he would later call philosophy of culture: its subject (certainly indebted to Grimm as well as to the general veneration of mediaeval Italy as the birthplace of modernity) and its major themes suggest that the essay is concerned with the philosophical appreciation of the conditions of modernity. On the other hand, the very scholarly style in which the essay is written (it is, in fact, the only long publication of Simmel which is heavily annotated), the journal in which it appeared and some unveiled references to *Völkerpsychologie* (e.g. GSG 1, p. 134) make it a work of historical-philological scholarship. I deal with the essay only from the first standpoint.
[4] See Grimm's essay 'Fiorenza: Anmerkungen zu einigen Gedichten Dante's und Michelangelo's', in Herman Grimm, *Fünfzehn Essays* (Gütersloh: C. Bertelsmann, 1822), pp. 1–61. Apart from Dante, the two other subjects mentioned in the title – Michelangelo's poetry and Florence – will later become topics subjects of Simmel's essays as well. See 'Michelangelo als Dichter' [1889], GSG 2, pp.

a juvenile work that did not make an impact. No wonder that a study dedicated to the reception of Dante in Germany does not mention Simmel's name even once, unlike, for example, that of Solzhenitsyn.[5] Nevertheless, the text is important for our story, because it is there that Simmel brought the problem of unity to the forefront for the first time, attempting to make sense of it by reproducing the worldview of a cultural genius.

Unlike Simmel's future works, the Dante essay has the appearance of a standard scholarly study, rich with citations and footnotes. Yet already there Simmel claimed for himself the approach that would mark all his future monographs. 'I do not want to write a chapter in Dantology', he said, 'but a chapter in the psychology of history'.[6] Dante, according to him, may be 'suitable after all for exemplifying the currents of the national spirit [*Volksgeistes*] of that time'.[7] The terminology of psychology and national spirit referred to the discipline of the psychology of peoples (*Völkerpsychologie*), propagated then by his teacher Moritz Lazarus. But in a sense this was misleading. There was nothing in the essay to offer an interpretation of Dante's work in terms of alleged traits of the Italian national character. What Simmel meant was rather that great figures should be studied not for exegetical or biographical purposes but in order to be made our guides into the worldviews and life-views they represented to the most intense degree. He wished to write the history of philosophy, where the emphasis was not on a particular *Volksgeist* but rather on a more general *Zeitgeist*, on the main philosophical tendencies identifying the age broadly conceived.

The age of Dante, according to Simmel, was characterised by the culmination of two very different spiritual tendencies. One of them found its purest expression in scholastics, the other in mysticism.[8] The former aimed at attaining the conceptual knowledge of things beyond their empirical immediacy; the latter aspired to direct contemplation of the absolute. Dante, taken as an exemplar of his own age, was impacted by both, and therefore, the study of his inner contradictions reveals to us the intellectual contradictions of his age as well as its spiritual possibilities.

Very soon it emerged, however, that this contradiction between two equally mediaeval tendencies that had reached their peak in Dante's times

37–48; 'Florence' [1906], trans. U. Teucher and T. M. Kemple, *Theory, Culture & Society* 24(7–8), 2007, pp. 38–41. [GSG 8, pp. 69–73.]

[5] Eva Hölter, *'Der Dichter der Hölle und des Exils': Historische und systematische Profil der deutsch-sprachigen Dante-Rezeption* (Würzburg: Königshausen & Neumann, 2002), p. 92.

[6] 'Dantes Psychologie', GSG 1, p. 96.   [7] GSG 1, p. 96.   [8] GSG 1, p. 94.

was not what interested Simmel the most. He even diminished the significance of the distinction by saying that 'that difference as appears in his writings is less than evidently appeared to his consciousness'.[9] In fact, 'it is not rationalism which is objectively the sharpest antithesis to mysticism, but empiricism; the difference between the first two concepts, despite its historical importance, is often just imaginary'.[10] This statement allowed Simmel to switch to a different claim: Dante was not really torn between two opposite currents belonging to the same age, although he himself lacked the required historical perspective that would let him realise that the tensions in his view were anything other than the conflict between the familiar paradigms of rationalism and mysticism. However, later times revealed that he had stood, so to speak, at the juncture between two ages. For, as the essay made clear, the aforementioned 'empiricism' signified the empirical individuality of sensual soul. And the main philosophical tension Simmel imputed to Dante was that between the mystical mediaeval tendency of the soul's self-abolition, of the perception of it as merely a reflection of the divine totality on the one hand and the more modern tendency towards individual self-assertion and empirical sensuality on the other.[11] This philosophical tension found its parallel in Dante's social thought, where the poet strove to reconcile the ideal of unity with a recognition of the emergence of constantly individualising social forms. In the end, 'in spite of this attempt at reconciliation between the general and the particular, by recognising the individuality of peoples he himself sharpened the weapon that was to destroy his idea of a universal empire'.[12] Dante was thus the figure of the transitional period, in which old mystical pre-individualised conceptions coexisted with the emerging vision of the new times.

The Dante monograph contained two motifs that would figure prominently in Simmel's subsequent works. One motif is that of modernity. Throughout the essay, modern times are alluded to as characterised by individuality, freedom, complexity and progress. This contrasts with the older times characterised by frozenness and dogmatism rather than free play of thought and intellectual curiosity and by the tendency of subjecting an individual soul to a larger totality (God or state) rather than celebrating its autonomy.[13]

The second motif is the assumption that great personalities are distinguished by their ability to absorb in themselves the totality of the opposing

---

[9] GSG I, p. 97.   [10] GSG I, p. 97.   [11] E.g. GSG I, pp. 105–106.   [12] GSG I, pp. 115.
[13] See GSG I, pp. 116–117, 134.

spiritual tendencies of their age, out of which they form coherent and comprehensive worldviews. Dante, said Simmel in the closing passage, 'expressed with accurate self-observation the different sides of his poetic individuality, even if not at one and the same time'.[14] In Dante's dualism, 'the divergent spiritual currents of his time, intersecting and culminating as it were in his powerful and ingenious personality, were brought together into a systematic consciousness before parting forever'.[15]

These two motifs are closely related. For if constant individualisation and ever-growing variety are the essential marks of modernity, then it is specifically for modern civilisation that the task of the harmonic resolution of variety becomes existential as well as increasingly difficult, perhaps even impossible without the intervention of a genius. And it is partly for this reason that Simmel will turn to study figures such as Kant, Schopenhauer, Nietzsche, Goethe and Rembrandt, looking for various patterns of reaching unity in the condition of variety.

In the text on Dante, however, the centrality of these two motifs was not yet apparent. In fact, the passage I just quoted is somewhat disconnected from the rest of the text. For in the essay those contradictions are not brought together into a systematic worldview. The study emphasised the tensions in Dante's thought by describing in detail his attitude to various aspects of metaphysics and ethics (such as soul, freedom, God, character, love etc.), but it did not aim to make them into the elements of a coherent disposition.

One reason for this restraint might be that Simmel still viewed himself in the role of a meticulous philologist who was not supposed to impose an artificial unity on his subject matter. His closing words, however, show that he was not entirely happy with these limitations. As he himself will later argue, even when the ideas of a great thinker appear contradictory, one has the right to derive a coherent worldview from them. With regard to his interpretation of Nietzsche, for example, he will claim much later that although 'it is possible to select quotations from Nietzsche's writings that uncompromisingly contradict' it, nevertheless 'it is sufficient that this interpretation be coherently argued from the texts and that its objective importance justifies the assumption that it constitutes the original core of Nietzsche's doctrines, which are so essential to the intellectual climate [*für die geistige Kultur*]'.[16]

---

[14] GSG I, p. 177.   [15] GSG I, p. 177.

[16] *Schopenhauer and Nietzsche* [1907], trans. H. Loiskandl, D. Weinstein and M. Weinstein (Urbana: University of Illinois Press, 1986), p. lv. [*Schopenhauer und Nietzsche: Ein Vortragszyklus*, GSG 10,

There may, however, be another reason as to why, despite the intention revealed in the last passage, Simmel failed to offer a fully integrated account of Dante's worldview. For what Simmel cared deeply about was the integration of the specifically modern mind. And Dante, unlike other thinkers and artists he would later write about, was not 'modern', in his view. Rather, he belonged to a 'great transitional epoch'.[17] It is only natural then that Simmel preferred to highlight Dante's incoherencies.

This does not mean that moderns have nothing to learn from 'pre-moderns' such as Dante. Never a one-dimensional writer, Simmel would occasionally adopt a mood of nostalgia for the pre-modern past. Thus he praised Dante's belief that love always brings love, contrasting this attitude with that of Heine who had once said: '[I]f any one would win my love, they must treat me en canaille.'[18] He regarded this attitude of Heine as assertive, egoistic and revealing the greatest fault of modernity: disintegration. As he wrote:

> How healthy and pure Dante's reciprocity of love appears in contrast to such unnaturally overstrung, inwardly poisoned emotions! But it is essentially the same psychological trait which, as opposed to the sentiment of earlier times, draws the *modern* man into the wildest alpine nature, preferably where it is most impassable, most repellent as it were.[19]

That is, the moderns with their insatiable individualism are ill-prepared for harmony and balance. They are always on the move as they seek new excitements and challenges.

The Alps theme did not appear accidentally. For the young Simmel, the fashion of Alpinism exemplified the self-delusion of the modern soul in its quest for inner integration.[20] It is the profound and spiritual people, he argued in his essay on this subject (1895),[21] who consider the alpine journey as part of *Bildung*, believing that it helps them cultivate the best parts of

---

pp. 171–172.] The English translation of the book does not always follow the literal meaning of the text closely, and therefore on most occasions I will use my own translation.

[17] 'Dantes Psychologie', GSG 1, p. 93.

[18] Heinrich Heine, 'Ideas: Book Le Grand', trans. Ch.G. Leland, in *Pictures of Travel* (New York: D. Appleton and Company, 1904), p. 131.

[19] 'Dantes Psychologie', GSG 1, p. 171. Italics mine – E. P.

[20] On Simmel's writings on the Alps, see Claudia Portioli, 'Alpen', in H.-P. Müller and T. Reitz (eds.), *Simmel-Handbuch: Begriffe, Hauptwerke, Aktualität* (Frankfurt am Main: Suhrkamp, 2018), pp. 105–110.

[21] 'The Alpine Journey', trans. S. Whimster, in D. Frisby and M. Featherstone (eds.), *Simmel on Culture: Selected Writings* (London: Sage, 1997), pp. 219–221. [GSG 5, pp. 91–95.]

their personality. This opinion is, however, false, as 'the educative value [*Bildungswert*] of alpine travel is very small'.[22] The Alps do indeed evoke the feeling of excitement, but this excitement is momentary, and the uplift is followed by the return to the mundane. The experience remains without any trace in the personality as a whole, which is the prerequisite for the true *Bildung*. The effect of the alpine journey is thus similar to that of music that takes us 'into the fantastic regions of the life of the senses', from which, however, we take little or nothing 'to adorn other areas of our inner life'.[23] Because of its physical challenges and risks, the alpine sport is believed to contain ethical values. Risk, however, becomes ethical only when undertaken for the sake of higher purposes. Assigning moral value to risk as such is a romantic delusion.[24]

There is then something disturbing, disquieting in modernity. Its endless possibilities, its search for new challenges, bring about pernicious side effects, be it egoism in love or senseless risk-taking in mountain sports. All this stands contrary to the ideal of harmony and perfection. But these discontents did not make Simmel reject the modern age altogether, and the occasional notes of nostalgia never developed into an intellectual statement in favour of the harmony of the past. This becomes clear if one compares Simmel's understanding of Dante with the turn Dante reception took in Germany in the subsequent decades.

Dante was indeed known and esteemed in Germany for a long time. The first signs of interest in Dante can be dated as early as the 1760s, and in 1791 his reputation was fully entrenched with the publication of August Wilhelm Schlegel's essay 'On Dante Alighieri's Divine Comedy'. From the 1820s onwards, a number of complete translations of the *Divine Comedy* were published, triggering the proliferation of scholarly research in Dante's work and leading to the establishment of the German Dante Society in 1865.[25] Nevertheless, by the 1880s, when Simmel wrote his study, Dante had not yet acquired a central place in the *Bildung* canon, if one compares him to figures such as Goethe and Shakespeare. For example, the number of citations from Dante with which an average cultivated German was supposed to become familiar remained at that time very limited.[26] Dante's reputation reached its peak only in the early twentieth century, culminating in the 1921 commemoration of the 600th anniversary of his death and even opening the way to rebranding him as a prophet of the 'Nordic'

---

[22] Ibid., p. 220. [GSG 5, p. 92.]   [23] Ibid. [GSG 5, p. 93.]   [24] Ibid., p. 221. [GSG 5, p. 95.]
[25] Hölter, '*Der Dichter der Hölle und des Exils*'; see also Walter Goetz, *Geschichte der Deutschen Dante-Gesellschaft und der deutschen Dante-Forschung* (Weimar: Hermann Böhlaus, 1940).
[26] Hölter, '*Der Dichter der Hölle und des Exils*', p. 69.

spirit.[27] As Dante was becoming a cult figure, he could be evoked as an alternative to the disintegration of modernity. 'What does Dante have to say about our spiritual troubles?'[28] – asked Ernst Troeltsch in 1921. Diagnosing the modern condition as that of 'formlessness, of the sceptical and critical dissolution and disemboweling of every traditional form and yet at the same time the eclectic and playful mixture of every form, style and thought',[29] he contrasted it with Dante's poetry, which he saw as 'an overwhelming archetype of solid form'.[30] Thus, for Troeltsch, Dante was the embodiment of form because he was unmodern! But for Simmel, four decades earlier, the opposite was true: Dante was not modern enough, and precisely because of this he was self-contradictory! It is in modernity itself that Simmel searched for the remedy for its own ills.

This affirmative attitude towards modernity is especially salient in Simmel's earlier period. Modernity indeed creates a differentiated, complex, constantly evolving and sometimes chaotic reality, but it also provides resources for dealing with this reality. Modernity is a challenge rather than a tragedy, and it is capable of transforming itself into a meaningful whole and producing integrated forms of living and thinking, exemplified by great individuals. And as early as 1890, Simmel pointed to such an individual. Somewhat unexpectedly, that person turned out to be Prussian general Helmuth von Moltke (1800–1891).

In October 1890, Simmel contributed a short essay entitled 'Moltke as Stylist' to the *Berliner Tageblatt*'s special issue on the occasion of the general's ninetieth birthday.[31] In it he claimed that Moltke was not only a great military commander but also a great master of literary style. In Simmel's praise, Moltke, whose publications consisted mainly of letters, diaries and reports on military campaigns, rose to the level of a universal genius of almost Goethe's proportions, a genius who achieved perfection in every field to which he dedicated himself:

> Just as the general was an expander (*Mehrer*) of the Empire, so the writer can be a teacher (*Lehrer*) of the Empire, from whom the stylistic anarchy of contemporary Germany, the thoughtlessness and fickleness of the language that pass as ingenious and interesting, would learn as much as a displaced Baroque artist would learn from the calm and strength of a Greek statue.[32]

---

[27] E.g. Wolf Meyer-Erlach, *Dante: Der Prophet der nordischen Sehnsucht* (Munich: J.F. Lehmann, 1927).
[28] Ernst Troeltsch, *Der Berg der Läuterung* (Berlin, E. S. Mittler & Sohn, 1921), p. 9.
[29] Ibid., p. 11. [30] Ibid. [31] 'Moltke als Stilist', GSG 2, pp. 103–107. [32] GSG 2, p. 103.

Simmel then described the virtues of Moltke's style: precision, inner freedom and flexibility, independence from any artificial cliché, and concluded the essay with a few general observations in which he spoke about the quiet greatness, the simplicity of Moltke which was the consequence of 'the total dedication of his person to his work'.[33] This devotion, however, did not seem to split his personality at all:

> Through this symmetry of perfect creations in such contrary fields, he delivers, in our times of specialisation in which dedication to one activity tends to exclude all others, a powerful warning, an irrefutable proof that the stubborn pursuit of a one-sided subject is by no means the condition for great achievement.[34]

Moltke was thus an embodiment of the *Bildung* ideal of the harmonious cultivation of the variety of human interests. He was not an embattled hero of a transitional period like Dante but a tranquil soul in whom classical balance coexisted with many-sidedness which was modern through and through.

It is not entirely clear to what extent Simmel was serious there. The suspicion that the essay could be at least partly ironic is raised by the timing of the publication: just a short time before, an anonymous book, *Rembrandt as Educator*, began to make waves in Germany. It protested against what it perceived as German anarchy and specialisation, looking for the remedy in a great artist on the one hand and a Prussian soldier on the other. As will be shown in the following section, Simmel strongly disliked the book. It is therefore strange that in his essay on Moltke he praised that Prussian solider in terms not unlike those of *Rembrandt as Educator*. Was this a jest on Simmel's part?

Be that as it may, the question of how to overcome the dangers of modern specialisation as well as the search for examples of such overcoming were a serious business for Simmel, and he dedicated his entire intellectual life to finding the answers. What distinguishes his early period from the rest is that he appeared to think that the answer lay at arm's length and that the wished-for unity would naturally emerge out of variety when it is properly lived and understood. And Simmel's most important intellectual pursuits in his earlier period were indeed dedicated to elaborating on the proper modes of living and understanding.

Two such pursuits stand out: Simmel's early social thought and his engagement with Kant's philosophy. In his writings on society and

[33] GSG 2, p. 106.   [34] GSG 2, pp. 106–107.

sociology, he inquired into the preconditions for living an integrated life in the conditions of modern civilisation. In his Kant studies, he investigated the preconditions for integrative thinking in the conditions of the modern fragmentation of knowledge. It is to elucidating these two aspects of Simmel's work in their respective contexts that I now turn.

2.2 Society

In 1890, the attention of the German readership was attracted to an anonymously published treatise titled *Rembrandt as Educator*.[35] Its author (Julius Langbehn) targeted what he considered to be the corrupting features of the age, such as growing technical specialisation and the pre-eminence of modern science over true art. These features threatened, in his opinion, the true ideals of spiritual life: individuality and universality.

The work and its lamentations were initially met favourably by most reviewers, even by leading art experts. But Simmel, then a relatively unknown *Privatdozent* at the University of Berlin, was not impressed. In a review he published the same year, he did not hide his dismissive attitude towards the book. 'The sparkling wit of the [book's] form', he argued, 'constitutes the greatest imaginable contrast to the obscurity and insignificance of its content'.[36]

Despite this attitude, the review was quite extensive. For although Simmel regarded the book's claims as insignificant, he nevertheless considered its broad appeal as symptomatic of the general intellectual mood which displayed signs of revulsion against the modern age. The review provided him with an opportunity to examine the nature of this revulsion and to point to what he believed to be its errors.

According to Simmel, the new era is characterised by the predominance of the natural scientific worldview, which imposes on us its atomistic mechanistic picture. This view leads to inner conflict between what we believe about the world and what we yearn to believe. For it opens the gap between the objectively indifferent picture of the world and the requirements of human feeling. This picture destroys the lyricism of the world, and today only 'the splendour of the results of natural science still saves us from disenchantment, from stripping the world of the lure of poetical appearance [*des poetischen Scheines*]'.[37]

---

[35] [Julius Langbehn], *Rembrandt als Erzieher: Von einem Deutschen* (Leipzig: C. L. Hirschfeld, 1890).
[36] Review of *Rembrandt als Erzieher*, GSG 1, p. 243.   [37] GSG 1, p. 235.

This situation evokes two possible responses. One is the rejection of modernity, stubborn devotion to the remnants of old cultural and artistic forms, as if they could help us escape the homelessness that we feel in the face of this cold world of scientific determinism.[38] The other response, by contrast, accepts the modern condition and makes use of it to create the type of art that would fit the new civilisational situation. This is the view with which Simmel associated himself, considering it to be the only worthy strategy in the contemporary condition.

He argued that this strategy implied redirecting human attachments from the fables and myths of metaphysics towards the interests of society. For once the physical world is known to be deterministic, there remains only one realm in which inner feelings and devoted actions do not turn out to be an illusion: the world of purely human interests. For 'instincts and feelings, whose vigour was previously squandered on superstitious phant-asms, and which now find for themselves no place in the heartless play of atoms', can live to the fullest only in these interests.[39]

In this world of human interests, human beings are of course not absolutely separate individual essences. On the contrary, 'the new histor-ico-sociological view considers the individual as a product of the historical development of his species, a mere intersection point of social threads'.[40] Yet individuality is not destroyed by this perception; rather, it is raised to a new level, at which a person becomes part of a greater whole. The exaggerated emphasis on individuality as something separate, isolated and unique has no value. In a world of growing specialisation and division of labour, dignity and the meaning of existence can be preserved only by means of devotion to social collectivity. One must be able to reconcile oneself with being a part of the social organism, and this can happen only when one becomes aware of being such a part. Just as a poem's words acquire their meaning only if read as part of the whole, so 'every individual and every specialised field of our culture only need to be considered as members of the greater whole, in order to obtain again the seemingly lost meaning and possibility of a poetic interpretation'.[41]

Modernity therefore is a source of much discontent for the individual, but it also offers a path to redemption: immersing oneself in society. The modern individual can overcome his own split existence by self-conscious attachment to social life. Society is the solution to the challenges of modernity.

The review of *Rembrandt as Educator* advocated social devotion as a pragmatic remedy to the loss of existential meaning. However, in other

---

[38] Cf. GSG I, p. 239.   [39] GSG I, p. 236.   [40] GSG I, p. 236.   [41] GSG I, p. 237.

of Simmel's publications this recipe also acquired an overtone of moral imperative, for example, in 'Infelices Possidentes', a short essay published three years later (1893) under the pseudonym Paul Liesegang.[42] The essay was written in the genre of the radical moral and aesthetic critique of modern society. In it, Simmel addressed what he regarded as a major symptom of the modern disease: the culture of entertainment. Modern entertainment, he asserted, consists only in achieving a sudden and short-lived effect on our nerves and is devoid of any serious content capable of affecting our minds. Shallow and not very different from intoxicating drugs, it is akin to ancient gladiatorial combat. Spectators are no longer capable of consuming serious art because their nerves are exhausted by the modern rhythm, constant competition, the hope of winning everything and the simultaneous anxiety about losing everything.

At first glance, this last point offered a diagnosis typical of the 'progressive' social criticism of the time. The decadent search for low pleasures was interpreted here as an escape from the disparities and anxieties of modern life, the causes of which lay in the economic structure of a society based on competition. These words sounded as if they were taken from the social democratic or, more specifically, Marxist vocabulary. One would expect Simmel to pursue this line in further detail. Yet he quickly put aside the economic explanation, arguing instead that 'the wild race of competition *and the awakening social conscience* are increasingly tending to vitiate the pleasures which make it worthwhile to be propertied'.[43] In other words, alongside economic reasons one can also find a *moral* cause for the unhappiness of the *possidentes* – their awakening social conscience:

> Since the upper ten thousand has become aware of the misery of the masses ... so the life of the better-off and higher strata has also experienced the kind of impediment which, on the one hand, leaves only the lower emotional energies for enjoyment, while on the other, if one is to enjoy oneself, tends to seek out the wildest intoxication, the most dazzling effects, so that one's own inner premonitions and admonitions may be drowned out.[44]

Or, to put it simply, the affluent classes are unhappy because they are tormented by pangs of conscience. Unwilling to follow the ethical imperatives of modernity, they find refuge in entertainment. This is, however, a deceptive refuge. Simmel did not say what they ought to do (the essay was

---

[42] '*Infelices Possidentes!* (Unhappy Dwellers)', trans. M. Ritter and D. Frisby, in Frisby and Featherstone (eds.), *Simmel on Culture*, pp. 259–262. [GSG 17, pp. 293–297.]
[43] Ibid., p. 262. [GSG 17, p. 297.] Italics mine – E. P.   [44] Ibid., p. 261. [GSG 17, p. 296.]

merely a work of criticism), but one conclusion appears fairly obvious. The remedy for the unhappiness of the affluent lies in working towards the removal of social ills, such as pauperism, immorality or widespread egoism.[45]

Thus, as in the review of *Rembrandt as Educator*, modernity was presented here as a problem and although the problematic character of modernity was outlined here from a different angle (in the review of *Rembrandt as Educator* the major problem was said to be intellectual disillusionment, while here it appeared to be moral disillusionment), the solution in both cases looked identical: ethical attachment to society.

Considered separately from Simmel's other works, these essays can be seen as adhering to the 'positivistic' approach, by which I do not mean the 'positivism' normally ascribed to the young Simmel (namely his anthropological and sociological pursuits in an attempt to develop a properly scientific method under the influence of both evolutionary theory and 'atomism'),[46] but 'positivism' in its original meaning coined by Auguste Comte.[47] Comte introduced the idea of three stages of social evolution, distinguished by the types of knowledge predominant in them. Knowledge, according to him, proceeds from the theological towards the metaphysical stage and then towards what he called the 'positive' stage. This last stage is distinguished by 'positive philosophy' which would reform sciences for the sake of bettering society.[48] Comte envisioned social cohesion based on the religion of humanity, and for him the altruistic attachment of the individual to the social whole constituted a central moral imperative.[49]

The ideas outlined in Simmel's two essays were quite similar to this view. Modernity, according to him, has destroyed the religious and metaphysical myths of the past and brought to our attention the problem of social disintegration. The way out of this predicament is to attach oneself

[45] Interestingly a similar critique of class egoism was among the driving sentiments of the German Society for Ethical Culture founded a year earlier (1892). Many of Simmel's university colleagues took part in its activities. Cf. Klaus Christian Köhnke, *Der junge Simmel: in Theoriebeziehungen und sozialen Bewegungen* (Frankfurt am Main: Suhrkamp, 1996), pp. 284–301.

[46] Cf. Lewis A. Coser, *Masters of Sociological Thought: Ideas in Historical and Social Context* (Long Grove, IL: Waveland Press, 1977), pp. 200–201; Hannes Böhringer, 'Spuren von spekulativem Atomismus in Simmels formaler Soziologie', in H. Böhringer and K. Gründer (eds.), *Ästhetik und Soziologie um die Jahrhundertwende: Georg Simmel* (Frankfurt am Main: Vittorio Klostermann, 1976), pp. 105–114.

[47] Parallels between Simmel's early sociology and Comte (though in a somewhat different respect) are also discussed in Heinz-Jürgen Dahme, *Soziologie als exakte Wissenschaft: Georg Simmels Ansatz und seine Bedeutung in der gegenwärtigen Soziologie* (Stuttgart: Ferdinand Enke, 1981), pp. 274–275.

[48] Mary Pickering, *Auguste Comte: An Intellectual Biography*, 3 vols. (Cambridge: Cambridge University Press, 1993–2009), vol. 1, pp. 561–690.

[49] Ibid., vol. 3, pp. 312–318.

to the interests of society as a whole. Social awareness is a counterpart to the progressive spirit of natural sciences. And if this constituted the young Simmel's view of society, then we would have to characterise him as a radical positivistic thinker, almost a Comtian, by then a rare phenomenon in the German intellectual landscape. Yet in order to see whether this is the case, one should look not only at Simmel's short articles but also at his theoretical work published in those years – *On Social Differentiation* – examining it in the context of contemporary traditions of social thought.

On the most general level, a large part of nineteenth-century European social thought was characterised by a number of common themes and idioms. Among its leading features one can include the notion of historical development from earlier to later stages (usually regarded as progress); the idea that the later stages are characterised by an ever-increasing differentiation of functions within society; and the use of biological metaphors such as 'growth', 'development' and 'organic'. Society was often said to be a kind of organism, and whatever specific meanings the word acquired, it normally connoted something positive (in contrast to 'mechanical'). At the same time, this common language was practised by thinkers of very different dispositions; consequently, it can be divided into a great variety of sub-traditions and idioms. To some extent, in the nineteenth century these idioms split according to national linguistic boundaries: British, French, German etc.[50] Since these traditions shared general postulates, it is at first glance unclear what was peculiar about each of them. Yet, when they are examined more closely, points of difference in their overall patterns of thinking begin to emerge.

I will focus here on one specific example, which is directly relevant to the discussion in the following pages. It pertains to the question of the relative weight of an individual versus society as a whole. In the context of nineteenth-century social thought, this problem was of particular significance because this thought was both organicist (perceiving society as a living unified system, an organism and not merely a sum of organisms) and liberal (or at least marked by the influence of liberalism, as it observed the growing importance of individuality in modern society). These two aspects could easily be seen as contradictory, and therefore one was called upon to address the issue of the potentially rocky relationship between the human and the social organism. The general answer of such theories was usually that no fundamental contradiction between the two existed: truly developed human individuality was fully congruent with truly organic

[50] Donald N. Levine, *Visions of the Sociological Tradition* (Chicago: University of Chicago Press, 1995).

society. However, in the context of different traditions this answer could mean many different things.

Consider the attitude of Herbert Spencer, arguably the most important figure in British sociology. Spencer's philosophical instincts were to a great degree utilitarian and his social and political convictions radically liberal and individualistic. His scientific system was indeed governed by the notion of evolution which formed the theoretical basis for the utilitarian and liberal aspects of his thought. Yet this evolutionism was endowed with strong individualistic overtones, characteristic of mainstream British social and political thought of the time.[51] Spencer argued, for example, that social organism was no more than a metaphor, a heuristic tool that enables us to understand society as a functional cooperation. Society, he said, is a 'discrete' rather than 'concrete' whole.[52] He emphatically assigned a greater value to the concrete individual organism than to the discrete social organism, claiming that the existence of the social body has no meaning or purpose apart from the interests of its members.[53] Spencer's organicism was thus marked by a strong individualistic bias with roots in the British philosophical traditions of empiricism and utilitarianism.

The approach of the leading currents in French social thought appears to be quite the opposite. While British organicist sociology emphasised the individual, the French tradition of social thought tended to treat the individual and his claims with suspicion.[54] This was true not only of the 'progressive' St. Simonian–Comtian tradition or the 'reactionary' Catholicism of de Maistre and Bonald but to some extent also of a number of liberal thinkers, especially Tocqueville.[55] French sociology usually assigned to society methodological pre-eminence over the individual.

How did German social thought address the same question? It appears that, when compared to the British and French traditions, it took the middle course. On the one hand, one can rarely find in it the unapologetic individualism of Spencer's kind. Nor, however, was it prone to French-like sermonising about altruism and social solidarity. If one were to name the attitude typical of the works of German social thinkers, one could call it 'complementarity'. Their writings are generally characterised by an attempt

---

[51] On Spencer's social and political thought, see David Weinstein, *Equal Freedom and Utility: Herbert Spencer's Liberal Utilitarianism* (Cambridge: Cambridge University Press, 1998).
[52] Herbert Spencer, *The Principles of Sociology*, 3 vols. (New Brunswick: Transaction Publishers, 2002), vol. 1, p. 457.
[53] Ibid., pp. 461–462.   [54] Levine, *Visions of the Sociological Tradition*, pp. 152–180.
[55] Cf. Lucien Jaume, *Tocqueville: The Aristocratic Sources of Liberty*, trans. A. Goldhammer (Princeton: Princeton University Press, 2013), pp. 115–128.

to draw some balance between the respective claims of the individual and society in which neither comes at the expense of the other. There is a disposition to recognise the rights of both the organic individual and the organic society. This disposition is marked by an ethical and intellectual individualism that goes back to Lutheran Protestantism and is also present in secularised traditions such as German Romanticism, with their emphasis on the uniqueness of individuality. At the same time, the concept of individuality is made to transcend the individual human being, achieving the status of a master concept applied to a variety of entities of a different order. Each human being is indeed an 'individuality' but so is each group, each nation, state or civilisation, and each has its own rightful claim to uniqueness. Thus the question of the relationship between the individual and society is conceived as one between two individualities of a different order, each with its own recognised claims to autonomy.[56]

This view can be traced back as far as Herder, whose thought emphasised both personal individuality and the individuality of social groups.[57] As for the period I am dealing with here, a relevant example would be the theory of 'national economist' and sociologist Albert Schäffle. His four-volume treatise *Structure and Life of the Social Body* (1876–1878) quite clearly follows the 'complementarity' model of the developmental organicist discourse which I just summarised. Within this mode of thinking, society as a whole and the individuals composing it are treated symmetrically: the development of both is a necessary condition for civilisational progress. Society is presented as a body, but it is a body in which a constant series of individualisations takes place according to race, temperament, age, gender and so on and ending with individualisation among individual human beings through the principle of personal freedom.[58] The most important aspect of personal freedom is, according to Schäffle, the freedom

---

[56] Hans-Peter Müller in 'Wie ist Individualität möglich? Strukturelle und kulturellen Bedingungen eines modernen Kulturideals', *Zeitschrift für Theoretische Soziologie* 4(1), 2015, p. 96 argues that Simmel follows the British and French traditions of social differentiation rather than the German one. But he reduces differentiation to the phenomenon of division of labour, viewing Marx and Engels as its main German theorists. Yet Marx's and Engels's thought was not, properly speaking, part of mainstream German social thought, being simultaneously too cross-national and too sectarian. The tradition to which I refer had nothing to do with Marxism. But since most German social thinkers of that period are all but forgotten, it is Marxism which is sometimes anachronistically perceived as representative of it.

[57] Frederick M. Barnard, *Herder's Social and Political Thought: From Enlightenment to Nationalism* (Oxford: Clarendon Press, 1965), p. 54. Cf. Michael N. Forster, *Herder's Philosophy* (Oxford: Oxford University Press, 2018), pp. 71, 76–77, 185–187.

[58] Albert Schäffle, *Bau und Leben des socialen Körpers*, 4 vols. (Tübingen: H. Laupp, 1876–1878), vol. 1, pp. 186–194.

of professional occupation. This freedom does not signify individuality in its egoistic sense but is a function of the division of labour in modern society.[59] A modern person is free and at the same time immersed in a network of numerous social relations: 'The same physical person is always a central point of several or many organisations or socially autonomous unities.'[60] Indeed, it is this variety of modes of everyone's social relationships which determines the peculiar character of the personality of each member.[61]

Thus Schäffle was careful in his theory not to discriminate the individuality of a lower order against that of a higher order, and vice versa. This was a central feature of the language of German social thought of the time, a feature which played a significantly less salient role, if any, in the writings of authors such as Comte or Spencer. And this is a feature one finds in Simmel's *On Social Differentiation*.[62]

From the outset, Simmel made the question of the relationship between individual entities of different orders into the treatise's major theme, mentioning the 'frequently observed peculiarity of complex structures: that the relation of one totality to another repeats itself among the parts of one of these totalities'.[63] This approach is already displayed in the book's first chapter, 'Towards the epistemology of social science', which deals with the general methodological problem of defining 'society' as the proper object of social science. Simmel rejects both the nominalist and the essentialist views of society. Society is neither a mere sum of its parts nor is it a mystical entity existing apart from its constituents. Instead, there is a third possibility which could be called relationist. Society, according to Simmel, is the interaction of its parts. This interaction endows an organism with relative unity, thus turning it into something qualitatively different from merely the sum of its elements. Yet at the same time this entity is dependent on those elements and cannot possess a separate existence.

Simmel's methodological rejection of both nominalism and essentialism implies an attempt to avoid the conflict between the claims of society and

---

[59] Ibid., pp. 198–199.   [60] Ibid., p. 278.   [61] Ibid., 275.

[62] 'The basic idea underlying Simmel's sociology is that of social interaction – and thus a conception of the social lying half-way between pure individualism and complete collectivism.' Hans Joas, *The Genesis of Values* (Chicago: University of Chicago Press, 2000), p. 71. For a brief summary of *On Social Differentiation*, see Frank J. Lechner, 'Social Differentiation and Modernity: On Simmel's Macrosociology', in M. Kaern, B. S. Phillips and R. S. Cohen (eds.), *Georg Simmel and Contemporary Sociology* (Dordrecht: Kluwert Academic Publishers, 1990), pp. 162–167. See also Gregor Fitzi, *The Challenge of Modernity: Simmel's Sociological Theory* (London: Routledge, 2019), pp. 9–13.

[63] *Über sociale Differenzierung: Sociologische und psychologische Untersuchungen*, GSG 2, p. 115.

those of the individual and consequently the need to express preference. This becomes clear when one examines the following five chapters of the book. They are based on a common theoretical postulate: social development is a twofold symmetrical process, which leads in parallel to the maturation of human individuality and to that of society.

Specifically, chapter two – 'On collective responsibility' – traces the transition from a primitive to a more differentiated society through the evolution of the phenomenon of guilt. Whereas originally the individual was not differentiated from the collective, and society as a whole was held responsible for the transgressions of its members, and vice versa, the gradually weakening bond and growing dissimilarity of conduct among the members led to a more individualised perception of guilt. Weaker primitive ties and a greater personal responsibility do not imply, however, that the individual's dependence on society is loosened in absolute terms. On the contrary, in a certain sense the individual has become even more dependent. For in the modern, thoroughly differentiated society, each member performs social functions for a great number of different social circles and is thus even more deeply embedded in the social network.

Chapter three – 'Group expansion and the formation of individuality' – establishes the fundamental twofold sociological principle which underlies the phenomenon described in the previous chapter. According to this principle, the extent of the development of a social group corresponds to the degree of individuality of those who belong to it: the larger and the more developed a group is, the stronger the individualism in it appears to be.

Chapter four – 'The social level' – deals with another paradoxical feature of differentiation. The bigger, the more complex, individualised and differentiated a society is, the more prone it is to levelling and reducing everyone to the average standard. In a primitive society, where differences between individuals are small, it is easy to distinguish oneself through even a slight deviation. In a highly differentiated society this becomes much more difficult because 'even if one rises above the average in certain respects, there are always others, developed in other aspects, who do the same in respect of those aspects'.[64]

Chapter five – 'On the intersection of social circles' – develops the point mentioned in chapter two: in a highly developed society any given individual can simultaneously belong to many social circles and is thus more tightly integrated into the network of social relations. On the other hand,

---

[64] GSG 2, p. 209.

this same fact allows the formation of one's own unique personality because the greater the number of these social circles, the less likely it is that there will be many other people who belong to exactly the same combination of circles.

Finally, the sixth chapter – 'Differentiation and the principle of economy of energy' – focuses on the question of how the ever more complex and many-sided goals of advanced civilisation are best achieved through the growing one-sidedness and simplification of the functions of its members.

As one can see, the book's structure does not form a linear argument. For example, the chapter dealing with collective responsibility precedes the one on group expansion and the formation of individuality; yet it is the latter which seems to deal with a more fundamental sociological principle, whereas the former is rather an exemplification of this principle. This does not, however, mean that the book lacks structure. Its chapters can be likened to different points on the periphery from which direct lines are drawn to the centre. The chapters are elucidations of the same central idea from different standpoints. The idea is parallelism: society and individuality are not necessarily two opposite concepts, and the relationship between the social whole and any of its parts is not a zero-sum game. On the contrary, the development of one necessarily requires that of the other. The more socialised a society becomes, the more individualised become its individuals. Individualisation and socialisation are two sides of the same coin, as can be concluded from observing the historical development of human society from its primitive to its more developed stages.

This approach seems to stand in sharp contrast to Simmel's polemical essays described earlier. There one finds 'progressive' rhetoric that emphasised the ethical, altruistic commitment to social welfare, reminiscent of the social theory of French positivism. *On Social Differentiation*, by contrast, was written in a much more native idiom with its judicious analysis of the advantages and disadvantages of modern differentiated society and its equal respect for the claims of society and those of the individual. For example, Simmel's major idea that the intersection of social circles leads to the development of individuality clearly followed the notion advanced by Schäffle several years earlier.

One could interpret *On Social Differentiation* as a purely academic work, unrelated to those writings of Simmel in which he acted as a (semi)-public moralist calling for the modern individual to redeem oneself via society. Such an interpretation would, however, overlook what the book and the essays have in common. For the question of the redemption of the modern individual was not exclusive to Simmel's polemical essays. On the contrary, this question lay at the heart of his philosophy, and it underlay the argument of *On Social Differentiation* no less than that of his other works.

Simmel scholarship is afflicted by a tendency to over-emphasise the theoretical-scientific aspects of his early thought, with its redemptive aspects only being noted – if at all – in his later writings.[65] I hold, however, the opposite view in respect of his sociology: it is his early rather than his mature writings in this field that bear the marks of a cultural redemptive project.

To explain why this is so, I would like to proceed to a closer contextualisation of the text and illustrate how it proves rather the opposite of what it is usually believed to prove. An important achievement of recent Simmel scholarship has been to reveal the immediate intellectual context of his early writings. If previously the accepted view was that Simmel's early social thought had been generally influenced by Spencerian 'positivism', it has by now been sufficiently proven that Simmel's main intellectual source was the German school of *Völkerpsychologie* (literally – 'psychology of peoples'), which was founded by Moritz Lazarus and Heymann Steinthal, centred around the *Journal for Völkerpsychologie and the Science of Language* and was originally conceived as a social psychology of ethnic and national character.[66] Lazarus was Simmel's teacher at the University of Berlin, and Klaus Christian Köhnke has convincingly shown how Lazarus's ideas were absorbed in Simmel's *On Social Differentiation*.[67] For example, the title of the third chapter on group expansion and the formation of individuality (*die Ausbildung der Individualität*) repeats almost literally Lazarus's programmatic pronouncement, made three decades earlier, according to which one of the tasks of *Völkerpsychologie* would be to examine the effect of the structure of the social whole on 'the formation of the individual' (*auf die Ausbildung der Einzelnen*).[68] There are many

---

[65] David Frisby, *Georg Simmel* (London: Routledge, 2002), pp. 91–93; Dahme, *Soziologie als exakte Wissenschaft*; Claudius Härpfer, *Georg Simmel und die Entstehung der Soziologie in Deutschland: Eine netzwerksoziologische Studie* (Wiesbaden: Springer, 2014).

[66] On *Völkerpsychologie*, see Egbert Klautke, *The Mind of the Nation*: Völkerpsychologie *in Germany, 1851–1955* (New York: Berghahn Books, 2016); '*Völkerpsychologie* in Nineteenth-Century Germany: Lazarus, Steinthal, Wundt', in Efraim Podoksik (ed.), *Doing Humanities in Nineteenth-Century Germany* (Leiden: Brill, 2019), pp. 243–263. On Simmel versus Spencer, cf. Elizabeth S. Goodstein, *Georg Simmel and the Disciplinary Imaginary* (Stanford: Stanford University Press, 2017), pp. 58–59.

[67] Cf. Köhnke, *Der junge Simmel*, pp. 337–338.

[68] M. Lazarus, 'Ueber das Verhältnis des Einzelnen zur Gesammtheit', in *Leben der Seele: in Monographien über seine Erscheinungen und Gesetze*, 2nd ed. (Berlin: Ferd. Dümmler, 1876), vol. 1, p. 361. [Based on a speech made in 1861, and first published in *Zeitschrift für Völkerpsychologie und Sprachwissenschaft* 2(4), 1862, pp. 393–453.]

other parallels. For example, Lazarus spoke about the lack of the notion of individual responsibility in primitive societies, claiming that this might have been a result of the similarity of conduct among its members.[69] He also suggested the idea of the intersection of different social circles, later discussed by Schäffle.[70]

Usually the influence of *Völkerpsychologie* on Simmel is presented as an episode in the history of the formation of the German science of society. The big story here is one of the rise of classical sociology from the spirit of *Völkerpsychologie* and early anthropology. Attention is normally drawn to theoretical concepts elaborated by this school and to their adoption by Simmel.[71] This line of interpretation is legitimate. *Völkerpsychologie* was indeed an attempt to introduce a new scientific discipline, and it did contribute to Simmel's own scientific pursuits. Yet the picture remains one-sided if one ignores the fact that for its founders, and especially for Lazarus, *Völkerpsychologie* was first and foremost a cultural project.[72] Lazarus's quest was not merely to provide suitable tools for the disinterested study of social processes but also to outline the road to redemption for the modern individual, and to do so by adhering to the prevalent mode of redemption within the German cultural context: to the ideal of self-cultivation, or *Bildung*. Moreover, *Völkerpsychologie* was a *Bildung* project not only because of its ideal but also because it subscribed to the general pattern of thinking associated with this ideal. The main feature of this pattern was constant dialectic between individuality and universality in the hope of finding resolution in some sort of totality under which both individuality and universality could be subsumed. *Völkerpsychologie* attempted to apply this pattern of thinking to the social realm. To

---

[69] M. Lazarus, 'Zum Ursprung der Sitte [1860]', in *Leben der Seele*, vol. 3, p. 381.

[70] Smaller social circles 'do not stand next to each other but touch and cut through each other in various ways'. Lazarus, 'Ueber das Verhältnis des Einzelnen zur Gesammtheit', p. 334. Dahme (*Soziologie als exakte Wissenschaft*, p. 355) suggested that Simmel's idea of the intersection of social circles was first introduced by Ludwig Gumplowicz in his *Grundriß der Soziologie*, and that it should be interpreted in terms of Gumplowicz's (and by implication, Simmel's) critique of the theories of older biologically oriented sociologists such as Schäffle. This, however, is not plausible, since this idea is clearly present in the works of authors such as Schäffle and Lazarus.

[71] E.g. David Frisby, *Simmel and Since: Essays on Georg Simmel's Social Theory* (London: Routledge, 1992), pp. 20–41; Alberto Meschiari, 'Moritz Lazarus and Georg Simmel', *Simmel Newsletter* 7(1), 1997, pp. 11–16; André Klein, *Simmel und Lazarus: Kulturwissenschaft und Völkerpsychologie in ihren Beziehungen*, PhD dissertation, University of Leipzig, 2004; Härpfer, *Georg Simmel und die Entstehung der Soziologie in Deutschland*, pp. 84–105.

[72] This fact was clearly recognised by contemporaries, such as those French thinkers who argued that Lazarus's and Steinthal's work was not rigorously scientific and described it as rather metaphysical or moralistic. See Egbert Klautke, 'The French Reception of *Völkerpsychologie* and the Origins of the Social Sciences', *Modern Intellectual History* 10(2), 2013, pp. 304–305.

a great extent, its purpose was to examine the possibility of the formation of a harmonious individuality within modern social conditions and, more specifically, to inquire how the requirement that a member of society dedicate himself to a narrow professional pursuit can be reconciled with the ideal of a many-sided well-cultivated personality.

If one takes, for example, Lazarus's three-volume collection of philosophical and anthropological writings *The Life of the Soul*, one finds that its first chapter is a long essay entitled '*Bildung* and Science'.[73] Written in 1856, it can be considered as a programmatic statement that serves as a background for his later work. Despite its title, it deals not only with the specific question of the relationship between *Bildung* and science but also with the notion of *Bildung* in general and its connection with morality and beauty.

Lazarus distinguishes between the narrow and the general aim of *Bildung*. The narrow aim is general education as such. It introduces a human being to what belongs to the sphere of common human interests. Although this education is distinct from the purely vocational one, every professional person must acquire it: 'a doctor is not just a doctor but also a human being'.[74]

At the same time, *Bildung* pursues a more general aim, which is to transcend the very distinction between the general and the particular and to connect general human interests with professional interests. This education not only allows one to see from the standpoint of one's own occupation (*Beruf*) that one is just 'a member in the great chain of general human aspirations' but also gives one insight into the general and the whole expressed in this very differentiation.[75]

The pattern of thinking that aims at the reconciliation of particularity with generality is also applied by Lazarus to the relationship between the individual and society. He claims that personal *Bildung* cannot be achieved in social isolation. True self-cultivation requires social progress, and vice versa.[76] The mutual connection between the development of individuality and that of social life is a constant motif in many of his works. He argues, for example, that the ancients knew only the value of collectivity and did not understand that the pursuit of individual aims also serves the general or national good.[77] For him, individuality does not equal egoism; rather, it means uniqueness contributing to the whole. Lazarus calls individuality 'a valuable peculiarity'[78] and formulates the purpose of society as follows: that

---

[73] M. Lazarus, 'Bildung und Wissenschaft [1856]', in *Leben der Seele*, vol. 1, pp. 3–123.
[74] Ibid., p. 33.   [75] Ibid., p. 35.   [76] Ibid., p. 21.   [77] Ibid., p. 25.
[78] Lazarus, 'Ueber das Verhältnis des Einzelnen zur Gesammtheit', p. 348.

'every individual attains the highest possible *freedom and individuality*, and yet at the same time there will be the highest intimacy and *strength of unity*'.[79]

It is important to realise that Lazarus never conceived *Völkerpsychologie* as a methodologically holistic discipline, despite what its name may suggest. It is true that he moved beyond methodological individualism in order to discover how to make social collectivity a unit of scientific analysis. He used the expression 'objective spirit', by which he meant mental phenomena, such as language, which are produced in the course of interaction between individuals, yet which also exist beyond the subjective awareness of each particular individual.[80] At the same time, Lazarus never dissolved the individual into the social whole. On the contrary, he always acknowledged the uniqueness of individual personality and took great care to emphasise the individualistic aspect of modern society. He never fully detached collective psychology from individual psychology, as he believed that 'objective' spirit could exist only through constant interaction with 'subjective' spirit.[81] He even argued that the ultimate criterion for determining one's national belonging was not the objective form – language, however important it might be – but the subjective decision – self-determination.[82]

Lazarus's *Völkerpsychologie* thus clearly represents the type of thinking which I attributed to German social thought with its concern for maintaining symmetry or balance between individualities of different degrees. It was never a merely scientific discipline. Similar to many other academic pursuits of that time, it was equally a cultural redemptive project, influenced by the persistent ideal of self-cultivation with its emphasis on the value of individuality and its development.

Now, a similar concern can also be seen in Simmel's *On Social Differentiation*. His most explicit discussion of the issue is found in the book's final chapter. The tendency in the evolution of organisms, argues Simmel, is towards economy of energy. The more developed an organism is, the less power it must exercise in order to achieve a certain purpose. The reason for this is the differentiation of functions within the organism. Such a differentiation allows it to perform the whole variety of functions required by the environment. The most differentiated organism is therefore the highest organism, and 'the most superior, intelligent individuals

---

[79] Ibid., p. 410.

[80] M. Lazarus, 'Einige synthetische Gedanken zur Völkerpsychologie', *Zeitschrift für Völkerpsychologie und Sprachwissenschaft* 3(1), 1865, pp. 41–43.

[81] Ibid., pp. 56–64.   [82] M. Lazarus, *Was heißt national?* (Berlin: Ferd. Dümmler, 1880).

have an outstanding capacity to adapt to any situation and to take on any manner of functions'.[83]

Economy of energy can be also achieved by the differentiation of time units. One can dedicate oneself completely to only one task in each time slot, whereas the exercise of the whole variety of capacities is enabled by a periodical change of tasks. Such change is crucial for the individual's performance. Continuously performing the same task reduces a person's effectiveness because monotonous activity exhausts and deadens him. Man is 'change-oriented',[84] and only a variety of stimuli can maintain his interest and attention.

Thus, already at the level of the individual organism, there is a potential tension between two contrary demands: that of the concentration of activity and that of variety. And when one considers the individual as part of society, the tension between the whole and a part seems to turn into an overt contradiction:

> The fact is that the differentiation of the social group is evidently directly opposed to that of the individual. The former requires that the individual must be as specialised [*einseitig*] as possible, that some single task must absorb all his energies and that all his impulses, abilities and interests must be made compatible with this one task, because this specialisation [*Einseitigkeit*] of the individual makes it both possible and necessary to the highest degree for him to be different from all other specialised individuals.[85]

This is, then, the greatest problem of differentiated society: the contradiction between the ideal of a harmonious many-sided personality and that of a harmonious many-sided society; the contradiction between the demand that an individual becomes a highly differentiated creature and the simultaneous demand that one exercise one's own social role, which can usually be met only 'by the utmost concentration on one special field to the exclusion of all other intellectual interests [*Bildungsinteressen*]'.[86]

Simmel believes, however, that there is a solution to this contradiction. For differentiation is not an endless process. After a certain point, the parts of the whole no longer contribute to it, and the unity falls apart. This is true both of society as a whole and of the individual as a whole. In both, therefore, the process of differentiation has its limits and it is possible in

---

[83] 'Differentiation and the Principle of Saving Energy', trans. D. E. Jenkinson, in P. A. Lawrence (ed.), *Georg Simmel: Sociologist and European* (Sunbury-on-Thames: Thomas Nelson and Sons, 1976), p. 126. [GSG 2, p. 279.]

[84] Ibid., p. 129. [GSG 2, p. 283.]   [85] Ibid., p. 130. [GSG 2, pp. 283–284.]

[86] Ibid. [GSG 2, p. 284.]

principle to find the most distant point at which the differentiation of functions within an individual will be most conducive both for the purpose of self-cultivation and for the cultivation of society: 'Up to a point, therefore, the interest of the individual in his own differentiation as a whole will coincide with the interest of society in his differentiation as a part.'[87] It is the task of culture 'to push that point further and further back and progressively to give to social and individual tasks a form that will demand the same degree of differentiation from both of them'.[88]

Thus, in *On Social Differentiation* Simmel believed that there existed the point at which the differentiation of the lower individuality could be compatible with that of the higher, and the more advanced a civilisation was, the higher degree of differentiation could it allow in both. This way of approaching the matter was different from Simmel's attitude in the essays I mentioned earlier. There the remedy for the individual appeared to be a change in consciousness, an acceptance of oneself as being just a part of a greater whole. Here, however, it was claimed that individuality could and should regard itself as a whole. Self-cultivation, and not only social altruism, was a necessary component in the redemption of the modern individual.

Simmel did not follow this line entirely consistently, and there are passages in *On Social Differentiation* which overlap with the sentiment of those essays. For example, in the fifth chapter Simmel describes the predicament of modernity in the following way:

> Meaningful, profoundly significant institutions and modes of behaviour are replaced by others which *per se* appear utterly mechanical, external and mindless. Only the higher purpose which lies beyond the earlier stage lends to their combined effect or later consequence a spiritual significance, which each individual element in itself entirely lacks.[89]

One could compare, for example, the activity of the modern soldier with that of the mediaeval knight, or modern mechanised work with a more ancient artisanal labour. Taken by themselves, these modern activities are less meaningful and enriching than their ancient counterparts. What endows them with organic meaning is their integration with other activities: 'Thus social institutions, gradations and associations can become more mechanical and external and yet serve the progress of

---

[87] Ibid., p. 131. [GSG 2, p. 285.]   [88] Ibid. [GSG 2, p. 285.]
[89] 'The Intersection of Social Spheres', trans. D. E. Jenkinson, in Lawrence (ed.), *Georg Simmel: Sociologist and European*, p. 108. [GSG 2, p. 254.]

culture, if a higher social aim arises to which they simply have to be subordinated.'⁹⁰

Yet ideas of this kind play only a secondary role in *On Social Differentiation* and are overshadowed by the central motif of reconciliation between social and individual cultivation. The prevalent idiom of Simmel's early sociology seemed to be that of German social thought in general and of *Völkerpsychologie* in particular. This idiom was characterised by the emphasis on the harmonious cultivation of individuality. With regard to society, it adopted the commonplace analogy of 'organism', yet it tended to perceive this analogy more literally than other idioms, conceiving of the individual and society as entities of the same kind and, therefore, assigning to both the same imperative of 'cultivation'. The conflict implied in this twofold assignment was resolved either through compromise or, more often, by means of some dialectical synthesis, symbolised by formulae such as 'unity in variety'.

It is, however, important to note in Simmel's ideas of that period, or more precisely in his style of thinking, at least one feature where he differed from his predecessors. Simmel was influenced by the generation of thinkers whose intellectual formation had occurred in the mid-nineteenth century. This intellectual generation, to which Lazarus (1824–1903) and Schäffle (1831–1903) belonged, was characterised by a particular disposition towards German cultural ideals, a disposition which can be described as a naive and yet pragmatic optimism. This generation spoke in idioms shared by other generations too: the idioms of tension between individuality and universality, identity and difference, unity and variety. But of all generations, this one was particularly prone to considering the cultural task of finding the solution to this conflictual feature of modernity as essentially unproblematic. It lacked the parental anxiety of the philosophically sophisticated *Blütezeit* generation and did not yet begin to develop the symptoms of disappointment so characteristic of later generations. It was just performing the cultural mission left to it by previous generations. The pattern of thinking that presupposed the 'unity in variety' answer to the contradiction between whole and part was so natural to it that the only thing apparently left for it to do was to demonstrate how this formula was embodied in different aspects of reality, for example, in social life.

Besides, for many Jewish intellectuals of the time, such as Lazarus and Steinthal, the ideal of *Bildung* signified the hope of integration within mainstream German culture and society. For this reason, they generally

⁹⁰ Ibid. [GSG 2, p. 255.]

continued to perceive it in a very optimistic manner even when cultural pessimism began to creep in. This was also true of the young Simmel. The fashion of cultural pessimism in Germany showed its first signs at some point after 1870. Although at the beginning the most vocal in this regard were iconoclasts such as Nietzsche, the tone of cultural discontent was also adopted by more respectable figures such as Windelband or even Treitschke. Yet Simmel did not seem to share these doubts up until the late 1890s. Once a student of Lazarus, Grimm, Droysen and Zeller, in *On Social Differentiation* he still adhered to the classical 'unity in variety' answer regarding the compatibility of the ideal of self-cultivation with the modern condition. Thus if the perception of Simmel as a typical 'Jewish' intellectual of the time has any basis, it is precisely in his initial attachment to the ideal of cultural harmony which a great number of Jewish German intellectuals continued to espouse even when it came under increasing attack.

Nevertheless, even then something was different in the way Simmel addressed these doubts. His reflections seemed on the whole less naive. In Lazarus, the synthesis of the social and the individual appeared as the only solid reality, whereas extreme individualism and extreme social essentialism were just two abstract tools of analysis paving the way towards the point of synthesis. In Simmel, by contrast, the 'synthetic' conclusion was very rarely stated explicitly at any specific stage of the argument and normally could only be derived from the general impression left by his work as a whole. He tended to offer a series of arguments and counterarguments, in which the theory, instead of resting in the golden middle, constantly vacillated between favouring the advancement of the individual and that of society.

Simmel generally avoided any overt expression of unqualified optimism. Rather, the advantages and disadvantages of modern civilisation were presented in a series of conflicting observations. Consider, for example, his treatment of the subject of social levelling (chapter four). Is levelling good or bad for cultivation (of both the individual and society)? On the one hand, it is detrimental to what is qualitatively best because in a mass of people levelling is achieved not by raising the level of the lower strata but by forcing the higher to come down.[91] On the other hand, that very property which produces levelling – the increase of the group – contributes also to its civilisational development.[92] At the same time this development leads to the demand for the equalisation of conditions, hence to socialism, which

---

[91] GSG 2, p. 210.   [92] GSG 2, p. 224.

may be problematic. Yet, psychologically speaking, the demand for equalisation may not necessarily conflict with the urge for differentiation.[93] For
such a demand does not necessarily indicate that the highest value is
attached to the principle of equality; it just reflects the immediate desire
of the lower classes simply to better their economic conditions. For this
reason, socialism provides neither a sure hope for those who want to
overcome the harmful effects of differentiation nor does it necessarily
endanger what others consider as differentiation's good effects.[94]

It seems, however, that behind this constant vacillation of argument
a general normative position can be discerned. *On Social Differentiation* on
the whole stood for modernity and differentiation. There, Simmel was
optimistic about the possibility of finding the most distant point of
compatibility between the differentiated individual and the differentiated
society. This kept him within the limits of the idiom of 'unity in variety'.
Yet, at the same time, this view revealed itself not in a stable synthetic
position but through constant fluctuation between two extremes, a quasi-
dialectical movement without any resting point. To use a metaphor which
Simmel would have liked, his approach to ideas was akin to the physicist's
approach to matter. What naive human perception sees as a solid motionless body, the physicist considers as the total sum of movements of an
innumerable amount of the smallest particles. Similarly, Simmel dissolved
what had once appeared as a solid synthesis into the perpetual pendulum-
like movement of thought.

However, this style of reflection potentially threatened the stability of
Simmel's initial view. In the course of constant fluctuation, the game can
only continue as long as certain limits are not crossed. In the late 1880s
and early 1890s, Simmel still remained within these limits. Despite all
vacillation, 'society' still appeared in his theoretical writings as the main
mode of redemption for the confused modern individual. That period
was also marked by the peak of Simmel's *practical* interest in social affairs.
In those years, he published a number of pieces on topical matters
(though mostly anonymously or under pseudonyms), dealing with issues
such as the emancipation of peasants in Prussia,[95] prostitution (he
favoured its legalisation, but only in officially licensed brothels),[96] trade
unionism (he suggested that 'state welfare' was a higher principle than

---

[93] GSG 2, p. 232.   [94] GSG 2, pp. 235–236.
[95] 'Die Bauernbefreiung in Preussen' [1888], GSG 17, pp. 195–222.
[96] *Ex malis minima! Reflexionen zur Prostitutionsfrage* [1891], GSG 17, pp. 251–260; 'Einiges über die
Prostitution in Gegenwart und Zukunft' [1892], GSG 17, pp. 261–273.

formal freedom)[97] or spiritism (in his view, a ghostly remnant from the pre-scientific past).[98]

Yet once the limits are crossed, the whole structure disintegrates; the solid body dissolves into fragments. And this is what happened to Simmel's vision of society both in theory and in practice in the course of the 1890s. The stream of opinionated publications on social topics slowed down. Simmel established his position as a public intellectual but at the same time avoided overtly political or socially partisan themes. He chose the role of a detached diagnostician of the general cultural situation.

Similarly, in his theoretical work society gradually ceased to play the role of the fundamental mode of redemption for the modern individual, and consequently it no longer figured as the focal point of his thought. It is true that even in his early period Simmel did not fully subscribe to sociological reductionism. Yet he came very close to it. For if 'society' is the main venue for human reconciliation with modernity, then all other spheres of human interest should be reduced to the social question. However divergent the spheres of human interest may be, in some profound, redeeming sense they are all reflections of social life. Traces of this approach are discernible even in some publications of the late 1890s, such as 'Sociological Aesthetics' (1896) and 'Towards the Sociology of Religion' (1898).[99] The spheres of aesthetics and religion were considered there from the standpoint of 'society'. The content of these essays is, of course, richer and more ambiguous than the titles suggest. In the former, the relationship between the aesthetic and the social is not one-directional or hierarchical but interactional: 'It is possible to discover ... how [seemingly] purely aesthetic interests are called forth by materialistic purposes [*Zweckmäßigkeit*], and how, on the other hand, aesthetic motives affect forms which seem to obey only functional purposes.'[100] And in the essay on religion, the autonomous value of religious ideals is asserted.[101] Nevertheless, the very fact that these two spheres were analysed in the framework of sociology points to certain rudiments of social reductionism in Simmel's thinking even in those years.

Just a few years later these last rudiments disappeared completely, as Simmel came to conceive the idea of the radical autonomy of every cultural

[97] 'Ein Wort über soziale Freiheit' [1892], GSG 17, pp. 21–25.
[98] 'Etwas vom Spiritismus' [1892], GSG 17, pp. 274–283.
[99] 'Sociological Aesthetics', trans. K. P. Etzkorn, in *The Conflict in Modern Culture and Other Essays* (New York: Teachers College Press, 1968), pp. 68–80. [GSG 5, pp. 197–214.]; 'A Contribution to the Sociology of Religion', trans. H. J. Helle, in *Essays on Religion* (New Haven: Yale University Press, 1997), pp. 101–120. [GSG 5, pp. 266–286; also GSG 18, pp. 387–404.]
[100] 'Sociological Aesthetics', p. 72. [GSG 5, p. 202.]
[101] 'A Contribution to the Sociology of Religion', p. 120. [GSG 5, p. 286; also GSG 18, p. 404.]

sphere, thus denying the notion of one pre-eminent mode of cultural redemption. The thinker from whom he apparently learned this insight was Friedrich Nietzsche, with whose writings he was increasingly preoccupied from the mid-1890s onwards, and it is in the context of his reception of Nietzsche that Simmel voiced the strongest repudiation of sociologism. In Simmel's view, one of Nietzsche's major achievements was the demonstration that not every moral ideal in respect of humanity must be a 'social' ideal.[102] Nietzsche envisaged the ideal of breeding the ever-improving human type. The moral task of humanity is to allow such a type to come into existence. Yet, from the point of view of this ideal, it does not really matter if only one such individual is produced, or if the development of this individual is made possible at the price of the suppression of all other members of the species.

By advancing such an alternative view, Nietzsche, according to Simmel, made an important intellectual contribution. For he repudiated the intellectual position which was becoming popular towards the end of the nineteenth century, according to which 'the social – socio-historical, socio-psychological, socio-ethical – point of view, which is one among many possible points of view, became simply *the* point of view'.[103] Simmel claimed that the popularity of this position reflected the profound needs of modern man:

> When the modern man in his search for values looks beyond the individual, he generally stops at 'society' as the last authority in the formation and award of values; perhaps because the class, which has become a bearer of considerable and real power and an object of ethical interest, is the one with which those who belong to higher strata tend to be connected only through the fact that they belong with it to *one* 'society'.[104]

As I see it, the class to which Simmel refers is the working class, and the meaning of the passage is that the members of the higher classes are capable of developing a sense of solidarity with the working class only by constructing the concept of 'society'.

It is not difficult to recognise that when Simmel described this worldview and explained the reasons for its popularity he spoke about his own past beliefs. For it was the young Simmel himself, who had tended to regard the social view as *the* point of view and it was Simmel who had appealed to the sentiment of social solidarity of the affluent classes! His repudiation of this attitude seemed therefore to be a repudiation of his own

[102] 'Zum Verständnis Nietzsches' [1902], GSG 7, pp. 58–59.
[103] *Schopenhauer und Nietzsche*, GSG 10, p. 359.   [104] GSG 10, p. 358.

past convictions that were now replaced by a new vision in which 'society' appeared only as 'one of the forms in which humanity, its powers, contents and interests live'.[105]

For the mature Simmel, society was no longer *the* mode of redemption. It was one of many possible modes because man was more than just a member of society. This would in fact become a presupposition of Simmel's *Sociology* (1908), in which society's second a priori would be formulated as follows: '[E]very element of a group is not only a social part but, in addition, something else.'[106]

Simmel worked on the development of his social science between 1894 and 1908, starting with the programmatic essay 'The Problem of Sociology',[107] which signalled a retreat from his earlier view of society. The fact that there is a difference between his approach in *Sociology* and that in *On Social Differentiation* has been noticed by scholars who have interpreted this change in various ways. Otthein Rammstedt, for example, pointed to a more individualistic turn in Simmel's later sociology.[108] Uta Gerhardt suggested that Simmel's subject matter in the two works is different: the analysis of modern society versus the analysis of forms of sociation.[109] To these I would like to add another interpretation. In my view, the basic difference between the two works lies in the abandonment of the quest for comprehensive cultural integration in favour of a purely scientific sociology. Precisely because 'society' was now seen as only one of many possible modes, it could become the subject of disinterested scientific investigation. It is often pointed out that Simmel lost interest in sociology soon after he had finished his *Sociology* in 1908.[110] It would, however, be more correct to say that Simmel's loss of *existential* interest in sociology occurred much earlier: before 1894. And it is precisely because he became *uninterested* in sociology as the way to cultural redemption that he could formulate a *disinterested* methodology for the study of social interactions, the project which he himself came to acknowledge as secondary to his main

---

[105] GSG 10, p. 358. As Simmel noted elsewhere, social enthusiasm 'has left behind a feeling of quiet disappointment in wide circles because it estranges the soul from its ultimate and deepest sense of belonging to itself.' '[Über:] *Karl Joël*, Professor in Basel: *Philosophenwege. Ausblicke und Rückblicke*. Berlin, Heyfelder, 1901' [27 April 1901], GSG 17, p. 328.

[106] 'How Is Society Possible?', trans. K. H. Wolff, in Kurt H. Wolff (ed.), *Essays on Sociology, Philosophy and Aesthetics* (New York: Harper & Row, 1959), p. 345. [GSG 11, p. 51.]

[107] 'Das Problem der Sociologie'. GSG 5, pp. 52–61.

[108] Otthein Rammstedt, 'Editorischer Bericht', in GSG 11, p. 902.

[109] Uta Gerhardt, 'The Two Faces of Modernity in Georg Simmel's Social Thought', *Simmel Studies* 16(1), 2006, p. 62.

[110] E.g. Frisby, *Simmel and Since*, p. 25.

interests.[111] From a *Bildung* project his sociology thus became a *Beruf* project.

2.3 Kant

For the young Simmel, the way to integrated life in the condition of modernity ran through modern 'society'. The regulative idea of the modern society was the ideal point where the activities and interactions of highly individualised personalities contributed to the life of society taken as a whole, whereas each personality itself constituted a complex unity balancing the variety of pursuits and interests. This was, however, redemption only on the level of living and doing. The other aspect of human existence threatened by modern fragmentation – that of thinking and understanding – also demanded attention. And Simmel's answer to the question of how to integrate thought in the condition of modernity was Kant.

It is difficult to overestimate the significance of Kant for Simmel's thought. One of his close friends, Margarete Susman, wrote that 'despite all numerous demonstrable intellectual influences of another kind and despite his changing attitude to *Kant*, he remained determined by him until the end'.[112] In fact, Simmel's intellectual career began with Kant. Kant's theory of matter was the subject of his student dissertation, for which he was awarded the Royal Prize in 1880, and on the basis of which he was awarded a doctoral degree.[113] His subsequent *Habilitation* essay analysed Kant's ideas of synthetic judgement, pure perception and pure will and was regarded by the examination committee as a better work than his initial study on the origins of music.[114] Simmel's first course as *Privatdozent* at the University of Berlin was on Kant's ethics, and he continued teaching Kant for many years.[115] Kant was also a recurring theme in many of his publications, culminating in *Kant: Sixteen Lectures Delivered at Berlin*

---

[111] Simmel, Letter to Célestin Bouglé, 13 December 1899, GSG 22, p. 342. For a recent contribution on the issue of disciplinary boundaries in Simmel's thought, see Elizabeth S. Goodstein, 'Sociology as a Sideline: Does it Matter that Georg Simmel (Thought He) Was a Philosopher?', in T. Kemple and O. Pyyhtinen (eds.), *The Anthem Companion to Georg Simmel* (London: Anthem Press, 2016), pp. 29–57.

[112] Margarete Susman, *Die geistige Gestalt Georg Simmels* (Tübingen: J. C. B. Mohr, 1959), p. 3.

[113] The first part of the dissertation was published as Georg Simmel, *Das Wesen der Materie nach Kant's Physischer Monadologie* [1881], GSG 1, pp. 9–41. See also Köhnke, *Der junge Simmel*, pp. 42–49.

[114] Michael Landmann, 'Bausteine zur Biographie', in K. Gassen and M. Landmann (eds.), *Buch des Dankes an Georg Simmel* (Berlin: Duncker & Humblot, 1958), p. 20; Köhnke, *Der junge Simmel*, pp. 51–77.

[115] Gassen and Landmann (eds.), *Buch des Dankes*, pp. 345–349.

University, read in the winter semester of 1902–1903 and published as a book in 1904.[116] *Kant* was Simmel's most popular work; none of his other books enjoyed four editions during his lifetime.[117]

In addition to his promotion of Kant's philosophy as a teacher and writer, Simmel regularly cooperated with Kant scholars: he contributed an article on Kant's philosophy to the first issue of *Kant-Studien*,[118] became a life member of the Kant Society and was among the founders of the philosophical journal *LOGOS*, perceived as the tribune of the Southwest neo-Kantian School, and he was initially apprehensive that he would be perceived as a representative of that particular school.[119]

These worries were exaggerated. His contemporaries did perceive Simmel as a neo-Kantian, but they also recognised the peculiar nature of his engagement with Kant. Thus in the eleventh edition (1916) of Friedrich Ueberweg's *Outline of the History of Philosophy*, its editor Konstantin Oesterreich acknowledged that Simmel represented a separate trend in neo-Kantianism alongside six others, such as the Marburg and Baden schools.[120]

But what kind of a neo-Kantian was he, after all? 'Neo-Kantianism' was a blend of activities of at least three different kinds.[121] First, it was a scholarly movement, the aim of which was to pursue a detailed philological, historical and interpretative study of Kant's philosophy. Second, it was an attempt at reformulating, developing and improving Kant's philosophical system. Finally, it was a public philosophical movement which aimed to create its own cultural worldview. Simmel's work encompasses all three aspects. When one mentions Simmel's 'neo-Kantianism', one is

---

[116] *Kant: Sechzehn Vorlesungen gehalten an der Berliner Universität*, GSG 9, pp. 7–226.
[117] The second edition appeared in 1905, the third in 1913, and the fourth in 1918.
[118] 'Ueber den Unterschied der Wahrnehmungs- und der Erfahrungsurteile: Ein Deutungsversuch', GSG 5, pp. 235–245.
[119] Rüdiger Kramme, 'Brücke und Trost? Zu Georg Simmels Engagement für den "Logos"', *Simmel Newsletter* 3(1), 1993, p. 65.
[120] Friedrich Ueberweg, *Grundriß der Geschichte der Philosophie*, part 4: *vom Beginn des neunzehnten Jahrhunderts bis auf die Gegenwart*, 11th ed., ed. K. Oesterreich (Berlin: Ernst Siegfried und Sohn, 1916), pp. 398–401.
[121] On neo-Kantianism see Frederick C. Beiser, *The Genesis of Neo-Kantianism 1796–1880* (Oxford: Oxford University Press, 2014); Klaus Christian Köhnke, *The Rise of Neo-Kantianism: German Academic Philosophy between Idealism and Positivism* (Cambridge: Cambridge University Press, 1991); Helmut Holzhey, 'Der Neukantianismus', in H. Holzhey and W. Röd (eds.), *Die Philosophie des ausgehenden 19. und des 20. Jahrhunderts 2: Neukantianismus, Idealismus, Realismus, Phänomenologie* (Munich: C. H. Beck, 2004), pp. 11–129. On neo-Kantianism and culture, see Stephan Nachtsheim, 'The Concept and Philosophy of Culture in Neo-Kantianism', in Nicholas Boyle and Liz Disley (eds.), *The Impact of Idealism: The Legacy of Post-Kantian German Thought*, vol. 2: *Historical, Social and Political Thought*, ed. John Walker (Cambridge: Cambridge University Press, 2013), pp. 136–160.

usually referring only to his cultural-philosophical contribution, without considering his role in the two other aspects of neo-Kantianism: the interpretation and modification of Kant's philosophy. Yet only by considering these can Simmel's peculiar place within neo-Kantianism be made clear.

Simmel's engagement with Kant can be split into two periods. In the first, he considered Kant not only as a great philosophical mind but also as the creator of the only adequate intellectual basis for resolving the contradictions of the modern era. In the second period, he came to believe that Kant's response to the problems of modernity was not fully satisfactory, although he continued to hold him in great esteem. This turn in Simmel's position happened between 1896 and 1902; that is, between the publication of his essay 'What Is Kant to Us?' (1896),[122] in which he outlined in detail his initial position, and his public lectures on Kant (1902), in which he voiced his new attitude. If one were to look for a more precise date for the change, I would suggest 1899. Two things happened then. First, Simmel stopped offering annual classes on Kant. From this point on he would lecture on Kant only occasionally.[123] Second, in the same year he published the essay 'Kant and Goethe', in which he spoke for the first time about an alternative way – Goethe's – to resolve the contradictions of modernity.[124]

But Simmel's overall interpretation of the meaning of Kant's philosophy did not change. Its main parameters were determined by what he had learned from the work of early neo-Kantians. To make it intelligible therefore one should look at the main landmarks of Kant reception during the neo-Kantian period.

In the latter half of the nineteenth century, Kant's philosophy attracted a great deal of attention in Germany.[125] The renewed interest had begun in the late 1850s and the 1860s with the publication of important studies by Kuno Fischer, Otto Liebmann and F. A. Lange. It spread in the 1870s and 1880s, with the term 'neo-Kantianism' first appearing around 1875.[126] In 1896, Hans Vaihinger launched the journal *Kant-Studien*, and shortly afterwards (1904) the Kant Society was founded.[127] In the last two decades

---

[122] 'Was ist uns Kant?', GSG 5, pp. 145–177.

[123] E.g. in the winter semester 1909–1910. See Gassen and Landmann (eds.), *Buch des Dankes*, p. 348.

[124] 'Kant und Goethe', GSG 5, pp. 445–478. See also Ingo Meyer, *Georg Simmels Ästhetik: Autonomiepostulat und soziologische Referenz* (Weilerswist: Velbrück, 2017), pp. 43–44, for the reference to the letters dated 1908 and 1912, where Simmel distances himself from Kant.

[125] Beiser, *The Genesis of Neo-Kantianism*, p. 1.

[126] Helmut Holzhey, 'Neukantianismus', in J. Ritter and K. Gründer (eds.), *Historisches Wörterbuch der Philosophie* (Darmstadt: Wissenschaftliche Buchgesellschaft, 1984), pp. 747–748.

[127] That the society was very important to Simmel until the end of his life is indicated by his letter to Margarete Susman (von Bendemann) dated 23 October 1917 (see GSG 23, p. 853), where he

of the *Kaiserreich*, neo-Kantianism established itself as a leading philosophical current in Germany.

The cultural project of neo-Kantianism in general can be described as an attempt to find in Kant the foundations for restoring the unity of the worldview vis-à-vis diversified modern civilisation. The diagnosis of modernity was disunity, and Kant was supposed to have provided the answer to this disunity. However, the kind of answer expected of Kant depended on the kind of disunity perceived to exist in modernity.

The first period of the Kantian revival (late 1850s–1880s) was affected by the legacy of Kant's reception by the first generation of post-Kantian Idealists. The specific kind of disunity that troubled these Idealists was that between the phenomenal and noumenal worlds. The central initial question of post-Kantian German Idealism was the question of dualism between the world as appearance and the world as it really is, symbolised by the famous expression 'thing-in-itself'.

Neo-Kantians, such as Liebmann and Lange, attacked this preoccupation with the thing-in-itself, which they considered futile.[128] They believed that emphasis on the thing-in-itself turned Kant into a metaphysician, whereas the most valuable aspect of his philosophy, the one that ensured its coherence, was his rejection of metaphysics. Kant's philosophy, in their eyes, was critical rather than metaphysical. It focused on what governs our experience and not on what may lurk behind it. These neo-Kantians regarded 'thing-in-itself' as a 'transcendental' (in the Kantian sense) rather than metaphysical term. In other words, 'thing-in-itself' is a term evoked to outline the limits of possible experience rather than to point to things that may exist beyond our experience. 'The "thing in itself" is a mere limit-concept', claimed Lange,[129] while Hermann Cohen called it 'ominous', arguing that, from the standpoint of our experience, it should be considered as nothing.[130]

Having thus disposed of the obnoxious thing-in-itself and its set of associated problems (antinomies, Ideas, God etc.), neo-Kantians concentrated on what they regarded both as the heart of Kant's theory and as his most relevant philosophical idea: that our mind always grasps the world actively, and that the forms in which the world appears to our perception

mentions the growth of the society's membership among the cultural moments that console him during the war.

[128] On Liebmann, see, for example, Beiser, *The Genesis of Neo-Kantianism*, pp. 289–290.

[129] Friedrich Albert Lange, *Geschichte des Materialismus und Kritik seiner Bedeutungen in der Gegenwart*, 2nd ed., vol. 2 (Iserlohn: J. Baedeker, 1875), p. 49.

[130] Hermann Cohen, *Kants Theorie der Erfahrung*, 2nd ed. (Berlin: Ferd. Dümmler, 1885), p. 167.

and to our understanding exist a priori. It is impossible for us to experience the world other than in time, in space, under the category of causality etc. The purpose of philosophy is to outline the presuppositions under which the world can be known by experience and thus to determine the proper sphere of modern science.

Neo-Kantians diverged in their views as to why our experience is determined by a priori forms and why specifically by these and not other forms. The earlier generation (e.g. Liebmann and initially Lange) offered a physiological explanation, arguing that the a priori is determined by our biological organisation.[131] Certain categories are necessary for the human race, whereas other intelligent beings may possess a different system of categories. Cohen, by contrast, believed that the categories possessed logical necessity: for all mental organisms there is only one way to pursue truly scientific knowledge. Kant's own view in this respect is a subject of historical interpretation, though it appears that he did not clearly differentiate between the two positions.[132] But this did not have to concern neo-Kantians, whose aim, even as they proclaimed the importance of studying Kant's texts scrupulously, was mainly to reformulate and improve upon Kant. The task of the new scholarship was precisely to return to Kant's basic problems in order to solve them in a better way than Kant himself had done.[133] As Wilhelm Windelband would later say, 'to understand Kant means to surpass Kant'.[134]

The way in which Kant was surpassed regarding the question of a priori was this: Kant himself believed that the system of categories outlined by him was complete and eternally valid. Neo-Kantians, however, could not accept this closed system; they considered it inadequate and outdated. It did not matter whether the a priori was a function of our biological organisation or of logical necessity. In both instances, Kant's system was finite, for he did not foresee any significant changes either in the organisation of human beings or in the Aristotelian and Newtonian basis of the natural sciences; and in both instances Kant would be challenged by the end of the nineteenth century. First, evolutionary biology implied that the contemporary form of the human race was not the final or the only possible

[131] Friedrich Albert Lange, *Geschichte des Materialismus und Kritik seiner Bedeutungen in der Gegenwart*, 1st ed. (Iserlohn: J. Baedeker, 1866), p. 264.
[132] Manfred Pascher, *Einführung in den Neukantianismus: Kontext – Grundpositionen – Praktische Philosophie* (Munich: Wilhelm Fink, 1997), p. 55.
[133] Otto Liebmann, *Kant und die Epigonen: Eine kritische Abhandlung* (Stuttgart: Carl Schober, 1865).
[134] Wilhelm Windelband, *Präludien: Aufsätze und Reden zur Einführung in die Philosophie* (Tübingen: J. C. B. Mohr, 1911), vol. 1, p. iv.

one, that new forms would develop in time and that consequently the nature of experiencing by future human beings may differ from ours. Second, and more central to the history of neo-Kantianism, the principles of natural and exact sciences evolved significantly, which allowed Cohen to suggest that Kant had based his a priori system on a scientific situation that was becoming increasingly irrelevant. Science is an open-ended activity. The science of the future would modify the principles universally accepted in Cohen's time, just as the science of his time modified the principles of Newtonian physics. For this reason, it is impossible to formulate a finite system of a priori categories. The system must remain open enough to accommodate future scientific progress.[135]

At the same time, neo-Kantians did not consider this criticism to be a repudiation of Kant. On the contrary, they saw themselves as completing Kant's work. For them, the most significant thing was first of all that Kant's philosophy presupposed unity rather than dualism and secondly that this unity was quintessentially modern because it welcomed variety and open-endedness. Kant paved the way towards a unified philosophical worldview that could accommodate open-endedness and progress. Thus, in the eyes of early neo-Kantians, his theory entailed, in principle, an adequate response to the intellectual demands of the modern age; it built a unified system valid for the condition of modern variety.

The project of reformulating Kantian doctrine was all but over by the early 1880s, the time of Simmel's first intellectual endeavours. His understanding of Kant's epistemology and metaphysics was preconditioned by this reformulation. His initial view of Kant developed in the context of the interpretation advanced by the early neo-Kantians, to whom he was greatly indebted even if he rarely mentioned their names expressly.[136] In his eyes, as in the eyes of many of his contemporaries, this was not *an* interpretation but *the* interpretation: the last word of scholarship.

For Simmel, Kant's philosophy was mainly the philosophy of knowledge and experience. Simmel did everything he could to remove any remnants of the noumenal world from Kant's philosophy. In 'What Is Kant to Us?', for example, he argued that Kant's teaching about the thing-

---

[135] Pascher, *Einführung in den Neukantianismus*, p. 56.

[136] I disagree with Kurt Röttgers's dismissive attitude regarding the extent of Simmel's scholarly acquaintance with Kant ('Die "große" Soziologie und die "große" Philosophie', in H. Tyrell, O. Rammstedt and I. Meyer [eds.], *Georg Simmels große 'Soziologie': Eine kritische Sichtung nach hundert Jahren* [Bielefeld: transcript, 2011], p. 69). Simmel's interest in Kant was certainly philosophical rather than exegetical. However, his Kant texts clearly display good knowledge of Kant as well as of contemporary scholarship, and the hearsay testimony according to which he once said that he could not understand Hermann Cohen's works should not count for much.

in-itself was generally misunderstood. It was commonly believed that Kant had argued that 'I' – our mind – had something beyond itself which was fundamentally different from it: the world of objects to which one was denied direct access. According to this belief, 'there exists an unbridgeable abyss between representation and the thing-in-itself, and the former can never reach the latter but instead will always remain just itself'.[137] This understanding, however, is false. The reason for our inability to know the thing-in-itself is not the incommensurability of our mind with what lies outside it (for thinking has no limits and can in principle push towards things-in-themselves); it is, rather, that pure thinking, detached from sensual perception, cannot be a means of knowledge at all, for the only existing reality is the one already entailed in sensual appearance. 'This mere appearance of the world that we see is not an illusion or error', for 'the sensible, intelligibly ordered representation *is* precisely reality'.[138] It is all the more certain to us, as we do not imagine anything beyond it:

> Thus the stable world's apparent evaporation and uprooting through reduc-
> tion to a sensible representation actually bestows on it a kind of stability and
> certainty which it never had as long as one assumed as the real and true
> world a world of things in themselves which exists beyond our senses and
> can be reached only in thought.[139]

This was the gist of Simmel's interpretation of Kant's theory of knowledge and experience: the very notion that the world was appearance determined by forms entailed in our own mind actually bestowed upon reality an earlier unachievable degree of certainty and thus freed us from the danger of scepticism. The radical subjectivism of Kant led to the radical assertion of objectivity and of certainty with regard to the known world. One could speak meaningfully about objectivity only once the thing-in-itself had been deprived of its status as an independent object.

According to Simmel's interpretation, from which he never deviated, the question of the existence of something beyond the realm of experience was simply irrelevant to the Kantian critique of reason.[140] Like other neo-Kantians, Simmel was well aware that this had not been exactly the view of the historical Kant, who had been very interested in the problem of God's existence and other 'metaphysical' subjects. Yet Simmel believed that these questions had lost their appeal for modern man, for whom the critical aspect of Kant's philosophy was of greater consequence. It is this critical

---

[137] 'Was ist uns Kant?', GSG 5, p. 152.   [138] GSG 5, p. 153.   [139] GSG 5, pp. 153–154.
[140] *Kant*, GSG 9, p. 86.

aspect which constituted the philosophical essence of Kant's ideas.[141]
Therefore it was important not to succumb to the 'danger of converting
into a *world* the absolutely unrecognisable [quality] of the thing-in-
itself'.[142] This substantialisation of the thing-in-itself was merely an unfortunate error of Kant's: 'The crossing of self-imposed limits undertaken by
Kant through the metaphysical use of the thing-in-itself is based on the fact
that he solidifies its purely functional meaning into a substantive entity.'[143]

The relevant context for the term 'function' vis-à-vis the term 'substance', as they were used in *Kant*, is the school of 'empiricism' (or
'empirio-criticism') of Ernst Mach and Richard Avenarius.[144] It was
Mach who popularised the idea that modern physics replaced the older
understanding of matter as substance with the newer notion of matter as
energy. By using these terms, Simmel was pushing his interpretation of
Kant in a strongly empiricist direction, apparently deviating from the
orthodox neo-Kantian position. In the intellectual context of the late
nineteenth century, Mach's critical positivism was seen as opposed to neo-
Kantianism, which focused on the logical rather than the sensual presuppositions of knowledge. Simmel regarded this opposition as unfortunate
and considered both approaches complementary. He wrote that 'the
intellectual-historical situation in the 1870s, in which the renaissance of
Kantian theory occurred, meant that one perceived in it above all its
opposition to ordinary empiricism without properly emphasising that in
fact, in respect of the *practice* of understanding, it did not depart that far
from empiricism'.[145]

Instead of postulating the dualism of empirical perception on the one
hand and necessary mathematical and logical judgements on the other,
Simmel thus described these as the two poles of possible experience: pure
perception as its lowest limit and pure understanding as its highest limit.
All judgements of experience occur within these limits, being in fact
mixtures of perception and understanding in different proportions.[146]
There is, then, no dichotomous distinction between valid objective experience and sensual perception. Valid objective experience means merely the
guarantee of the repetition of sensual perception for everyone and at all
times.[147]

---

[141] GSG 9, p. 85.   [142] GSG 9, p. 180.   [143] GSG 9, p. 182.
[144] Gideon Freudenthal, '"Substanzbegriff und Funktionsbegriff" als Zivilisationstheorie bei Georg
Simmel und Ernst Cassirer', in L. Bauer and K. Hamberger (eds.), *Gesellschaft denken: Eine
erkenntnistheoretische Standortbestimmung der Sozialwissenschaften* (Vienna: Springer, 2002), pp.
251–276.
[145] *Kant*, GSG 9, p. 56.   [146] GSG 9, p. 55.   [147] GSG 9, pp. 51–52.

This empiricist bias does not, however, place Simmel outside the neo-Kantian tradition. Some other prominent neo-Kantians, especially those with a scientific bent, such as Helmholtz and Riehl, were strongly influenced by empiricism as well. In addition, in Simmel's texts this empiricist side coexists with another motif: considering the mind as an active construction of reality. This motif was characteristic of more stringent currents in neo-Kantianism, represented, for example, by the Marburg School of Cohen and Paul Natorp.

One of the central tasks of the Marburg neo-Kantians was to purge Kantian teaching of any elements of passivity or of receptivity.[148] For if the mind is just a passive perceiver of external reality, then the question – what is reality in itself? – is not eliminated. These thinkers therefore suggested that even time and space (i.e. those a priori forms which, according to Kant, are perceived intuitively and not conceptually) are nothing other than functions of the active mind itself. This is exactly the line Simmel pursued to its extreme. He described space as an activity of experiencing. According to him, it would be false to say that we exist in space. Rather, it is the mind's activity which is spatial. And this is what actually makes space perfectly 'objective': 'Space possesses the entire reality about which one can speak at all within the limits of our knowledge, precisely because it is the form of and condition for our empirical representations.'[149] Similarly, time is 'the form of self-perception, of the knowledge of one's own self'.[150] In other words, as Simmel said in the fourth edition of *Kant* (1918), the essence of Kantian Idealism lay not in the formula 'the world is my representation [*die Welt is meine Vorstellung*], but in the more profound: the world is my [activity of] representing [*die Welt ist mein Vorstellen*]'.[151]

Yet, again, this formula does not presuppose any subjectivism. On the contrary, it bestows complete certainty on our experience. Already in the first edition of *Kant*, Simmel claimed that the Kantian subject 'is definitely not personal, definitely not the "soul"'.[152] Kant succeeds in combining the subjective and the objective into a fully coherent whole: 'After subjectivity and objectivity have thus become for him the [opposite] poles of the world of knowledge, he bends them together again.'[153] Kant's teaching substitutes representations of things for the things themselves. Yet by this 'the world is indeed intellectualised, but not subjectivised'.[154]

---

[148] Paul Natorp, 'Kant und die Marburger Schule', *Kant-Studien* 17, 1912, pp. 193–221.
[149] *Kant*, GSG 9, p. 83.   [150] GSG 9, p. 94.   [151] GSG 9, p. 61.   [152] GSG 9, p. 71.
[153] GSG 9, p. 69.   [154] GSG 9, p. 103.

Later, in the third edition (1913), this point was reinforced by an additional statement: that the relevant conscience in experience is not that of the individual but the unity of conscience as such, which is 'not individual, not force-like [*kraftmäßig*], but is the meaning, the form for the mental coherence of the contents of the world, coherence that resides in the currently active individual, similar to how the logical meaning of a written sentence resides in the material pieces of that sentence'.[155]

Thus, even in his later writings, Simmel continued to follow the initial programme of the neo-Kantian movement in general and of the Marburg scholars in particular: that of removing any remnants of dualism from Kant's epistemology. Whenever he sensed the danger of dualism sneaking back in, he spoke against it. For example, without naming him explicitly, he criticised Vaihinger's interpretation of Kant. In 1911, Vaihinger published *The Philosophy of As If*, in which he argued that human knowledge advances by inventing convenient fictions: mental tools employed to acquire knowledge of reality. A significant portion of the treatise was dedicated to Kant and his usage of the 'as-if' formula.[156] It is to this image of Kant as an 'as-if' philosopher that Simmel replied in his 1913 edition of *Kant*:

> This category of 'as if', introduced by Kant among philosophical methods, was proclaimed as the necessary fiction for human understanding and action, a conscious self-deception, so to speak, which is a stage on the way towards what is theoretically and practically correct. I consider this to be a misconception ... It can appear as fiction only because we are used to attuning our elements of knowledge to the harsh and extraneous alternative: subjective or objective. As a matter of fact, this structure belongs to a third layer which cannot be divided into those two, but is rather a self-sufficient synthetic unity of them.[157]

In Simmel's eyes, the major achievement of Kant's philosophy was to achieve unity out of extreme dualism. This unity had to be guarded.

Another aspect in which Simmel followed the neo-Kantian interpretation was the notion of a priori. Like other neo-Kantians, he considered the idea of the synthetic a priori one of the most important and promising

---

[155] GSG 9, p. 62.

[156] Hans Vaihinger, *Die Philosophie des Als Ob: System der theoretischen, praktischen und religiösen Fiktionen der Menschheit auf Grund eines idealistischen Positivismus* (Berlin: Reuther & Reichard, 1911). On Kant, see pp. 613–733.

[157] *Kant*, GSG 9, p. 25. On the philosophy of 'as if' in Simmel, see also Henry Schemer and David Jary, *Form and Dialectic in Georg Simmel's Sociology: A New Interpretation* (New York: Palgrave Macmillan, 2013), pp. 196–221.

elements of Kantian teaching, and like them he criticised Kant's specific scheme of a priori categories. The history of knowledge, argued Simmel, can be reduced to two contrasting tendencies. One is governed by 'the architectonic instinct', which attempts to reduce all parts of our knowledge to a closed system.[158] The other and more modern tendency, of which the quintessential expression is the theory of evolution, sees the world as an incessant development, an endless line rather than a circle. Kant's view is a surprising mixture of both. On the one hand, he postulates that the world given to our sensual experiences is infinite, and so knowledge of it develops endlessly. On the other hand, this endless development of knowledge is governed by the systematic structure of our mind. The satisfaction of the architectonic inclination is thus achieved not in extraneous reality but within the mind itself, whereas the developmental inclination can satisfy itself in an endless exploration of the world.[159]

According to Simmel, this solution was a stroke of genius; sadly, it became unsatisfactory for the modern mind. There is no reason why the mind's structure itself should remain closed and limited and why the infinite development attributed to the world should not also be attributed to the forms of our knowledge.[160] The system of a priori should become more flexible, developing together with advancing knowledge. It should assign 'to each domain of experience its general norms and forms'.[161] On a number of occasions, Simmel tried to develop new a priori postulates for specific sorts of knowledge himself, such as historical knowledge or social knowledge.[162]

With regard to the origin of the a priori, Simmel also seemed to follow the general neo-Kantian approach, as his suggestions vacillated between the two aforementioned possibilities: that the a priori is determined either by our physiological organisation or by the logic of scientific inquiry. The former position was most explicitly presented in 'On the Relation of the Theory of Selection to Epistemology', an article published in 1895 in *Archiv für systematische Philosophie*, edited by Natorp.[163] Simmel suggested there a synthesis between pragmatism and evolution theory. The truthfulness of our knowledge is based on its usefulness. Usefulness is the primary category. The objection to this view would be that it appears to advocate

---

[158] GSG 5, p. 158.   [159] GSG 9, p. 43.   [160] GSG 9, p. 44.   [161] GSG 5, p. 150.

[162] *Die Probleme der Geschichtsphilosophie: Eine erkenntnistheoretische Studie*, 1st ed. [1892], GSG 2, pp. 304–308. Cf. the second edition (1905) – *The Problems of the Philosophy of History: An Epistemological Essay*, trans. G. Oakes (New York: The Free Press, 1977), pp. 42–51. [GSG 9, pp. 237–248]; 'How Is Society Possible?'.

[163] 'Ueber eine Beziehung der Selectionstheorie zur Erkenntnistheorie', GSG 5, pp. 62–74.

arbitrariness in knowledge: truth is subject to our subjective desires. Yet, in Simmel's view, this is an erroneous objection. The emphasis on usefulness does not need to presuppose subjectivity. In order to explain why this is so, Simmel draws an analogy with Kant's philosophy. The fact that, for Kant, 'space' is not some independent reality but is embedded in the process of intuition itself does not make it any less objective or real. Similarly, the requirement of usefulness does not lead to epistemological chaos. On the contrary, the process of evolution has established for us norms of 'truth' that we recognise as objectively valid and from which we cannot absolve ourselves at our own discretion:

> The dualism between the world as appearance as it logically and theoretic-
> ally exists for us and the world as that reality which responds to our practical
> action is overturned by the fact that those forms of thought which produce
> the world as representation are also determined by the practical actions and
> counteractions that are shaped, in accordance with evolutionary necessities,
> by our mental as well as our physical constitution.[164]

Simmel goes on to suggest that evolutionism can be the postulate of the Kantian worldview. The validity of Kant's system does not originate in abstract logical necessity, he argues, but is rather a result of the evolutionary development of the human race. Our experience today is indeed governed by the limits drawn by Kant. However, this is only because in the course of evolution these specific limits turned out to be the most useful for our existence.

This radical evolutionism is not characteristic of Simmel's thought as a whole. The article emerged from the philosophical explorations of a younger Simmel, and he later partly abandoned the position outlined in it. In *Kant*, he did not venture into the exploration of the biological 'in-itself' of our experience but instead took a rather more standard line. The Kantian a priori is described there not as a product of the biologically conditioned state of the human organism but as an abstraction derived from the practice of existing sciences. Yet this interpretation was no less neo-Kantian, as it seemed similar to the view of Cohen, who argued that the a priori was based on logical necessity.[165]

In any case, be the nuances of Simmel's view of Kant's epistemology what they may, his principal position reflected the line of mainstream neo-

---

[164] GSG 5, p. 74.
[165] On Simmel's interpretation of Kant's epistemology, especially in relation to that of Cohen, see Heinrich Adolf, *Erkenntnistheorie auf dem Weg zur Metaphysik: Interpretation, Modifikation und Überschreitung des Kantischen Apriorikonzepts bei Georg Simmel* (Munich: Herbert Utz, 2002), pp. 59–94.

Kantianism. His interpretation was based on two major ideas. First, there is no irreconcilable dualism in Kant's theory of knowledge. Second, the specific form that this theory takes in Kant's writings is out of date and should be modified in accordance with the state of modern knowledge.

But whatever modifications might be required, it is difficult to overestimate the cultural-philosophical significance of Kant's theory. Kant provides a response to intellectual discrepancies created by the modern age. Before him, early modern thinking was torn between rationalism and sensualism. Pushing both elements to their extremes, Kant managed to create a true synthesis, a true unity. He showed the way to accomplish 'the *unification* of the manifold'.[166] Simmel might have had reservations about some details in Kant's worldview, but, especially in his younger years, he considered Kant's philosophy in general as *the* outline for the philosophy of modernity and his method of thinking (even when used in a very non-Kantian way in the context of the theory of evolution) as *the* way to find unity in variety.

Simmel almost never reneged on this appraisal of Kant's *theory of experience*. Although doubts about Kant's epistemology crept into the 1918 edition of *Kant*, where Simmel suggested that 'at the foundation of a priori . . . there lurks a clandestine scepticism towards life', on the whole he tended to grant Kant his due with regard to this aspect of his philosophy.[167] Yet in the late 1890s Simmel began to modify his reading of other aspects of Kant's teaching, sounding more sceptical about whether the Kantian kind of 'unity in variety' was sufficiently encompassing to provide a comprehensive response to modern disunity. At that point, Simmel's interpretation of Kant began to diverge from that of many of his fellow neo-Kantians. In order to show in what way Simmel differed from the other neo-Kantians, I will first outline some developments which occurred in neo-Kantianism from the 1880s onwards.

In the 1880s, one could detect a certain redirection of attention by many neo-Kantians from critical philosophy towards ethics, driven by the hope of developing a positive worldview on the basis of Kant's teaching. The entire Kantian system began to be perceived as directed towards questions of morality, and this perception found support in the Kantian formula of 'the primacy of practical reason'.[168] Already in 1877, Cohen referred to ethics as the safe ground to which experience steers

---

[166] Cf. *Kant*, GSG 9, p. 65.   [167] GSG 9, p. 39.

[168] See the chapter 'On the Primacy of Pure Practical Reason and Its Connection with Speculative Reason', in Immanuel Kant, *Critique of Practical Reason*, in *Practical Philosophy*, trans. M. J. Gregor (Cambridge: Cambridge University Press, 1996), pp. 236–238.

itself as its last anchor[169] and in 1881 Friedrich Paulsen, in his essay 'What Can Kant Be to Us?', assigned to Kant a crucial moral-cultural significance. He argued that during the preceding decades the German nation had lost its unifying idea and expressed the hope that a future philosophy built on Kantian foundations would restore the unity of the national ideal and thus lead the nation. The questions to be dealt with, however, did not pertain to epistemology but to faith and morality.[170]

It is sometimes believed that the main point of difference between the two most famous schools of neo-Kantianism – the Marburg School represented by Cohen and Natorp and the Southwest (Baden) School represented by Windelband and Rickert – is the weight assigned to different aspects of Kant's philosophy; that while the latter attributed greater significance to questions of value and morality, the former focused on Kant's logic and its role in the foundation of the natural sciences. This account cannot be considered satisfactory and it has, in fact, been challenged by commentators.[171] Neither school posited a sharp dichotomy: ethics or knowledge. Cohen and Natorp professed a keen interest in moral philosophy and in practical issues arising from it, while Windelband and Rickert paid serious attention to general epistemological questions (they used the terms 'norm' and 'value' as meta-concepts governing every aspect of Kant's philosophy – epistemology no less than morality).[172]

A gradual shift towards an exploration of the foundations of Kantian ethics took place in both schools. The major difference seems to lie rather in the way they addressed the new questions that arose as a result of their growing attention to ethics. As I pointed out earlier, neo-Kantianism was driven by the hope of forming an integrated worldview in the condition of diversified modernity. This hope underlay the aspiration of the early generations of neo-Kantians: to remove incoherencies from Kant's epistemology. The same search for unity and certainty in the condition of diversity initially triggered the cultural-ethical pursuits of the following generations.

But the peculiarity of Kant's ethics and the neo-Kantian diagnosis of the modern cultural situation presented a new set of problems. First, Kant's practical philosophy was intimately connected with the notion of freedom,

---

[169] Hermann Cohen, *Kants Begründung der Ethik* (Berlin: Ferd. Dümmler, 1877), p. 271.

[170] Friedrich Paulsen, 'Was uns Kant sein kann?', *Vierteljahrsschrift für wissenschaftliche Philosophie* 5(1), 1881, pp. 1–96.

[171] E.g. Thomas E. Willey, *Back to Kant: The Revival of Kantianism in German Social and Historical Thought, 1860–1914* (Detroit: Wayne State University Press, 1978), p. 132.

[172] E.g. Wilhelm Windelband, 'Immanuel Kant: Zur Säkularfeier seiner Philosophie', in *Präludien*, vol. I, pp. 112–146.

which belonged to the 'noumenal' world, to the realm of the 'thing-in-itself'. To dismiss the 'thing-in-itself' in this respect was much more difficult than in the context of Kant's theory of knowledge. Dualism threatened to return.

Second, the emphasis on ethics highlighted the problem of the relationship between the field of ethics and the field of knowledge, and consequently the even broader problem of how different fields in Kant's philosophy relate to each other. To find a unified system in Kant's *Critique of Pure Reason* was easy. But was it possible to envision a unified worldview encompassing all three *Critiques*? The three spheres outlined in them – knowledge, action, non-reflective judgement – seemed to be independent, each governed by its own set of postulates. And thus, even if earlier neo-Kantians had managed to correct the epistemological dualism of Kant, there remained the problem of the pluralism of the forms of experience. Plurality of cultural forms and the question of the possibility of achieving unity out of *this* plurality became, then, the central question of neo-Kantianism.

As I see it, the main difference between the Marburg and Southwest Schools lies in the way they addressed this problem. The two schools differed on the question of to what extent, if at all, is it possible to contemplate unity in the condition of the variety of cultural spheres? The Marburg scholars' answer tended to be 'optimistic'. Cohen, for example, argued as follows: '*Culture is unified* [*einheitlich*] because it is possible, even necessary, to discover in it a unified law on the basis of a unified methodology. This is the task of systematic philosophy: to make culture unified in what is really its methodological lawfulness.'[173] Once a student of Lazarus, Cohen even in his old age adhered to the classical *Bildung* optimism.

This was, of course, an extreme statement; the philosophical position of the Marburg scholars was more nuanced, and their relative optimism regarding the possibility of unity was due to the fact that their criteria for it became less stringent in the course of time and involved an open-ended logic which did not require a closed totality.[174] Still, it is not philosophical nuances which concern us here but the public language of the two intellectual movements. It is significant that Cohen was still writing like this at a time when such language was already unimaginable for Southwesterners,

---

[173] Hermann Cohen, *Ästhetik des reinen Gefühls* (Berlin: Bruno Cassirer, 1912), vol. I, p. 18.
[174] Cf. Jakob Gordin, *Untersuchungen zur Theorie des unendlichen Urteils* (Berlin: Akademie Verlag, 1929), pp. 94–100, 114, 132–133.

who gradually adopted a rather pessimistic discourse on the issue. If in 1881 Windelband was able to suggest that all spheres of experience could be subsumed under the concept of 'rule',[175] and if a decade later Rickert could still claim that the concept of 'ought' was the governing category, the end of every judgement and therefore of knowledge,[176] then in their later publications these two authors admitted that even if something unifies different cultural spheres, it belongs either to the transcendent realm unknown in principle or is discoverable only in a very distant future.[177] Windelband and his followers doubted, therefore, whether modern culture could be integrated into a unified whole. They introduced a degree of cultural 'pessimism' into neo-Kantianism.

The Marburg and Southwest Schools thus symbolise two diverse approaches to the question of cultural integration within neo-Kantian discourse. Yet these approaches did not carry equal weight in neo-Kantianism understood as a cultural movement. Current studies of the field pay much attention to the ideas of the Marburg neo-Kantians. Yet, historically speaking, their cultural role was relatively marginal. Hermann Cohen enjoyed the reputation of a great Kant commentator, but his role as a public intellectual was limited mainly to the Jewish audience. Moreover, politically, Cohen and Natorp were adepts of a certain kind of 'idealistic' socialism, which put them far to the left of the political mainstream but did not endear them to orthodox Social Democrats who were committed, at least in rhetoric, to Marxist 'materialism'. The ideas of Marburg scholars may have influenced a number of prominent figures on the left, such as 'revisionist' leader Eduard Bernstein, but this influence was indirect and, in any case, what Marburg scholars were saying on the subject of the unity of culture remained off the mainstream public radar. Ernst Cassirer, a younger Marburg scholar, played a significant role as a public intellectual, but with regard to the notion of the variety of cultural spheres he tended to adopt a pluralistic tone more reminiscent of Rickert than of Cohen.

Now, whereas the Marburg philosophers were known and respected as scholars rather than intellectuals, the story of the Southwest School seems to be the exact opposite. In the field of Kant commentary they wrote nothing comparable in scope to Cohen's works (unless one counts Windelband's teacher, Kuno Fischer, who published his commentary on

---

[175] Windelband, 'Immanuel Kant'.

[176] Heinrich Rickert, *Der Gegenstand der Erkenntnis: Ein Beitrag zum Problem der philosophischen Transcendenz* (Freiburg im Breisgau: J. C. B. Mohr, 1892), pp. 66–67.

[177] Wilhelm Windelband, 'Kulturphilosophie und transzendentaler Idealismus', *Logos* 1, 1910/1911, pp. 186–196; Heinrich Rickert, *Kant als Philosoph der modernen Kultur* (Tübingen: J. C. B. Mohr, 1924).

Kant in the 1860s).[178] But they were much more vocal in their role as public intellectuals, setting the tone in debates on the state of modern culture. As a cultural phenomenon, therefore, neo-Kantianism as a whole began to be associated with the specific position taken by Windelband and his followers. They emphasised above all the idea of the radical plurality of cultural spheres in the modern world, believing that the role of philosophy was to theorise the axiological postulates of these spheres.

But what was the role of Kant in this story? We have seen that neo-Kantians initially perceived Kant as the guide to the integration of the modern mind. But now, as the focus of attention moved towards the issue of the pluralism of cultural spheres, Southwest neo-Kantians moved away from this ideal. At the same time, though, they were not prepared to break with Kant. They carried him with them as far as they could, presenting him as the source of their pluralism, although admitting that the historical Kant may not have been as radical as they.[179] The neo-Kantian reading of Kant which began with Kant as a great unifier thus turned into a perception of Kant as a codifier of plurality. And it is in the context of this general change that we should now examine what happened to Simmel's interpretation of Kant.

Initially Simmel regarded Kant's practical philosophy as the basis for solving the dilemmas of the modern age. In the essay 'What Is Kant to Us?' (1896), he argued that Kant laid out presuppositions for the truly empirical science of ethics, which could produce an antidote to the prevailing scepticism.[180] In his appraisal of Kant's ethics, Simmel did not differ from many other neo-Kantians. Indeed, the title of the essay was reminiscent of Paulsen's essay from 1881.[181] Paulsen might be slightly suspicious of the term 'empirical'. Many neo-Kantians believed that 'empiricism' was just a euphemism evoked to conceal overall nihilism. Yet they would have hardly disagreed with the main message of Simmel's essay, according to which Kant was the founding father of the kind of morality that was able to rebuff modern scepticism.

Simmel's initial view of Kant's ethics paralleled his view of Kant's epistemology: just as Kant's epistemology established the principles of

---

[178] Kuno Fischer, *Geschichte der neuen Philosophie*, vols. 3–4, 2nd ed. (Heidelberg: Friedrich Bassermann, 1869).

[179] Wilhelm Windelband, 'Nach hundert Jahren', *Kant-Studien* 9, 1904, pp. 5–20.

[180] 'Was ist uns Kant?', GSG 5, pp. 170, 173. Scattered references to Kant's moral philosophy also appear in many of Simmel's earlier publications, but there his main aim is to develop his own approach to ethics rather than provide a coherent interpretation of Kant's ethics.

[181] Paulsen, 'Was uns Kant sein kann?'.

our knowledge, his ethics established the principles of moral judgement and conduct. In both cases, the solution is achieved by creating a great synthesis from two contradictory tendencies. In respect of epistemology, the two tendencies were rationalism and sensualism. Analogously, 'Kant's moral teaching is a curious attempt to decide between social and individualistic tendencies.'[182] The synthesis between the two is achieved by means of the categorical imperative that requires us to act in such a way that would enable our actions to become a universal law. And 'here is the point where the Kantian formula links the complete individualisation of action with its complete socialisation'.[183] On the one hand, an action must be completely free; that is, it must come from the depths of one's own personality, from the determination of one's will. On the other hand, this self-determination is supposed to follow the broadest principles of social welfare. Therefore the apparent dualism between the personal and the social is abolished. To be part of social collectivity and at the same time a free individual is in fact one and the same thing. This approach also conformed perfectly to Simmel's own theory of the simultaneous progress of individuality and sociality, as was outlined in *On Social Differentiation*.

Simmel admitted, though, that there appeared to be another dualism within Kant's moral teaching: that between the quest for happiness and the requirements of duty. Kant denied any possibility of reconciliation between the two in this world. By depriving us of this, 'he caused a rift in the world of ideals which runs right through the middle of the human heart'.[184] But even here dualism was not Kant's last word. The possibility of reconciliation was implied in his view of God and immortality, so that dualism could be overcome by the unity of a higher order, at least hypothetically.[185]

Thus, according to Simmel, the task of Kant's moral philosophy was analogous to that of his theory of knowledge: to show the way to overcome modern dualism and reach coherent unity. An integrated worldview is achieved within both the sphere of action and the sphere of thought. But what about their relation to each other? Does the perfect unity characterising each of these spheres separately also exist when they are considered together? And if they are part of the same unity, do they both enjoy equal status or does one of them have primacy over the other (e.g. does practical reason have primacy over theoretical reason, as many neo-Kantians claimed)?

---

[182] 'Was ist uns Kant?', GSG 5, p. 160.   [183] GSG 5, p. 160.   [184] GSG 5, p. 172.
[185] GSG 5, pp. 174–177.

Simmel occasionally touched on this question in his early writings. Sometimes he appeared to think that the two spheres were fully independent of one another. For example, in the *Introduction to Moral Sciences* (1892), where he advocated the autonomous standing of the category of 'ought', he argued that

> the Kantian assertion that [moral will] is practical reason, and that it is 'in the end one and the same reason' which operates in understanding and in practice, was the expression and is still the cause of countless obscurities and errors. I cannot see at all what the act of will of renouncing my advantage for the sake of that of another person or of a collectivity has in common with the ability to draw a conclusion from certain premises, unless one extends the notion of the reason common to them to that of consciousness or of the soul in general whereby, however, this connection loses any specific sense.[186]

On other occasions, like in the aforementioned essay on knowledge and the theory of selection, he suggested that there is a sort of connection between the two spheres and that primacy belongs to practice: truth appears to be a function of practical usefulness.[187]

Yet generally the question of the relationship between the sphere of knowledge and the sphere of action in Kant's philosophy did not bother Simmel too much in his early writings. He seemed to be satisfied enough with the manner in which the paths to unity *within* the realm of scientific knowledge and *within* that of moral conduct were outlined, and this was everything he needed at that time. His own philosophical position was that the two spheres were mutually irrelevant, and therefore, he did not envisage a grand system encompassing the two.

It is with regard to this issue that Simmel's attitude underwent an important change when he later developed an interpretation which put him at odds with the neo-Kantian one. He did this in *Kant*, arguing there that Kant's thought *as a whole* is characterised by a unified disposition, that the inner unity found within each sphere of Kant's thought also exists between the spheres and that in this unified worldview the theoretical attitude appears to be primary and all the rest derivative.

This interpretation was of the utmost importance to Simmel and he presented it in many places in the book. Already at the beginning he criticised the tendency, as it were, to regard 'will' rather than 'thought' as the central interest of the Kantian system. This view was erroneous because 'Kant and his system are fully intellectualistic; his interest ... is to prove

[186] *Einleitung in die Moralwissenschaft: Eine Kritik der ethischen Grundbegriffe*, GSG 3, p. 104.
[187] 'Ueber eine Beziehung der Selectionstheorie zur Erkenntnistheorie', GSG 5, pp. 62–74.

that the norms valid for *thinking* are valid in *all* spheres of life.'[188] In another chapter, Simmel claimed that 'the modern tendency to adjust or subordinate knowledge itself to other ruling powers in life is completely foreign to Kant'.[189] The famous primacy of practical reason means little. And if one still had any doubts, Simmel decided to be utterly provocative:

> The Kantian 'primacy of practical reason' over the theoretical – the legitim-isation of the theoretically unprovable ideas of God, freedom and immor-tality because of ethical needs – has often been greatly exaggerated in respect of its significance for the image of life. Yet it means nothing more than that science, itself not knowing what to do with a couple of concepts, leaves them to the practical need to give them shape, thus making sure that this practical need never interferes in its own affairs. To call this a primacy of practical reason was not a very happy choice of words.[190]

The primacy of practical reason was thus reduced by Simmel to 'a couple' of concepts relegated to practice, as if they were a cookie given by parents to an obnoxious child to shut him up.

The primacy of intellect over will in Kant was demonstrated through the analysis of his justification of the categorical imperative. Simmel posited the question of why, according to Kant, was it inherently impossible to wish that certain actions were a universal norm? Why was it impossible to wish that stealing or lying became a general law of conduct? Simmel claimed that two divergent answers could be found in Kant, even if Kant himself had not always clearly differentiated between them. One answer was based on the notion of one's own interest: when hurting others, one cannot really want the others to behave similarly towards oneself. Simmel considered this answer inadequate and incomprehensible, reproaching Kant for 'ethical pettiness [*Kleinlichkeit*]'.[191] Kant must never have been able to imagine a strong rebellious character bent on suppressing others who at the same time would be prepared to submit to someone stronger than he. Similarly, Kant did not seem to realise that the most altruistic natures are precisely those who, while always being ready to sacrifice themselves for the sake of others, would never want anyone else to behave like them in similar situations.

However, there was another answer in Kant which was based not on considerations of interest but on those of logic. It is inherently impossible to want to universalise certain actions because this would constitute a logical contradiction. For example, to turn 'lying' into a universal law would entail contradiction. To lie is to make a false utterance. A law is also

---

[188] *Kant*, GSG 9, p. 15.   [189] GSG 9, p. 50.   [190] GSG 9, pp. 171–172.   [191] GSG 9, p. 129.

a type of utterance, and according to the general maxim of 'lying' the law prescribing lying would be false too.[192] Such a law would therefore contradict itself.

Unlike in the case of the first argument, Simmel was not sparing in his praise for the second. He called it 'Kant's most important *purely speculative* thought ... it is a truly superb idea that the intellectual coherence, the inwardly logical unity of our actions, constitutes the criterion of their moral value as well'.[193] Simmel claimed that in this argument 'the Kantian intellectualism reveals itself as the ultimate authority of moral decisions too'.[194] This determination of ethics by logic does not abolish Kant's moralism. On the contrary, Kant's intellectualism is the surest foundation of his moralism: 'By morality entering next to it as an absolute value, a difficult dualism of the ultimate principles [*Dualismus des Definitiven*] would have emerged, which Kant solved by allowing the moral norm to be structured by logic.'[195]

Simmel's interpretation of Kant thus reached its logical completeness. Kant's philosophical method, according to him, was based on attaining certainty by means of a radical synthesis of two seemingly opposing tendencies. Long before *Kant*, Simmel had explained the way this synthesis worked separately within the world of knowledge and the world of action. Now it appeared that a similar synthesis occurred in Kant's thought as a whole. On an even higher level of abstraction, Kant's 'intellectualism' seemed to govern both his ethics and his epistemology, regardless of whether both these fields enjoyed full autonomy or whether (as seemed to be implied in Simmel's argument) Kant's philosophy tended towards the primacy of theoretical reason.

Simmel offered this intellectualist reading of Kant in connection with other fields too, even if only in passing, since he focused mainly on epistemology and ethics. Thus, in his discussion of Kant's theory of religion, he argued that Kant, because of intellectualism, 'could not acknowledge religiosity as a unified structure, as a shoot with its own roots'.[196] Rather (said Simmel in 1913), 'religion is to him a sum of theoretical conclusions from morality'.[197] The same intellectualism is found in the field of aesthetics. The mind of the genius, argued Simmel, led Kant to great insights about art and beauty. Yet these insights coexisted with errors which sprang out of Kant's very limited knowledge of true art and his very limited ability for aesthetic feeling. Kant's aesthetic

---

[192] See GSG 9, p. 129.   [193] GSG 9, p. 130.   [194] GSG 9, p. 131.   [195] GSG 9, p. 132.
[196] GSG 9, p. 172.   [197] GSG 9, p. 171.

philosophy, even when true, was constructed not through a positive relation to aesthetic objects 'but instead only indirectly, through the scientifically rational need to delimit with absolute precision the concept of the beautiful versus the sensually agreeable, the true and the morally good'.[198]

This interpretation was unusual in Simmel's time, and this did not remain unnoticed. One critic, for example, claimed that Simmel grasped Kant 'too intellectualistically'.[199] Simmel's interpretation was certainly at odds with the approach of other neo-Kantians, especially the Southwest School. Windelband once said (1881) that the significance of Kant in the history of philosophy consisted in his overcoming the entire philosophical tradition that had preceded him with its roots in ancient Greece. Greek civilisation, in his view, was characterised by 'intellectualism', and thus Kant's achievement consisted in overcoming Greek intellectualism.[200] Later, Windelband retreated somewhat from this formulation. He spoke about 'reason' (*Vernunft*) as the basis on which Kant built his vision of all spheres,[201] but he used the word 'reason' in an ambiguous and broad sense. It apparently signified for him simply the absence of irrationality, without suggesting any strong 'intellectualistic' connotations in the Simmelian sense.

From a certain perspective, Simmel's position can be seen as being close to that of the Marburg School. Marburg scholars envisioned a narrower distance between different parts of Kant's philosophy and placed greater emphasis on the guiding role of logic. But Simmel differed from them in at least two important respects. First, unlike Cohen, he did not play with the idea of the primacy of practical reason. At most he assigned to each sphere an equal standing, placing logic above them all, and on many occasions he sounded as if he put the sphere of knowledge above those of ethics and aesthetics. He even seemed to suggest at one point that Kant's theory of knowledge was the only truly satisfactory part of his teaching.[202]

Second, and crucially, Kant's coherence and intellectualism were, for Simmel, a reason for reproach rather than praise. Precisely because Kant's worldview was intellectualistic, it became inadequate for the present day. The unity it entailed was one-sided, not comprehensive. This fully coherent intellectualism was not competent to deal with the true variety of modern experience.

---

[198] GSG 9, p. 210.
[199] Otto Braun, 'Review of M. Kronenberg, *Geschichte des deutschen Idealismus*', *Kant-Studien* 22, 1918, p. 150.
[200] Windelband, 'Immanuel Kant', p. 118.   [201] Windelband, 'Nach hundert Jahren', p. 9.
[202] *Kant*, GSG 9, p. 77.

Here we come to the essence of Simmel's change in attitude. The young Simmel believed that Kant's philosophy was a peculiar mixture of coherence and open-endedness. It was coherent enough to serve as a basis for a unified worldview and open-ended enough to enable the adjustment of this worldview to new conditions. The principles of Kant's worldview were, in fact, the *only* satisfactory ones for the purpose of forming unity out of modern variety; this was true both of epistemology and of ethics.

In later years, however, Simmel began to regard Kant's worldview as outdated. He still considered Kant's theory of knowledge as fairly adequate,[203] but he questioned Kant's ethics, arguing that the intellectualism in it went far beyond its proper limits. The sphere of ethics belongs to life, he protested, and the norms of life cannot be reduced to the lifeless formulae of thought. In the 1913 edition of *Kant*, Simmel added the following statement:

> Modern pragmatism, whatever else one may think about it, has at least seen that the limitations of the critique of reason and of the entire intellectualism lie in this: that knowledge, even if it is the Kantian enthronement of the empirical, cannot protect itself by itself when the question of legitimacy is addressed to experience, and hence it is only within the total structure of life that one should seek the other elements that provide such legitimisation.[204]

It was, of course, Simmel himself who almost two decades earlier (1895) had brought up Kantian theory in the context of pragmatism.[205] As we have seen, in that early article Simmel argued that the truth of experience was dependent on the process of our biological evolution. Yet he did not think that this would make Kant's worldview inadequate. On the contrary, he attempted to integrate Kant's philosophy into the general framework of pragmatist philosophy. Later, however, the gap between pragmatism and Kant became clear to him, as Kant was becoming more and more intellectualistic for him, and 'life' more and more non-reflective.

This led Simmel to realise that Kant's philosophy could not be modified or improved, and that it should rather be abandoned. This realisation initially developed into a peculiar philosophical standpoint which to a great extent can be identified as neo-Kantian, as it included a distinctively neo-Kantian emphasis on the variety of the forms of experience, each governed by its own presuppositions. This Simmelian 'neo-Kantianism' was already based on the conscious decision to repudiate

---

[203] Compare 'Was ist uns Kant?', GSG 5, pp. 158–159 with *Kant*, GSG 9, pp. 42–44.
[204] *Kant*, GSG 9, p. 50.
[205] 'Ueber eine Beziehung der Selectionstheorie zur Erkenntnistheorie', GSG 5, pp. 62–74.

Kant, something that other neo-Kantians were not prepared to do, or at
least admit to.

Subsequently, Simmel added to this 'neo-Kantian' critique a more
radical one. Beyond the neo-Kantian variety, he postulated a synthesis of
another order to be based not on reason (like in Kant) but on 'life'. In the
fourth, 1918 edition of *Kant*, he summed up the two alternatives (the
Kantian and his own) in the following way: 'The *whole intellect* knows –
this was the Kantian overcoming of rationalism and sensualism. And now
this gets higher and broader: the *whole human being* knows.'[206] The author
of this synthesis, according to Simmel, was Goethe. One can also hear in
the expression 'the whole man' overtones from Wilhelm Dilthey. In the
Introduction to Human Sciences (1883), Dilthey protested the exaggerated
intellectualism of Locke, Hume and Kant, who, he alleged, constructed the
knowing subject but forgot to pour blood into its veins. Instead, there is
only 'the diluted extract of reason as a mere activity of thought'.[207] Dilthey
argued that true human sciences should be based on the whole human
being. It was Dilthey who formulated the idea of living experience
(*Erlebnis*) as the integrating moment in culture. Towards the end of his
life, Simmel adopted many elements from this notion of *Erlebnis*.

Indeed, the motif of life, or experience, in its integrating function began
to appear in Simmel's writings long before. Already in 1899, as he grew
disillusioned with Kant, he suggested in one of his publications that
Goethe could be seen as a more satisfactory alternative.[208] But the peculiarities of this alternative were then still unclear to Simmel. It would take
time until he came back and offered a comprehensive analysis of Goethe's
life-view. Meanwhile – during the first decade of the twentieth century –
Simmel became more and more sceptical regarding the very possibility of
attaining encompassing unity. It is to an analysis of this period in his
thought that I now turn.

---

[206] *Kant*, GSG 9, p. 28.
[207] Wilhelm Dilthey, *Einleitung in die Geisteswissenschaften: Versuch einer Grundlegung für das Studium
    der Gesellschaft und der Geschichte* (Berlin: Duncker & Humblot, 1883), p. xvii.
[208] 'Kant und Goethe', GSG 5, pp. 445–478.

CHAPTER 3

Unity versus Variety

In the previous chapter, I described the cultural ideals of the young Simmel in terms of the classical *Bildung* model of unity in variety. This model could be applied on two levels: that of the cultivation of the multi-faceted self into a harmonious unity and that of attaining the harmony of an individual with the manifoldness of the outward world.

That the notions of self-cultivation and harmonisation were a central moment in the imagination of the young Simmel often escapes notice, for in his early writings they are not presented in the languages in which the *Bildung* ideal was usually expressed: neo-humanistic art and classical Idealist philosophy. Playing in tune with his own times, Simmel spoke the languages that would have seemed foreign to Goethe or Wilhelm von Humboldt: those of sociological positivism and neo-Kantianism. But as I have tried to show, by means of these languages he expressed the classical longing for unity, searching for the keys that open the gates to the totality of the world. One such key was provided by attachment to society. Society reconciled everything and subsumed everything under itself. Art, religion, law were just different idioms in which social life expressed itself. The other key was Kantian philosophy that brought about the fusion of the multiplicities of the world of representation into an ultimate coherent worldview.

Now, it is this ideal that began to disintegrate in Simmel towards the end of the 1890s. Simmel came to realise that society was not everything, and that sociological reductionism was actually false. There will always remain something untouched by social life and its values, which is, however, valuable for human life as such. And there will always remain something in itself beyond the neo-Kantian world of pure representation, which Kantian philosophy, as he took it, had no means to account for.

This realisation, however, did not cause Simmel to abandon the search for unity altogether. On the contrary, once unity revealed itself as a much more difficult ideal to attain, Simmel became even more obsessed with it in his writings. He was certainly not prepared to let it go, especially when it started to look illusory.

In respect of contemplating unity in the condition of variety, Simmel's writings of the middle period follow a common pattern, which is characterised by an attempt to retreat into inwardness and envision the possibilities of forming a unified cultural world untouched by the ills of exterior fragmentation. Such a world would act on the level of personal culture as a symbol of comprehensive unity. Its unity would be a unity in miniature, a microcosmic copy of the macrocosmic harmony. This subjective unity would still appear harmonious but at the price of giving up a great measure of complexity and variety. Rather than absorbing the world with its manifoldness, unity would stand outside it and be opposed to it, protecting itself against chaotic variety. This is the true significance of what is often described in scholarly literature as Simmel's subjectivist turn.[1]

3.1   Schopenhauer and Nietzsche

The clearest sign of this turn was Simmel's growing interest in Schopenhauer and Nietzsche, on both of whom he published a book three years after *Kant*.[2] Not accidently, it is in respect of Schopenhauer that Simmel first defined philosophy as 'a temperament, seen through a worldview'.[3] To say that philosophy is a temperament already meant to renege on the ideal of an ultimate philosophical truth. Different temperaments produce different but equally valid and comprehensive images of the world. For the young Simmel, Kant was the ultimate philosopher. Now he

---

[1] E.g. Klaus Lichtblau, *Georg Simmel* (Frankfurt am Main: Campus, 1997), p. 81.

[2] *Schopenhauer und Nietzsche: Ein Vortragszyklus*, GSG 10, pp. 167–408. It is dated 1907 but appeared already at the end of 1906.

[3] GSG 10, p. 190. On Simmel's interpretation of Schopenahuer and Nietzsche, see Klaus Lichtblau, 'Das "Pathos der Distanz": Präliminarien zur Nietzsche-Rezeption bei Georg Simmel', in H.-J. Dahme and O. Rammstedt (eds.), *Georg Simmel und die Moderne* (Frankfurt am Main: Suhrkamp, 1984), pp. 231–281; Uwe Justus Wenzel, 'Unter Null: Simmel, Nietzsche, Schopenhauer, Kant und die "ewige Wiederkehr"', *Neue Rundschau* 111(1), 2000, pp. 43–46. Dirk Solies, 'Ist Simmel ein Schopenhauerianer?', in F. Ciracì, D. M. Fazio and M. Koßler (eds.), *Schopenhauer und Schopenhauer-Schule* (Würzburg: Königshausen & Neumann, 2009), pp. 327–333; Davide Ruggieri, *Il conflitto della società moderna: la ricezione del pensiero di Arthur Schopenhauer nell'opera di Georg Simmel (1887–1918)* (Lecce: Pensa multimedia, 2010); Dominika Partyga, 'Simmel's Reading of Nietzsche: The Promise of "Philosophical Sociology"', *Journal of Classical Sociology* 16(4), 2016, pp. 414–437; Roger Häußling, 'Nietzsche, Friedrich', in H.-P. Müller and T. Reitz (eds.), *Simmel-Handbuch: Begriffe, Hauptwerke, Aktualität* (Frankfurt am Main: Suhrkamp, 2018), pp. 398–405; Denis Thouard, 'Schopenhauer, Arthur', in ibid., pp. 503–508.

became just one thinker among many, on par with Schopenhauer or Nietzsche.[4]

It is not accidental either that *Schopenhauer and Nietzsche* appears to be a more personal, 'subjective' book, where, in contrast to *Kant*, Simmel conducted his own philosophical dialogue with the two writers, thus adding to it his own philosophical temperament. His preoccupation with Schopenhauer and Nietzsche was an explicit preoccupation with the questions that troubled him personally, the central one being the problem of retaining harmonious unity. The book's first chapter focused on this problem.

There Simmel argued that Schopenhauer and Nietzsche represented two different responses to the cultural condition of modernity characterised by lack of unity. He specifically emphasised one aspect of this condition: the conflict of ends and means.[5] According to Simmel, the discontent of modern civilisation springs from the feature that can be found in every advanced civilisation: its immense complexity. The ultimate goals of human life in a complex civilisation become increasingly more distant, and the way to them becomes more circuitous. Life in such a civilisation therefore becomes overwhelmed by technique, that is, by doing things which are perceived as means towards ends, and when these ends are realised, they immediately turn into simply other means for a farther end, so that sight of the final purpose is completely lost: 'The higher man is civilised, the more indirect a being he is.'[6] This domination of means over ends in modern civilisation generates both the feeling that life has lost its purpose and a longing for the perfect unity to redeem man from this purposeless existence. This longing is the inheritance of Christianity to the modern mind that, however, lost its belief in the purposes that Christianity once postulated: the salvation of the soul and the entrance into God's kingdom.[7]

This is the stage at which Schopenhauer and Nietzsche found the modern man. Both addressed in their philosophies the fundamental problem of purposelessness longing for purpose, both diagnosed it in similar terms, but each of the two displayed a different attitude towards it. For

---

[4] 'On the Nature of Philosophy', trans. R. H. Weingartner, in Kurt H. Wolff (ed.), *Essays on Sociology, Philosophy and Aesthetics* (New York: Harper & Row, 1959), p. 284. [*Hauptprobleme der Philosophie*, GSG 14, p. 15.]

[5] On the emancipation of means from ends as one aspect of estrangement in modern culture, see Willfried Geßner, *Der Schatz im Acker: Georg Simmels Philosophie der Kultur* (Weilerswist: Velbrück Wissenschaft, 2003), pp. 158–164.

[6] *Schopenhauer und Nietzsche*, GSG 10, p. 176.   [7] GSG 10, pp. 177–178.

Schopenhauer, the final purpose was merely an illusion. The world for him was 'will', a constant striving that has no real object to which it can attach itself and that can never be satisfied. Schopenhauer the pessimist believed therefore that salvation lay in the abnegation of all striving.

Nietzsche too accepted that an extraneous purpose was an illusion. However, being less of a metaphysician and more of a moralist, and also influenced by Darwin's teaching, he focused specifically on human life (rather than on that of the universe) and claimed that it could still be redeemed if, instead of looking for an external purpose, it made its own development and self-overcoming into its purpose.[8] Simmel regarded Nietzsche as representative of the most radical affirmation of life, attributing to him 'immense optimism'.[9] Nietzsche, he argued, taught the modern mind to console itself through the belief that the inner energies of life continuously pushing it forward are valuable as such. For this reason, in the controversy between Nietzsche and Schopenhauer 'modern man's sympathies will lie with Nietzsche'.[10]

This approach made some of Simmel's contemporaries and more recent commentators see in his turn to Nietzsche a symptom of his general turn towards the philosophy of life that dominated his later period.[11] This would, however, distort the overall significance of Nietzsche for Simmel and his intellectual development. Of course, some elements of Simmel's interpretation of Nietzsche later found their place in Simmel's life-philosophical vocabulary. For example, it is in *Schopenhauer and Nietzsche* that Simmel introduced the notion of 'more-life' that would later play a prominent role in his last treatise *The View of Life* (1918).[12] But on the whole, Nietzsche's impact on Simmel recedes during the later period. The figures from whom Simmel derived his life-philosophy were Bergson, Goethe and Rembrandt. Nietzsche was mentioned rarely and often with critical intentions.[13] And when Simmel occasionally adopted a Nietzschean air, such, for example, as in the essay 'Become What You

---

[8] GSG 10, pp. 178–180.   [9] GSG 10, p. 182.   [10] GSG 10, p. 188.

[11] E.g. Karl Joël, 'Erinnerungen an Simmel', in K. Gassen and M. Landmann (eds.), *Buch des Dankes an Georg Simmel* (Berlin: Duncker & Humblot, 1958), pp. 166–169; Helmut Loiskandl, Deena Weinstein and Michael Weinstein, 'Introduction', in G. Simmel, *Schopenhauer and Nietzsche* (Amherst, NY: University of Chicago Press, 1986), p. xxix.

[12] *Schopenhauer und Nietzsche*, GSG 10, p. 180. See *The View of Life: Four Metaphysical Essays with Journal Aphorisms*, trans. J. A. Y. Andrews and D. N. Levine (Chicago: University of Chicago Press, 2010), pp. 1–17. [GSG 16, pp. 212–235.]

[13] Cf. 'The Dialectic of the German Spirit', trans. A. Harrington, *Theory, Culture & Society* 24(7–8), 2007, p. 65. [GSG 13, p. 229.]

Are' (1915), this was in order to abandon for a while his quest for encompassing totality which lay at the basis of his life-philosophy.[14]

For Nietzsche was in Simmel's eyes a philosopher of plurality rather than unity. He taught Simmel the possibility of the coexistence of conflicting values without any higher unity. And since Simmel came close to espousing this view during his middle period, it is not surprising that almost all of Simmel's publications on Nietzsche (and Schopenhauer) are dated between the years 1896 and 1911, which roughly corresponds to that period.[15] Simmel's emphasis on Nietzsche's life-affirmation is less related to his subsequent life-philosophy but should be understood in the context of his critique of Schopenhauer's pessimism.[16] This pessimism was strongly related to Schopenhauer's view of the world of representation as the world of plurality, and Simmel's purpose was to overcome the pessimistic attitude towards plurality. To make this point clear, one needs to take a closer look at the story of Simmel's reception of Nietzsche and Schopenhauer and at the context in which it developed.

By the time Simmel was making his first intellectual steps in the 1880s, Schopenhauerian philosophy had been flourishing in Germany for at least two decades. It had an especially great impact on a broad intellectual and artistic public. However, some important mavericks among contemporary philosophers, such as Eduard von Hartmann, Friedrich Nietzsche and Ferdinand Tönnies, also became committed to at least some of its central tenets. The term of recognition for these trends was 'pessimism'.[17] The word itself had already been known for more than a century, but it was

---

[14] "'Become What You Are'", trans. U. Teucher and T. M. Kemple, *Theory, Culture & Society* 24(7–8), 2007, pp. 57–60. [GSG 13, pp. 133–137.] See Chapter 4 of this book for my interpretation of this essay in the context of Simmel's war writings.

[15] Apart from *Schopenhauer and Nietzsche* and two excerpts from it published as separate articles, Simmel's writings on Nietzsche include: 'Elizabeth Försters Nietzsche-Biographie' [1895], GSG 1, pp. 338–346; 'Friedrich Nietzsche: Eine moralphilosophische Silhouette' [1896], GSG 5, pp. 115–129; Review of F. Tönnies, *Der Nietzsche-Kultus* [1897], GSG 1, pp. 400–408; 'Zum Verständnis Nietzsches' [1902], GSG 7, pp. 57–63; 'Nietzsches Moral' [1911], GSG 12, pp. 170–176.

[16] On Simmel and pessimism, see Davide Ruggieri, 'Georg Simmel and the Question of Pessimism: A Sociophilosophical Analysis between "Wertfrage" and "Lebensphilosophie"', *Simmel Studies* 16 (2), 2006, pp. 161–181.

[17] This was probably first used by Lichtenberg in 1776. Only in 1878, however, was it officially accepted by the French Academy. See Michael Pauen, *Pessimismus: Geschichtsphilosophie, Metaphysik und Moderne von Nietzsche bis Spengler* (Berlin: Akademie, 1997), p. 15. On the pessimism controversy in philosophy, see Frederick C. Beiser, *Weltschmerz: Pessimism in German Philosophy, 1860–1900* (Oxford: Oxford University Press, 2016). On pessimism among artists and intellectuals, see Gabriele von Heesen-Cremer, 'Zum Problem des Kulturpessimismus: Schopenhauer-Rezeption bei Künstlern und Intellektuellen von 1871 bis 1918', in E. Mai, S. Waetzoldt and G. Wolandt (eds.), *Ideengeschichte und Kunstwissenschaft: Philosophie und bildende Kunst im Kaiserreich* (Berlin: Gebr. Mann, 1983), pp. 45–70.

Schopenhauer's thought and its philosophical grandeur that proved to be the pivotal factor in its growing respectability. The most notable popular-iser of philosophical pessimism was Eduard von Hartmann (1842–1906), who in his *Philosophy of the Unconscious* (1869) attempted to construct a Schopenhauerian-Hegelian synthesis in the fashionable language of the natural sciences.[18]

To a great degree, pessimism remained the philosophy of institutional outsiders. This does not mean that Schopenhauerian philosophy took on the role of outcast. Even many of those professional philosophers who disagreed with it tended to treat it with respect, and in the second half of the nineteenth century several important monographic studies on Schopenhauer written by professional philosophers were published.[19] On the whole, however, Schopenhauer and his pessimism received a cold shoulder from institutional philosophers. Friedrich Paulsen expressed this attitude well, when he claimed that neither Schopenhauer nor Nietzsche but Jesus of Nazareth was worthy of being an educator![20]

The reason for this was that for Paulsen and many of his colleagues there seemed to be a close connection between pessimism and moral nihilism, despite protestations from such adherents of pessimism as Hartmann and his wife and colleague Agnes Taubert.[21] The defenders of pessimism argued that far from destroying moral ideals, pessimism was the surest foundation which might cause one to seek the good and the beautiful, without expecting any pleasurable effect from those moral activities. Yet to more conventional contemporaries this justification looked suspect, especially given that Hartmann's justifications of pessimism were embedded in scientific and sometimes utilitarian phraseology, according to which the world contained a quantitative surplus of pains over pleasures.[22] This combination of pessimism and utilitarian scientism could be considered inimical to the objective validity of moral ideals.

It was with this background in mind that Simmel joined the debate on pessimism in one of his first publications, dated 1887,[23] and continuously

---

[18] Eduard von Hartmann, *Philosophie des Unbewussten: Versuch einer Weltanschauung* (Berlin: Carl Duncker, 1869); See also his *Zur Geschichte und Begründung des Pessimismus* (Berlin: Carl Duncker, 1880). On Hartmann's 'optimistic pessimism', see Beiser, *Weltschmerz*, pp. 122–161.

[19] Kuno Fischer, *Arthur Schopenhauer* (Heidelberg: C. Winter, 1893); Johannes Volkelt, *Arthur Schopenhauer: Seine Persönlichkeit, seine Lehre, sein Glaube* (Stuttgart: Fr. Frommann, 1900).

[20] Friedrich Paulsen, 'Arthur Schopenhauer' [1882], in *Schopenhauer, Hamlet, Mephistopheles: Drei Aufsätze zur Naturgeschichte des Pessimismus* (Stuttgart: J. G. Cotta, 1911), p. 111.

[21] E.g. A. Taubert, *Der Pessimismus und seine Gegner* (Berlin: Carl Duncker, 1873), p. 145.

[22] Hartmann, *Zur Geschichte und Begründung des Pessimismus*, pp. 65–85.

[23] 'Über die Grundfrage des Pessimismus in methodischer Hinsicht', GSG 2, pp. 9–20.

returned to this subject over the course of the following twenty years.[24] The attitude he adopted towards pessimism was consistently critical. For example, he called Schopenhauer 'the prophet of modern pessimism' and 'the most arrogant writer'.[25] The main target of Simmel's criticism, however, appeared to be Hartmann rather than Schopenhauer, even if he did not mention Hartmann by name, for the pessimistic argument to which Simmel paid most attention was the one framed in the scientific language of the quantitative surplus of pains. Simmel argued, for example, that it was impossible to find a common criterion on the basis of which one could weigh pains against pleasures, for the two categories were not commensurable. Hartmann probably found Simmel's arguments powerful, as he felt the need to respond to them and included a chapter debating Simmel's critique in the second edition of his *Towards a History and Foundation of Pessimism*.[26]

Simmel thus positioned himself from the beginning as a critic of pessimism. Yet his critique was of a different kind than that of mandarins such as Paulsen, who argued in defence of faith, or Windelband, who sought a countermeasure to pessimism in the world of values.[27] In fact, Simmel found himself in a precarious situation. For he too was often suspected by his colleagues of advocating the same kind of moral nihilism for which the adherents of pessimism were reproached. The young Simmel appeared not to believe in the possibility of objective justification of moral ideals. He separated the world of moral obligation from the world of knowledge and denied the latter any prescriptive role, arguing that the task of the science of ethics was merely to elucidate the character of the world of obligation. He already made this position known in 1886[28] and subsequently elaborated upon its premises in the two-volume treatise *Introduction to Moral Sciences* (1892/1893).[29]

---

[24] Other writings on pessimism include: 'Zur Psychologie des Pessimismus' [1888], GSG 17, pp. 223–233; 'Zu einer Theorie des Pessimismus' [1900], GSG 5, pp. 543–551; 'Socialismus und Pessimismus' [1900], GSG 5, pp. 552–559; the fourth chapter of *Schopenhauer and Nietzsche* [1907], GSG 10, pp. 241–268.

[25] 'Zur Psychologie des Pessimismus', GSG 17, p. 230.

[26] Eduard von Hartmann, *Zur Geschichte und Begründung des Pessimismus*, 2nd ed. (Leipzig: Wilhelm Friedrich, 1891), pp. 263–277.

[27] Windelband analysed the phenomenon of pessimism in his speech 'Pessimismus und Wissenschaft' [1876], see Wilhelm Windelband, *Präludien: Aufsätze und Reden zur Einführung in die Philosophie* (Tübingen: J. C. B. Mohr, 1911), vol. 2, pp. 195–220.

[28] Review of H. Steinthal, *Allgemeine Ethik*, GSG 1, pp. 192–210.

[29] *Einleitung in die Moralwissenschaft: Eine Kritik der ethischen Grundbegriffe*, GSG 3–4. On the reception of this work, see Klaus Christian Köhnke, *Der junge Simmel: in Theoriebeziehungen und sozialen Bewegungen* (Frankfurt am Main: Suhrkamp, 1996), pp. 265–284. Interestingly, Paulsen's opinion seems to have been generally unfavourable (ibid., p. 360n).

Therefore, by criticising pessimism, Simmel might have wished to distance himself from any suspicion of moral nihilism. Yet given the kind of approach to ethics he espoused at the time, this critique could not take the form of a defence of 'old-fashioned' moral ideals. The proper way to address pessimism was to understand its causes, adopt what is valuable in it and move forward. Pessimism, according to him, reflected the transitory stage of the mind's work: the stage of negation. The task of negation was to free one's mind towards positive activity. In this regard, the pessimistic attitude, common especially among the young, is of educational value. The danger is, however, that one remains stuck at this stage, and it is especially great in the case of those whose education is half-baked: 'half-educated' (*Halbgebildete*). For 'negation is the form in which even an inferior mind can make judgements about the universality of being, without possessing the scope and power of intellect to judge it positively'.[30] What was therefore needed for overcoming pessimism was a more accomplished *Bildung*.

At some point in the mid-1890s, Simmel found a model for such intellectual development: Nietzsche. After falling under the spell of pessimism in his youth, Nietzsche found the inner resources to move beyond it not via restoring obsolete moral ideals but via absorbing its premises and turning them into a philosophy that affirms life. It was precisely because of this that Nietzsche fit the role of educator denied him by thinkers such as Paulsen. Earnest 'professional thinkers' (*Berufsdenkern*) were unable to take him seriously, but this is because as a true philosopher-educator 'he could do more than be serious'.[31]

That Nietzsche attracted Simmel's attention in those years was hardly surprising. Beginning from around 1890, Nietzsche's popularity grew quickly, and in just a few years a new fashion emerged in artistic circles: the 'Nietzsche cult'.[32] Nietzsche's popularity crossed political and ideological lines. He was admired by rebellious socialists, middle class liberal aesthetes and frustrated nationalists. There was, however, one thing common to all those who made him their new hero: their disenchantment with what they saw as the respectable and at the same time mediocre social and cultural order of the German Empire.

As with Schopenhauer a generation later, many institutional outsiders found Nietzsche attractive. But now the spirit of the times was different: in

---

[30] 'Zur Psychologie des Pessimismus', GSG 17, p. 226.
[31] 'Friedrich Nietzsche: Eine moralphilosophische Silhouette', GSG 5, p. 115.
[32] See Steven Aschheim, *The Nietzsche Legacy in Germany 1890–1990* (Berkeley: University of California Press, 1992), pp. 33–34.

the post-Bismarck German Empire avant-garde and counter-culture voices grew more confident, taking the offensive against a more official culture which in its turn could not ignore the Nietzsche phenomenon. By the late 1890s, the philosophical establishment began to accept Nietzsche as a philosopher. Thus, in 1897 philosopher Alois Riehl published a monograph on Nietzsche's thought.[33] Yet it was Simmel one year earlier who was the first professional philosopher to promote Nietzsche.

In those years, Simmel was not, of course, the authoritative voice of the academic establishment. Still a *Privatdozent*, he was unsure about his own professional future and felt somewhat disillusioned with the university world. He seemed to have been considering changing the course of his life. The idea of turning to artistic activities crossed his mind, and it appears that he even considered joining Elisabeth Förster-Nietzsche in establishing the Nietzsche archive in Weimar.[34] Were this to happen, we would probably hear not of Simmel the philosopher but of Simmel the Nietzsche prophet. But none of this materialised. Simmel stayed in academia and became associate professor in 1900. And although he was not 'respectable' enough for many of his older and high-brow colleagues, for students and the outside public, his recommendation of Nietzsche as a philosopher carried weight.

Simmel was trying to make Nietzsche respectable as a thinker. But what sort of 'respectability' did he bestow on him? This was certainly not the respectability of the kind Förster-Nietzsche would later try to establish: that of bourgeois conservatism with racial overtones. Among those who attributed to Nietzsche a racial vision was the young Heinrich Mann, who claimed in his article 'Towards Understanding Nietzsche' (1896) that Nietzsche's *Übermensch* should be seen as 'a social and a race symbol'[35] and as a new moral ideal 'which issues from the perfection of the race and the species'.[36] Simmel, however, argued in an article with a similar title and contrary views that Nietzsche's aristocratism 'must not be interpreted as a means for the welfare of society' and that it presupposes no 'social aristocracy'. Rather, 'it is an end in itself: the existence of society in general is justified through the formation of the aristocratic man, and not vice versa'.[37] Similarly, Simmel was not attracted to Nietzsche's early, more Germanic writings that had earned him the respect and admiration of

[33] Alois Riehl, *Friedrich Nietzsche: Der Künstler und der Denker* (Stuttgart: Fr. Frommann, 1897).

[34] Otthein Rammstedt, 'On Simmel's Aesthetics: Argumentation in the Journal *Jugend*, 1897–1906', *Theory, Culture & Society* 8(3), 1991, p. 139, n. 4.

[35] Heinrich Mann, 'Zum Verständnisse Nietzsches', *Das Zwanzigste Jahrhundert* 6(9), 1896, p. 246.

[36] Ibid., p. 251.   [37] 'Zum Verständnis Nietzsches', GSG 7, pp. 61–62.

Ferdinand Tönnies. Simmel's Nietzsche was the Nietzsche of *Zarathustra* and other later writings that Tönnies rejected.[38]

Nor was it, however, liberal respectability, which would be in tune with Nietzsche's reception in literary middle-class circles, where emphasis was placed on Nietzsche's advocacy of individual authenticity. Simmel, otherwise sympathetic to the liberal quest for individuality, was plainly aware that Nietzsche did not preach equality, and that his teaching was incompatible with liberalism, which in the end is also 'by all means a social ideal, except that it relies on the freedom of the individual, the accentuation of the individual condition, as a technique to pursue social goals'.[39] Besides, it was clear to Simmel that Nietzsche's 'pathos of distance' presupposed extreme social inequalities for the sake of breeding the highest exemplar of the human species. Therefore, if one wished to focus on the individual qualities of common people, one had to go not to Nietzsche but to poet and mystic Maeterlinck and sculptor Meunier.[40]

It is, rather, two other features that made Nietzsche respectable in Simmel's eyes. First, for Simmel, Nietzsche was not a utopian transformative thinker. He did not postulate any substantive ideal in a distant future to which some revolutionary change should lead, for such an ideal did not exist. Life has no other purpose than itself and its own continuous development. Therefore, '*Übermensch* is nothing other than the idea in its crystalline form that man can and therefore should develop beyond his present state'.[41] *Übermensch* is thus merely a regulative idea that underlies the continuous march of the human species. The highest representative of humankind today is the *Übermensch* in relation to such a person yesterday, and the even more improved exemplar of tomorrow will be its *Übermensch* in relation to the *Übermensch* of today.

Second, Nietzsche was not an egoist or nihilist. Contrary to what Nietzsche's vulgar friends and enemies believed, Nietzsche was a moralist through and through. The source of Nietzsche's individualism was not self-gratification but 'personalism':[42] the sense of responsibility towards oneself and towards the imperative of the constant overcoming of oneself. In this sense, there are even similarities between Nietzsche's and Christian ethics, for both assign 'the soul's entire value to its purely internal *qualities*, to its mode of being [*So-Sein*] that never emerges'.[43] There are also similarities between Kant's categorical imperative and Nietzsche's eternal

---

[38] Ferdinand Tönnies, *Der Nietzsche-Kultus: Eine Kritik* [1897] (Berlin: Akademie, 1990).
[39] *Schopenhauer und Nietzsche*, GSG 10, p. 361.   [40] GSG 10, p. 372.   [41] GSG 10, p. 399.
[42] 'Friedrich Nietzsche: Eine moralphilosophische Silhouette', GSG 5, p. 121.
[43] *Schopenhauer und Nietzsche*, GSG 10, p. 353.

recurrence. In parallel to Kant's dictum – act the way you wish everyone would act in the same situation – Nietzsche preaches: Act the way you wish the same action would be repeated by you an infinite number of times.[44]

The central moral ideal of Nietzsche is 'distinction' (*Vornehmheit*). It includes leading motifs of Nietzsche's thought, such as the value of qualitatively different personalities, the notion of individual responsibility and the idea of the pathos of distance, that is, of distinguishing oneself from others. The importance of 'distinction' is what Simmel learned from Nietzsche's philosophy. And this term appears in Simmel's articles precisely when Simmel emancipated himself from his earlier social ideas and opened himself to the idea of radical plurality. Plurality signifies not only the autonomy of distinguished personalities but also the autonomy of cultural objects and values produced by such personalities 'whose importance lies in a functional performance separated from their subjective life, in a contribution to the objective spirit'.[45] The objectivity of Nietzsche's moral imperative lies therefore not only in the responsibility to develop oneself but also in the creation of objective values that transcend the subjective significance of one's own life.

In Simmel's later terminology, the continuous self-overcoming of life is called 'more-life', and the production of objective values is called 'more-than-life'. With regard to these two notions, Klaus Lichtblau has argued that in his later philosophy Simmel remained faithful to Nietzsche when he perceived life as a process of continuous ascent, whereas he abandoned Nietzsche when he focused on the notion of objective cultural forms: the sphere of 'more-than-life'.[46] This claim would be correct if Simmel took Nietzsche to be a 'naturalistic monist',[47] but in fact Nietzsche does not appear in Simmel in a 'monistic' context. On the contrary, he normally appears in Simmel's texts in the context of the subversion of unity.

This is the way many contemporaries read Simmel.[48] To take one example, as Eugène Fleischmann argued, it was from Simmel that Max Weber, who heavily annotated *Schopenhauer and Nietzsche*, learned the significance of Nietzsche as a philosopher.[49] This thesis is worth paying attention to. Wolfgang Schluchter criticised it in a number of

---

[44] GSG 10, pp. 354–355.   [45] GSG 10, p. 376.   [46] Lichtblau, 'Das "Pathos der Distanz"', p. 264.

[47] Wolfgang Schluchter, 'Zeitgemäße Unzeitgemäße: Von Friedrich Nietzsche über Georg Simmel zu Max Weber', *Revue Internationale de Philosophie* 192(2), 1995, pp. 107–126.

[48] *Schopenhauer and Nietzsche* enjoyed broad popularity. See Thomas Mann, who approvingly quotes from it in *Reflections of a Nonpolitical Man*, trans. W. D. Morris (New York: Frederick Ungar, 1983), p. 58.

[49] Eugène Fleischmann, 'De Weber à Nietzsche', *Archives Européennes de Sociologie* 5(2), 1964, pp. 190–238.

respects.[50] First, he argued, Weber appears to have been influenced by Nietzsche long before reading Simmel's book. Second, Simmel's interpretation of Nietzsche was not a faithful rendering of Nietzsche's work, as it ignored Nietzsche's reduction of all values to life as biologically understood and to its brutal demands.[51] Whatever Weber might have learned from Simmel, it was not Nietzsche. Finally, there were important differences between the positions of the older Weber and Simmel. Yet there is no doubt that Weber read Simmel's book carefully and was influenced by it. And the positions of Schluchter and Fleischmann should be reconciled in the following way. If it is true that Simmel's interpretation departed in many respects from the spirit of Nietzsche, this means that Simmel influenced Weber in his *mis*interpretation, the result being their shared non-monistic reception of Nietzsche.[52]

Nietzsche's legacy vis-à-vis Simmel should thus be understood in terms of his emphasis on the plurality of cultural and human forms: the aspect of 'more-than-life'. Nietzsche, the philosopher of life-drive, entered Simmel's world precisely at the moment when Simmel felt that the architectonic grandeur of unity in variety did not suffice for the demands of modern life with its radical variety. There was no unity that could incorporate this variety. Nevertheless, Simmel did not abandon the quest for unity altogether. Instead, he tried to envision another kind of unity and another mode of its relation to variety. To understand what this implied, we should look back at Schopenhauer.

Towards the 1900s, as Simmel grew increasingly sceptical towards unity in variety, and as he adopted Nietzsche as his guide in this retreat, he began to pay closer attention to the philosophy against which Nietzsche had rebelled: the grand system of Schopenhauer. If, in his earlier period, Simmel had taken issue with Schopenhauer on account of his pessimism, which Simmel regarded as incompatible with the ideals of *Bildung*, now it was Schopenhauer's philosophical monism that began to trouble him. Simmel reproached Schopenhauer for 'the deep alienation of his worldview from all individuality'.[53]

Yet at the same time this monism attracted Simmel, for it was of a very different kind than the one he attributed to Kant. Schopenhauer, as is known, argued that there are two ways to conceive the world. One is the

---

[50] Schluchter, 'Zeitgemäße Unzeitgemäße', pp. 110–111n.
[51] On the contrast between Nietzsche's rejection of dualism and Simmel's emphasis of it, see also Rammstedt, 'On Simmel's Aesthetics', p. 139, n. 3.
[52] Cf. Schluchter, 'Zeitgemäße Unzeitgemäße', pp. 121, 126.
[53] *Schopenhauer und Nietzsche*, GSG 10, p. 226.

world of representation, governed by a number of fundamental presuppositions ('principles of sufficient reason'), which form the way in which our world perception takes place.[54] The fundamental condition of this perception is the division into object and subject, and the secondary conditions are categories through which the world of objects is represented to the subject: time, space, matter and causality. This world of representation existing in space and time consists of individual objects occupying a specific slot in time and space.

Behind this veil of appearance there is, however, another world: the world in itself, the world as will. We can never know what the essence of this world is. We can, however, raise the veil just a bit and with the help of philosophy draw a number of conclusions about it, of which the fundamental ones are first of all that that world exists and secondly that it is qualitatively different from the world as it appears to us. 'Will' is unlike 'representation' and is devoid of the forms under which representation takes place. The categories of time and space are thus irrelevant to it, and therefore it does not consist of separate individualities. The will is not plural, and therefore it is 'one', although it is 'one' not in the numerical sense but in the sense of transcending every kind of division.

The logic of this philosophical vision seems to force upon us pessimistic conclusions. For our world is the will that constantly objectivises itself into representations. These representations are necessarily plural, yet they represent one and the same will. The result is that they find themselves in eternal discord with each other. There can be no peace among them because in essence they do not live, as it were, in separate compartments. They all want a full share of the same thing: to represent the will in its primordial unity. Through these representations the 'will' therefore incessantly struggles with itself. The foundation of Schopenhauer's pessimism is the irreconcilable conflict between unity ('will') and variety ('representations'). Schopenhauer constructed a metaphysic of unity, but this metaphysic was built on repudiating the ideal of unity in variety. The final salvation may come only through the complete abolition of variety, by switching off desire and plunging into the mystical nothingness of the 'one'.

And it is at this point that Simmel accuses Schopenhauer of having made a fallacious syllogism. For even if one accepts that the world 'in-itself' is absolutely unlike the world as representation, it does not have to follow

---

[54] Arthur Schopenhauer, *The Will as World and Representation*, 2 vols., trans. E. F. J. Payne (New York: Dover Publications, 1966).

that the metaphysical world is the absolute 'one' that recognises no individuality. It is possible and does not entail any contradiction for this world to also consist of individual entities, even though such entities would be of a completely different kind than the individualities of the world of representation:

> This absolute *may* indeed be unity, but it *may* just as well possess a degree and a kind of individuality and of separate being-for-itself, which is just as far removed from the character of the world of appearance, just as little empirically demonstrable, just as much something absolute and indeterminable through knowing consciousness, as that unity.[55]

The metaphysical world can therefore also be a world of variety. But what kind of individualities will this variety consist of? These metaphysical individualities cannot, of course, be the material objects of our world of representation, for those can exist only in time and space. Yet variety can be conceived as consisting of the units of mental activity, which exist beyond time and space: 'Our soul has a mysterious and at the same time empirically by all means effective ability to combine a great number of elements of which it has become successively conscious into an absolutely unified thought.'[56] As their existence is independent from them being thought in time, these units can at least give us a hint as to the kind of individuality which is possible in the world 'in itself'.

Such units can be single dicta, for example, 'life is suffering'.[57] They can, however, form more general systems of experience through which the world is addressed in its entirety. According to Simmel, the contents or results of different spheres of our activities – aesthetic, intellectual, practical or religious – 'form separate empires governed by their own laws, each producing the world (or a world) in its own way and language'.[58] Simmel makes this claim in the fifth chapter of *Schopenhauer and Nietzsche*, which deals with Schopenhauer's aesthetics, and with good reason. For it is in relation to aesthetics that Schopenhauer introduces his conception of 'Ideas' that are very similar to Simmel's 'worlds'.[59] Ideas for Schopenhauer are like ideal types, in which the will first objectifies itself before these ideal types are further objectified in the plurality of the objects of representation. Ideas are beyond the limits of the principles of sufficient reason, and therefore they cannot be perceived through scientific knowledge. Instead, they should be accessed through aesthetic intuition.

---

[55] *Schopenhauer und Nietzsche*, GSG 10, p. 221.   [56] GSG 10, p. 219.   [57] GSG 10, p. 219.
[58] GSG 10, p. 269.
[59] Schopenhauer, *The Will as World and Representation*, vol. 1, book 3, pp. 168–267.

Schopenhauer does not make Ideas into real self-sufficient entities. Like the individual objects governed by the principles of sufficient reason, they are merely different aspects of 'one'. For him, true plurality among them is therefore impossible. But for Simmel, the contrary is the case. For the Ideas that signify forms of our experience can be seen not as fighting with each other but as standing alongside each other. They are foreign to each other but for this very reason, none interferes with the others and each is fully satisfactory in its own terms: 'One grasps the richness of structure in the motions of our mind only when one learns to affirm the autonomy of these manifold strata, of which each imparts a different meaning, a different truth value, a different kind of nexus to the same content.'[60]

Thus, according to Simmel, Schopenhauer's problem was his drive for unity which led him in the end to accept the unavoidability of the conflict between unity and plurality and hence to adopt the stance of pessimism. Simmel, however, did not want to replace this pessimism with its opposite. What Simmel looked for was an optimism informed by Schopenhauer's insights: a restrained optimism of hope. Thus, whereas Schopenhauer argued that striving signifies dissatisfaction and hence suffering, Simmel evoked Plato's description of love as a mixture of having and not-having at the same time, arguing that it is not only real possession that can be enjoyed but also the idea of being on the way to possession, so that 'the hope of happiness becomes for us the happiness of hope'.[61] Curiously, this restrained optimism was closer to the real position of Nietzsche, whose philosophy can be interpreted as transcending the entire dichotomy of optimism and pessimism,[62] than to the aforementioned image of Nietzsche as an optimist.

Be that as it may, the important point is that for Simmel, Nietzsche was first and foremost a philosopher of difference. Simmel seems to have been looking for a philosophical insight which would free him from the ideal of comprehensive unity that, as Schopenhauer showed, ends in despair. And the vision of the plurality of individuals and forms of experience independent from each other, worked out by Simmel as a consequence of the impression Nietzsche had made on him, provided him with such an insight.

Things were, however, not that simple, for Simmel, while moving philosophically towards an affirmation of variety without unity, was

---

[60] *Schopenhauer und Nietzsche*, GSG 10, p. 295.   [61] GSG 10, p. 245.

[62] Hartmann Tyrell, 'Pessimismus: Eine begriffsgeschichtliche Notiz', *Simmel Newsletter* 2(2), 1992, p. 140.

nevertheless attracted to the philosophical grandeur of Schopenhauer's system. Acknowledging the superiority of Schopenhauer as a philosopher over Nietzsche, he claimed that Schopenhauer 'defends the worse cause with better powers'.[63] On closer inspection, it appears that Simmel's rejection of Schopenhauer's worldview was not unambiguous.[64]

First, one can see that in *Schopenhauer and Nietzsche*, despite Simmel's praise of Nietzsche, the conflict between unity and plurality is not resolved in favour of plurality, if at all. Our soul, Simmel says, is ruled by one fundamental dualism which transcends all other derivative dualisms and constitutes its rhythm: 'the division [*Parteiung*] between unity and plurality [*Vielheit*]'.[65] Schopenhauer represents one side of this dualism: the side of unity, which cannot be simply dispensed with for the sake of plurality. Discussing ethics, but with broader philosophical implications, Simmel argues that 'perhaps it is not impossible to perceive duality and unity as poles of our moral conduct and every single moral occurrence as possessing them both to a certain degree, as its form, so to speak'.[66]

Second, the very way in which Simmel formulates the idea of the variety of forms of experience is in fact more Schopenhauerian than Nietzschean.[67] For he understands these units not only as fragments coherent in themselves but as reflections and symbols of the comprehensive unity, each addressing the *entirety* of the world under its specific categories. And although the grand synthesis of unity in variety disintegrates, each unit of this variety claims this unity for itself. This just reinforces the sense of a tragic conflict, as each form of experience is at the same time the whole and one fragment; each carries in itself the opposition of unity and variety.

When one examines Simmel's intellectual endeavours of his middle period, one can see this conflict at its sharpest, as Simmel constantly vacillates between making a certain sphere of human experience into the symbol of the world unity on the one hand and recognising its inadequacies and inner contradictions on the other.

Three such attempts are especially significant, and each is intimately related to the leading motifs of *Schopenhauer and Nietzsche*. These are

[63] *Schopenhauer und Nietzsche*, GSG 10, p. 188.
[64] Stjepan Mestrovic, e.g., argues that in respect of the concept of 'will to life', Simmel 'seems to have been a more faithful follower of Schopenhauer' than of Nietzsche: Stjepan G. Mestrovic, 'Simmel's Sociology in Relation to Schopenhauer's Philosophy', in M. Kaern, B. S. Phillips and R. S. Cohen (eds.), *Georg Simmel and Contemporary Sociology* (Dordrecht: Kluwert Academic Publishers, 1990), p. 185.
[65] *Schopenhauer und Nietzsche*, GSG 10, p. 321.   [66] GSG 10, p. 322.
[67] Cf. Thouard, 'Schopenhauer, Arthur', p. 507.

inquiries into the nature of beauty, religion and the feminine. Each was in a sense an attempt to overcome Schopenhauer's tragic dichotomy between the world as will and the world as representation. Simmel suggested that Schopenhauer had missed the third sphere: the word as 'feeling'.[68] This claim was unavoidably reminiscent of the proverbial tripartite division into the true, right and beautiful, of which the three critiques of Kant were the most famous philosophical illustration. Defining the beautiful was a central moment of Kant's third critique, and Simmel's world of 'feeling' could thus point to the sphere of art and aesthetics. Or, in a slightly different tripartite taxonomy, 'feeling' could be perceived as the domain of religion, as in Schleiermacher, for example.[69] The experience of unity could therefore be looked for in religion. And finally, given Simmel's aforementioned argument about love and hope, the world of 'feeling' could be relegated to the erotic sphere, which for Simmel was intimately related to the philosophy of the feminine and the relationship between the sexes. But as Simmel explored these three possibilities, in each case he appeared to arrive at aporia. Neither religion, nor art, nor the feminine brought about the wished-for harmony and abolished the inner conflict between unity and variety. This would be no surprise to Schopenhauer. In his vision, 'the totality of life separates from the sum of its particulars and turns into that only real unity, which we indeed sense in that particular as its substance, but at the same time and behind it as the dark fate of life in general – the fate which is not an addition to life but life itself'.[70]

Let us then turn to a detailed examination of Simmel's philosophy of these three spheres: beauty, religion and the feminine.

3.2   Beauty

The subject of art, aesthetics or the beautiful does not belong exclusively to any particular period of Simmel's thought. Like many other subjects, issues related to aesthetics accompanied him from his young years, when he studied the history of art and began to participate in various artistic clubs and societies, up to his last years, when many of his published and unpublished works, including the monographs on Goethe and Rembrandt, touched directly or indirectly on the philosophical significance of the beautiful.

---

[68] *Schopenhauer und Nietzsche*, GSG 10, p. 249.
[69] Friedrich Schleiermacher, *On Religion: Speeches to Its Cultural Despisers* [1799], trans. John Oman (London: Kegan Paul, 1893), p. 47.
[70] *Schopenhauer und Nietzsche*, GSG 10, p. 213.

In this section, however, I will not deal with the entirety of Simmel's contribution to aesthetics[71] but only with the way his writings on art and the beautiful reflect on his preoccupation with the problem of unity and variety. In this respect, the changes in Simmel's thought from his early to middle periods, as well as the central place that art occupies in his search for unity unencumbered by and standing apart from variety, deserve special attention.

Towards his middle period, Simmel began to deal intensively with aesthetic issues. This does not mean Simmel was not interested in art beforehand. But if earlier his artistic sensibilities found expression mainly in his private pursuits, whereas his academic and public work focused on issues of society, morals and economy, from the mid-1890s onwards aesthetics played a key role in his persona as a public intellectual.

This increase in intensity corresponded to a change in Simmel's attitude to art. On the whole, his sporadic statements on art before the mid-1890s quite expectedly provide yet another illustration of his overall ideal of 'unity in variety' and of his view of society as the means to redemption in the condition of modernity. Thus, in a piece on art exhibitions published in 1890, Simmel presented exhibitions as embodiments of the modern artistic spirit. According to him, artistic activity is characterised by the same features that characterise all modern activities: growing specialisation and the division of labour. As a result, an individual production loses in uniqueness, originality and significance, which, however, does not mean that these disappear as such: rather, they now become the features of collective artistic activity: 'In the modern world, the great is done by the masses and not by the individual.'[72] Thus the value and greatness of art lie today not so much in individual artistic achievement as in the totality of artistic production, and it is by means of art exhibitions that this totality reveals itself to the public.

---

[71] For a comprehensive survey of Simmel's writings on aesthetics, see Ingo Meyer, *Georg Simmels Ästhetik: Autonomiepostulat und soziologische Referenz* (Weilerswist: Velbrück, 2017). See also Emil Utitz, 'Georg Simmel und die Philosophie der Kunst', in P. U. Hein (ed.), *Georg Simmel* (Frankfurt am Main: Peter Lang, 1990), pp. 85–124; Klaus Lichtblau, 'Ästhetische Konzeptionen im Werk Georg Simmels', *Simmel Newsletter* 1(1), 1991, pp. 22–35; Barbara Smitmans-Vajda, *Die Bedeutung der Bildenden Kunst in der Philosophie Georg Simmels* (Aachen: Shaker, 1997); Ute Faath, *Mehr-als-Kunst: Zur Kunstphilosophie Georg Simmels* (Würzburg: Königshausen und Neumann, 1998); Dirk Solies, *Natur in der Distanz: Zur Bedeutung von Georg Simmels Kulturphilosophie für die Landschaftsästhetik* (St. Augustin: Gardez!, 1998); Eduardo de la Fuente, 'The Art of Social Forms and the Social Forms of Art: The Sociology-Aesthetics Nexus in Georg Simmel's Thought', *Sociological Theory* 26(4), 2008, pp. 344–362.

[72] 'Ueber Kunstausstellungen', GSG 17, p. 242.

Like in other spheres of human activity, the division of labour in art brings with it a growing one-sidedness. Art exhibitions, however, mitigate or even compensate for this one-sidedness. Through them, the 'one-sidedness of modern human beings in the things they produce is offset by multi-sidedness in the things they consume'.[73] This solution is not without its problems. The enormous variety of impressions produced by the mixture of all sorts of works of art often leads to superficiality and a *blasé* attitude. This mixture of impressions is the greatest enemy of 'any deeper understanding of an individual artwork'.[74] Yet it would be wrong to adopt a pessimistic attitude on account of these negative effects of specialisation and the division of labour. Whether the final balance will be in favour of the positive aspects of modernity remains to be seen, but any attempt to resurrect the past is futile.

Within a few years, however, Simmel's enthusiasm regarding the collective artistic achievement somewhat dissipated. In his article on the Berlin Trade Exhibition, published in 1896,[75] one can notice a certain change in nuance, even if it still borrows many ideas from the earlier, 1890 article. For whereas the 1890 text begins and ends with the rejection of pessimism, while the disadvantages of modernity are mentioned in the middle, the 1896 article starts with discontent towards specialisation and only afterwards proceeds with a few positive words about the exhibition itself.[76]

The change in Simmel's attitude can in fact be spotted already in his essay on painter Arnold Böcklin, published a year earlier under the title 'Böcklin's Landscapes' (1895).[77] Signs of retreat from the grand 'sociological' vision of art are unmistakable in it. Art is no longer seen as a collective enterprise that satisfies the cultural needs of the members of the collective but as an individual activity that brings salvation to the 'soul'. Böcklin's landscapes are characterised by their solitude. This solitude is by no means tragic; rather, it indicates a sense of self-sufficiency, reminiscent of those people whose natural immovable fate is somehow to be 'solitary'.[78]

---

[73] 'On Art Exhibitions' [1890], in Austin Harrington (ed.), *Georg Simmel: Essays on Art and Aesthetics* (Chicago: University of Chicago Press, 2020), p. 138. ['Ueber Kunstausstellungen', GSG 17, p. 243.]

[74] Ibid., p. 140. [GSG 17, pp. 246–247.]

[75] 'The Berlin Trade Exhibition', in D. Frisby and M. Featherstone (eds.), *Simmel on Culture: Selected Writings* (London: Sage, 1997), pp. 255–258. [GSG 17, pp. 33–38.]

[76] On the context of this essay, see Dorothy Rowe, 'Georg Simmel and the Berlin Trade Exhibition of 1896', *Urban History* 22(2), 1995, pp. 216–228.

[77] 'Arnold Böcklin's Landscapes' [1895], in Harrington (ed.), *Georg Simmel: Essays on Art and Aesthetics*, pp. 205–211. [GSG 5, pp. 96–104.]

[78] Ibid., p. 210. [GSG 5, p. 103.]

Böcklin's landscapes grant us a feeling of timelessness, bringing us
'redemption and release from dull narrow realities'.[79] Simmel thus moves
towards appreciating the subjective value of art as a tool of redemption for
the individual. This redemption may now involve even a certain touch of
escape from reality.

Nevertheless, the essay still contains much of the logic of 'unity in
variety'. Thus the atmosphere of Böcklin's landscapes is said to be as if

> a part of the original unity of things had been rescued in the world of
> appearances from the two opposing sides into which conscious mind, on the
> one hand, and unconscious nature, on the other, have constituted them-
> selves, and as if the soul, pushed to and fro by these poles, had sought to
> return these sides to their lost unity.[80]

The kind of unity his paintings achieve is that in which all opposites are
united:

> Frequently we describe with contradictory and mutually exclusive attributes
> things we experience at first hand as intrinsically unitary and coherent. And
> in the sense in which [the reflective mediaeval philosopher] apostrophises
> the highest divine unity of things as the *coincidentia oppositorum*, or con-
> ciliance of all opposites and antitheses, so we are often incapable of describ-
> ing unity in the works and agency of man other than by speaking of the
> meeting of mutually contradictory elements.[81]

In 1895, therefore, Simmel, while no longer holding the view that
aesthetic greatness could be attained by bringing together various works
of art produced by numerous artists, still adhered more or less to the
pattern of thinking, according to which unity naturally comes out of the
contrasting elements of variety. Böcklin was a great painter precisely
because he produced unity which encompassed fundamental dualisms
such as that between soul and nature.

A similar motif can be also found in the essay 'Rome' published in 1898.
Rome's essential characteristic, according to Simmel, is its combination of
extreme multiplicity with unity, or, to be more precise, Rome's unity is
based on its multiplicity. Rome produces a natural feeling of immense
unity, which 'is not torn apart by the vast tension of its elements'; on the
contrary, this unity 'is displayed through this very tension'.[82] Simmel even
compared Rome with Goethe,[83] thus alluding to an immediately

---

[79] Ibid., p. 208. [GSG 5, p. 100.]   [80] Ibid., pp. 205–206. [GSG 5, p. 96.]
[81] Ibid., pp. 208–209. [GSG 5, pp. 100–101.]
[82] 'Rome', *Theory, Culture & Society* 24(7–8), 2007, p. 34. [GSG 5, p. 307.]
[83] Ibid., p. 35. [GSG 5, pp. 307–308.]

recognisable set of connotations: Goethe the universal genius was by that time commonly depicted as having embodied the classical *Bildung* ideal of forming oneself into a harmonious and consistent whole out of the greatest possible variety.[84]

To summarise, before the mid-1890s, art played a secondary role in Simmel's work and was subservient to the ideal of social progress. In the mid-1890s, its significance began to increase, as Simmel's attention turned to the value of the individual. But the initial pattern through which art was understood was that of unity in variety. Simmel spoke about art in the language of synthesis, accommodation and unity that emerge out of contrasts, opposites and manifold elements. The release that beauty offers to an individual is that which society or Kantian philosophy may offer: that of attaining unity out of the vastly differentiated reality.

However, by the turn of the century, signs of change can be seen in Simmel's approach towards art. As he spent more time thinking, teaching and writing about it, new nuances emerged, at first almost imperceptibly. Simmel continued, of course, to regard art as a path to redemption for the modern individual who yearns for unity, but this unity was now understood in a somewhat different way.

On the surface, many of Simmel's statements on art continue to fit the pattern of unity in variety. For example, in 'The Aesthetic Significance of the Face' (1901) he suggested that the inner unity of the face is the function of the interaction of its parts.[85] But there is something else in his words, as he referred to this unity as 'unity out of and *above* diversity'.[86] The word 'above' points to a certain incommensurability between unity and the elements of which it consists. Unity is not only the sum of its parts; in a sense, it stands opposite to the mere sum of its parts.

That the use of the word 'above' here is not a stylistic inadvertence but reflects Simmel's position on the matter may be gathered from other nuances that can be found in his writings of the same period. Thus Simmel began to use the word 'grace' and its synonyms quite often when referring to the redemptive function of art. Already in 'Rome' he said that 'our perception of beauty as mysterious and gratuitous – something that reality cannot claim but must humbly accept as an act of grace – may be

---

[84] For the detailed elucidation of Simmel's depiction of Rome and other Italian cities, see Efraim Podoksik, 'In Search of Unity: Georg Simmel on Italian Cities as Works of Art', *Theory, Culture & Society* 29(7/8), 2012, pp. 101–123.

[85] 'The Aesthetic Significance of the Face', trans. L. Ferguson, in Wolff (ed.), *Essays on Sociology, Philosophy and Aesthetics*, pp. 276–281. [GSG 7, pp. 36–42.]

[86] Ibid., p. 276. [GSG 7, p. 36.] Italics mine – E. P.

based on that aesthetic indifference of the world's atoms and elements in which the one is only beautiful in relation to the other'.[87] There 'grace' seemed to be used in the context of the formula of unity in variety. Similarly, in 'The Aesthetic of Portrait' (1905) one reads of art 'gracing us with a harmony of elements'.[88]

Nevertheless, the overtones of the word 'grace' already point in a different direction. For grace is not usually the word used to signify universal comprehension and accommodation. On the contrary, it is a term meant to distinguish, to grant redemption to the chosen. Simmel is indeed aware of these connotations when he applies this word to the work of art. As he says, 'the feeling of an undeserved gift with which it delights us originates from the pride of this self-sufficient closure, with which it now nevertheless becomes our own'.[89]

The mystery associated with the act of grace is not really compatible with the logic of unity in variety. For unity in variety, properly speaking, does not imply any fundamental mystery; rather, it presupposes a natural process. Comprehensive unity is just the other side of a high level of differentiation and is no more mysterious than the latter. A highly developed organism is equally more differentiated and unified: the one is the counterpart of the other, and therefore no special, let alone 'undeserved' gift is required. For Simmel, however, aesthetic harmony is that provided by 'a happy [feeling of] coalescence of two heterogeneous orders of being and possibility [*Seins- und Kraftreihen*], arising not from any natural process but only [from] art'.[90]

Consequently, grace presupposes arbitrary choice, whereas unity in variety does not. In the latter case, unity is in a sense the *telos* of development and differentiation. Yet if unity is the work of grace, then differentiated variety does not by itself presuppose unity and does not necessarily lead to it. Such unity remains in a sense a riddle, something which is inexplicable, like the feeling of unity in art, according to Simmel, who speaks about the soul's 'fundamental and [therefore] irreducible capacity to knit together its own manifold levels and orders of being into the unitariness of an ego, of a self-consciousness'.[91] As he says in 'The Philosophy of the Dramatic Actor', art 'resembles a kind of preestablished harmony or

---

[87] 'Rome', p. 31. [GSG 5, p. 301.]
[88] 'Aesthetics of the Portrait: Part I', in Harrington (ed.), *Georg Simmel: Essays on Art and Aesthetics*, pp. 243–244. [GSG 7, p. 325.]
[89] 'The Picture Frame: An Aesthetic Study', in ibid., p. 149. [GSG 7, p. 102.]
[90] 'Theatre and the Dramatic Actor: Part I', in ibid., p. 266. [GSG 8, p. 431.]
[91] 'Aesthetics of the Portrait: Part I', p. 244. [GSG 7, p. 326.]

state of grace *above* life and not deriving from any forces of life's individual elements'.[92]

The change in Simmel's position is most clearly illustrated if one juxtaposes his essay 'Rome' with 'Florence', published eight years later (1906).[93] Like Rome, Florence bestows a feeling of unity. But this unity is not, like in the case of Rome, the other side of its multiplicity. Rather, unity is achieved through a miraculous disappearance of contrasts. Thus, in it the very opposition between nature and mind has become void ('*sei . . . nichtig geworden*'[94]).

The unity of Florence is thus a 'mysterious unity'[95] or, one could say, it is a unity defined by the act of grace that redeems the righteous elect from the ills of the secular world with its disorders. In Simmel's account, Florence appears as a city untouched by usual contradictions. Somehow it managed to remain untainted by the dualisms of life even in its maturity. It is not a city that absorbs everything into an encompassing unity. On the contrary, in order to achieve unity, it must select. This city admits only what is fit for harmony and perfection, gathering 'from every corner of the soul all that is ripe, cheerful and alive'.[96] It has become 'the good fortune of those fully mature [*reifen*] human beings who have achieved or renounced what is essential in life, and who for this possession and renunciation are seeking only its form'.[97]

Simmel does not tell us more about these mature people.[98] But the expression itself evokes Nietzsche's name and his pathos of distance.[99] Florence can be seen as the best kind of retreat for the Nietzschean ideal man. The *Bildung* ideal of harmonious personality is not abandoned here, but it comes to characterise only a special kind of individual, living in a special kind of city.

The redemptive character of art for Simmel in his middle period seems therefore to be as follows. Although it is now impossible to envision unity as arising naturally out of variety, art can provide a substitute for it: a snapshot of unity, in the form of a specific work of art, of an instant

---

[92] 'Theatre and the Dramatic Actor: Part I', p. 264. [GSG 8, p. 429.] The italics are in the English translation.

[93] 'Florence', trans. U. Teucher and T. M. Kemple, *Theory, Culture & Society* 24(7–8), 2007, pp. 38–41. [GSG 8, pp. 69–73.]

[94] GSG 8, p. 69.   [95] 'Florence', p. 39. [GSG 8, p. 69.]   [96] Ibid., p. 40. [GSG 8, p. 72.]

[97] Ibid., p. 41. [GSG 8, p. 73.]

[98] On the community of foreign lovers of art in fin-de-siècle Florence, see Bernd Roeck, *Florence 1900: The Quest for Arcadia*, trans. S. Spencer (New Haven: Yale University Press, 2009).

[99] Cf. Friedrich Nietzsche, *On the Genealogy of Morality*, trans. C. Diethe (Cambridge: Cambridge University Press, 1994), pp. 80–85.

aesthetic experience at a specific point in time, of a harmonious city unlike other cities. This snapshot is, however, felt as something unnatural and hence inexplicable and transitory. The aesthetic experience becomes a symbol of unity, a temporary escape from chaos and contradictions, but it hardly offers a comprehensive and permanent solution to the yearning for unity. Art is still governed by the ideal of beautiful harmony, but this beauty and this harmony ignore or abolish conflictual reality instead of absorbing it.

This approach did not characterise only Simmel's philosophical essays on art. It was also displayed in the cultural and social attitudes he adopted. For example, in 1903 he became involved in founding an association of artists, which became the Union of German Artists (*Deutscher Künstlerbund*).[100] The intention was to bring together leading avant-garde figures in order to form an alternative to what the organisers perceived as the obscurantism of both official art and the popular 'philistine' taste. 'Day by day it becomes clearer', explained Simmel in the invitation letter to Stefan George, 'that we live among barbarians'.[101] In the attached draft of the association's mission statement, which was at least in part, it seems, composed by Simmel, the rationale of the initiative was described as the founding of 'a circle of highest cultivation [*Bildung*] which, despite all individual diversity, would feel itself to be the bearer of the unified totality of culture [*Gesammtkultur*]'.[102] Examples of cultural life in Athens, Weimar, Paris, as well as in Florence, were evoked. With regard to the cultural purpose, the following was proclaimed:

> For versus the specialisations of science, the hostilities of political and social existence, the alienation of life through the domination of economic and technological advances, there is only artistic interest that is the bearer of a culture which is both inward and personal and at the same time extends beyond interpersonal contradictions.[103]

And when another invitee, writer Ricarda Huch, apparently expressed some scepticism regarding the possibility of artists acting as a collective, Simmel, in order to allay her reservations, clarified his position: 'Since art is not subject to the division of labour but always creates a whole, the artist

---

[100] On the Union, see Martina Wehlte-Höschele, *Der Deutsche Künstlerbund im Spektrum von Kunst und Kulturpolitik des Wilhelminischen Kaiserreichs*, PhD dissertation, University of Heidelberg, 1993.
[101] Letter to Stefan George, 24 February 1903, GSG 22, p. 446.
[102] Supplement [*Anlage*] to the letter to Stefan George, 24 February 1903, GSG 22, pp. 449–450.
[103] GSG 22, p. 450.

cannot have any substantial relationship to "unions" where a whole is created only through the cooperation of the many.'[104]

These pieces of correspondence thus openly express what was merely implied in Simmel's more abstract philosophical pieces: that by that time he fully rejected the view he had espoused in his earlier publications, according to which the enterprise of modern art had to be based on the principle of the division of labour. Now Simmel concurred that art was fundamentally an individual activity, to which only the initiated and talented were called. Artistic associations were just the means of cultivated individuals to protect themselves against surrounding barbarism. These artists needed a shelter where they could pursue their individual creative activities, not unlike Florence. It was the harmony of seclusion that they sought and not the ultimate unity arising out of full-fledged specialisation.

In principle, this position was relatively coherent, and if Simmel wished he could have made it his credo. However, this is not what happened. On the contrary, as its contours became clearer to him, he grew more and more sceptical towards it. As he was writing about art as a path to the mysterious unity that offers an escape from variety, his other texts showed that he also considered this escape into aestheticism a puristic illusion or at least a solution that could not satisfy his own complex and multi-faceted nature.

As follows, for example, from his other essays of the same period, art can hardly turn itself into an experience free from contradictions. In 'The Picture Frame' (1902), for example, Simmel noted:

> The work of art is in the actually contradictory position of being supposed to form a unified whole with its surroundings, whereas it is itself already a whole. In this way, it repeats the general difficulty of life, that the elements of totalities nevertheless lay claim to being autonomous totalities themselves.[105]

And another essay of the same period – 'The Aesthetics of Gravity' (1901) – also emphasised conflict rather than harmony. In it, Simmel argued that two different artistic styles can be identified on the basis of the way they address the eternal conflict in which human beings find themselves: the fight between physical gravity and the soul's impulse to overcome gravity. Human movements are the stage where this conflict takes place, and there are two principal forms in which it can be presented: 'grace' (in the sense of

---

[104] Letter to Ricarda Huch, 5 March 1903, GSG 22, pp. 455–456.
[105] 'The Picture Frame: An Aesthetic Study', p. 153. [GSG 7, p. 107.]

graciousness, *Anmuth*, not grace in the aforementioned theological sense of *Gnade*) and 'dignity' (*Würde*). We move ourselves with grace when the opposition of matter seems to be virtually non-existent, so that there is an impression that nothing stands in the way of movement. In the realm of the ethical, this is similar to the 'beautiful soul', whose conduct flows easily out of its own nature. Movement with dignity, by contrast, suggests that the whole weight of matter's resistance is on display, but this resistance is overcome by the victorious spirit. In ethics, this is signified by the notion of merit which means worthiness as a result of overcoming the seductions of flesh.[106]

The source of this distinction was Friedrich Schiller's essay 'On Grace and Dignity' (1793).[107] Schiller defined grace as the moral aspect of the body's beauty. Morality belongs to the realm of freedom, and graciousness allows this freedom to express itself in the natural world otherwise governed by the principle of causality, as if action proceeded without fighting, instinctively and with ease. A dignified action is, on the contrary, one in which resistance is explicit. For example, one can suffer pain with dignity, refusing to succumb to the natural reflexes it usually produces.

Thus far it seems that Simmel appropriated Schiller's distinction between graciousness and dignity quite faithfully. However, on closer inspection, one can notice a difference in emphasis. For the classicist Schiller, the fundamental concept was 'grace', which was congruent with his ideal of beauty that was supposed to lead humankind gently into the realm of morality. Consequently, it is to the elucidation of grace that he paid the most attention.

By contrast, the emphasis of Simmel's essay was on conflict rather than harmony. He appeared to think that quiet harmony was an exception rather than a common occurrence. The resistance of matter was not an enemy to be taken lightly. He was informed not only by Schiller's classicism but also by Schopenhauer's more acute sense of tragic senselessness. For Schopenhauer too had something to say about the aesthetics of gravity and resistance. In general, he understood aesthetic contemplation as the way to intuit the primary ideal-typical objectifications of the will: Ideas. Different Ideas reflect different grades of the will's objectification. Natural

---

[106] 'Aesthetics of Gravity', in Harrington (ed.), *Georg Simmel: Essays on Art and Aesthetics*, pp. 146–147. [GSG 7, pp. 47–48.]

[107] Friedrich Schiller, 'On Grace and Dignity', trans. J. V. Curran, in J. V. Curran and Ch. Fricker (eds.), *Schiller's 'On Grace and Dignity' in Its Cultural Contexts: Essays and a New Translation* (Rochester, NY: Camden House, 2005), pp. 123–170. This is not the first time that Simmel used these terms. See 'The Berlin Trade Exhibition', p. 257. [GSG 17, p. 36.]

forces are Ideas of the lowest level, and they are followed in ascending order by species of plants, species of animals and individual human characters. The aesthetic experience is that in which one reaches the vision of Ideas beyond the world of appearances. But since Ideas find themselves in an eternal struggle with each other, the vision of Ideas is therefore a vision of struggle, of discord. The task of every kind of art is to transmit the clearest image of this discord.

Different arts can be categorised by the grade of Ideas they display. Among them, architecture displays the Ideas of the lowest grade, producing aesthetic contemplation of the struggle between natural forces. Or more precisely, as Schopenhauer put it: '[T]he conflict between gravity and rigidity is the sole aesthetic material of architecture; its problem is to make this conflict appear with perfect distinctness in many different ways.'[108] A building is therefore beautiful when it produces a clear feeling of the struggle between two polar forces: gravity and rigidity.

The title of Simmel's essay clearly alludes to Schopenhauer, especially to his emphasis on discord and the inner tragedy transmitted by art. Of course, in Schopenhauer this aesthetic experience itself is not painful. On the contrary, the vision of discord is supposed to raise us above our own subjectivity as willing subjects and to grant us calm. However, this kind of release from discord is a temporary illusion that ends once the aesthetic contemplation is over. In Simmel, this transitory character of aesthetic experience is most clearly seen in his essay on Venice (1907).[109]

Like Rome and Florence, Venice is a work of art and, like them, it displays unity. Yet Venice's unity is not real. It is a lie, the purpose of which is not to remove the basic dualism of existence but to conceal it. That is the core difference between Venice and Florence. Florence's unity may not be universal and may not be available to everyone, but at least it produces true unity between nature and art. Venice's sort of unity, by contrast, does not aim at reconciliation with nature at all. Venice is a city of appearance, artifice, mask. In it, 'all that is cheerful and bright, free and light, has only served as a face [*Fassade*] for a life that is dark, violent and unrelentingly functional'.[110]

Venice aims at the unity of singleness rather than variety. Its life is carried out fully 'in a single tempo', as 'no draught animals or vehicles attract the attentive eye with their alternating speeds, and the gondolas

[108] Schopenhauer, *The Will as World and Representation*, vol. 1, p. 214.
[109] 'Venice', trans. U. Teucher and T. M. Kemple, *Theory, Culture & Society* 24(7–8), 2007, pp 42–46. [GSG 8, pp. 258–263.]
[110] Ibid., p. 44. [GSG 8, p. 260.]

entirely follow the pace and rhythm of people walking'.[111] From a certain viewpoint, it can be seen as the aesthete's release, for it represents an aesthetically complete form, disconnected from life and belonging solely to the realm of pure appearance. Yet this release turns out to be deception. For instead of bestowing a feeling of unity, Venice radiates an air of ambiguity [*Zweideutigkeit*] which is a symptom of the duality of life as such. Life is merely a foreground behind which stands death as the only certainty. When torn out of 'being', life is in constant danger of becoming a rootless appearance. Salvation can come only from art, but art can perform this role only in those rare moments in which it brings 'being' into appearance. This happens when art, though remaining itself, goes beyond artifice, connecting itself with reality: when it is 'more than art'.[112] Venice, however, cannot be more than art: it exists merely for the sake of beauty. But this beauty is rootless, and our soul cannot build in Venice a home [*Heimat*] for itself.[113] To support this claim, Simmel refers to Schopenhauer's words that life is 'ambivalent through and through'.[114]

This description of the discord between Venice's ambition to impart unity apart from reality and its inability to do so reveals the central dilemma of Simmel's approach to the question of unity in his middle period. In that period, he saw unity and variety as standing in opposition towards each other rather than in concord. Yet on some fundamental level they nevertheless cannot exist without each other. Venice, for example, chooses unity over variety up to the point of extreme monotony. It aims at aestheticism that brings with it full release from the fragmentariness of reality. But this unity turns out to be a false unity. True harmony must include variety or dissonance at least in some form, as is the case with Florence. Yet once art incorporates variety, it necessarily becomes more than just art; it comes back to reality.

But then art as such cannot be the way to harmonious self-cultivation in the fragmented world; it cannot be a symbol of perfect unity. It needs something beyond itself. Beauty must be related to something else. This logic will guide Simmel in his writings of the later period. For example, in 1913, when he will discuss Goethe and present him as the embodiment of the principle of perfect artistic autonomy, as one whose '"primordial phenomenon" [*Urphänomen*] in respect of his life phenomenon [*Lebensphänomen*] is that he is an artist',[115] he will also claim that beneath

---

[111] Ibid. [GSG 8, p. 261.]   [112] Ibid., p. 45. [GSG 8, p. 263.]   [113] Ibid., p. 46. [GSG 8, p. 263.]
[114] Ibid., p. 45. [GSG 8, p. 262.]   [115] *Goethe*, GSG 15, p. 261.

this artistic phenomenon there should lurk something even more fundamental:

> But he himself indicated that behind the primordial phenomena [*Urphänomenen*], the final things which we are capable of grasping and investigating, there is still something ultimate that eludes all sight and description. And thus the artistic basis and operating law of his nature has something deeper behind it, an unnameable entity that also bears and enfolds his entire artistically determined appearance.[116]

This ultimate and deepest something is no longer an autonomous unity that opposes variety. It is another form of unity that somehow must involve variety, even if their relationship is rather more complex than that of unity *in* variety.

The nature of this more complex relationship will be discussed in the next chapter. Meanwhile, it is important to take note of Simmel's hopes and disappointments in his middle period with regard to the role of aesthetic experience as the gate to unity and as a mode of self-cultivation. Simmel went a long way towards this realisation. Initially, he considered art as part of the great fabric of modern differentiated society. Afterwards, he emphasised its role for the individual but in its capacity to produce unity emerging out of variety. Then he began to consider the experience of the beautiful as that which grants harmony by a mysterious act of grace. Yet almost immediately he also started to suspect that this harmonious release may be just an illusion. Aestheticism turns out to be a self-destructive lie, for art should somehow relate to the fundamental reality of life.

Simmel's examination of aestheticism thus led him to a kind of aporia. But what if art was just a wrong mode of redeeming oneself? What if the release from chaotic multiplicity were better attained via another experience: religiosity? To examine this possibility, I turn now to Simmel's approach towards religion.

3.3   Religiosity

Simmel dedicated the second edition of his *Religion*, published in 1912, to two female friends: Gertrud Kantorowicz and Margarete Susman (von Bendemann). When he sent the copy to Bendemann, he added: 'How much is still wanting – no one knows this better than I. Anyway, take it

---

[116] GSG 15, pp. 261–262.

again in this imperfect form – perhaps the dedication is the only perfect thing in it.'[117]

Today, the reader's first instinct would be to treat this display of outward modesty with a grain of salt. *Religion* was certainly not a failure: like other of Simmel's books it was both engaging and enlightening. Being a sort of summary of his thoughts on the subject for over a decade, it offered the reader fresh and interesting insights on various questions relating to religion, among them the notion of religiosity as an autonomous category of experience which stands prior to and independent from objects of faith (God, dogmas etc.), and the analogy between religious beliefs and social attachments.[118]

On closer examination, however, Simmel's self-assessment in this case may be correct. The book's main problem seems to be the lack of inner coherence. It consists of a number of themes, each one pushing the argument in a somewhat different direction, and it is not easy to find any common denominator between them. If any of Simmel's works deserves the reproach of 'fragmentariness', which was often unjustly levelled against him, it is this one.

To a degree, this incoherence can be explained by extraneous factors, such as that this was a work commissioned at the request of Martin Buber, who in 1906 launched a series of monographs under the title *Society* in order to familiarise the general public with the major concepts of sociology. Simmel was instrumental in promoting this series and helping Buber commission other contributions, and the first edition of *Religion* was the second book in the series.[119] Simmel compiled in it various lines of thought on religion that he had developed in previous years, without caring too much about producing a fully coherent work.

---

[117] Letter to Margarete von Bendemann, 4 August 1912, GSG 23, p. 93.

[118] On Simmel's theory of religion, see Horst-Jürgen Helle, 'Introduction', in G. Simmel, *Essays on Religion* (New Haven: Yale University Press, 1997), pp. xi–xx; Volkhard Krech, *Georg Simmels Religionstheorie* (Tübingen: Mohr Siebeck, 1998); idem, 'Die "Soziologie der Religion": Neu gestehen', in R. Lautmann and H. Wienold (eds.), *Georg Simmel und das Leben in der Gegenwart* (Wiesbaden: Springer, 2018), pp. 325–346; Christine Pflüger, *Georg Simmels Religionstheorie in ihren werk- und theologiegeschichtlichen Bezügen* (Frankfurt am Main: Peter Lang, 2007); Austin Harrington, 'Simmel und die Religionssoziologie', in H. Tyrell, O. Rammstedt and I. Meyer (eds.), *Georg Simmels große 'Soziologie': Eine kritische Sichtung nach hundert Jahren* (Bielefeld: transcript, 2011), pp. 275–299; Hartmann Tyrell, 'Das *Religioide* und der *Glaube*: Drei Überlegungen zu einer Religionssoziologie der Zeit um 1900', in Lautmann and Wienold (eds.), *Georg Simmel und das Leben in der Gegenwart*, pp. 347–362; Francesca E. S. Montemaggi, *Authenticity and Religion in the Pluralistic Age: A Simmelian Study of Christian Evangelicals and New Monastics* (Lanham: Lexington Books, 2019), pp. 53–60.

[119] See Michael Behr, Volkhard Krech and Gert Schmidt, 'Editorischer Bericht', in GSG 10, pp. 410–413.

However, this is not a fully satisfactory answer because this would just mean that Simmel struggled to arrive at an ultimate philosophical position with regard to religion, and the question of the reasons for this would have to be asked. As I see it, the answer is that, like in the case of art, Simmel both hoped that religiosity might provide a path to the redemption of modernity and suspected that by itself it was not up to the task, and something rather more fundamental was required. Simmel's *Religion* includes both sentiments, and in addition it incorporates Simmel's earlier sociologist attitude towards religion. All this resulted in a product full of inconsistencies. The purpose of this section is to support and explain this claim by examining the development of Simmel's philosophy of religion in its context.

Simmel dealt with religion throughout his entire intellectual life. His first extensive analysis of religion can already be found as early as the first volume of his *Introduction to Moral Sciences* (1892),[120] and the discussion of religion played an important role in one of his last texts: 'The Conflict of Modern Culture' (1918).[121] But the bulk of his work on religion belongs to the period between 1898 and 1912 that roughly corresponds to his middle period. In 1898, he published an essay on the sociology of religion. This was followed in the early 1900s by a series of essays on religion that discussed a variety of topics, such as pantheism and the salvation of the soul. In 1906, the first edition of *Religion* was published. Two more essays – on the personality of God and the modern religious condition – appeared in 1911 and were included in the same year in *Philosophical Culture*. A year later, a revised version of *Religion* (1912) appeared, which should be regarded as Simmel's more or less final word on the subject, even though a discussion of religion occasionally took place in his later writings, such as the essay on religiosity in Rembrandt (1914).[122]

Given that Simmel began to publish extensively on the topic of religion only towards the end of his early period, it is no surprise that these writings were coloured by a combination of the residues of his earlier attitudes and the mood of his middle period. This is most clear in the first edition of *Religion* which was a compilation of two parallel arguments. One originated in the 1898 essay on the sociology of religion. It presented religion in its social role as the means and symbol of the inner unity of social groups.

---

[120] *Einleitung in die Moralwissenschaft*, GSG 3, pp. 422–441.
[121] 'The Conflict of Modern Culture', trans. D. E. Jenkinson, in Frisby and Featherstone (eds.), *Simmel on Culture*, pp. 87–89. GSG 16, pp. 201–205.
[122] Almost all of Simmel's writings on religion can be found in English in Simmel, *Essays on Religion*, trans. H. J. Helle.

This view was the rudiment of Simmel's earlier sociologism. The purest form of such sociologism was represented by Émile Durkheim, who considered religion first and foremost a means of social solidarity, of making individuals identify with their group.[123] In fact, it is in the context of scholarly cooperation with Durkheim that Simmel began to reflect on the sociological functions of religion, and Durkheim certainly borrowed those of Simmel's insights that corresponded to his own sociological approach.

But in 1898 Simmel was already on the way to abandoning his earlier sociologism, as even in the essay on the sociology of religion he was not fully prepared to accept the primacy of the social. Rather, he suggested that religious sentiment might have an independent origin and that the value and truth of religion was a category independent of its social function. This caveat was unacceptable to Durkheim, and it became one of the reasons for the fallout between him and Simmel as well as his subsequent unwillingness to admit his intellectual debt to Simmel.[124]

In a certain sense, Durkheim's instincts did not deceive him. For the seed of the idea of the autonomy of religious experience that could already be spotted in the 1898 essay and even earlier, for example, in the treatise on ethics,[125] grew in the 1900s into a central postulate from 'The Contribution to the Epistemology of Religion' (1902)[126] onwards. Simmel began to advance the claim that human experience consists of a number of mutually independent and incommensurable categories, each of them forming its own special world, and that religiosity is just one among such worlds. This was the second major argument of *Religion* (1906), alongside that of the social function of religion, and apparently it was more important to Simmel, as it is his insistence on the categorial autonomy of religious experience that opened and closed the book.

This argument was further expanded in the second edition (1912). Moreover, there, drawing on the two essays on religion published in the *Philosophical Culture*, Simmel included a third motif: that religiosity,

[123] Cf. Émile Durkheim, *The Elementary Forms of Religious Life* [1912], trans. C. Cosman (Oxford: Oxford University Press, 2008). For an earlier example of a 'scientific' approach to religion in Germany, see Paul v. Lilienfeld, *Die Religion betrachtet vom Standpunkte der real-genetischen Socialwissenschaft, oder Versuch einer natürlichen Theologie* (Hamburg: Gebr. Behre, 1881).

[124] See Horst Firsching, 'Émile Durkheims Religionssoziologie – Made in Germany? Zu einer These vom Simon Deploige', in V. Krech and H. Tyrell (eds.), *Religionssoziologie um 1900* (Würzburg: Ergon, 1995), pp. 351–363.

[125] *Einleitung in die Moralwissenschaft*, GSG 3, p. 440.

[126] 'Contributions to the Epistemology of Religion', trans. H. J. Helle, in Simmel, *Essays on Religion*, pp. 121–133. [GSG 7, pp. 9–20.]

rather than being primordially autonomous, may point to something more fundamental beyond itself, such as life process.

In other words, this edition encapsulated, in the area of religion, the three different periods of Simmel's thought. His sociological approach towards religion reflected the sociologism that had been so prominent in his earlier period. His view of religion as an autonomous experience was part of the idea of the plurality of the worlds of experience that characterised his middle period. And the notion of life as the underlying metaphysical aspect beneath various spheres of experience, such as religion, became prominent in his later period, which will be discussed in the next chapter.

We have seen a somewhat similar development in the sphere of art and the beautiful. Simmel's view of art evolved from sociologism towards the notion of the autonomy of the beautiful and then to doubts about the ideal of pure beauty. Indeed, in the middle period Simmel himself on several occasions suggested that the role of religion might be analogous to that of art, that it might be just another autonomous way to unity. It is in this sense that he spoke in 'Christianity and Art' (1907) about 'the similarities of religious and artistic behaviour',[127] noting that 'in themselves, religion and art are in fact unconnected. Indeed, in their ideal forms, so to speak, they cannot meet or overlap with each other, because each expresses the whole of existence in its own particular language'.[128]

But were the two really analogous to Simmel? His writings point to at least one important difference: although Simmel rejected aestheticism in the end, for a while he did consider it a satisfactory attitude, and in some of the essays of his middle period he was quite happy with it. In respect of religion, however, he hardly ever came forward with an unambiguous theory of its categorial autonomy. It appears that for him the idea of the autonomy of religiosity constituted a tremendous challenge. The reason for this appears to be that religion is an experience more difficult to tame and confine to its own epistemological limits.

Here is, for example, a typical description of the function of art in one of Simmel's essays: the man (unlike the woman) 'knows how to create the semblance and shimmer of a solution [to the conflict between law and freedom] only in the form of art'.[129] The statement that art is merely 'semblance and shimmer' does not sound very provocative, for even artists and art lovers, with the exception of fanatics who believe that art should

---

[127] 'Christianity and Art', trans. H. J. Helle, in ibid., p. 64. [GSG 8, p. 264.]

[128] Ibid., p. 76. [GSG 8, p. 275.]

[129] 'Bruchstücke aus einer Psychologie der Frauen', GSG 7, p. 294. For Simmel's view of gender differences, see the last section of this chapter.

rule, can accept that art performs the modest function of a symbol or even shadow of the universe and even accept the fact that there may be other forms of experience, equally capable of being such a shadow. But would a similar view of religion sound plausible to its devotees?

Religious sentiment, as long as it is professed earnestly, seems to possess an inherent claim to pre-eminence and comprehensiveness. It is usually inimical for religion to recognise its own relativity. The young Simmel acknowledged this when he mentioned (1892) those 'tormenting inner doubts ... which are inseparable from religiosity at the moment when the progress of culture has made its territory autonomous alongside those of social, intellectual and moral interests'.[130] Much later, in an unpublished manuscript on art (written apparently in 1913–1914), Simmel formulated the difference between art and religion in the following way. Art's exclusivity, he argued, is stronger than that of religion, for religion 'is inconceivable outside a religious life in which its timeless contents are interwoven in a manner that cannot be compared to any other'.[131]

This difficulty appears even greater if one takes into account not only the characteristics of religion in general but also the historical legacy of the Christian religion. For Christianity was not merely one of many candidates that claimed to perform the redeemer's role for the modern individual: it was a candidate with a problematic past. For it had already been dethroned after serving as the custodian of spiritual integration for the mediaeval age, providing it with a sense of unity and purpose. After its place became vacant, there appeared many other candidates which considered themselves more suitable for the secularised age, such as art, philosophy or the natural sciences.

Nevertheless, over the course of the nineteenth century, there were many who held the view that a reformed sort of Christianity was compatible with modernity and, moreover, that it was the solution to modernity's discontents. Generations of 'liberal theologians', from Johann Salomo Semler to Ernst Troeltsch, believed that religion could accommodate the findings of science and critical biblical scholarship without demolishing itself.[132] Christianity, in the view of at least some of these theologians, was perfectly capable of playing a unifying role for modern culture and, more specifically, providing the spiritual basis for the German nation state. This

---

[130] *Einleitung in die Moralwissenschaft*, GSG 3, p. 440.
[131] 'Zum Problem der Naturalismus', GSG 20, p. 233.
[132] Gottfried Hornig, *Johann Salomo Semler: Studien zu Leben und Werk des Hallenser Aufklärungstheologen* (Tübingen: Niemeyer, 1996); Mark D. Chapman, *Religion and Cultural Synthesis in Wilhelmine Germany* (Oxford: Oxford University Press, 2001).

trend is known as *Kulturprotestantismus*,[133] and its main proponent was the theologian and scholar Albrecht Ritschl (1822–1899), author of the magisterial three-volume *Christian Doctrine of Justification and Reconciliation* (1870–1874).

Ritschl assigned to the Lutheran religion the great task of performing the synthesis of modern culture that would reconcile the demands of wholes and parts: between human spirit and nature, between the individual and society, between a particular quality of human mind and the entirety of its qualities. Ritschl, like Lazarus and Schäffle, belonged to the same generation of scholars who through their work and convictions symbolised the apparent triumph of the *Bildung* institutions. In their lives and work they aimed at, and considered themselves as having achieved, a synthesis between personal cultivation and scientific scholarship. Their ideal was the totality of human culture and experience. It is just that, whereas for social thinkers Lazarus and Schäffle the glue that held the elements of modern experience together was 'society', for the theologian Ritschl it was, unsurprisingly, religion. Giving modernity its due, Ritschl accepted modern individualism and the principle of the division of labour. At the same time, Lutheranism was for him a social and ethical religion through and through, and he considered the commitment to ethical life and conscientious work not as inimical to harmonious self-realisation but as the surest path to it. Modern differentiation was a challenge to which religion had an adequate response.[134]

Ritschl's great synthetic vision and his emphasis on the sphere of willing, ethics and good work at the expense of knowledge or even to some extent faith did not, however, remain unchallenged. For liberal theology contained another tradition that referred to religion less as a synthesis and more as a distinct sphere of human experience, and that appealed to the authority of Friedrich Schleiermacher. Schleiermacher tried to delineate a special sphere of religion which would be distinct from knowledge and morality, and he found it in feeling. Feeling was the seat of religiosity. Other aspects of religion, such as teaching, practices and institutions, depended on feeling. Ritschl was critical of Schleiermacher's subjectivism, and many others concurred with him.[135] But some theologians took the side of Schleiermacher,

---

[133] On *Kulturprotestantismus*, see Friedrich Wilhelm Graf, 'Why Theology? Strategies of Legitimation: Protestant Theology in German Protestantism', in Efraim Podoksik (ed.), *Doing Humanities in Nineteenth-Century Germany* (Leiden: Brill, 2019), pp. 40–58.

[134] E.g. Albrecht Ritschl, *Die christliche Lehre von der Rechtfertigung und Versöhnung*, vol. 3: *Die positive Entwickelung der Lehre*, 3rd ed. (Bonn: Adolph Marcus, 1888), pp. 193, 473, 630–632.

[135] E.g. A. Dorner, 'Über das Wesen der Religion', *Theologische Studien und Kritiken* 56(1), 1883, pp. 217–277.

criticising Ritschl in turn. It was argued, for example, that 'in religion, the feelings are more fundamental than teaching and actions'.[136] Of course, neither side in this theological debate fully rejected the preferences of the other. Schleiermacher certainly did not mean to banish external religious practices from his vision of religion. The question was rather about the relative pre-eminence of one aspect over the other in the definition of the essence of religion. The debate thus highlighted the inner conflict between two separate but interrelated aspects of religion: 'subjective' and 'objective'. These, or some other synonymous distinctions, such as that between 'religiosity' and 'religion',[137] often appeared in contemporary accounts of religion.

Academic theologians were thus relatively cautious while pursuing their claims. The same issues were, however, also discussed by lay intellectuals, and these were less constrained by the expectations of theological propriety. They tended to formulate the question of the place of religion on the map of human experience in bolder ways. Some dared suggest that one should not expect a comprehensive worldview from religion at all, and that it offered only one epistemological perspective among many. Often this argument was designed for the purpose of defending religion in the condition of growing secularisation. For if religion was an independent worldview, it could not be refuted by modern science. The question arises, however, as to what extent this approach could truly satisfy devoted religious consciousness.

In April 1898, the Viennese newspaper *Die Zeit* published an essay titled 'Religion and Culture'.[138] The essay was written by Lou Andreas-Salomé, a St.-Petersburg-born writer who had once been a friend of Friedrich Nietzsche. In the late 1890s she resided in Berlin and maintained close intellectual contact with Simmel. She and her husband paid visits to Simmel's house during coffee soirees, sometimes meeting other invitees there, such as one of Simmel's young students: Rainer Maria Rilke.[139] One extant letter from Simmel to Salomé indicates that her writings on religion figured quite prominently in their discussions.[140] It is also worth noting

---

[136] Julius Kaftan, *Das Wesen der christlichen Religion* (Basel: C. Detloff, 1888), p. 33. For a Schleiermacherian reading of religion, see also Ernst Brausch, 'Das psychologische Wesen der Religion', *Zeitschrift für wissenschaftliche Theologie* 37(2), 1894, pp. 161–174.

[137] Hermann Siebeck, *Lehrbuch der Religionsphilosophie* (Freiburg im Breisgau: J. C. B. Mohr, 1893), pp. 263–268. See also Rudolf Schulze, 'Religion: Eine philosophische Skizze', *Zeitschrift für Missionskunde und Religionswissenschaft* 16(9–12), 1901, pp. 257–261, 289–305, 335–338, 358–365.

[138] Lou Andreas-Salomé, 'Religion und Cultur: Religionspsychologische Studie', *Die Zeit* 183, 2 April 1898, pp. 5–7.

[139] Cf. Georg Simmel, letter to Rainer Maria Rilke, 20 January 1898, GSG 22, p. 280.

[140] Letter to Lou Andreas-Salomé, 10 May 1896, GSG 22, p. 203. In this letter Simmel mentions her article 'Jesus der Jude' [Jesus the Jew] published in *Neue Deutsche Rundschau* 7, 1896, pp. 342–351.

that many of Simmel's essays and reviews in the period between 1895 and 1909 were published in *Die Zeit*.[141]

One should therefore not be surprised to find many ideas in Salomé's article that Simmel himself would later put forward in his writings on religion. The modern condition, she argued, is characterised by the growing differentiation of cultural spheres. Each such sphere originally belonged to religion, but then separated from it. Those spheres were like sisters born to the same mother who grew up and each went their own way. This separation signified contrary things to the daughters and the mother. The daughters were on their way to maturity and full development of their own powers, yet for religion the separation meant 'living within empty walls that are cold and dead if they were not allowed to encompass all the life that was born within them'.[142] Religion cannot turn itself into just a specialised field like other activities. It is forever looking for the unity of human life.

In this situation, religion can find consolation in two considerations. First, even in the modern differentiated world, it can retain the meaning of its own existence if it retreats into inwardness. This means abandoning the religiosity of faith, by which Salomé understood attachment to the external attributes of a particular religion, such as God, dogma etc., and becoming 'the religious outside of faith but within life itself and its various forms of expression as the finest and utmost blossom of human sentiment in them'.[143] Religion thus becomes merely a sentiment, and the religious sentiment may reside within each human activity. Whatever a person's specialisation may be – science, art or the life of practice – these activities can be performed with the religious sentiment in the background. Thus, even if objective religion has been discredited and become obsolete, the subjective religious sentiment can survive and even flourish in the condition of modernity.

There is also another consolation. The salvation of which religion dreams is that of God becoming the life of life. But this happens only at two extreme points of human development: 'deep down in the dark, where man was born as man, while imagining himself to descend from a god – but also at the finest and highest peaks of culture, where man only then imagines himself to be truly human when he begets God'.[144] Salomé envisioned therefore that religion would in the future retain its power

---

[141] See David Frisby (ed.), *Georg Simmel in Wien: Texte und Kontexte aus dem Wien der Jahrhundertwende* (Vienna: WUV, 2000).
[142] Andreas-Salomé, 'Religion und Cultur', p. 5.   [143] Ibid.   [144] Ibid., p. 7.

not by playing according to the rules of contemporary fragmentariness but by overcoming it and imposing upon it a spiritual integration of the highest order. This was an unmistakably Nietzschean motif, that of the *Übermensch*, and not in its Simmelian but rather in its transformative revolutionary interpretation, apparently more faithful to Nietzsche's own position. This conformed to the times, as the talk about Nietzscheanism becoming a new religion on the basis of 'the faith in the *Übermensch*'[145] was very much in the air.

Besides this point, however, the parallels between Salomé's essay and Simmel's explorations of religion are striking. Simmel's central motif was the distinction between two aspects of religion: 'religion' and 'religiosity', as he called them in *Religion*,[146] or 'objective religion' and 'subjective religion', as he called them later in *Rembrandt*.[147] Like Salomé, when using this distinction Simmel did not aim at reconciling religiosity with religion but at clearly differentiating between the two and assigning fundamental priority to the subjective aspect: religiosity.

According to Simmel, religiosity is in general the principal (even if not necessarily historical) origin of every religion: '[R]eligion does not create religiosity, but religiosity creates religion.'[148] Religiosity is the only thing that all religions possess in common, for in all other respects – their deities, dogmas, moral teachings etc. – they greatly differ from one another. But for the modern condition, the notion of the priority of religiosity is of special importance. As Simmel argued in 'The Problem of Religion Today' (1911), religious faith lost its force and was no longer capable of satisfying the religious needs of the soul that remained as strong as ever. The only way of satisfying these religious needs was by emancipating religious living from its connection to the belief-systems of all positive religions.

Simmel was aware that he had suggested something very far-reaching and that this change would involve 'a radical reconstruction of spiritual life'.[149] The rejection of all dogmas would mean going much further than

---

[145] Hans v. Liebig, 'Nietzsches Religion', *Die Umschau* 4(42), 1900, p. 823. Simmel was familiar with Andreas-Salomé's description of Nietzsche and even defended it against her critics. He argued that whatever its shortcomings, the value of Salomé's portrait of Nietzsche lay in her attempt to outline the psychological image of the entire person. ('Elizabeth Försters Nietzsche-Biographie' [1895], GSG 1, pp. 345–346.)

[146] *Religion*, trans. H. J. Helle, in Simmel, *Essays on Religion*, p. 150. [GSG 10, p. 54.]

[147] *Rembrandt: An Essay in the Philosophy of Art*, trans. A. Scott and H. Staubmann (New York: Routledge, 2005), pp. 111–113. [GSG 15, pp. 451–454.]

[148] *Religion*, p. 150. [GSG 10, p. 54.]

[149] 'The Problem of Religion Today', trans. H. J. Helle, in Simmel, *Essays on Religion*, p. 9. [GSG 12, p. 150.]

even religious 'liberalism', which confined 'the religious person to specific objects [*Inhalte*], merely permitting freedom of choice between them', was prepared to go.[150] Such liberalism was associated in those years with Adolf Harnack (1851–1930) and Ernst Troeltsch (1865–1923). Harnack, a historian of the Christian dogma and Ritschl's disciple, was Simmel's colleague at the University of Berlin. They were personally acquainted, and Simmel even attended Harnack's lectures on the essence of Christianity, held in 1899–1900.[151] It was after attending these lectures that Simmel started writing extensively on religious philosophy and, as has been demonstrated by commentators, many of his specific claims, including interpretations of biblical passages, were indebted to Harnack.[152] One of Harnack's central ideas was that original Christianity should be understood as a way of life of small communities rather than an ordered system of beliefs.[153] Harnack held a strongly anti-Catholic view, regarding the Reformation as a return to the religion of the Gospel. Jesus's Gospel meant for him not any specific positive religion but religion as such.[154] This corresponded, of course, to Simmel's emphasis on religiosity rather than positive religion and even, in a certain sense, to his earlier ideas about the social meaning of religion as the expression of the inner unity of a social group. As for the Simmel-Troeltsch relationship, the two were even closer. They thought along parallel lines and influenced each other in many respects.[155] Troeltsch's ideas about the importance of the subjective element of religion strongly resembled those of Simmel.[156]

Nevertheless, Simmel's attitude was not only more radical than theirs but in a sense qualitatively different. Harnack's intention was certainly not to demolish Christian dogma. For him, a specific form of belief – Lutheran Christianity – and the specific texts belonging to it – the Gospels – still constituted the highest and most correct religion. And even Troeltsch, who was, on the whole, more radical than Harnack, criticised Simmel for the excesses of his 'psychologism'.[157] For Simmel, however, religious liberalism

---

[150] Ibid., p. 17. [GSG 12, p. 158.]
[151] Adolf Harnack, *Das Wesen des Christentums* (Leipzig: J. C. Hinrichs, 1900).
[152] Cf. Pflüger, *Georg Simmels Religionstheorie*, pp. 279–337.
[153] E.g. Adolf Harnack, *Lehrbuch der Dogmengeschichte*, vol. 1: *Die Entstehung des kirchlichen Dogmas*, 3rd ed. (Freiburg im Breisgau: J. C. B. Mohr, 1894), pp. 141–142, 156.
[154] Harnack, *Das Wesen des Christentums*, pp. 41, 165.
[155] See Friedemann Voigt, '*Die Tragödie des Reiches Gottes'? Ernst Troeltsch als Leser Georg Simmels* (Gütersloh: Gütersloher Verlagshaus, 1998).
[156] E.g. Ernst Troeltsch, 'Der Begriff des Glaubens', *Religion und Geisteskultur* 1(3), 1907, pp. 191–201.
[157] Ernst Troeltsch, 'Zur modernen Religionsphilosophie', *Deutsche Literaturzeitung* 28(14), 6 April 1907, p. 841.

that still adhered in one way or another to Christian dogma, was merely a shaky compromise. He was concerned with the question of the redemptive potential of religion *per se*. And to him, unaffiliated subjective religiosity appeared as the only mode in which the modern mind could express its religious longings, even if this solution threatened Christianity itself.

This subjectivist approach had, however, its own share of difficulties that were related not to the issue of the preservation of Christian articles of faith but to the coherence of Simmel's own philosophy. To make his case for religiosity Simmel had to define its features, to explain what constitutes the religious disposition and the religious personality as such versus the scientific, moral or aesthetic disposition. In 'Contributions to the Epistemology of Religion' (1902), Simmel suggested that religiosity was a fundamental category communicating significance to all contents of experience, similar to other categories, such as being, duty, willing.[158] But what was this religiosity?

Now, what is striking in Simmel's account of religion is that he was reluctant to provide a clear definition of what religious sentiment actually involved. In the 1902 essay, he offered a rather impressionistic description. He attributed to religiosity a particular psychological tone that could be described as a 'characteristic interchange of aspiration and enjoyment, of giving and talking, of humility and exaltation, of fusion and separation', but he also immediately added that the unity of this tone cannot be conceived 'as composed of those elements'.[159]

Likewise, in *Religion* (1906), he approached the matter somewhat hesitantly and after a while. He mentioned 'fervour and dedication' as illustrating 'an act of religiosity'.[160] Further on he stressed the feeling of dependence: 'The individual feels bound to some general, higher principle [*an ein Allgemeines Höheres gebunden*] from which he originates and to which he ultimately returns . . . from which he is distinct and to which he is yet identical.'[161] Finally, he introduced the notion of piety, however again not as the defining component but just as a common characteristic: 'This particular type of emotion can perhaps be described in *most cases* as a piety: the attitude of the soul which becomes religion as soon as it is projected onto social norms.'[162]

In emphasising piety (*Frömmigkeit*), Simmel followed Schleiermacher. It was Schleiermacher who defined the religious attitude in terms of piety

---

[158] 'Contributions to the Epistemology of Religion', p. 124. [GSG 7, p. 12.]
[159] Ibid., p. 126. [GSG 7, p. 13.]   [160] *Religion*, p. 153. [GSG 10, p. 57.]
[161] Ibid., p. 156. [GSG 10, p. 60.]   [162] Ibid., p. 161. [GSG 10, p. 65.] Italics mine – E. P.

which he understood as the feeling of dependence. He described piety as a disposition of mind separate from either knowledge or action, the essence of which is 'the consciousness of being absolutely dependent, or, which is the same thing, of being in relation with God'.[163] Yet Simmel was not prepared to anchor his view of religiosity in the theory of piety. He mentioned this definition of religiosity-as-piety merely as a possibility, and just a few pages later he retreated into an impressionistic description, speaking of religiosity as the 'synthesis of restraint [*Gebundenheit*] and expansion of the self, of clear-sightedness and blindness, of spontaneous will [*Spontaneität*] and *dependence*, of giving and receiving'.[164] Similarly, in 'The Problem of Religion Today' (1911), Simmel spoke about the combination of 'the feelings of *dependence* and hopefulness, humility and yearning'.[165]

Simmel's writings also contain other terms that could potentially constitute the conceptual core of religion, such as faith. For Simmel, faith did not mean a set of theoretical beliefs about the world. Such beliefs are merely the lower level of the domain of knowledge, truth. Rather, faith referred to the emotional state of mind of a religious person, regardless of the theoretical validity of that person's beliefs.[166] Here too, however, Simmel spoke of faith not as the defining quality of religiosity but as merely one aspect of it, and he mentioned it not in the context of the definition of religiosity as such but within his discussion of the analogy between the social and religious.

In other words, despite the fact that Simmel's central claim with regard to religion was that it was a particular sphere of experience governed by its own specific categories, and despite the fact that the intellectual traditions with which he was clearly familiar offered him conceptual ways to formulate the constitutive components of this particularity (such as Schleiermacher's notion of piety), he was very reluctant to delineate the special characteristics of religiosity. This was hardly mere inadvertence. One should rather interpret it as a sign of the inner conflict within Simmel's approach to religion: the conflict between the whole and a part.

---

[163] Friedrich Schleiermacher, *The Christian Faith* [1830–1831] (London: Bloomsbury, 2016), p. 12. On the parallels between Simmel and Schleiermacher, see Krech, *Georg Simmels Religionstheorie*, pp. 181–185.

[164] *Religion*, p. 170. [GSG 10, p. 74.] Italics mine – E. P. Cf. Pflüger, *Georg Simmels Religionstheorie*, p. 175.

[165] 'The Problem of Religion Today', p. 10. [GSG 12, p. 151.] Italics mine – E. P.

[166] Cf. 'Contributions to the Epistemology of Religion', pp. 126–133; [GSG 7, pp. 14–20.] *Religion*, pp. 166–173. [GSG 10, pp. 69–77.]

When one examines Simmel's view of religion, one can see that his understanding of its essence was difficult to reconcile with his general claim that religiosity was just one world of experience among others. He imputed to religion the striving for comprehensive unity. In 'Religion and the Contradictions of Life' (1904), Simmel evoked Nicholas of Cusa's definition of God as '*coincidentia oppositorum*', arguing that, in addition to unifying the contradictions within our worldview, an even more fundamental quest for religion was to unify the contradictions of life.[167]

For those who, like Ritschl, adhered to the classical *Bildung* model of 'unity in variety', this would mean that religion was the ultimate or highest sphere of human experience that reconciled the contradictions among other spheres. This was not, however, Simmel's view. Rather, according to him, religion's striving for unity contained an irreconcilable dualism.

> Religion is one of the elements of life: it must take its place among other elements and must develop a relationship with them if life is to be an integrated whole. At the same time, religion is a counterpart to that which we would otherwise call our empirical life. It stands besides life as an equivalent power, expressing and balancing out the whole of life in its own right. Religion therefore is a limb and a whole organism at the same time – a part of our existence, and yet also that whole existence itself on an elevated, spiritual [*verinnerlichten*] plane.[168]

Thus the conflict between whole and part which the *Bildung* ideal was supposed to solve, and which in Ritschl's scheme was indeed solved by religion, reappeared here in the domain of religion itself. Religion claims to be both a part that possesses special spiritual characteristics and the whole that acts as the arbiter between all possible characteristics. This conflict between part and whole is a fundamentally irreconcilable contradiction.[169] Simmel's unwillingness to define religiosity in specific terms may have been the outcome of his realisation that such a definition would satisfy only the aspect of religion as a part, one world of experience among many.

Furthermore, even when Simmel occasionally did speak about religion in its role as arbiter between contradictions, this did not imply the optimistic formula of unity in variety. For example, Simmel argued that the idea of God originated in 'the absolute *within our soul*'.[170] God thus signified the absolute dimension of particular spiritual qualities: not love of a particular person but love as such, not the quest for a specific ideal but the

---

[167] 'Religion and the Contradictions of Life', in Simmel, *Essays on Religion*, p. 36. [GSG 7, p. 295.]
[168] Ibid., p. 43. [GSG 7, p. 302.]   [169] *Religion*, pp. 187–188. [GSG 7, p. 91.]
[170] Ibid., p. 172. [GSG 7, p. 76.]

quest as such, and so forth. This understanding of God as *absolute* may indeed be synonymous with the idea of unity in variety, but it need not be. And certain passages in Simmel's writings on religion in his middle period suggest that the highest unity he assigned to religion did not include variety but stood in opposition to it.

Two examples will elucidate this. First, when in his discussion of religion Simmel touched on the subject of the division of labour, his assessment of the phenomenon was significantly more pessimistic than in his earlier period. The division of labour, he argued, leads to the growing one-sidedness of individuals that prevents their formation into harmonic wholes. This one-sidedness is 'the flow of all very complex cultures',[171] in which the perfection of society is paid for 'with the imperfection of the individual'.[172] Religion may, however, avoid this one-sidedness, but it is because it is capable of avoiding differentiation. For when it is considered in terms of its most profound subjective purpose – the salvation of the soul – it creates sameness rather than difference among members of the religious community. 'This type of religious relationship precludes any essential differentiation,'[173] for none of the members of such a community contributes to the others' perfection. Simmel was, of course, aware that the social structure of religions often led to the division of labour, and he analysed in detail the phenomenon of priesthood: God's officials by vocation.[174] But his normative view of Christianity was essentially Protestant. Like Harnack, he saw in Christianity the religion of individual salvation. He clarified this point even further in the 1912 edition of *Religion* in the context of his discussion of the 'spiritual socialisation' offered by Christianity.[175] 'The idea of the invisible church' and 'the symbolic kinship [*Geschwisterlichkeit*] of all Christians', he claimed, are 'the most significant attempt ... to achieve unity without employing the means of differentiation'.[176] This does not mean that Christianity is a kind of mechanistic communism: its unity remains 'organic', it is just some sort of undifferentiated organism.[177]

Second, with regard to the question of the salvation of the soul, Simmel argued that the essence of the salvation offered by Christianity is each soul following its own individual nature.[178] However, given that all souls are equal in God's eyes and coexist in perfect harmony, the question arises as to

---

[171] Ibid., p. 189. [GSG 7, p. 93.]   [172] Ibid. [GSG 7, p. 93.]   [173] Ibid., p. 190. [GSG 7, p. 94.]
[174] Ibid., pp. 191–194. [GSG 7, pp. 95–98.]   [175] Ibid., p. 190. [GSG 7, p. 94.]
[176] Ibid. [GSG 7, p. 94.]   [177] Cf. ibid., p. 191. [GSG 7, p. 95.]
[178] In the 2nd edition of *Religion*, Simmel, apparently inspired by Buber, also brought a Hassidic story to illustrate his position (p. 195; [GSG 7, p. 99]). However, on the whole Simmel was uninterested

whether this equality is compatible with the emphasis on the distinct individuality of each soul. Simmel's answer in *Religion* was that this was possible due to the absence of competition that arises out of the division of labour. Without presupposing this competition, it is possible for religion to represent 'the distinctive individuality and the coexisting diversity in a *single* harmonious realm'.[179] In this condition there is 'differentiation' which is *not* a 'division of labour'.[180] In the 1912 edition, he tried further to clarify this somewhat obscure idea, suggesting that the value differences between souls on the empirical level do not bear on their ultimate 'being', through which they are all same, or equal.[181]

All these distinctions may appear confusing to the reader, since Simmel spoke on the one hand about 'organic' unity which is not differentiation and on the other hand about differentiation which is not the division of labour. I believe it would be pointless to draw far-reaching abstractions from these distinctions. *Religion* is not the most consistent of Simmel's texts, and it is not clear whether he envisaged any elaborate theory behind all these distinctions. They are useful, however, as indications of the general direction of his thinking. They show that in assigning unity to religion he was torn between two contrary vectors.

On the one hand, the unity embedded in religion could not be the comprehensive unity in variety in the proper sense, for such unity arises out of contradictions. This becomes clear if one juxtaposes Simmel with the following passage from Ritschl:

> In a community, the individual operates under two conditions inasmuch as he is equal to others or unequal, alternately dependent on them or acting upon them. Therefore, a psychological explanation of religion is not exhaustive, for it centres solely on the spiritual manifestations in which all humans are equal, and one person is the type for all.[182]

Ritschl postulated here the true synthesis of unity in variety, rejecting psychologism that, in his view, considered human beings only in their spiritual aspect where they are all equal. The latter was, however, precisely the position that Simmel adopted. The unity he attributed to religion was one that lay in the spiritual realm and did not recognise contradictions.

---

in Judaism, and even with regard to mysticism he was more familiar with its Christian variety. E.g., he read Meister Eckhart closely.
[179] Ibid., p. 199. [GSG 7, p. 103.] For an earlier instance of this insight in Simmel, see *Einleitung in die Moralwissenschaft*, GSG 3, p. 436.
[180] *Religion*, p. 198. [GSG 7, p. 103.]   [181] Ibid. [GSG 7, p. 102.]
[182] Ritschl, *Die christliche Lehre*, vol. 3, pp. 188–189.

On the other hand, this unity had to include some kind of variety in order to be organic and differentiated rather than monotonous. Simmel took religion into the realm of purely spiritual phenomena, yet for him the sameness on this level somehow managed to escape homogeneity.

To return to the analogy between religion and art, a similar tension existed in Simmel's view of the beautiful. The beautiful had to evoke a harmonious organic image of unity in order to avoid monotony and deception. That is why Florence was preferable to Venice. At the same time, this unity could not encompass variety fully, in all its contradictions. Contradictions could not really be absorbed and had to disappear as if by magic. Religiosity likewise offered organic unity without actually making it into comprehensive unity. It avoided contradictions rather than absorbing them. In the end, and despite Simmel's own words, religion could not really represent *coincidentia oppositorum*. In both cases, therefore, the retreat into the citadel of autonomous worlds of experience was not fully successful. In each case, the closed unity that was opposed to variety and contradictions was felt to be insufficient and to require something beyond itself.

In the domain of art, as I have shown, this consideration led Simmel to hint at the possibility of the existence of some kind of primordial unity from which artistic experience springs. Unsurprisingly, the same motif also entered his writings on religion. Consider, for example, a telling contrast between the first and second editions of *Religion*. In 1906, Simmel suggested that religion was autonomous from society: religious phenomena could not be reduced to social ones, nor vice versa; but in 1912 he spoke differently. He suggested the possibility of the existence of 'some profound moving forms of spiritual life that take effect in moulding both religious and social reality, so that the uniformity of certain phenomena derives from a single, common root that determines its shape'.[183] And in the concluding part of the treatise, which he completely revised, he described the work's argument as marked by two different motifs. One motif considered religiosity as a fundamental a priori category alongside many others. There was, however, another one. As he wrote, 'it might be possible to postulate processes and states that are *formal* in a purer sense. They manifest themselves in religious phenomena on the one hand and in social phenomena on the other'.[184]

There are thus more fundamental processes beneath religion which become religiosity only when they reach a certain threshold. This

---

[183] *Religion*, p. 165. [GSG 7, p. 69.]   [184] Ibid., p. 211. [GSG 7, p. 115.]

fundamental origin of experience remains as yet beyond our reach. No one has managed to gain an insight into it. Therefore, according to Simmel, it is preferable to recognise religiosity as a primary quality. This is why in *Religion* he adopted mainly the standpoint of the former motif, which considers religion an autonomous sphere of experience.[185] Elsewhere in publications of the same period, however, Simmel threw hints as to where to look for the primordial quality that transcends all dualisms and contradictions. Religion, he suggested, can be reduced to the more fundamental concept of life as a whole.[186]

In other words, the plurality of unities no longer worked for Simmel. Simmel was again trying to envision a comprehensive unity which would, however, be different from and superior to 'unity in variety'. But before this emerging outlook can be discussed, one should examine yet another subject that was of principal importance to Simmel during his middle period: the feminine and its essence.

3.4   Women

We have seen by now that in his middle period Simmel, growing more sceptical about the possibility of cultural redemption through comprehensive unity in variety, began instead to look for a symbol of unity that could be experienced by means of a single worldview, such as religion or art. We have also seen that these attempts turned out to be not entirely coherent and did not equip Simmel with an ultimate solution to the questions he was asking. But what if the problem of disparity was not a universal problem of modern human beings but a peculiar characteristic of only half of humanity: men? What if the other half – women – were free by virtue of their nature from the inability to maintain an integrated existence? What if only men needed art (or religion) to attain unity, whereas women possessed a quasi-aesthetic unity within their own experience? In his second period, Simmel accepted this at least as a possibility. As he put it in one of the texts of that period:

> By the over-personal becoming the directly personal way of feeling and creating for the woman, she resolves through experience the conflict between law and freedom, in which the man, having risen above the unity

---

[185] Ibid., p. 212. [GSG 7, pp. 115–116.]
[186] These passages appear in the non-translated version of 'The Problem of Religion Today' published in *Philosophische Kultur* [1911], GSG 14, pp. 376–377.

of her nature, so often exhausts himself and knows how to create the semblance and shimmer of a solution only in the form of art.[187]

If this was the case, could not feminisation be seen as a solution? The subject of the feminine was certainly of great significance to Simmel. Although within his entire corpus the amount of text dealing specifically with women is not very large, his writings on this subject are nevertheless quite salient and spread over more than two decades. Moreover, advancing women's welfare, especially in the sphere of education, was among the rare topics on which Simmel took a public stance. These philosophical and political interventions regarding the role of women in modern culture had an impact on the intellectual debates in Wilhelmine Germany.[188]

But what did Simmel want to say through these interventions? The answer to this question is not at all clear, as interpretations of his writings on women are very conflicting. On the one hand, it is sometimes argued that Simmel on the whole anticipated the feminist approaches of today,[189] with some commentators even making him into a radical representative of the feminist avant-garde.[190] On the other hand, there are scholars who insist that Simmel espoused a sharply anti-feminist or even anti-feminine view.[191]

Sometimes this conflict of interpretations is the consequence of the ambiguous implications of the theoretical views espoused by Simmel.[192]

---

[187] 'Bruchstücke aus einer Psychologie der Frauen', GSG 7, p. 294.

[188] Cf. Ingrid Gilcher-Holtey, 'Modelle "moderner" Weiblichkeit: Diskussionen im akademischen Milieu Heidelbergs um 1900', in R. M. Lepsius (ed.), *Bildungsbürgertum im 19. Jahrhundert*, III: *Lebensführung und ständische Vergesellschaftung* (Stuttgart: Klett-Cota, 1992), pp. 176–205.

[189] Lewis A. Coser, 'Georg Simmel's Neglected Contributions to the Sociology of Women', *Signs: Journal of Women in Culture and Society* 2(4), 1977, pp. 869–876; Suzanne Vromen, 'Georg Simmel and the Cultural Dilemma of Women', *History of European Ideas* 8(4/5), 1987, pp. 563–579; Lieteke van Vucht Tijssen, 'Women and Objective Culture: Georg Simmel and Marianne Weber', *Theory, Culture & Society* 8(3), 1991, pp. 203–218; Rita Felski, *The Gender of Modernity* (Cambridge, MA: Harvard University Press, 1995), p. 45; Janet Wolff, 'The Feminine in Modern Art: Benjamin, Simmel and the Gender of Modernity', *Theory, Culture & Society* 17(6), 2000, pp. 33–53; Marcel Stoetzler, 'Intersectional Individuality: Georg Simmel's Concept of "The Intersection of Social Circles" and the Emancipation of Women', *Sociological Inquiry* 86(2), 2016, pp. 216–240.

[190] Ralph M. Leck, *Georg Simmel and Avant-Garde Sociology: The Birth of Modernity, 1880–1920* (Amherst, NY: Humanity Books, 2000), pp. 131–165.

[191] Marianne Ulmi, *Frauenfragen, Männergedanken: Zu Georg Simmels Philosophie und Soziologie der Geschlechter* (Zurich: efef, 1989); Anne Witz, 'Georg Simmel and the Masculinity of Modernity', *Journal of Classical Sociology* 1(3), 2001, pp. 353–370; Ilya Parkins, 'Fashion, Femininity and the Ambiguities of the Modern: A Feminist Theoretical Approach to Simmel', in D. D. Kim (ed.), *Georg Simmel in Translation: Interdisciplinary Border-Crossings in Culture and Modernity* (Newcastle: Cambridge Scholars Press, 2006), pp. 28–49.

[192] For a theoretical analysis of Simmel's feminism, see Guy Oakes, 'Introduction: The Problem of Women in Simmel's Theory of Culture', in G. Oakes (ed.), *Georg Simmel: On Women, Sexuality, and Love* (New Haven: Yale University Press, 1984), pp. 35–55. For a more recent examination of

In general, Simmel postulated a radical incommensurability between the feminine and masculine characters, and such a view can be pushed in two opposite directions: feminist or anti-feminist. But there is also a simpler explanation. One does not need to go into the depths of philosophical interpretation in order to notice that Simmel's attitude to women as it was put forward in many of his writings was highly ambiguous or even incoherent.[193] Expressions of respect were often followed by disparaging and even hostile remarks, and calls for equality for women coexisted with denial of this equality in many aspects of life and scepticism regarding women's abilities.

One can, however, make sense of this apparent incoherence if one notes that Simmel's attitude depended on the kind of text he was writing. Usually, polemical texts, or those intended as contributions to political debates specifically on the topic of women, tended to be much more pro-feminist than texts which approached the question of women philosophically as part of a more general metaphysical project.

As for the more political texts, they belong mainly to the 1890s: the first Wilhelmine decade, which was marked by remarkable social-cultural fermentation when new moral-cultural issues came to the forefront of social life and the German women's movement experienced fast growth.[194] It was then that Simmel enlisted, albeit sometimes anonymously, in various causes related to the rights and social conditions of women.[195] As has already been mentioned, in the early 1890s Simmel flirted with socialism, and his publications on women-related issues in those years bear socialist overtones and reveal interest in the socialist debates on the women question. For example, he agreed with a socialist author whose book he reviewed that the inferior social conditions of women did not indicate that women were doomed to those conditions by nature.[196] Two of his essays published anonymously in socialist periodicals (Karl Kautsky's *Neue Zeit* and *Vorwärts*, the official paper of the Social Democratic Party),

---

Simmel's writing on gender, see Cornelia Klinger, 'Geschlecht', in Müller and Reitz (eds.), *Simmel-Handbuch*, pp. 241–246; and 'Simmels Geschlechtertheorie zwischen kritischer Beobachtung und Metaphysik', in ibid., pp. 828–843.

[193] 'Simmel's writings on women combine sociological observation with philosophical speculation in ways that often make his arguments appear contradictory, surprising, confusing, or simply wrong.' Thomas Kemple, *Simmel* (Cambridge: Polity Press, 2018), p. 92.

[194] See Richard J. Evans, *The Feminist Movement in Germany, 1894–1933* (London: Sage, 1976), pp. 39–53.

[195] In these years, he also made the social status of women part of his sociological research as can be seen from his historical overview of the connection between militarism and the status of women: 'Der Militarismus und die Stellung der Frauen' [1894], GSG 5, pp. 37–51.

[196] Review of Machetes: *Das Unrecht des Stärkeren in der Frauenfrage* [1892], GSG 1, p. 283.

dealt with the delicate topic of prostitution, suggesting a policy of outlaw-
ing street prostitution while keeping legal brothels under strict control.[197]
There, Simmel also discussed the centuries-long oppression of women and
protested against the ostracism of prostitutes. Prostitution, he argued, was
a social ill rather than an individual sin. Using Darwinist and socialist
idioms, he suggested that with the 'elimination of capitalism'[198] in the
future, these ills would be ameliorated even if prostitution would not
disappear altogether.

A more general overview of Simmel's outlook can be found in his 1892
review of Theodor Gottlieb von Hippel's pamphlet *On the Civil Betterment
of Women* (1792).[199] Hippel was a Prussian writer who in the wake of the
French Revolution called for an eventual recognition of the individual
rights of women, arguing that their inabilities were the consequence of
their oppression. Simmel related Hippel's argument with sympathy, especially emphasising his comparison of the historical condition of women
with slavery and the assertion that the absence of rights leads one to inner
debasement and habituates one to slavery.[200] Simmel mentioned the
impact of the eighteenth century on Hippel's ideas, his Rousseauan belief
that nature was good and therefore simply could not make man and
woman into such unequal beings and his gradualist view that proper
education for women would eventually make them fit for legal emancipation. Yet Simmel argued that Hippel's approach was not completely
adequate for modern tendencies. Hippel's analysis of the discrimination
of women contained two important lacunas. First, to Hippel 'the demand
for an economic independence of women does not occur'.[201] Using a kind
of Hegelian-Marxist language, Simmel argued against Hippel that 'the
realisation that personal and social values are economically conditioned,
which found its concrete expression in the modern women's movement,
escapes him'.[202] That is, the liberation of women is intimately related to
their place in the economic structure of society. The other sphere in which
Hippel was wrong was that of marriage. Simmel reproached him for
restricting the freedom of women within marriage by denying them
equality with men in respect of spouse fidelity. Whereas Hippel took the

---

[197] *Ex malis minima! Reflexionen zur Prostitutionsfrage* [1891], GSG 17, pp. 251–260; 'Some Remarks on
Prostitution in the Present and in Future' [1892], trans. M. Ritter and D. Frisby, in Frisby and
Featherstone (eds.), *Simmel on Culture*, pp. 262–270. [GSG 17, pp. 261–273.]
[198] 'Some Remarks on Prostitution', p. 269. [GSG 17, p. 270.]
[199] Theodor Gottlieb von Hippel, *Über die bürgerliche Verbesserung der Weiber* (Berlin: Vossische
Buchhandlung, 1792).
[200] 'Ein Jubiläum der Frauenbewegung', GSG 1, pp. 288–289.   [201] Ibid., p. 292.   [202] Ibid.

infidelity of men relatively lightly, that of women was damned with the harshest words.[203]

Thus, in 1892, Simmel argued that the emancipation of women, in addition to a legal aspect, should also contain economic and moral aspects. Quite soon, however, Simmel appears to have lost interest in the purely economic side of the matter. One can notice that even when he wrote on prostitution in the socialist papers, his primary concern was moral rather than economical. And as he soon abandoned socialism completely, it seems that he even developed hostility towards the arguments based on economics. This became clear during the Berlin Women's Congress that took place in 1896. This congress witnessed sharp conflict between the middle-class majority and the social-democratic wing. In his report about the congress, Simmel did not hide his aversion towards social-democratic factionalism. He accused Social Democrats of 'blind hatred, which rejects every [social] reform coming from bourgeois circles'.[204]

This does not mean that Simmel's feminism became more moderate. On the contrary, in the course of the 1890s social-democratic feminism turned out to be culturally more conservative and less avant-gardist than the feminism that developed in the left-liberal women's circles. The feminism promoted by social democratic activists was subordinated to the principles of class struggle. As the left-liberal urban intelligentsia often adopted a generally more apolitical and even anti-political stance, this enabled some of them to focus specifically on the question of women and develop a more radical attitude by far, in purely feminist terms. It was in these circles that the search for new moral and cultural forms developed, including 'the erotic movement', to use the expression of Terry Kandal,[205] that challenged the moral puritanism of mainstream bourgeois society. As Simmel clearly settled in those years for the passive support of the liberalism of the left, he became at the same time drawn into various personal lifestyle experiments, such as vegetarianism,[206] or riding a bicycle to work.[207] Cultural feminism was certainly part of the package, and henceforth Simmel focused on topics related to the cultural role of women. He

---

[203] Ibid., pp. 292–293.
[204] 'The Women's Congress and Social Democracy', trans. M. Ritter and D. Frisby, in Frisby and Featherstone (eds.), *Simmel on Culture*, p. 272. [GSG 17, p. 42.] On Simmel's dismay towards the socialist arguments put forth during the congress, see Köhnke, *Der junge Simmel*, pp. 462–468.
[205] Terry R. Kandal, *The Woman Question in Classical Sociological Theory* (Miami: Florida International University Press, 1988), pp. 108–118.
[206] Michael Landmann, 'Bausteine zur Biographie', in Gassen and Landmann (eds.), *Buch des Dankes*, p. 33.
[207] Edith Landmann, 'Erinnerungen an Simmel', in ibid., p. 208.

supported causes such as the foundation of girls' grammar schools[208] and the admission of women to universities.[209]

However, even this story has its nuances. For even in respect of the causes Simmel supported, his personal attitude towards women and the feminine was ambiguous. He did care about the social conditions of prostitutes, but his main concern in his advocacy of reform in the sphere of prostitution was protecting the health of men who used the prostitutes' services. And although he was disparaged for having too many women and 'oriental people' (that is, Jews) in the audience,[210] this testimony should not be taken at face value, as some commentators do, as if it testifies to Simmel's belief in the intellectual equality of women and his full respect of them. Some of his assertions actually suggest the opposite. Even in the published texts where he praised foreign female students as being, on the whole, 'serious, diligent and intelligent personalities',[211] he was overtly critical of the Berlin women 'who are seeking entry to the lectures not in order to pursue studies as a professional calling but in order to perfect their general "education" [*"Bildung"*]'.[212] And in private correspondence he was even blunter. Thus, after relating in a letter to Heinrich Rickert (1898) that he had many foreigners and women in his class, he added:

> I cannot say that I am very happy about the high percentage of female listeners: they disturb for me the uniformity of the audience. Since in fact I speak not at all to the listeners but to myself, I like it when the audience is as colourless and neutral as possible. The duality of appearances and the colourful clothes disturb me.[213]

All this shows that on the personal level Simmel's attitude towards women was often marked by uneasiness and condescension. This did not preclude him from speaking on behalf of women's causes, but it coloured those texts where immediate practical impact was not the primary purpose. These were the philosophical essays on the nature of womanhood.

Simmel's philosophical texts on women are often read by commentators in terms of the women's question. It appears to me, however, that these texts are less about women than about Simmel's own philosophical journey. When Simmel wrote in this mode about women, his point of

---

[208] [Gutachten über die Petition zur >Gestattung bzw. Errichtung vollständiger Mädchengymnasien<, 27 March 1903], GSG 17, p. 64.
[209] 'Frauenstudium an der Berlin Universität.' [Lesebrief vom 21 December 1899], GSG 17, pp. 326–327.
[210] See the letter of Dietrich Schäfer, quoted in Landmann, 'Bausteine zur Biographie', pp. 26–27.
[211] 'Frauenstudium an der Berlin Universität.', p. 326.   [212] Ibid.
[213] Letter to Heinrich Rickert, 15 August 1898, GSG 22, p. 305.

reference was not specifically women or the women's movement. He was rather concerned with a set of metaphysical questions, in which feminine nature was merely an object of reflection through which those questions could be re-examined, a convenient abstraction, like other abstractions discussed in his numerous essays: God, beauty, society etc. For this reason, Simmel's writings on women are perhaps less of value for gender philosophy than is often assumed. Yet for the same reason they are important as another brick with which Simmel's cultural philosophy in general, and his understanding of modernity in particular, was built. In other words, in his philosophy of women, the subject – women – is secondary and accidental, whereas the form – philosophy – is primary and essential.

The sources of Simmel's perception of women are therefore not so much contemporary public debates and feminist explorations but the commonly assumed cultural stereotypes about the feminine and the prevalent attitudes towards women of leading German philosophers. In respect of the view of women, everyday discourse and high-brow philosophical texts were actually quite similar. For German thought as it developed in the eighteenth and nineteenth centuries reflected the cultural context of the society and culture in which it emerged, and this society and culture were among the most women-excluding of the major European countries. This was partly the consequence of the origins of classical German culture, which were simultaneously middle-class and illiberal. For on the one hand, the non-bourgeois sources of many other cultures – mainly French, but also Russian, and to some extent English – offered more space for the active role of women, given that the aristocratic or even peasant life sometimes provided social opportunities for the emergence of independent and powerful female characters. On the other hand, the bourgeois elements of the cultures to the west of Germany developed within a political setting that quickly took the path of liberalisation and democratisation, which also included significant elements of the legal emancipation of women. Germany had the worst of both worlds. It was less liberal than France and Britain, but the predominantly middle-class cultural paradigm entrenched the burgher emphasis on the division of labour in the family where the male head enjoyed complete legal and cultural dominion. In many respects, in Germany of the mid-nineteenth century, the prevalent cultural attitude towards the standing of women in society was more patriarchal than during the age of Enlightenment with its Berlin salons or that of early Romanticism with its cult of love and humanity.[214]

---

[214] Cf. Matthew Jefferies, *Imperial Culture in Germany, 1871–1918* (Basingstoke: Palgrave Macmillan, 2003), p. 18.

The common view was that there existed fundamental differences between men and women, which were assumed to be of both biological and spiritual nature. These differences were expressed in everyday language by a series of dichotomies of masculine versus feminine qualities, such as 'active' versus 'passive', 'doing' versus 'being', 'rational' versus 'emotional' etc.[215] These differences, figuring prominently in contemporary lexicons, also entered the refined levels of high culture. German philosophers even used them as metaphors in their metaphysical arguments. When Schopenhauer, for example, wanted to emphasise the passivity of reason [*die Vernunft*], its inability to create of itself, he spoke about it as 'feminine in nature', which 'can give only after it has received'.[216]

Most classical German thinkers, such as Kant, Fichte and Wilhelm von Humboldt, espoused the 'polarised philosophy of sexes', which reflected this dichotomy.[217] This polarised philosophy did not always lead to the postulate of the inferiority of women. The Romantic generation, for example, strived to elevate the significance of the feminine. In their view, the feminine, while qualitatively different from the masculine, contributed together with it, and often on equal terms, to the elevation of humanity.[218] Respect often evolved into veneration. And towards the end of the nineteenth century, critics of modern social dislocation, such as Ferdinand Tönnies, even used the alleged polarity between the sexes to emphasise the aspects of woman which the cold *Gesellschaft* lacks: the importance of conscience, the orientation towards home, the rejection of the calculating world of trade and business.[219]

Yet the negative attitude springing from polarised philosophy was no less common among nineteenth-century thinkers. Hostile outbursts towards women, such as Schopenhauer's essay 'On Women' or Nietzsche's various statements from *Thus Spoke Zarathustra* onwards, are well known.[220]

---

[215] Karin Hausen, 'Family and Role-Division: The Polarisation of Sexual Stereotypes in the Nineteenth Century: An Aspect of the Dissociation of Work and Family Life', in Richard J. Evans and W. R. Lee (eds.), *German Family: Essays on the Social History of the Family in Nineteenth- and Twentieth-Century Germany* (London: Croom Helm, 1981), pp. 55–57. Cf. Ute Frevert, *Women in German History: From Bourgeois Emancipation to Sexual Liberation* (Oxford: Berg Publishers, 1989), p. 18.

[216] Schopenhauer, *The Will as World and Representation*, vol. 1, § 10, p. 50.

[217] Hausen, 'Family and Role-Division', p. 60.

[218] On a similar view in Schlegel, see, e.g., Hannelore Scholz, *Widersprüche im bürgerlichen Frauenbild: Zur ästhetischen Reflexion und poetischen Praxis bei Lessing, Friedrich Schlegel und Schiller* (Weinheim: Deutscher Studien, 1992), p. 112.

[219] Ferdinand Tönnies, *Community and Civil Society*, trans. J. Harris and M. Hollis (Cambridge: Cambridge University Press, 2001), pp. 162, 165–171.

[220] Arthur Schopenhauer, 'On Women', trans. E. F. J. Payne in *Parerga and Paralipomena* (Oxford: Clarendon Press, 1974), vol. 2, pp. 614–626. On Nietzsche's attitude to women, see, e.g.,

And as is usually the case in such things, the most common-held attitude lay somewhere in between. Stylistically more polite than Schopenhauer and Nietzsche, the typical German writers of the nineteenth century likewise avoided Romantic indiscretions and confined women to the inferior position. It is important to stress that this attitude was not 'reactionary' in the proper sense of the word. More often than not it coexisted with the assertive middle-class drive for modernisation. It was precisely because women were not considered consonant with the dynamism of modern society that they were confined to the protection of the bourgeois house. It was rather the critics of modern individualistic industrial society, such as Tönnies, who sometimes recommended 'feminine' qualities as an antidote for the ills of modernity.

Whatever direction this polarised view took, its fundamentals were widely shared throughout the nineteenth century, testifying again to the remarkable continuity of major cultural postulates. A quotation from a late eighteenth-century text by the proto-Romantic Wilhelm von Humboldt, in which he spoke about woman as the custodian of family relations and morality, would be as good an example of this view as many others:

> Wholly exempt as she is from most outward occupations, and absorbed almost entirely only by those which leave the soul untouched – stronger in what she can be than in what she can do ... more richly endowed with all the means of immediate, indefinable expression, a more delicate frame, a more moving eye, a more winning voice – destined rather, in her relations with others, to expect and receive, than to initiate ... ceaselessly striving in her union to experience and grasp what the other experiences ... inspired at the same time with the courage which loving care and the consciousness of strength infuse into soul ... woman is strictly speaking, nearer to the ideal human nature than man ... As the poet profoundly says, 'Nach Freiheit strebt der Mann, das Weib nach Sitte.'[221]

Now, when a century later Simmel began to write his essays on women, the basic parameters of his estimation were not very different. Like Humboldt, he spoke about the orientation of woman to custom and to home and argued that the potential in her being was more significant than the actualised. Like Humboldt, he occasionally appealed to the authority of Goethe whose line from *Torquato Tasso* about men seeking freedom and

Julian Young, 'Nietzsche and Women', in Ken Gemes and John Richardson (eds.), *The Oxford Handbook of Nietzsche* (Oxford: Oxford University Press, 2013), pp. 46–62.

[221] Wilhelm von Humboldt, *The Limits of State Action*, trans. J. W. Burrow (Indianapolis: Liberty Fund, 1993), p. 25.

women seeking good morals (*Sitte*) he liked to quote.[222] Of course this does not necessarily mean that Simmel took these opinions directly from Humboldt. It means only that Simmel was stepping into a well-trodden path of reflection by German theorists on gender differences and relationships between the sexes.[223]

This philosophical reflection, however, was presented by him in the language of late nineteenth-century European anthropology and sociology and was akin to the argument put forward by leading social thinkers of the time.[224] Generally speaking, his argument was that modernity is differentiation, and differentiation is the domain of men. It was outlined in Simmel's first attempt to theorise the feminine in his essay 'Towards the Psychology of Women', published in 1890 in Lazarus's and Steinthal's *Zeitschrift für Völkerpsychologie und Sprachwissenschaft*.[225] In this text, Simmel, clearly influenced by his early Spencerianism and by Schmoller, was careful to distance himself from dogmatic essentialism. This does not mean that the young Simmel necessarily rejected essentialism. On the contrary, he even applied the notion of differentiation to the sphere of physiology, suggesting that the female sex might be by nature less differentiated than the male sex. In the entire world of nature, 'the female is more similar throughout to the young members of her own species than is the male', and 'the surface of the male body is more differentiated than that of the female'.[226] He did not deny therefore that biological factors might contribute to the prevalence of certain psychological traits among women. And as we shall see later, the mature Simmel would be driven even more strongly towards the essentialist view. Yet in this early essay he put aside the question of whether this condition of lesser differentiation among women 'should be attributed to inner necessity and immutability or to a possible continuous development through changed living conditions'.[227] He noted that his analysis dealt with averages and that there might be deviations in particular cases. Therefore, when one speaks about women 'in plural', one 'should be content with dealing at best with a mere majority'.[228]

---

[222] E.g. 'The Relative and the Absolute in the Problem of the Sexes', trans. G. Oakes, in *On Women, Sexuality, and Love*, p. 126. [GSG 14, p. 249.]

[223] Cornelia Klinger is right when she suggests that Simmel's approach can be read as a sum of gender theories that emerged between the late eighteenth and the turn of the twentieth centuries. Klinger, 'Simmels Geschlechtertheorie', p. 842.

[224] Cornelia Klinger, e.g., points to parallels in this respect between Simmel and French thinkers such as Durkheim and Le Bon. Klinger, 'Geschlecht', p. 243.

[225] 'Zur Psychologie der Frauen' [1890], GSG 2, pp. 66–102.   [226] GSG 2, p. 67.

[227] GSG 2, p. 68.   [228] GSG 2, p. 66.

The features common to this majority of women contain no surprises. Simmel spoke about the predominance of feeling and disregard for objectivity in women and hence their indifference to the value of objective truth, their inability to be good critics of art, as well as their preference for moral custom over impartial justice. He merely tried to explain these traits as consequences of the deficit in differentiation. Non-differentiation makes women into more unified beings than men. In them there is no wide gap between part and whole, and therefore to whatever object they turn their attention, they approach it with the entirety of their being.

Simmel's interpretation sometimes bore a tone of empathy and understanding, such as, for example, when he tried to explain to frustrated men that 'feminine' traits should not be taken for what they seem. Thus indifference towards the value of truth does not imply any deficit in logical abilities.[229] On occasion he even suggested that this feminine 'unity' had something positive in itself, and that moving towards the condition of a more developed differentiation might entail a loss for women, at least for most of them:

> The defenders of emancipation, who wish to release women from their bondage to knitted stocking and cooking pot, care not to consider that since one cannot do without the functions described here or, for very good reasons, take them away from women, increasing differentiation among women can indeed liberate a number of them so that they dedicate themselves to higher and more intellectual professions, but only at the price of binding the rest more tightly and with a much greater degree of specialisation to those functions.[230]

Progress in differentiation might also harm the institute of marriage, for the more differentiated women would likely display less fidelity and precisely for the same reason that infidelity was common among men and generally forgiven by society: where the whole personality is not involved in every specific action, as with differentiated beings, guilt for an action is less directly related to the entirety of that personality.[231]

This weighing of the pros and cons of differentiation for women and for gender relationships in general did not, however, affect the fundamental position that the state of non-differentiation is one of evolutionary inferiority, even if it produces significant abilities absent from more differentiated beings. Thus the remarkable ability of foresight that Simmel attributed to women 'points to the lower level of perceptiveness which is characteristic of animals and less-developed peoples [*niedere Völker*]'.[232]

---

[229] GSG 2, p. 70.   [230] GSG 2, p. 88.   [231] GSG 2, p. 89.   [232] GSG 2, p. 74.

Women, in his view, were indeed endowed with unity, but this was not the unity Simmel was looking for in that period. His unity was that which crowned the process of differentiation: unity in variety. The primordial unity of women was, however, of a different sort, and he felt that he needed to explain the difference between the two:

> Here is one of the frequent cases, when the final link of the process displays the same form as its opening link. *After* full specialisation and differentiation of the entity's parts has been attained, *after* each faculty has gained the state of the perfectly developed autonomy, it is of course the life task of the higher order to bring this manifold again into unity ... But if that process has not taken place, if unification does not proceed on the enriched material, it is obvious that the precondition for that advantage which is granted to women has not to a degree been fulfilled among them.[233]

Thus, for the young Simmel, unity in variety as the ideal and task of modernity had nothing to do with the specifically feminine unity which precedes differentiation rather than resolves it. Therefore, women at this stage had nothing to offer to the dilemmas of modernity. It appeared that attaining truly fruitful unity still remained the business of men, and women could partake of it only if and when they developed into differentiated beings.

Not that such development was impossible. Although at the beginning of the essay Simmel said that he would suspend judgement about the possibility of differentiation for women, later, as the argument proceeded, it appeared that the historical and cultural facts he mentioned spoke in favour of such a possibility. Thus he referred to Burckhardt regarding the cases where 'the woman ... enjoys more diversified development and thus more closely approaches the male type'.[234] He also discussed the nature of the phenomenon of flirtation (*Koketterie*), which, according to him, springs from the same source: the decrease in the degree of feminine unity in the periods of 'increase in culture [*Steigerung der Kultur*]'.[235] To the high level of differentiation 'in the male mind that conditions the susceptibility to flirtation, there should correspond a similar degree of differentiation in the female temperament when doing the same'.[236]

Yet, in the final account, differentiation is not only possible but also desirable and recommended. It may lead to an increase in infidelity, but it may also result in the increase of its opposite, encouraging a life of monogamy and love. Simmel spoke about 'the refinement through love',

[233] GSG 2, p. 84.   [234] GSG 2, p. 89.   [235] GSG 2, p. 95.   [236] GSG 2, p. 99.

which consists partly 'in the cultivating [*höherbildenden*] differentiation through a relationship on the basis of expressed individuality'.[237]

To summarise Simmel's position so far: he suggested that women were on the whole different from men; that this difference was the consequence of social conditions rather than embedded in their essence; that they were at an inferior stage on the evolutionary path towards comprehensive unity, a unity which should not be confused with the primordial unity of the feminine character; and that despite the fact that the process of differentiation in and among women might have its negative sides, on the whole this was the only plausible path forward for women in the modern world. Philosophically, therefore, this view postulated that modernity was gender-coloured: it was masculine. From the standpoint of the requirements of modernity, the feminine character was flawed, and it could be remedied only through integration into the world of differentiation.

This view in itself was not necessarily anti-emancipationist. The project of the social, legal and political integration of women into the rules of the game of modernity was not confined merely to Enlightenment tracts, such as that of Hippel, or to liberal Anglo-American feminism. Calls for equality on the basis of the principal identity of human nature were occasionally made in nine-teenth-century Germany as well.[238] And although feminism there took, for historical reasons, mainly the democratic deficit in the Second German Empire, on the whole a different form, caring less about political rights and emphasising the essential differences between men and women, this approach should not be seen as the opposite of the former. The German feminist movement did care about integrating women into the rules of the games of modernity where it mattered, especially for the middle-class women who formed the backbone of this movement, calling, for example, for the broadening of the range of professions into which women were allowed.[239]

Therefore, the conceptual postulates formulated by Simmel in his 1890 essay were all he might need if he wished to advance the ideal of the emancipation of women into modernity. This emancipation would produce women as more differentiated beings who at the same time would become more similar to men. For according to the logic of the theory of social differentiation, growing differentiation within groups also implies growing similarities between members across groups.[240]

---

[237] GSG 2, p. 92.
[238] E.g. Hedwig Dohm, *Der Frauen Natur und Recht* (Berlin: Wedekind & Schwieger, 1876).
[239] On the feminist movement in Germany, see, e.g., Evans, *The Feminist Movement in Germany*; Frevert, *Women in German History*.
[240] *Über sociale Differenzierung: Sociologische und psychologische Untersuchungen* [1890], GSG 2, p. 169.

In fact, over the course of the 1890s and 1900s, there were authors whose starting points were similar to that of the young Simmel and who envisioned the integration of women into the modernised world without reneging on the principles of modernity. Consider the popular writer Wilhelm Bölsche who considered the process of evolution as leading to the integration of woman in cultural life. In his *Love Life in Nature* (1898–1902), Bölsche developed a peculiar kind of Darwinism, where instead of a competitive struggle for existence he envisioned the universe grounded in the universal principle of erotic attraction, and argued that women by nature were similar to men in their physical and intellectual capacities, and that the main problem was merely the physical degeneration of their bodies. He called upon women, as well as men, to take care of their bodies, which would lead as a result to their 'growing participation in the ever-increasing spiritualisation of culture'[241] and to the blossoming of their intellectual powers.

A few years later, sociologist Franz Müller-Lyer linked the emancipation of women to the dynamics of differentiation even more directly. In his *Phases of Culture and Directions of Progress* (1908), he divided history into three epochs on the basis of the kind of differentiation prevalent in each. In the first epoch, he argued, one observes the initial division of labour between men and women; in the second there is a growing differentiation among men themselves. Finally, in the third period, differentiation takes place also among women. Contemporary civilisation, Müller-Lyer suggested, finds itself at the beginning of the third phase.[242] In this approach, therefore, the connection between modernity and masculinity turns out to be contingent, and women are supposed to find their place and role in the overall process of modernisation.

The same conceptual postulates could, however, bring about a very different kind of feminism. Instead of suggesting that women should become more differentiated beings, one could also argue that differentiation itself was a problem. One could reject the liberal masculine *Bildung*,[243] arguing instead that women should cultivate their harmonious essence in order to shape an alternative and superior culture. This view was

---

[241] W. Bölsche, *Das Liebesleben in der Natur: Eine Entwickelungsgeschichte der Liebe*, vol. 3 (Leipzig: Eugen Diederichs, 1903), p. 289.

[242] Franz Müller-Lyer, *The History of Social Development*, trans. E. Coote Lake and H. A. Lake (London: George Allen & Unwin, 1920), pp. 205–219. [*Phasen der Kultur und Richtungen des Fortschritts: Soziologische Überblicke* (Munich: J. F. Lehmann, 1908).]

[243] Cf. Peter Davies, *Myth, Matriarchy and Modernity: Johann Jakob Bachofen in German Culture 1860–1945* (Berlin: Walter de Gruyter, 2010), pp. 175–176.

more esoteric than the mainstream bourgeois position, but in the course of the 1890s it spread among radical and bohemian intellectuals.

The vision of the feminine as an alternative to modernity was not a new ideal. Some early Romantics professed it. Their language, however, was socially too naïve for the post-Romantic late nineteenth century. In that age, such a vision had to be expressed in the language of human anthropology and acknowledge the well-entrenched motif of social evolution. The writer who enabled such a transformation was Swiss thinker Johann Jakob Bachofen. On the basis of his study of ancient myths, Bachofen argued that patriarchy had been preceded by a matriarchic social and legal order.[244] He himself did not propagate the idea of a return to matriarchy, considering the masculine order as the peak of human civilisation. According to him, it was patriarchalism that was responsible for the emergence of individualism,[245] for creating the world of becoming and multiplicity.[246]

On some occasions, Bachofen adopted the commonplace evolutionary approach, arguing that 'the development of the human race knows no leaps, no sudden progression, but only gradual transitions',[247] and he considered the patriarchal stage to be the end result of this long process. Matriarchy was only an intermediate stage in this evolutionary development. Yet at the same time he presented a different story: not that of a gradually evolving human civilisation but of swift and often bloody upheavals[248] or, as one could say today, of paradigm changes. Considered from this point of view, matriarchy was a self-sufficient way of life that contrasted with patriarchy. It was an ordered, gentle and peaceful human condition that endowed matriarchic peoples with the feeling of unity of life.[249] The matriarchic world was the world of being rather than becoming.

The motif of matriarchy as the alternative to masculine modernity had a great impact on the intellectual fringes on both the left and right who aspired to supersede the existing order. Thus Friedrich Engels considered Bachofen to be a genius who started a real revolution, even if he had no patience for what he took as Bachofen's 'Idealism'.[250] On the opposite side

---

[244] Johann Jakob Bachofen, *Das Mutterrecht: Eine Untersuchung über die Gynaikokratie der alten Welt nach ihrer religiösen und rechtlichen Natur* (Stuttgart: Krais und Hoffmann, 1861).

[245] Johann Jakob Bachofen, *Myth, Religion and Mother Right: Selected Writings of J.J. Bachofen*, trans. R. Manheim (Princeton: Princeton University Press, 1967), p. 110.

[246] Ibid., pp. 125, 146.   [247] Ibid., p. 98.   [248] Ibid., p. 93.   [249] Ibid., p. 91.

[250] Cynthia Eller, *Gentlemen and Amazons: The Myth of Matriarchal Prehistory, 1861–1900* (Berkeley: University of California Press, 2011), p. 110.

of the ideological spectrum, the idea of matriarchy inspired the members of the Munich Cosmic Circle around Ludwig Klages and Karl Wolfskehl who worshipped Mother Earth.[251]

Furthermore, from the 1890s onwards, elements of this vision began to appeal to broader metropolitan cultural circles who played with the notion of the primordial mother figure as an alternative to the discontents of modernity. Such revaluation of values can be found, for example, in the writings of Lou Andreas-Salomé. As has already been mentioned, in those years Salomé kept in close intellectual contact with Simmel and her 1899 piece 'The Human Being as Woman' can be plausibly interpreted as engaging with the ideas of the young Simmel. She accepted the view that women were undifferentiated beings but refused to see this as a defect. For this lack of differentiation grants the feminine 'more intact harmony, safer consensus'.[252] The feminine relates to the masculine as 'a piece of the most ancient, in the oldest sense noblest aristocracy'.[253] It is this lesser differentiation which constitutes the creative power of woman.[254] It protects her from the tragic split characterising men. As if woman, as a totality, lived in a primordial dream.[255]

It is against the backdrop of such radical ideas that the crystallisation of Simmel's position in his second period took place. His modified position with regard to women found its expression in the essays published in the early and mid-1900s, which included the first version of 'Female Culture' (1902), 'Fragments from a Psychology of Women' (1904) and 'Philosophy of Sexes: Fragments' (1906).[256] These essays display continuity with his earlier writings on the same subject, adopting the same principal view of women as undifferentiated beings, although there is a certain change in terminology: the word 'differentiation' – previously the key marker of modernity – takes a back seat, whereas some other terms signifying the peculiarity of modernity, such as 'objective', take a more prominent place in Simmel's vocabulary.

More significant, however, is the change in mood. Instead of the earlier civilisational optimism, now the phenomenon of modern specialisation is understood as an almost tragic condition that leads to a disconnect between the subject and his product.[257] Hence Simmel is less interested

---

[251] Cf. Davies, *Myth, Matriarchy and Modernity*, pp. 177–182.

[252] Lou Andreas-Salomé, 'Der Mensch als Weib: Ein Bild im Umriß' [1899], in *Die Erotik: Vier Aufsätze* (Frankfurt am Main: Ullstein, 1992), p. 7.

[253] Ibid., p. 10.   [254] Ibid., p. 14.   [255] Ibid., p. 37.

[256] 'Weibliche Kultur' [1902], GSG 7, pp. 64–83; 'Bruchstücke aus einer Psychologie der Frauen' [1904]; 'Philosophie der Geschlechter: Fragmente' [1906], GSG 8, pp. 74–81.

[257] Cf. 'Weibliche Kultur' [1902], GSG 7, p. 67.

in harmonising variety than in circumventing it. He is searching for
a direct path to unity, void of conflicts and contradictions. But then the
harmony of the feminine soul, previously considered as a sign of its
civilisational inferiority, can indicate that at least half of humanity is, by
virtue of its intrinsic mental structure, redeemed from the condition that
plagues the other half. What if this effortless unity of the feminine, its
'beautiful soul' that does not require any dialectical engagement with the
world in order to flourish, is the blueprint for overcoming the discontents
of modernity? If this is the case, the individualised and objectivised nature
of man should not be considered necessarily superior. This superiority is an
illusion due to the fact that 'our set of values was created by men and thus
their way of building the world and experiencing life became the top
values'.[258] And if the feminine nature is no longer seen as the consequence
of incomplete modernisation but rather represents a civilisational alternative, then it is only natural that Simmel's thought should take a more
explicit essentialist turn, in which the feminine is considered
a fundamental category in itself.

The essential in woman, according to him, is that there is no separation
in her between inner subjectivity and outer objectification. On the contrary, woman engages the world with the totality of her personality:

> The whole depth and beauty of the feminine nature, which make it the
> redemption and reconciliation of the masculine mind, is grounded in this
> unity [*Einheitlichkeit*], in this organic, immediate connection of the person-
> ality with all of its expressions, in this indivisibility of 'I' which knows only
> of 'all or nothing'.[259]

Even those features that seem to contradict this assertion are now explained
as confirming it. Consider again the case of flirtation, earlier described as
a phenomenon of an advanced cultural stage and signifying a peculiar form
of feminine differentiation. In the article 'Psychology of Flirtation' (1909),
flirtation is now explained in terms of the basic unity of feminine nature.
Although it seems to be 'a consciously dualistic form of conduct' that
'stands in complete contradiction to [the] "uniformity" of the female
nature',[260] in fact, women's nature 'does not run counter to the dualism
of flirtation'.[261] Refusing and conceding, which are embedded in flirtation,

---

[258] 'Philosophie der Geschlechter', GSG 8, p. 81.   [259] 'Weibliche Kultur' [1902], GSG 7, p. 68.
[260] 'Psychologie der Koketterie', GSG 12, p. 40. Quoted from the translation of the identical passage in
the later version of this essay: 'Flirtation', trans. G. Oakes, in *On Women, Sexuality, and Love*,
p. 138. [GSG 14, p. 262.]
[261] GSG 12, p. 40. Or 'Flirtation', p. 138. [GSG 14, p. 262.]

are not two distinct heterogeneous elements. Rather, the woman's 'relationship to the male in flirtation represents a distinctive synthesis of the crucial aspect of this relationship. This is because ... it is precisely the relationship of the woman to the man that is exhausted by the processes of concession and denial'.[262] Conceding and refusing is thus what women and only women can do in a perfect manner.[263] In other words, flirtation is part of their unified primordial character when this character is considered from the perspective of women's relationship to men.

This uniformity and lack of disparity between the inner and the outer grants women a peculiar cultural role. First, with regard to the specific contribution of women to cultural activities, this means that instead of copying activities suitable to men, who are much more capable of distancing themselves from their inner self, women should concentrate on those spheres that best fit the unity of their nature. Such are the cultural fields where the sense of empathy is more important than that of pure objectivity or where imitation is valued more than creativity.

In his specific remarks about the fields suitable to women, Simmel was sometimes ahead of his time, as he included among them the writing of history which requires empathy towards historical personalities, or even mathematics. The latter was said to possess a kind of abstractness that stands above the psychological differences among human beings and between genders.[264] More often, however, Simmel's practical attitude was very conservative, as he listed activities where the presence of women was long acknowledged, such as medicine or composing novels, one of few literary genres in which, in his opinion, women perform well. For, according to him, they are generally not very skilled in literature, and it would be utopian to speak about specifically feminine poetic forms.[265] Another important activity in which women excel is that of house managing, for which they have a special aptitude.[266] On the whole, therefore, Simmel was very cautious with regard to expanding the range of cultural activities to be opened to women. And his position was regarded as too conservative even by those contemporaries, such as Marianne Weber, whose own feminism was relatively moderate.[267]

---

[262] GSG 12, p. 40. Or 'Flirtation', p. 139. [GSG 14, p. 262.]
[263] GSG 12, p. 41. Or 'Flirtation', p. 139. [GSG 14, p. 263.]
[264] 'Weibliche Kultur' [1902], GSG 7, p. 73.
[265] Cf. 'Female Culture', trans. G. Oakes, in *On Women, Sexuality, and Love*, p. 81. [GSG 14, p. 524.]
[266] 'Weibliche Kultur' [1902], GSG 7, p. 77.
[267] Cf. Marianne Weber, 'Die Frau und die objektive Kultur' [1913], in *Frauenfragen und Frauengedanken: Gesammelte Aufsätze* (Tübingen: J. C. B. Mohr, 1919), pp. 95–133. On the intellectual dialogue between Simmel and Marianne Weber, see Katja Eckhardt, *Die*

However, listing the cultural activities that would be most appropriate for women was of secondary significance to Simmel. What was more important for him was to examine the role of women in remedying the defects of modern culture in general. For the principle of objectivity embedded in modern culture was not necessarily an advantage, and lack of objectivity did not need to be considered intellectual insufficiency. As Simmel argued in 1906, 'the man's inward dividedness and differentiation allows perhaps the purely intellectual in him to rise higher, but in return makes the purely sensual sink deeper. It often cuts the threads by which this purely sensual could be raised to the level of the essential and noblest in his nature'.[268] Therefore, a strong injection of subjective culture was perhaps what the alienated world of masculine objectivity needed. And here the woman's harmonious inwardness, previously conceived as a disadvantage in terms of the civilisational process, could actually be the way forward.

Occasionally, Simmel went as far as to claim that the spirit of the times and the artistic feeling springing from it had already begun to be influenced by the 'feminine' principle.[269] He suggested this in an article on Rodin (1902) in the context of a comparison he drew between the French sculptor and Michelangelo. Here, Simmel imputed to modern experience the quality of fleeting dynamism, and this fleetingness, salient in the art of Rodin, he considered a specifically female trait. More frequently, however, Simmel imputed to the feminine the opposite characteristic: women are redeemers of culture because they are a symbol of settled harmony. Thus, in 1904, he argued that the woman possesses the features of a house: 'solidity, closeness [*Geschlossenheit*], unity'[270] and this closeness gives the woman 'where she can be presented purely, something of the character of the work of art'.[271] This aestheticist moment can still be found in Simmel's texts as late as 1911, when he wrote: 'The constitutive idea of the woman ... is the unbroken character of her periphery, the organic finality in the harmony of the aspects of her nature, both in their relationship to one another and in the symmetry of their relationship to their centre. This is precisely what epitomises the beautiful.'[272]

Auseinandersetzung zwischen Marianne Weber und Georg Simmel über die 'Frauenfrage' (Stuttgart: ibidem, 2000).

[268] 'Philosophie der Geschlechter', GSG 8, p. 80.

[269] 'Auguste Rodin: Part I', in Harrington (ed.), *Georg Simmel: Essays on Art and Aesthetics*, p. 303. [GSG 7, p. 93.]

[270] 'Bruchstücke aus einer Psychologie der Frauen', GSG 7, p. 289.   [271] GSG 7, p. 290.

[272] 'Female Culture', p. 88. [GSG 14, p. 445.]

Such a view puzzled Rita Felski, one of the most perceptive commentators on Simmel's thought on gender: 'It is perhaps surprising that Simmel's often subtle and complex engagements with the contradictory dimensions of modernity [give] way in the context of his account of femininity to a view of a static and unchanging female nature.'[273] But when this view is placed within the overall logic of Simmel's intellectual journey, all the pieces of the puzzle fall into place. For as we have seen, in the 1900s Simmel was looking for relief from the contradictions of the world, and one of the paths he explored was aestheticism. This aestheticist turn was not fully coherent. For alongside a yearning for the classic ideal of harmonious beauty it also included the opposite tendency, towards aesthetic modernism. Hence the allegedly impressionist motif in Simmel's writings of the period of *The Philosophy of Money*,[274] which in respect of women found its expression in the aforementioned Rodin essay. This motif in his thought was, however, relatively short-lived. The side of harmonious tranquillity appeared to prevail, and women too were made into objects of this purified aestheticism. They turned into a world in itself which was a fragment and at the same time a symbol of cosmic unity.

This coexistence of two contrary tendencies in Simmel's aesthetic approach to women is also a sign of his general intellectual drifting in that period, which was merely the outward appearance of his inward aporia, of his feeling of losing direction on the way towards unity. And even the ideal of aestheticist harmony taken by itself was, as we have seen, an illusion full of contradictions. Motionless beauty was simply the opposite of the flow of life, and apparent tranquillity turned out to be the flipside of death: the ripe happiness of Florence unavoidably led to the deceptive aestheticism of Venice.

Simmel was looking for a way out of this condition. Any return to the older scheme of unity in variety was of course impossible: for him it was now too naïve. However, if unity were to be regained, it had to accomplish some kind of reconciliation with variety, a reconciliation which would endow it with dynamism and life. And it appears to me that it is his writings on the subject of women that contain the first seeds of the general intellectual solution at which Simmel arrived.

The crucial moment here is the turn of the 1910s. The central texts on women belonging to this period are two essays included in *Philosophical*

---

[273] Felski, *The Gender of Modernity*, p. 57.
[274] Cf. David Frisby, *Fragments of Modernity: Theories of Modernity in the Work of Simmel, Kracauer and Benjamin* (Cambridge, MA: The MIT Press, 1986); David Frisby, *Sociological Impressionism: A Reassessment of Georg Simmel's Social Theory* (London: Routledge, 1992).

Culture (1911): the significantly revised and expanded version of the earlier essay 'Female Culture' and the essay entitled 'The Relative and the Absolute in the Problem of the Sexes'.[275] Although there is an apparent continuity between these pieces and the essays of the previous decade, it is here, it seems, that a new paradigm began to emerge, before it attained full shape and spread across the other themes of Simmel's later thought.

The main thrust of these two essays is familiar to us: the feminine world of unity, harmony and subjectivity is very unlike the masculine world of objectivity and differentiation, and hence the cultural significance of women is qualitatively different from that of men. But consider nuances. For example, now in addition to examining the possibility of women's independent contribution to cultural production, Simmel placed more emphasis on their role as inspirers of the masculine culture. Already in 1902 Simmel spoke about the objectivisation of the woman's essence in man.[276] Now he referred more explicitly to the negative aspect of this role, to what she cannot be. Woman, according to him, is the fundamental condition of the masculine culture, but she herself does not share in the culturally creative life: '[T]he idea of an objective female culture is a contradiction in terms.'[277] Through her embeddedness in 'being' she communicates to men something that cannot be expressed in words, something that in them becomes 'culture'.[278]

Generally, Simmel appears to have moderated his admiration for the feminine. The first version of 'Female Culture' (1902) spoke of 'the marvellous connection with the unbroken unity of nature which the feminine soul still seems to have and which distinguishes the entire formula of her existence from the man who is so fissured, differentiated and thrives on objectivity'.[279] As Marianne Ulmi has noticed, this passage is absent from the 1911 version; probably such praise now went way too far for Simmel.[280] The reason for this seems to me to be that in this period Simmel no longer looked for ways to escape from the contradictions of modernity through singular modes of experience. The feminine unity of harmonious beauty also ceased to be conceived as the principal alternative to the modern masculine variety.

---

[275] 'Female Culture', pp. 65–101; [GSG 12, pp. 251–289 and GSG 14, pp. 417–459.] 'The Relative and the Absolute in the Problem of the Sexes', pp. 102–132. [GSG 12, pp. 224–250 and GSG 14, pp. 219–255.]
[276] 'Weibliche Kultur' [1902], GSG 7, p. 80.   [277] Cf. 'Female Culture', p. 100. [GSG 14, p. 457.]
[278] Cf. ibid., p. 97. [GSG 14, p. 454.]   [279] 'Weibliche Kultur' [1902], GSG 7, p. 68.
[280] Ulmi, *Frauenfragen, Männergedanken*, p. 101.

Yet at the same time a somewhat different kind of unity began to be assigned to women. There was a subtle change in terminology. In order to conceptualise the dichotomy between men and women, Simmel began to use the words 'being' and 'becoming' more often, a conceptual pair that figures prominently in the tract *Main Problems of Philosophy* published a year earlier.[281] In some places, this usage was in line with his earlier approach: 'In the symbolism of metaphysical concepts', he argued, 'woman represents being and man represents becoming'.[282] The masculine mode of existence is 'dualistic, oriented to becoming, knowledge, and volition'.[283] It objectivises the contents of its life, whereas the feminine mode must search for perfection within the contents of its life themselves. But the opposite usage was also apparent in the same essay. Simmel suggested that in respect of artistic activity, being and becoming in man and woman swap roles. Whereas man is especially successful in fields where strict form is required (music, architecture, drama), woman devotes herself to the fleeting life.[284]

As has been shown, there were already occasions when Simmel linked the feminine nature to the notion of fleetingness. Previously, however, this was merely a fragment of thought that did not square coherently with other aspects of his philosophy of women, whereas now other insights joined it to push the argument in the direction of the view that stressed the dynamic character of women's unity. Thus Simmel rejected the idea that women possess their own world which is incomparable to that of men.[285] For Simmel, to argue that someone's experience is a 'world' would mean imputing to that person an escape from plurality into a coherent even if fragmentary experience. In his vocabulary, 'world' signified a stable mental structure enabling one to conceive reality through a coherent system of postulates. A 'world' is a one-sided contemplation of the entire universe. In other words, it is a unity that reflects totality without encompassing the entire variety embedded in that totality; it is unity versus variety. Therefore, when Simmel claimed that woman was not a world, it meant

---

[281] *Hauptprobleme der Philosophie*, GSG 14, pp. 44–79.

[282] 'Female Culture', p. 88. [GSG 14, p. 445.]   [283] Ibid., p. 101. [GSG 14, p. 458.]

[284] Ibid., pp. 93–94. [GSG 14, p. 451.] One can find usage of the word 'becoming' in respect of women in his earlier writings as well, e.g., in the 1902 version of 'Female Culture', where Simmel spoke about the lack of pure objectivity in women, of life in the timelessness of the impersonal. With woman, not the values of objective culture but their carrier is of importance, a function: 'not the being but the mode of her becoming' (GSG 7, p. 83). However, this is just an incidental point which is not brought into full coherence with the rest of the points Simmel was making. What changes in the later stage is that this idea that had so far carried merely fragmentary existence, now became a formula more clearly related to Simmel's general life-philosophy.

[285] Cf. 'Female Culture', p. 101. [GSG 14, p. 458.]

that her experience was not static or closed. Her totality was not that of a 'world' but that of 'life'. It was a primordial dynamism. The metaphysical nature of her psyche was 'conclusively defined in a consummate state of being and life itself'.[286]

This dynamism was inward-oriented. But as follows from Simmel's later revision of 'Female Culture',[287] the inward-oriented existence is less static than the outward-oriented one. For whereas the life governed by outward goals actualises itself in one determined reality, the inward existence does not set determinate goals for itself and is actually more open and dynamic, being based on a limitless number of potentialities. And potentialities, as Simmel noted, are 'not just something trussed or seemingly dead, but something constantly active'.[288]

All this could have led Simmel to suggest that the feminine would indeed be the solution for the question of unity, only that this unity would be of a less static sort than imagined by him previously, less of a 'beautiful soul'. This is, however, not the path he took. Whereas in his later stage he did attempt to envision a very different scheme of unity and variety which incorporated this inner dynamism, he did not try to attribute this newly conceived unity specifically to the phenomenon of the feminine. To the extent that women symbolise in Simmel's philosophy the way to redemption, they belong to his second period, and even his later texts touching on the subject of women remain within the framework drawn earlier.

Nevertheless, it seems that it is in one of Simmel's texts on women that a new idea, crucial for that new vision, first appeared, even if its far-reaching metaphysical implications were not yet clearly outlined. This was the idea that the way to approach the dualisms and contradictions of modernity was not by harmonising or circumventing them but rather by developing a kind of double view. In it, one and the same concept plays both the relative and absolute function. As the relative concept, it is immersed in the world of contradictions and dualisms, and as the absolute concept it encompasses them. This is an insight of the essay 'The Relative and the Absolute in the Problem of the Sexes'. According to Simmel, neither man nor woman should be seen as merely relational concepts each postulating the dividing line between itself and the other. Rather, the male

---

[286] Cf. ibid. [GSG 14, p. 459.]

[287] The second revised edition of *Philosophische Kultur* appeared in November 1918 but was officially dated 1919. It is not known when, precisely, the revisions were made. See Rüdiger Kramme and Otthein Rammstedt, 'Editorischer Bericht', in GSG 14, p. 480.

[288] 'Weibliche Kultur', in *Philosophische Kultur*, GSG 14, p. 426.

can also be understood as including in himself both the relatively male and the relatively female because 'objective norms themselves are male'.[289] Likewise, the absolute female stands beyond the opposition of the two sexes because the woman, in her being, 'lives directly at and by means of the source from which both sides of this opposition flow'.[290]

Taken in isolation, this formula does not say much to the reader yet. It appears at first glance as just another adventure of Simmel's dialectical mind. However, more so than many other ingenious insights, this one should be given special attention. It is not an accidental idea that cropped up in Simmel's texts only to disappear. Already in *Philosophical Culture* some other essays contain the same formula.[291] And over the course of the following years this formula would become that which enabled him to formulate new answers to his old questions. In order to examine all this in detail, I now move to the third – final – stage of Simmel's intellectual development, a stage which proceeds under the ideal of unity above variety.

---

[289] 'The Relative and the Absolute in the Problem of the Sexes', p. 127. [GSG 14, p. 250.]

[290] Ibid., p. 127. [GSG 14, p. 251.] Simmel also said that the absolute male stands *above* the dualism of the sexes whereas the absolute female stands *beyond* it. This distinction is not important in the context of my discussion, and I doubt whether it is something more than just a game of wit.

[291] E.g. 'On the Aesthetics of the Alps' [1911], in Harrington (ed.), *Georg Simmel: Essays on Art and Aesthetics*, pp. 216–217. [GSG 12, p. 168; GSG 14, p. 302.] 'The Handle', trans. R. H. Weingartner, in Wolff (ed.), *Essays on Sociology, Philosophy and Aesthetics*, p. 273. ['Der Henkel', in *Philosophische Kultur*, GSG 14, p. 284.] On various uses of 'absolute' and 'relative' in Simmel's texts in general, see also Henry Schemer and David Jary, *Form and Dialectic in Georg Simmel's Sociology: A New Interpretation* (New York: Palgrave Macmillan, 2013), pp. 165–195.

CHAPTER 4

Unity above Variety

As I have shown in the previous chapter, Simmel's quest for unity in his middle period took the form of escape from variety. Instead of postulating unity as emerging naturally from the diversified world, he searched for it as an alternative to such a world. Unity was supposed to be reached through a symbolic immediate experience in which fragmentation disappears, while one acquires an intuitive, even if imperfect, insight into what the never-reachable comprehensive unity may look like. Simmel examined the possibility of such unity in a certain kind of religiosity, in aesthetic feeling or in the feminine experience.

It is to this period that Simmel's first significant publications on Goethe belong. Taken apart from his other Goethe writings, these seem to provide yet another example of his search for unity versus variety, achieved by means of the aesthetic experience. Goethe's unity, Simmel argued in 1906, may be more suitable to the contemporary generation than Kantian unity, as it incorporates aesthetic interests:

> The perceived need for a synthesis that transcended both in their opposition to each other gave rise, in the 1870s, to the call: 'Back to Kant!'. But the *science-oriented* solution, which he alone was able to provide, then demanded a balancing. This seemed to be offered by aesthetic interests. They had generally come to assume leadership in intellectual life at the beginning of the century and their further development, whatever forms it took, could not be effaced from coming changes within the German spirit. As they offered a way for re-accepting Spirit back into the real world, opposed to Kantianism but also somehow complementing it, these aesthetic interests condensed into the call: 'Back to Goethe!'.[1]

The figure of Goethe was thus evoked by Simmel at that time as yet another example of what I call 'unity versus variety'.

---

[1] 'Kant and Goethe: On the History of the Modern *Weltanschauung*', trans. J. Bleicher, *Theory, Culture & Society* 24(6), 2007, pp. 163–164. [GSG 10, p. 127.]

Yet during that period Goethe did not stand at the forefront of Simmel's own cultural preoccupations. The most important thinker for him then was Nietzsche. It was only several years later that Simmel's interest in Goethe would bear its principal fruit in the form of a long monograph. But by that time his view of the poet would change substantially: in that final period, Simmel's attitude to the problem of *Bildung* would evolve from 'unity versus variety' to what I call here 'unity above variety', and Simmel would make Goethe the prime representative of this new position.

Yet this powerful image would be depicted only towards the end of Simmel's life.[2] It would be the final outcome of a life-long preoccupation with the poet. His earlier attempts at interpretation were perhaps less original and more indebted to the surrounding intellectual environment. But in order to understand Simmel's later achievement properly, one should start with the story of what preceded it, both in Simmel's own works and in the reception of Goethe in Germany in general.

4.1 Goethe

The reception of Goethe in the German *Kaiserreich* has a complex but distinct physiognomy.[3] In the first decades after 1871, it was marked by two main features: the entrenchment of his status as a classical figure on the one hand and the extensive scholarly study of almost all aspects of his work and life, known as 'Goethe philology', on the other.

Veneration of Goethe as an Olympian classic was of course not something new. It drew on an existing line of interpretation, the main

---

[2] The literature on Simmel's interpretation of Goethe is scarce. The best and most detailed account is in Italian: Paola Giacomoni, *Classicità e frammento: Georg Simmel Goethiano* (Naples: Guida, 1995). A more recent analysis, especially in respect of the notion of 'symbol' can be found in Annika Schlitte, *Die Macht des Geldes und die Symbolik der Kultur: Georg Simmels Philosophie des Geldes* (Munich: Wilhelm Funk, 2012), pp. 69–88, 390–414. See also Hans-Martin Kruckis, '*Ein potenziertes Abbild der Menschheit': Biographischer Diskurs und Etablierung der Neugermanistik in der Goethe-Biographik bis Gundolf* (Heidelberg: Universitätsverlag C. Winter, 1995), pp. 284–291; Josef Bleicher, 'From Kant to Goethe: Georg Simmel on the Way to *Leben*', *Theory, Culture & Society* 24(6), 2007, pp. 139–158; Wilhelm Voßkamp, '"Diese Rastlosigkeit von Selbstentwicklung und Produktivität": Georg Simmels *Goethe*-Buch', *Simmel Studies* 19(1), 2009, pp. 5–19; Donald N. Levine, '*Soziologie* and *Lebensanschauung*: Two Approaches to Synthesizing "Kant" and "Goethe" in Simmel's Work', *Theory, Culture & Society* 29(7–8), 2012, pp. 26–52; Ingo Meyer, *Georg Simmels Ästhetik: Autonomiepostulat und soziologische Referenz* (Weilerswist: Velbrück, 2017), pp. 113–126.

[3] I have drawn here, generally, on the magisterial study by Karl Robert Mandelkow, *Goethe in Deutschland: Rezeptionsgeschichte eines Klassikers*, vol. 1: 1773–1918 (Munich: C. H. Beck, 1980); vol. 2: 1919–1982 (Munich: C. H. Beck, 1989). For a study in English, see Wolfgang Leppmann, *The German Image of Goethe* (Oxford: Clarendon Press, 1969). With regard to the early twentieth century, Mandelkow's work can be supplemented with Heinz Kindermann, *Das Goethebild des 20. Jahrhunderts* (Darmstadt: Wissenschaftliche Buchgesellschaft, 1966), pp. 9–167.

representatives of which were Wilhelm von Humboldt and Carl Gustav Carus. Already during Goethe's lifetime, Humboldt attempted to interpret him as an embodiment of spiritual harmony, whose creativity, by success-fully overcoming the antithesis between the old and the new, created a new synthesis of *Bildung*.[4] And half a century later, Carus drew an image of Goethe as a happy and healthy spirit, who exemplified a way of life much preferable to the discontents of the modern hectic existence.[5]

In their generations, however, Humboldt and Carus were exceptions, as for their contemporaries Goethe was a contested figure, praised or criti-cised depending on the place they attributed to him in their artistic and political controversies. Goethe was engaged with rather than venerated. Yet all this was over by 1871. The foundation of the empire brought the era of struggle for German unification to an end, and Goethe – a reserved, quasi-aristocratic, sometimes esoteric spirit – was taken to be the perfect symbol of the emerging national consensus, a spiritual founder of the nation, the history of which had come full circle.

The person who, perhaps, best symbolised this final classicisation of Goethe was Herman Grimm. Grimm (1828–1901) epitomised, as it were, the German tradition of *Bildung* and was personally related to several important acquaintances of Goethe. He was the son of Wilhelm Grimm (one of the two Grimm brothers) and close to the circle of Bettina von Arnim, a friend and admirer of Goethe, whose daughter Gisela, herself a prominent writer, he married. He taught history of art at the University of Berlin, working on famous artists of the past, such as Raphael and Dürer. His 1874 lectures on Goethe were made into a book which became one of the most popular works on the poet, reprinted many times over the course of subsequent decades.[6] Towards the end of the nineteenth century, a great number of Goethe biographies followed, the most popular of them being a two-volume work by Albert Bielschowsky.[7] Bielschowsky aptly summar-ised what became the conventional view of Goethe in the first decades of the *Kaiserreich*. Goethe, he argued, was marked by the special ability to combine and harmonise in himself all the different features of humankind.

---

[4] Cf. Mandelkow, *Goethe in Deutschland*, vol. 1, pp. 54–56. On Schiller and F. Schlegel's interpret-ations as precursors to Simmel, see also Voßkamp, "'Diese Rastlosigkeit von Selbstentwicklung und Produktivität'", p. 8.

[5] Carl Gustav Carus, *Goethe: Zu dessen näheren Verständnis* [1842] (Dresden: Wolfgang Jess, 1955). On Carus's reception of Goethe, see Mandelkow, *Goethe in Deutschland*, vol. 1, pp. 141–145.

[6] Herman Grimm, *Goethe: Vorlesungen gehalten an der Kgl. Universität zu Berlin*, 2 vols. (Stuttgart: J. G. Cotta, 1903).

[7] Translated by W. A. Cooper into English in three volumes as *The Life of Goethe* (New York: G. P. Putnam's Sons, 1905–1908).

He was characterised by the completeness of his nature; he was 'the most human of all human beings [*menschlichste aller Menschen*], because he had been endowed with a portion of everything human'.[8]

This deification of Goethe as the most universal man – the peak of human *Bildung* – was accompanied by a vast research enterprise in which hardly any available text of Goethe's or about Goethe escaped scholarly scrutiny. This was the enterprise of what Wilhelm Scherer called 'Goethe philology'.[9] Classical philology, as was noted earlier, played a major role in the German *Bildung* project: the ancient ideal could be reconquered by intimate knowledge of classical culture, and the path to acquiring this knowledge ran through impartial scholarship. Goethe philology strove to replicate this quest of classical philology, only replacing the ancients with Goethe as the object of emulation discovered and maintained by means of scholarly knowledge.

Attempts to examine Goethe's works 'philologically' had already been undertaken in the mid-nineteenth century,[10] but the real breakthrough in Goethe scholarship took place in the 1880s. In 1880, Ludwig Geiger, a colleague of Grimm's at the University of Berlin, founded the *Goethe-Jahrbuch* and remained its editor for almost 35 years. These annual volumes, edited in accordance with the highest academic standards, become a major focus for Goethe scholarship, especially after the opening of the Goethe archives in Weimar in 1885 and the establishment of the Goethe Society in the same year, of which it became the official publication.

The dual thrust of Goethe's reception of the time – cultivation of him as a classical figure and historical-philological dissection of his life and work – resembled, of course, the general duality of the German cultural ideal in the nineteenth century. This duality was not without its contradictions, and those in charge of projects on Goethe occasionally had to make up their minds as to which side to emphasise, that of edification or of scholarship. For example, how were Goethe's works to be edited? Should they be presented to the reader in their final form (*Ausgabe letzter Hand*) without any additional material, so

---

[8] Ibid., vol. 1, p. 1. Intellectuals of Jewish origin played a major role in the formation of the Goethe cult at the turn of the century. Ludwig Geiger was a son of the founder of Reform Judaism Abraham Geiger. Bielschowsky too was Jewish-born. This brings us again to the issue of Simmel's 'Jewishness'. Like in the case of his early sociology, his continuous fascination with Goethe was in conformity with the common outlook of the educated German Jewish middle class who adopted the *Bildung* ideal and its symbols as the basic element of their identity: German and universalist at once.

[9] Wilhelm Scherer, 'Goethe-Philologie', in *Aufsätze über Goethe* (Berlin: Weidmannsche Buchhandlung, 1900), pp. 3–27.

[10] By authors such as Heinrich Düntzer. See Heinrich Düntzer, *Goethes Leben* (Leipzig: Fues's Verlag [R. Reisland], 1880).

that the reader could have immediate contact with the corpus as Goethe had left it? This was the approach taken in the Weimar complete edition of Goethe's works that consisted of 143 volumes.[11] Or should Goethe's works be provided with an extensive scholarly apparatus, with commentaries, and also include earlier versions of his works? This was the approach of the Cotta Jubilee edition which comprised 40 volumes.[12]

In general, however, these two sides coexisted in quite remarkable harmony. While cracks had already begun to appear in the general ideal of *Bildung*, as synthesis between cultivation and professionalisation started to be increasingly perceived of as problematic, if not impossible, the Goethe enterprise was still on the whole protected from these new doubts. Goethe research was still driven by the assumption that cultural self-cultivation and scholarly criticism could go hand in hand.

This double approach to Goethe did not, however, remain completely unchallenged, as towards the 1890s one can notice the rise of new opposition to the Goethe cult. Unlike the earlier cases of opposition (such as that of the Young Germany group) or the later ones (such as that of Thomas Mann in older age), this did not and could not develop into a criticism of Goethe himself. Goethe remained beyond reproach.[13] Rather, this opposition took the form of a defence of Goethe against the self-complacent image imposed upon him. Of course, Goethe had to remain an ideal, but not one that affirmed everything and synthesised all the contrasting tendencies of his life and time. Rather, he was an ideal because he separated himself from the world's philistinism. Nietzsche was one of the most eloquent advocates of this position, considering Goethe a heroic and even tragic figure and emphasising Goethe's more esoteric 'classicism' rather than his popular proto-Romantic lyrics and *Faust*, with which much of the scholarship of the time was concerned.[14] He spoke about 'Goethe's noble isolation',[15] contrasting him with Kant: 'What he wanted was *totality*; he fought against the separation of reason, sensibility, feeling, will (– preached in the most forbiddingly scholastic way by *Kant*, Goethe's antipode).'[16] Thus, for

---

[11] Mandelkow, *Goethe in Deutschland*, vol. 1, p. 220.   [12] Ibid., p. 222.

[13] Except for within the Catholic sub-culture represented by the Swiss Alexander Baumgartner. See ibid., pp. 168–173.

[14] Ibid., p. 237.

[15] From Friedrich Nietzsche, 'Aus dem Nachlaß', in Karl Robert Mandelkow (ed.), *Goethe im Urteil seiner Kritiker: Dokumente zur Wirkungsgeschichte Goethes in Deutschland*, part III: 1870–1918 (Munich: C. H. Beck, 1979), p. 137.

[16] Friedrich Nietzsche, 'Twilight of the Idols or How to Philosophize with a Hammer', trans. Judith Norman, in *The Anti-Christ, Ecce Homo, Twilight of the Idols, and Other Writings* (Cambridge: Cambridge University Press, 2005), § 49, p. 222.

Nietzsche, it was the noble secluded totality of Goethe which epitomised true artistic calling.

A similar stance was adopted by Stefan George. In 1899, he wrote the poem 'Goethe Day', in which he lashed out at the philistine and self-complacent Goethe admirers who could never appreciate the true Goethe.[17] Himself an aestheticist, many of whose early poems are examples of refined form and emotional detachment, George saw Goethe as a poet of 'happy measure' who epitomised the achievement of self-mastery.[18]

This trend thus aimed not at demolishing the Goethe cult but at redesigning it by replacing the image of a harmonising man with that of a secluded artist. Yet both these trends in the early decades of the *Kaiserreich* shared the quest for unity in Goethe, whereas the difference between the two was related to the kind of unity attributed to him. I would suggest that the difference in this respect corresponds to the distinction outlined in the previous chapters: the distinction between unity in variety and unity versus variety. In the former, Goethe is seen as a harmonious man absorbing the differentiated world in its totality, whereas in the latter, Goethe is seen as a refined classicist escaping from the contradictions of lower reality into the beautiful form or immediate perception.[19]

Now, we have already followed the evolution of Simmel's approach towards unity from 'unity in variety' to 'unity versus variety' over the course of his early and middle periods. Therefore, one should not be surprised to discover that the development of his view of Goethe in those years corresponded both to the changes in his own approach and to the parallel changes in Goethe reception in Germany. Simmel in fact witnessed the history of this reception at first hand, as he was personally close to many of its main protagonists. As a student at the University of Berlin, for example, he is reported to have been close to Herman Grimm. He must also have attended the classes of Ludwig Geiger,[20] and later he became a close friend of Stefan George.

---

[17] Stefan George, 'Goethe-Tag', in Mandelkow (ed.), *Goethe im Urteil seiner Kritiker*, pp. 308–309.

[18] See Kindermann, *Das Goethebild des 20. Jahrhundert*, pp. 87–89.

[19] This second trend was also related to the growing interest in Goethe's studies in natural philosophy and science. One of the main figures in this sphere was Rudolf Steiner, the future founder of anthroposophy, who edited and commented on Goethe's scientific writings (Rudolf Steiner, *Goethes naturwissenschaftliche Schriften* [Dornach: Philosophisch-Anthroposophischer Verlag, 1926]). Goethe's scientific theories and methodological approach were rejected by most mainstream scientists. Yet towards the turn of the century they again became a matter of curiosity, especially in conservative-minded circles, who found in them an alternative to what they perceived as the prevailing scientific positivism of the time. It was another way of doing science, science through the eyes of an artist.

[20] Klaus Christian Köhnke, *Der junge Simmel: in Theoriebeziehungen und sozialen Bewegungen* (Frankfurt am Main: Suhrkamp, 1996), pp. 40–41.

Simmel's interest in Goethe dates at least to his university years, if not earlier. He even twice suggested Goethe's philosophy as one of three possible topics for a public lecture as part of his habilitation procedure.[21] In the end, a different subject was approved by the committee – the relation of ethical ideals to logical and aesthetical ones[22] – so we do not know what Simmel intended to say. However, this shows that the figure of Goethe was intellectually important for the young Simmel.

Simmel joined the Goethe Society in 1885 immediately after it had been founded (although he appears to have left four years later).[23] In 1887 he published a review of a volume of correspondence between Goethe and Carlyle which provides some clues as to his view of Goethe in those years. He distinguished between two conceptions of philosophy: 'scholar-conception' (*Schulbegriff*) and 'world-conception' (*Weltbegriff*), arguing that whereas in respect of the former, the philosophy of his time was oriented towards Kant, in respect of the latter it was much indebted to Goethe.[24] Simmel, then a modernist with socialist sympathies and a believer in positivist science, saw a divide 'between the *content* of his [Goethe's] thought and that of the modern age'.[25] Yet although the content of Goethe's ideas was outdated, the poet nevertheless had something to offer to Simmel's contemporaries: 'It is in respect of *formal* coherence, of the maturity and inner satisfaction of his worldview that he remains for us an eternal model, an ideal for every comprehension of things even if it deviates in terms of the content.'[26] In other words, Goethe is a model for personal cultivation. He teaches how to reach a state of perfect harmony and a unity of mind. He teaches the form of *Bildung*, even if the content of this *Bildung* belongs to the past.

The young Simmel thus seemed to reiterate somewhat naively the typical *Bildungsbürgertum* attitude to Goethe in the early *Kaiserreich*. However, by the time he published his article 'Kant and Goethe' a decade later, his view had undergone a metamorphosis. This article, produced in 1899 (the 150th anniversary of Goethe's birth), was Simmel's first extensive treatment of Goethe's worldview. Together with his book of the same title – *Kant and Goethe* (1906), which is just an expanded version of the earlier text – it

---

[21] Ibid., pp. 154–155. Simmel did so twice because he failed his first habilitation exam and had to complete the procedure a second time.

[22] Ibid., pp. 114–115.

[23] Simmel is listed as a member of the Goethe Society in 'Jahresbericht der Goethe-Gesellschaft', *Goethe-Jahrbuch* 7, 1886, p. [26]. His name is absent starting from 'Fünfter Jahresbericht der Goethe-Gesellschaft', *Goethe-Jahrbuch* 11, 1890, p. [26].

[24] 'Einige Bemerkungen über Goethes Verhältnis zur Ethik', GSG 1, p. 215.   [25] GSG 1, p. 215.

[26] GSG 1, p. 216.

represents Simmel's view of Goethe in his second period. Importantly, three editions of *Kant and Goethe* were published during his lifetime, the third of which (1916) included a number of changes and additions that reflected the further evolution of his position in his third period.[27] In order to obtain an accurate picture of Simmel's position during his second period, one should therefore consult the 1906 version.

Now, by the end of the nineteenth century, Goethe and Kant were unmistakably the two most venerated figures in German culture, and it was only natural that on many occasions they were mentioned together, especially given that they had been near contemporaries and that Goethe's worldview had in some respects been strongly influenced by Kantian philosophy. Kant's influence on Goethe and the affinities between the two were studied extensively in those years by Karl Vorländer, a neo-Kantian and historian of philosophy.[28]

However, significant differences clearly existed between the views and dispositions of the two men, as some critics, such as Friedrich Paulsen, did not fail to mention in reference to Vorländer's study.[29] These differences were especially emphasised by critics of modern culture who came to see Kant as symbolising its most problematic aspects. We have already seen that Nietzsche considered Goethe an antipode to Kant. Yet hardly anyone was clearer or more outspoken in postulating the contrast between the two than Simmel.

His argument ran as follows. The condition of advanced civilisations in general, and certainly of the modern civilisation that developed out of Christianity and the Renaissance, is one of dualism. Whereas at the outset there existed a primordial unity, distinct elements subsequently developed out of it and found themselves in opposition to each other. One could consider, for example, the opposition between subject and object or any other major dualism of our consciousness. The spiritual task of modernity is to find a way to unify the divided world in which we live.

The modern era produced two thinkers capable of suggesting a way out of this dualism towards unity: Kant and Goethe. Their solutions were, however, different from or even opposed to one another, both in the theoretical and practical spheres. For example, in the theoretical sphere, Kant unified subject and object from the side of the subject (conceiving of the world of objects as our representation), whereas Goethe unified them

---

[27] The second, 1907 edition is identical to the first.
[28] Karl Vorländer, 'Goethes Verhältnis zu Kant in seiner historischen Entwicklung', *Kant-Studien* 1(1–3), 1897, pp. 60–99, 315–351; 'Goethe und Kant', *Goethe-Jahrbuch* 19, 1898, pp. 167–185.
[29] Friedrich Paulsen, 'Goethes ethische Anschauungen' *Goethe-Jahrbuch* 23, 1902, p. 6n*.

from the side of the object (conceiving of the subject as being part of the world).[30] Kant presupposed the mind as actively imposing unity on the world, Goethe the congeniality and harmony of the self with nature.[31] Furthermore, to conceive the unity of the world, Kant had to presuppose a transcendent God beyond things, whereas Goethe saw such unity as embedded in the things themselves. For Kant, ultimate reality remains unknown because it belongs to a categorically different sphere that is beyond us; for Goethe, there is no such separation: ultimate reality exists at a deeper mystical layer of the phenomena themselves, which we abstain from reaching not because of a fundamental impossibility but because of piety.[32]

Kant's basis of thinking is analysis, a drawing of limits. Goethe's is contemplation of the universal nature in every detail.[33] And this is also true in the practical sphere. Kant completely separates the moral and sensual sides of man, so that in this life duty is unrelated to happiness and superior to it. Reconciliation between the two is to be hoped for only in the afterlife. But such separation is anathema to Goethe, who considers the moral and the sensual as comprising the unity of the whole man in this world. And thus, whereas Kant separates value and being (in order to reconcile them in some other dimension), for Goethe their unity is already given in immediate reality.[34]

To summarise Simmel's argument in one sentence, Kant overcomes duality by constructing a mediated unity which is placed prior to or after nature, whereas Goethe does so by contemplating the immediate unity of nature in appearance. That is, in his description of Goethe, Simmel placed emphasis on the act of immediate harmonious perception, which is an aesthetic act. Therefore, whereas the ultimate foundation of the Kantian worldview is scientific, that of Goethe's is artistic,[35] and the aesthetic motif in him is pre-eminent over all other motifs.[36]

This aesthetic emphasis was in line with Simmel's general approach of 'unity versus variety' in those years. This sort of unity was generally found in specific spheres of experience, such as the sphere of the beautiful. Now, as was often the case with Simmel, some of his passages, even in that period, appeared to point in a different direction. For example, he also said that there was something deeper in Goethe's personality than the aesthetical motif.[37] But in those years this was merely a fragmentary observation.

---

[30] 'Kant und Goethe', GSG 5, p. 454.   [31] GSG 5, p. 455.   [32] GSG 5, p. 457.
[33] GSG 5, pp. 459–460.   [34] GSG 5, pp. 465–468, 475–476.   [35] GSG 5, p. 461.
[36] GSG 5, p. 472.   [37] GSG 5, p. 473.

Simmel's focus was on Goethe as an embodiment of the aesthetical. As he said in the 1906 book, 'Goethe is from beginning to end an *artist*';[38] 'the whole artistic ecstasy of the unity of internal and external, of God and world, erupts within him and from him'.[39]

In his interpretation of Goethe in those years, Simmel seemed to follow the aestheticist line of Nietzsche and George. He even explicitly compared Goethe and Nietzsche in the context of the indifference of both to social issues: 'In a similar way, Nietzsche, despite or because of his passionate interest in human beings and the general development of humankind, has now displayed an absolute indifference to all social questions.'[40] Perhaps it would not be an exaggeration to say that during that period Simmel looked at Goethe with Nietzschean eyes, as earlier he had looked at him with the eyes of Grimm or Geiger. His view of Goethe was still in embryonic form, and like an embryo it recapitulated in the process of its formation the two already existing interpretations. It was only in later years – with the publication of the *Goethe* monograph (1913) – that his attitude to Goethe reached its fully fledged form, in which the poet became the pivotal figure for his own philosophical quest.

Goethe was Simmel's first work in a planned series of monographs to be dedicated to the worldviews of great artists and which, apart from the book on Goethe, was supposed to include works on Rembrandt, Beethoven and Shakespeare.[41] As he worked on it, he immersed himself in studying Goethe's writings anew, having purchased the forty-volume jubilee edition and reading the extensive material it contained, an undertaking attested to by the numerous passages he quoted from the various types of Goethe's writings: poems, prose, essays, letters. Having thus engaged himself in an inner dialogue with Goethe, Simmel developed a view which differed significantly from what he had thought before. As will be shown, in this work Simmel continued to be receptive to developments in the overall reception of Goethe in Germany. But now he was also making an original contribution to the field. Rather than simply reflecting his context, Simmel began to shape it.

The book consists of eight chapters. Each of them can be read as a self-contained essay, approaching Goethe from a particular angle, yet all are related to one and the same core basis of Simmel's view of Goethe. Simmel believed that there is no way to attain a 'view of individuality' apart from indirectly: by 'reproduction through a sum of partial images'.[42] 'I would

---

[38] 'Kant and Goethe', p. 163. [GSG 10, p. 126.]   [39] Ibid., p. 166. [GSG 10, p. 130.]
[40] 'Kant und Goethe', GSG 5, p. 469.   [41] Of these only the Rembrandt book was written.
[42] *Goethe*, GSG 15, p. 10.

take it as the opposite of a reproach against this book', he argued, 'if one were to read in each of its chapters the same things as in all the others'.[43]

We have already seen this manner of composition, which is characteristic of Simmel's early writings, such as his study on social differentiation. This kind of writing is often perceived as fragmentariness. Indeed, it presents a challenge for any author, for giving up on linear structure demands maintaining a high discipline of thought to prevent the argument from disintegrating. But Simmel was up to the challenge, as each of the chapters exemplifies and is related to the coherent set of conceptions which constitute Simmel's view of Goethe.

The most basic aspect of this view was the assumption that Goethe's personality was philosophically significant. As Simmel claimed, his purpose was to examine '*what is the spiritual meaning of Goethe's existence in general?*'[44] This was not supposed to be yet another description of Goethe's life and work but an attempt to attain knowledge of 'Goethe as *Urphänomen*' or 'Goethe as Idea'.[45]

This assumption reflected the changes in Goethe reception of the time. Goethe was a great poet, and this was of course the main reason why Germans had always admired him. Moreover, he was a man of culture whose life was meticulously documented. This enabled the sense of familiarity that helped to turn his life into a public performance from which the educated middle classes could learn how to live an exemplary life. For the educated Germans of the nineteenth century, therefore, Goethe was an artist and a teacher of life. But he was not a philosopher. Goethe indeed professed keen interest in philosophy and philosophers, such as Spinoza, Jacobi or Kant, but he never pretended to be a philosopher himself. And though his philosophical attitudes were noticed by nineteenth-century scholars, they were generally treated as just further background to his artistic development. As late as 1895, philosopher Moritz Brasch lamented that very little had been said by scholarship on Goethe's philosophy.[46] Yet in the same article he himself argued that Goethe had not been a system builder and thus limited his treatment of the subject to the question of the influence of other philosophers on some of Goethe's ideas.

The younger Simmel apparently agreed with that. In 1899, he argued in 'Kant and Goethe':

> One cannot speak of Goethe's philosophy using the trivial formula that he possessed an integral philosophy but did not lay it down in a systematic and

---

[43] GSG 15, p. 10.   [44] GSG 15, p. 9.   [45] GSG 15, p. 9.
[46] Moritz Brasch, 'Goethes Beziehungen zur Philosophie', *Die Gegenwart* 48(36), 1895, p. 152.

professional form. He lacked not only a system and a scholarly technique but also the whole purpose of philosophy as science, which is to raise into the sphere of abstract concepts our feeling of the value and coherence of the world as a whole through which we generally inwardly relate to it.[47]

However, when one examines his later writings, one finds an important change. The passage just quoted still appears in the 1916 edition of *Kant and Goethe*, but the crucial first sentence is left out.[48] It seems that by then Simmel no longer held the view that Goethe did not possess a complete philosophy; not because he came to think that Goethe operated with abstract concepts but because his own notion of philosophy no longer required such operation, as it had moved beyond science into the *lebensphilosophische* sphere.

Now, this evolution in Simmel's position corresponded to a new trend in Goethe reception that emerged around the turn of the century when one suddenly notices a surge of attention to the subject of 'Goethe's philosophy'. Thus, in 1900, Rudolph Eucken delivered a keynote speech on 'Goethe and Philosophy' at the general meeting of the Goethe Society,[49] and in 1902 Frommann press published a volume on Goethe's thought penned by Hermann Siebeck as part of a series on the classics of philosophy,[50] thus placing the poet alongside thinkers such as Plato, Aristotle, Hobbes and Kant. The idea of Goethe as a philosopher began to attain respectability.

In a certain sense, this development was inevitable. After the cult of Goethe as the most exemplary human being had spread so widely and after he had been claimed as an authority by practitioners of many different disciplines, from science to theology, it was no wonder that philosophers too would try to appropriate him for their purposes. The form which this appropriation took, however, was a historical contingency which emerged out of the interplay between certain characteristics of Goethe's own thought, the general heritage of German philosophy and some peculiar qualities of early twentieth-century philosophical discourse.

When one examines the manner in which philosophers of that time approached Goethe, one notices the prevalence of a peculiar philosophical

---

[47] 'Kant und Goethe', GSG 5, pp. 448–449. In the mid-1880s, Simmel proposed a habilitation lecture on the topic of Goethe's philosophy. We do not know, however, what he planned to say. If one were to judge from his early writings, this would hardly have gone beyond platitudes about Goethe's general worldview.

[48] 'Kant and Goethe', p. 162. [GSG 10, p. 125.]

[49] Rudolph Eucken, 'Goethe und die Philosophie', *Goethe-Jahrbuch* 21, 1900, pp. 3*–22*.

[50] Hermann Siebeck, *Goethe als Denker* (Stuttgart: Fr. Frommann, 1902).

problem to which Goethe, in their opinion, might provide an answer, either because he was allegedly preoccupied with it or because his manner of thinking pointed to the proper way of addressing it. The problem was the question of unity between the universal and the individual.

Apparently every developed tradition of philosophical reflection includes a set of questions regarded by its practitioners as most important not because the tradition has managed to solve them but precisely because no reflective solution appears in sight, and thus the flavour of mystery seems to forever be attached to them. And in the domain of mystery, visionaries, mystics and poets seem to possess an advantage. What is regarded as a handicap with regard to ordinary questions suddenly becomes a source of hope when the great antinomies of the world and of life refuse to disappear before the tribunal of reflection. In the Christian tradition, for example, such issues include trinity and theodicy.

German philosophical tradition had its own share of such questions as well. As I have already claimed, one primary perpetual issue, from Leibniz onwards, was the reconciliation between generality and particularity. When this question was explicitly posed, it was often felt that satisfactory answers to it could only be given in approximation, by means of analogy or appeal to intuitive perception, rather than by means of rigorous logical analysis. And a poet with metaphysical interests might be a more suitable candidate to proceed in this way than a systematic thinker.

Goethe was such a poet. And at the turn of the century, his name began to be evoked when the relationship between the universal and the individual came under consideration. This issue was not contemplated exclusively within the domain of philosophy. For example, it could also be tackled in respect of Goethe's artistic achievement. As literature scholar Otto Harnack argued in 1894:

> If I were to emphasise again where I see the greatness of Goethe's art as well as its overwhelming and purpose-giving significance for the art of our times, it is in the union of the true and the beautiful, of the individual and the typical, of the personally free and the ethical that he accomplished with such confident ingenuity.[51]

Yet almost imperceptibly this metaphysics of art evolves into a general metaphysics, when one begins to reflect on the possibility of reconciliation between the universal and the individual in general.

---

[51] Otto Harnack, 'Goethes Kunstanschauung in ihrer Bedeutung für die Gegenwart', *Goethe-Jahrbuch* 15, 1894, p. 205.

Goethe was claimed to have addressed or even solved this problem, for example, by suggesting the notion of *Urphänomen* as representing the *type* to which an empirical individual belongs and at the same time being an individual itself or through his peculiar understanding of law as allowing empirical exceptions. A number of commentators stressed the older Goethe's interest in Leibniz and a certain affinity between his views and the theory of monads – intelligent atoms, each of which contain the world in its totality – while criticising certain biographers of Goethe for placing too much emphasis on his Spinozism and pantheism, causing the significance of the 'individual' and the unique for him to remain underestimated.[52]

A major role in the development of this perception of Goethe was played by the new trend of life-philosophy.[53] The principal purpose of life-philosophy, as propagated in Germany by thinkers such as Rudolph Eucken and Wilhelm Dilthey, was to attain unity by enlarging the domain of philosophy. Whereas reflection was no longer capable of resolving the contradictions of thought and life, philosophy had to go one step beyond reflection to find the true spring of unity in the stream of life, the flow of activity. This was, according to Eucken, Goethe's answer to the world of contradictions:

> It is not a single dichotomy [*Gegensatz*] that governs Goethe's work and thought. Rather, the world's plenitude is divided in him into a series of opposites [*Gegensätzen*]. These opposites are not treated as if one component overpowers and oppresses the other, but rather the different sides assert their peculiarity towards each other with clear boundaries and find an equilibrium not through some theory but through the work itself, which brings the one into the most fruitful interaction with the other, and which achieves the greatest by letting life connect between them as it playfully vacillates between the one and the other.

Moreover, as Eucken made clear, these contradictions existed not only between different aspects of life but also between life as a whole and objects beyond life. He spoke about the life which 'gravitates into the distance and yet remains with itself'.[54] The conflict is thus not only within variety but

---

[52] Bruno Bauch, 'Ueber Goethes philosophische Weltanschauung', *Preußische Jahrbücher* 115(3), 1904, pp. 518–529; Georg Schneiderreit, 'Die individualistische Grundzug in Goethes Weltanschauung', *Goethe-Jahrbuch* 33, 1912, pp. 31–42.

[53] On life-philosophy, see David Midgley, 'After Materialism – Reflections of Idealism in *Lebensphilosophie*: Dilthey, Bergson and Simmel', in Nicholas Boyle and Liz Disley (eds.), *The Impact of Idealism: The Legacy of Post-Kantian German Thought*, vol. 2: *Historical, Social and Political Thought*, ed. by John Walker (Cambridge: Cambridge University Press, 2013), pp. 161–185.

[54] Eucken, 'Goethe und die Philosophie', p. 7*.

between unity and variety, and it 'is then overcome in the most fruitful way when the whole with its immeasurable abundance enters each individual constituent and turns it into its own expression, and yet in a special way in each case and not without that constituent's participation'.[55]

This life-philosophical reading of Goethe was further developed by Dilthey in *Experience and Poetry*. Goethe's poetic phantasy, he argued, sprang out of life experience. This notion of life experience should be taken not in a biographical but in a deeper philosophical sense, for it is the fundament even of those phantasies and images through which Goethe tried to overcome himself, to break away from his immediate experience.[56] The universal – the totality of life – produces the particularities of poetic imagination which release themselves from it and oppose it, and yet both life and its poetic creations are united in Goethe within the same harmonious whole. According to Dilthey, life 'is growth according to an inner law . . . Out of his view of the formative power of Nature, Goethe recreates for it the life which is the object of poetry. On the basis of the inner system of laws that he discovered here, he forms his poetic world and moulds himself – these both making an inseparable whole'.[57]

In his review of Friedrich Gundolf's book on Goethe (1917), Simmel spoke of Dilthey with a mixture of admiration and condescension, saying that he 'never got beyond half-clarity', and therefore 'he always jumped too short of his ingeniously conceived aims'.[58] Yet the parallels between Simmel and Dilthey, as well as between Simmel and Eucken, are numerous and noticeable even in details. Thus Dilthey quoted a sentence of Goethe from a letter to Schiller in which he confessed to having been afraid to write tragedy because he felt that even a mere attempt would destroy him,[59] and the same sentence was quoted by Simmel;[60] Dilthey drew a comparison between Shakespeare and Goethe,[61] and Simmel did the same, although perhaps in a more integrative and philosophically profound manner.[62] Likewise, Eucken cited Goethe's claim that he was the 'liberator of the Germans'[63] and so did Simmel.[64]

The essential thing is, however, that at first reading Simmel's main argument in *Goethe* seemed to follow along the same lines. I would emphasise three main points which, combined together, reflect the impact

---

[55] Ibid., p. 9*.
[56] Wilhelm Dilthey, *Das Erlebnis und die Dichtung* (Leipzig: B. G. Teubner, 1916), p. 196.
[57] Ibid., p. 200.   [58] 'Das Goethebuch', GSG 13, p. 233.
[59] Dilthey, *Das Erlebnis und die Dichtung*, p. 188.   [60] *Goethe*, GSG 15, p. 165.
[61] Dilthey, *Das Erlebnis und die Dichtung*, pp. 202–217.   [62] *Goethe*, GSG 15, pp. 160–166.
[63] Eucken, 'Goethe und die Philosophie', p. 19*.   [64] *Goethe*, GSG 15, p. 153.

of the Euckenian-Diltheyan life-philosophy on Simmel's interpretation of Goethe: first, the postulate of unity; second, the emphasis on the peculiar unity of the universal and individual in Goethe; and finally, the idea of life as the fundament of that unity.

Unity is the *Leitmotif* of Simmel's book. Goethe's ability to attain unity is emphasised in every chapter. Thus, in the first chapter – 'Life and Work' – Simmel argued that Goethe represents an exceptional unity between the two poles of spiritual life: the flow of subjectivity in the activity of life versus the objective content which results from that activity. It is 'the essence of genius', he argued, 'to present the organic unity of these so to speak mechanically separated elements'.[65] The remarkable feature of Goethe's personality was the perfect balance between his ability to receive from the world, work out within himself what had been received and give back to the world what had been produced. This ability attested to the 'health and instinctive confidence of his organs',[66] claimed Simmel, using the same imagery as Carus before him.[67]

In the second chapter – 'Truth' – Simmel attributed to Goethe 'the dynamic unity of life',[68] which reveals itself in the dialogue between the world and the spirit which is itself a world: microcosm.[69] The third chapter, unlike the preceding two that dealt with unity in respect of Goethe's *personality* and his attitude to the world, focuses on the content of Goethe's *thought*, arguing that unity was one of its guiding ideas.[70] Its title – 'Unity of the World Elements' – speaks for itself. But unity is no less the subject of the fourth chapter, even if it is entitled 'Division of the World Elements'. Its main task is to examine three different ways in which Goethe, over the course of his life, conceived the possibility of unity between art and reality.[71]

The fifth chapter – 'Individualism' – seeks to reconcile the universal ideal of humanity and the variety of unique individuals. As Simmel interpreted Goethe, 'unity and variety do not contradict each other's reality or value, for variety is the mode of existence of unity'.[72] The sixth chapter, entitled 'Accountability and Overcoming', deals with what Simmel described as the 'objectivisation of the subject' in Goethe's creative existence,[73] the ability to live one's own life fully and at the same time to give an account of this life to oneself. Such an account provides limiting norms which, far from hindering the free flow of life, become its necessary

---

[65] GSG 15, pp. 13–14.   [66] GSG 15, p. 26.   [67] Carus, *Goethe: Zu dessen näheren Verständnis.*
[68] *Goethe*, GSG 15, p. 56.   [69] GSG 15, p. 57.   [70] GSG 15, p. 76.   [71] GSG 15, p. 109.
[72] GSG 15, p. 171.   [73] GSG 15, p. 180.

counterpart. Goethe thus possessed the ability to live a life contemporary to itself without going astray in the formless yearning or hopeless nostalgia of the Romantics. The seventh chapter – 'Love' – argues that Goethe escaped two contrasting dangers of the erotic: leading a life entirely consumed by love or neutralising love by compartmentalising it in just one separate sphere of life. He could avoid both these extremes because of his exceptional ability to absorb from the world what was congenial to the direction of his life process while rejecting what was harmful to it.[74] And finally, the last chapter – 'Development' – refers to Goethe's life as that of a non-professional. His life was an exemplar of unity subject to its own all-encompassing norms and indifferent to the extraneous norms imposed by a specific profession or calling.[75]

Now, the specific kind of unity in Goethe especially stressed by Simmel is not a unity between various elements of equal standing but a unity of the general (total, universal) and particular (partial, individual). In the book, he mentioned Leibnizian monads on several occasions;[76] spoke about the 'idea', the divine, that lives in particulars;[77] referred to the interaction between life as totality and its particular specifications;[78] and drew attention to the concept of *Urphänomen*, which he described as 'timeless law itself within temporal perception, the universal that manifests itself without mediation in the form of the individual'.[79] The dynamics between the uniqueness of particular human individuality and the category of universally human is discussed at length in the chapter on individualism,[80] where he emphasised 'Goethe's ever-repeated demand to see the universal in the individual'.[81]

With regard to the question of what makes it possible to find the universal in the individual, Simmel also followed contemporary life-philosophical interpretations of Goethe, suggesting that this possibility is derived from the notion of life. 'The value of the individual', he argued, 'is not levelled out but exists further as such because *specification towards the infinite* is, like the unbroken oneness, the mode of life of the type; so that the valuation of the individual as well as of the general is the valuation of *the same* life process. Only the mechanistic view separates the two'.[82] Creative unity was possible for Goethe because 'he included existence [*Dasein*] under the category of life, and through the objectivity of this aspect acquired the right to interpret the relationship between the

---

[74] Cf. GSG 15, pp. 206–207.   [75] GSG 15, p. 218.   [76] See GSG 15, p. 15; GSG 15, p. 51.
[77] GSG 15, p. 106; GSG 15, p. 261.   [78] GSG 15, pp. 218–219.   [79] GSG 15, p. 68.
[80] See GSG 15, pp. 170–178.   [81] GSG 15, p. 178.   [82] GSG 15, p. 178.

individual and the general without anthropomorphism and according to the formula of his own existence [*Existenz*]'.[83]

Master idea of life is then what enables the unification of the universal and the individual. This is why Spinoza's pantheism turns out in the end to be inadequate: Spinoza lacked the concept of becoming and thus sacrificed plurality to unity.[84] Leibniz, a man of universal interests, addressed the question of the synthesis of the universal and the individual in his thought but could not make himself into a fully integrated personality. His intellectualism prevented this.[85] The true solution is life, and this is what Goethe teaches us. The life process 'offers perhaps a most general and conceptually ungraspable formula – different for each individual – that determines his mental processes as well as the way in which the world is taken into the "I" through experience [*Erlebnis*] and the "I" is given out into the world through creativity'.[86] A criticism of Dilthey seems to be implied here. *Erlebnis*, Simmel claimed, is not the source of artistic work. Rather, both the work and *Erlebnis* are different aspects of something more profound: the process of life. Simmel disliked the word *Erlebnis* because, in his view, it indicated merely a series of outward experiences; in his opinion, a more precise word would emphasise the inner flow of life as such. And only in life does restless becoming, the continuous forming and unforming, become apparent.[87] To characterise Goethe's worldview, Simmel used expressions such as: 'the living function',[88] 'dynamic life',[89] 'the will for the unity of life'.[90]

Moreover, at times Simmel seemed to impart to his notion of 'life' a meaning transcending that of individual life. For the world itself, the cosmos, is life of which human life is merely an aspect. Simmel rarely said this explicitly, but he clearly flirted with the idea. In *Kant and Goethe* (1916), for example, he spoke about 'a cosmic unity, pre-existing and infusing the whole process',[91] or about the 'all-encompassing Life' that 'admits of no further description or of being covered by a single concept'.[92]

I hope enough has been said to demonstrate the affinities between Simmel's view and the general life-philosophical interpretations of Goethe. Yet what has been described so far is no more than Simmel's

---

[83] GSG 15, p. 178.   [84] GSG 15, pp. 68, 81.
[85] GSG 15, p. 213. Cf. a similar reproach by Dilthey vis-à-vis the philosophers of the past in Wilhelm Dilthey, *Einleitung in die Geisteswissenschaften: Versuch einer Grundlegung für das Studium der Gesellschaft und der Geschichte* (Berlin: Duncker & Humblot, 1883), p. xvii.
[86] GSG 15, p. 28.   [87] GSG 15, p. 80.   [88] GSG 15, p. 35.   [89] GSG 15, p. 147.
[90] GSG 15, p. 260.   [91] 'Kant and Goethe', p. 172. [GSG 10, p. 139.]
[92] Ibid., p. 176. [GSG 10, p. 144.]

position at first approximation, and at that level it appears to be just another expression of a certain general intellectual trend. However, if one takes a closer look, a more complex and nuanced picture begins to emerge. A good place to start would be a more specific examination of the kind of unity Simmel attributed to Goethe.

The first thing to consider is that Simmel's approach to unity in Goethe did not remain the same. One specific passage can serve as good proof of this observation, as it was included in all of Simmel's Goethe writings, starting from his 1887 review. In this passage, Simmel referred to Goethe's aversion towards the Saint-Simonians 'which he . . . justified in such a way that each one has to start with oneself and pursue his own happiness, out of which without fail would arise the common good'.[93] Before the 1910s, Simmel constantly interpreted this position of Goethe as a 'liberal' individualistic criticism of social awareness, even if in his first publication Simmel was critical of such anti-socialism and in his later ones more sympathetic towards it.

But then he suddenly modified this interpretation. In *Goethe* he argued as follows:

> It is only the practical turn of this connection [between human beings and the objectivity of existence] and therefore its affirmation, when he remarks regarding the Saint-Simonians that each one nevertheless has to start with oneself and pursue his own happiness, out of which would arise without fail the common good. It is impossible that this is based on the trivial-liberal 'harmony of interests', which refers only to the individual phenomena on the surface. He can only mean that it is in a harmonious relationship to the world-being as such that the 'happiness' of the individual – in full accordance with his 'inclinations' – strikes roots or exists.[94]

And in the 1916 edition of *Kant and Goethe* he added, after quoting Goethe: 'There is, however, a profound metaphysical motive underlying this view. "Happiness" for Goethe does not mean isolated well-being but a harmonious relationship with the whole of existence that is itself a precondition for the full development of the individual.'[95]

These remarks indicate a very important change in Simmel's approach to unity. To understand it, let us briefly recall the preceding argument. Simmel's central question was how to reconcile unity and variety, and his

---

[93] 'Einige Bemerkungen über Goethes Verhältnis zur Ethik', GSG 1, p. 219. See similar sentences in 'Kant und Goethe', GSG 5, p. 469; 'Kant and Goethe', p. 181. [GSG 10, p. 153]; *Goethe*, GSG 15, p. 52.
[94] *Goethe*, GSG 15, p. 52.   [95] 'Kant and Goethe', pp. 181–182. [GSG 10, p. 153.]

answer to this question evolved over the course of his life. Initially, he subscribed to the formula of 'unity in variety', as if unity were simply the other side of apparent variety. The perception of Goethe as an exemplary man harmoniously combining in himself the whole variety of experience corresponded to this position, as did the liberal social utopia of the harmony of individual interests. This view was then replaced with that of 'unity versus variety', in which conflictual reality appears to be irreconcilable with transcendental unity. It is perhaps possible to get some sense of this unity by intuitively experiencing 'flashes' of it in specific experiences, such as aesthetic or religious experiences, but these intuitive flashes, while symbolising for us the encompassing unity, can never lead us to it. The perception of Goethe as a master of artistic form and of synthetic insight into the mysteries of nature is related to this view.

Now, in his later period, Simmel formulated a new answer to the problem of unity and variety, and his Goethe interpretation changed accordingly or, more precisely, it was his very engagement with Goethe which enabled him to find this answer. It can be described as 'unity above variety'. It differs from the two previous answers in the following way. On the one hand, unlike 'unity in variety', it does not presuppose harmony. Variety retains all its dualisms, conflicts and contradictions, whereas unity in some miraculous way becomes part of this conflict and at the same time floats above it. This is what Simmel meant in his claim that unity springing out of individual pursuits of happiness is not the result of any harmonious combination of various activities.

On the other hand, unlike in 'unity versus variety', the encompassing unity is no longer relegated to the transcendental realm. It is here and now, in the immanent process of life, and there is no gulf between us and it. And this is what is implied in Simmel's reference to our connection with the totality of the world.

His departure from 'unity versus variety' can be further illustrated by the changes in his usage of the term 'symbolic'. Thus in one of his earlier publications on Goethe (1908), Simmel spoke about action as 'the form by which that absolute foundation of the personality's being enters visible reality and creates its own (ultimately random) symbol'.[96] The symbol (in this case, human action) is just an accidental allegory of the whole. This was quite in line with the role of the symbolic in 'unity versus variety'. But a few years later, in *Goethe*, something different was claimed:

---

[96] 'Über Goethes und Kants moralische Weltanschauung: Aus einem Vorlesungszyklus', GSG 8, p. 423.

> The essential here is that a single form no longer reveals the idea in its immediate being-for-itself (which it in any case cannot do), but through mediation: it includes in itself the totality of the cases that make up the range of manifestations of the Idea. He then says about this category of the 'symbolic', 'eminent', 'significant' case, that it 'supersedes outright the contradiction that lay between my nature and immediate experience which in former times I could never solve'.[97]

Symbol is here a mediator rather than an image or allegory, implying a closer relationship between the idea and its expression. Likewise, Simmel spoke about the organism which becomes for Goethe 'the symbol of the world' and the world which becomes 'the symbol of the organism'.[98] The world is thus also a symbol! Clearly, unlike in the case of 'unity versus variety', here the symbolic is not merely an intuitive flash giving some sense of the unreachable transcendental unity. The symbolic is now directly related to unity.

An even clearer illustration of the change in Simmel's position can be found in his understanding of the relationship between particular modes of human experience and reality as a whole. In his second period, under the combined influence of neo-Kantianism and Schopenhauer, Simmel developed the view that reality is not accessible to us unconditionally but is formatted into various coherent systems, each determined by its own presuppositions – worlds – via which we approach it. Thus a practical person refers to reality in terms of practical life; the life of an aesthetical person is determined by aesthetic categories; and a religious person sees in every occurrence divine providence. Simmel postulated the complete integrity and self-sufficiency of each such world; for example, artistic experience is valid within the postulates of the aesthetic world, and it cannot teach us anything either about other worlds or about the ultimate reality. In *Goethe*, however, Simmel occasionally began to speak as if he now thought that there was no unbridgeable gap between particular worlds of experience and the whole. Thus:

> But the artist is not *just* an artist. The formation of experience implied here pervades the totality of his life in infinite quantitative gradations. That unity of individual wholes naturally never coincides in its character with the pure concept of the artistic as such, just as little as it does with that of the religious or the practical. Rather, the living reality crosses through these rigid and exclusive concepts, touching them in a very irregular and changing manner.

---

[97] *Goethe*, GSG 15, p. 138.   [98] GSG 15, p. 78.

Even when its core is fixed on one of them, its periphery can still be split up among others to varying degrees.[99]

In other words, although there is distance between a world of experience and totality, this distance is gradated rather than absolute and the connection to totality is felt in every aspect of life.

As we have seen, in his second period Simmel emphasised Goethe as an 'artist', contrasting him with the 'scientifically' oriented Kant, and it was then that he also developed the idea of categorically separated spheres of experience. But he now saw Goethe differently. Although he again stated that Goethe's whole life was coloured by the aesthetic worldview, and thus one can speak of Goethe the artist as *Urphänomen* Goethe, he argued at the same time that *Urphänomen* is not the ultimate point of Goethe's personality: There is something beyond it, something which is more profound and more universal. It may forever remain shrouded in mystery, but we know it is present, and without it the *Urphänomen* of artist would not exist:[100]

> Here we feel more clearly than toward any other historical figure this peculiar and yet little examined category which determines for us every living human being as soon as we know him to some extent: the generality of his personality, not as an abstraction derived from his individual traits and actions, but as a unity accessible only to an immediate mental knowing.[101]

Now, before we examine more closely the structure of the Simmelian view of 'unity above variety', I would like to draw attention to two things. First, in the passage just quoted, one can sense mystical, even demonic overtones that enter Simmel's descriptions of Goethe. Second, it is important to keep in mind what has been said about his new understanding of unity: that it does not eliminate conflicts and dualisms. In other words, unity now seems to distance itself from light and harmony. But can unity exist without harmony, can it be 'demonic'? To understand where Simmel stood on this question, let us look again at his intellectual context.

In the last decade before the war, German-speaking intellectuals began to display symptoms of a growing scepticism towards the perception of Goethe as a harmonious Olympic personality. This scepticism did not yet develop into full-scale criticism, but the doubts were already raised: was Goethe really so successful in reconciling all the sides of his multi-faceted personality? The change was noticed both in Goethe research and in the philosophical interpretation of his personality.

---

[99] GSG 15, p. 29.   [100] GSG 15, pp. 261–262.   [101] GSG 15, p. 263.

For a very long time, literary interest in Goethe focused on the works of his early and classical periods. Later works, such as *West-Eastern Divan* and *Faust II*, received less attention and their aesthetic value was often dismissed. However, by the early twentieth century, Goethe scholars, having exhausted other themes, turned their attention towards those works, especially *West-Eastern Divan* which became the subject of a number of prominent studies by Konrad Burdach.[102] This redirection of attention brought a new degree of complexity to the image of Goethe, for these works appeared to signify Goethe's retreat from the search for perfect classical form. Besides, *Divan* appeared to contain a strong emphasis on *polarity*, or duality of existence. Hugo von Hofmannsthal, for example, under the influence of *Divan*, stressed the polarity of elements in Goethe, such as closeness and distance, or immanence and transcendence.[103]

A similar emphasis on polarity can be found in the large volume on Goethe, published by Houston Stewart Chamberlain just one year before Simmel's monograph. Like most commentators before him, Chamberlain perceived unity as an important category in Goethe's thinking and similarly understood this unity in terms of the relationship between whole and part. He spoke about *Urphänomen*,[104] mentioned the name of Leibniz[105] and dealt with the interaction of totality ('idea') and limitation ('reality') in Goethe.[106] But unlike them, he turned disunity into a no less important category than unity, as he spoke about 'polarity' as Goethe's fundamental concept.[107] According to Chamberlain, this polarity does not create logical unity. Rather, it exists as a perpetual alternation: breathing in and breathing out, diastole and systole.[108]

Chamberlain, hardly a profound thinker, did not attempt a philosophical explanation of what this combination of unity and disunity involved. But Simmel, who placed the chapter on the division of world elements immediately after the chapter on the unity of world elements, as if he wanted to show that in his view too disunity stood on equal footing with unity in Goethe, and who also liked to cite Goethe's metaphor of breathing,[109] appeared to think that he was up to the task.

Simmel revealed his view of the way in which the combination of unity and disunity functions in Goethe in the second chapter of his book, which

---

[102] See, e.g. Konrad Burdach, 'Einleitung', in *Goethes sämtliche Werke: Jubiläums-Ausgabe in 40 Bänden* (Stuttgart: J. G. Cotta, 1902–1912), vol. 5 [*West-östlicher Divan*], pp. v–l.

[103] Mandelkow, *Goethe in Deutschland*, vol. 1, p. 239.

[104] Houston Stewart Chamberlain, *Goethe* (Munich: F. Bruckmann, 1912), p. 311.

[105] Ibid., p. 612.   [106] Ibid., p. 576.   [107] Ibid., pp. 569–570.   [108] Ibid.

[109] *Goethe*, GSG 15, p. 93.

dealt with Goethe's notion of truth. Quoting the poet's saying – 'What is fruitful is alone true'[110] – Simmel attributed to him a concept of truth 'so elevated, so broadly-encompassing, its absolute meaning, so to speak, that it equally includes the true and the false in the sense of their being relative opposites'.[111] In other words, there are two concepts of truth. One is a relative concept. It takes its meaning from being the opposite of 'false-hood'. The other is a higher, absolute concept. In some way it contains both truth and falsehood.

This was not an incidental remark but rather Simmel's favourite formula in his later period, which he began to employ in many other writings on various topics[112] and which played a central role in his mature interpret-ation of Goethe. It was valid not only for the notion of truth but in fact for almost every aspect of Goethe. Thus, Simmel argued in the same chapter, the absolute meaning of lawfulness includes in Goethe's mind both law and arbitrariness; the regular – both the relative rule and deviation from it; the highest norm – both normal and abnormal; the absolutely natural – both natural and unnatural; the absolutely appropriate – both right and wrong.[113] And he spoke elsewhere about the absolute synthesis as standing above the relative synthesis and antithesis;[114] the timeless youth of Goethe as being above his temporary young and old ages;[115] the all-encompassing unity as transcending the opposition between unity and disunity (*Entzweiung*)[116] and the absolute concept of life as containing the relative concept of life and its opposite: form.[117]

Simmel described the guiding principle of this formula as the 'culmin-ation of an encompassing value over its own relative meaning'[118] and as 'the dominance of a principle precisely over its opposite ... by its higher meaning and force overshadowing the relation between itself and that opposite'.[119] In this scheme, dualisms and contradictions are not trans-formed or abolished; they are transcended. Neither unity nor duality disappears, as they both continue to exist, so to say, on two levels. The

---

[110] GSG 15, p. 33. Chamberlain also cited this phrase. See Chamberlain, *Goethe*, p. 246.
[111] GSG 15, p. 35.
[112] E.g., he toyed with this scheme in some of his essays on *Philosophical Culture*, speaking about the beauty of the highest instance, of which beauty in the usual sense is only an element, or the absolute concept of 'high' which is above the opposition of 'high' and 'low'. See 'On the Aesthetics of the Alps' [1911], in *Georg Simmel: Essays on Art and Aesthetics* (Chicago: University of Chicago Press, 2020), pp. 216–217; [GSG 12, p. 168; GSG 14, p. 302.] 'The Handle', trans. R. H. Weingartner, in Kurt H. Wolff (ed.), *Essays on Sociology, Philosophy and Aesthetics* (New York: Harper & Row, 1959), p. 273. ['Der Henkel', in *Philosophische Kultur*, GSG 14, p. 284.]
[113] *Goethe*, GSG 15, p. 36.   [114] GSG 15, p. 95.   [115] 'Goethe und die Jugend', GSG 13, p. 104.
[116] 'Goethes Gerechtigkeit', GSG 13, p. 95.   [117] 'Werte des Goetheschen Lebens', GSG 20, p. 55.
[118] *Goethe*, GSG 15, p. 36.   [119] GSG 15, p. 93.

lower – the relative level – is that of a pair of opposite concepts. The higher – the absolute level – is that on which the 'positive' member encompasses totality. Unity is thus not found in variety nor is it opposed to variety; it is simply placed above variety, with variety remaining intact.

This is not a happy unity; it is always on the verge of falling apart. Even when Simmel specifically focused on the side of unity in Goethe, as, for example, in the chapter on the unity of world elements, he did not forget the other side, mentioning notions such as polarity, breathing in and out.[120] The idea of unity in Goethe, he argued, contains three aspects: continuity, totality, equilibrium.[121] He explained the aspect of equilibrium in the following way: 'Perhaps every entity, and at least the human being ... stands in its essence at the central point of many lines, so to speak, each of which ends in an absolute pole on this and on that side of it.'[122] He warned the reader not to interpret this in terms of the philistine happy harmony:

> Here appears the deepest meaning of that 'balance' which, if not the actuality, was the norm of Goethe's life and which appeared to a superficial glance as coldness, as a guarantee against the danger of extremes, as the 'golden middle way' of the philistine, as harmonisation at any price coming from an aestheticising and mindful classicism. In truth, the 'balance', the 'middle' he praises and for which he strives marks the point of sovereignty from which all the realms of life are governable to the maximum and in which his powers are most consummately available: a ruler usually tends not to reside at the border of his country but where possible in the centre, for corresponding reasons.[123]

To be in the middle is thus more like being apart or above, in some rarefied atmosphere from which one can encompass all the contradictions beneath. This has nothing in common with walking the broad path of moral certainty; it is rather like the balancing act of a tightrope walker, where even a small error may cause a fall.

But the most far-reaching examples of the fragile character of this unity can be found in chapters four and eight: 'The Division of World Elements' and 'Development'. The structure of the two chapters is essentially similar. In both, Simmel focuses on changes in Goethe; in both, the process of change is divided into three periods; and in both, the description of the third period is somewhat obscure: it seems as if Simmel himself had not made up his mind about that period and was offering a series of thoughts rather than a well-designed argument. Partly this reflects his understanding

---

[120] GSG 15, 93.   [121] GSG 15, pp. 85–86.   [122] GSG 15, p. 99.   [123] GSG 15, pp. 100–101.

that Goethe in his third period was never able to detach himself completely from the legacy of the second period.[124] But this may also reflect Simmel's difficulties in formulating an ultimate philosophical answer to the questions with which he himself was preoccupied in *his* third period, and especially that of unity and variety.

The subject of the fourth chapter is the changes in Goethe's perception of the relationship between nature (reality) and art (value). Although the genius of Goethe always combined these two poles into unity, the character of this unity was different in each of the three stages into which Goethe's life is traditionally divided: his younger years, the classical period and old age.

The young Goethe displayed a naive undifferentiated unity between natural reality and artistic value, governed solely from the side of the subject. Only what Goethe perceived as natural, real and true in his immediate subjectivity could trigger him in his artistic production. This was unity prior to any synthesis because 'the elements that composed the synthesis in which his later life passed, on the whole had not been yet differentiated'.[125]

After Goethe moved to Weimar, though, cracks began to appear in this naive unity. Suddenly faced with substantive reality for which he could not find a proper answer in his soul, he retreated into his inner self, feeling incapable of producing art which would be adequate to the demands of the world. The solution came during his travels to Italy, which initiated his second period: beauty is inherent in nature itself which is understood as original unity that 'stands *prior to* any singularity'.[126] This beauty, however, is not identical to the empirical individual appearances of nature. It reveals itself only by means of art, of which the highest example is the art of the Greeks. In other words, in contrast to the young Goethe who attained the unity of reality and art from the side of subjectivity, the mature Goethe attained it from the side of objectivity: instead of a synthesis of natural feeling and artistic production, he pursued a synthesis of nature and beauty. He found it in classicist art.

He never abandoned this outlook, but in the third period he added new elements to it, which, according to Simmel, signify an increasing emphasis on artistic value. This value, having previously reached an organic connection with reality, 'grows to a certain extent beyond the existing intertwining with the contents of reality'.[127] Now, the precise meaning of this description of Simmel's is unclear, as it seems to entail two very different

[124] GSG 15, pp. 125, 256.   [125] GSG 15, p. 113.   [126] GSG 15, p. 123.   [127] GSG 15, p. 126.

implications. On the one hand, he appears to be saying that Goethe moved towards a kind of aestheticism, in which art acquires autonomy for itself and simply does not require any reference to reality. The earlier classicist well-tempered aestheticism, where beautiful form was understood as a harmonious rendering of true nature, evolves into its own extreme, where the connection between art and reality is broken. Yet, on other hand, in an amazing twist Simmel said this:

> The 'artistism' [*Artistentum*] of his later years did not leave Nature behind as if it were a new enemy; the reconciliation with Nature was now embedded in Art itself; its idea had become for him now so vast and high that its autonomy no longer required a counterpart and antithesis, which is often otherwise the condition but also, for this reason, the barrier of autonomy. This is what he says as an octogenarian: the highest works of art are the ones that possess 'the highest truth but no trace of reality'.[128]

In other words, this apparent escape into the artistic does not necessarily mean the disintegration of unity; it is rather a sign of a higher unity, of a synthesis in which reality's otherness is simply not needed: art itself is absolute reality. One could be reminded here of the formula of 'unity above variety': absolute aestheticism floats above aestheticism and reality.

It seems, then, that two contrasting interpretations of Simmel's view of Goethe's attitude to art in his third period are possible: absolute apartness and absolute integration. One would expect that after pushing the two positions to their respective extremes, Simmel, as was his habit, would in the end reconcile them at a higher level of abstraction. But this is not what happened. Such reconciliation was natural with regard to Goethe's first period with its youthful effortless unity; it was also possible with regard to the second period, when the gap between subjectivity and objectivity had opened yet could still be bridged by the synthesis of nature and form; but in the third period, the two vectors found themselves so far apart from one another that Simmel's interpretation of Goethe's view of the relationship of art and reality began to seem obscure. The dissonance was now greater and more serious than that which had character-ised Goethe's early Weimar years. No travels to Italy would be sufficient to solve this 'divergence of the ideal and the real',[129] for here the problem was not personal, requiring not just a change in the direction of life, but profoundly metaphysical, solutions to which were at most fragmentary.

Simmel suggested a number of ways in which Goethe then confronted the division between art and reality. First, the notion of the 'symbolic case',

---

[128] GSG 15, p. 128.   [129] GSG 15, p. 137.

described as an attempt 'to find the infinite on the level of the finite'.[130] Or
the idea of the 'middle position': a human being finds itself between the
totality of the cosmic order and the particularity of real appearances. It is 'a
microcosm that repeats in its spiritual character the meaning of that totality
and for that very reason cannot fully belong to any of the individual parts of
the whole, neither to the idea nor to the real and empirical'.[131]
Furthermore, the notion of activity understood not teleologically, as if it
were directed to some external purpose, but in terms of life energy, as
depicted in *Faust II*.[132] Finally, the idea of the stream of life, in which the
life process is united with the individual law governing it, so that the
dichotomy of norm and exception is overcome.[133] Yet none of these is a
happy resolution. It is no accident that the chapter was called 'The
Division of World Elements'. In the search for ultimate unity we have
descended to a mystical level, and whatever unity can be found there must
stand beyond logic and reflection. Expressions such as 'symbolic case' or
'life process' are at most inadequate approximations of it. Going further
would lead us to frightening metaphysical depths which we instinctively
abhor. Referring to Goethe's saying that the perception of *Urphänomen*
provokes in us the feeling of fear, Simmel noted: 'It is always one of the
deepest horrors of the human soul when it sees that what it must consider a
logical contradiction has become reality.'[134]

And a similar dynamic takes place in chapter eight – 'Development'.
There, Simmel examines Goethe's attitude towards life. There are two
types of personalities: those whose existence is determined by a specific
norm, calling or profession and those who derive the imperative of their
existence from the totality of their life. Goethe always belonged to the
second type. Yet his totality of life was displayed differently in his three
periods. In his younger period, his life was an unhindered flow of energy
characteristic of a subjective lyricist. Everything is feeling, which is prior to
any norm or any distinction between good and evil. In the second period,
Goethe became more interested in humanity than in man. Objectivisation
takes place, and form emerges as something foreign to life, to be reconciled
with it later by means of the classical ideal. And in the third period, of
which we again perceive symptoms rather than a complete picture, a
process of radicalisation similar to that described in the fourth chapter
occurred. On the one hand, objectivisation gallops towards its own
extreme: 'As Goethe grows older, his veneration of "form" becomes more

---

[130] GSG 15, p. 138. [131] GSG 15, p. 140. [132] GSG 15, pp. 141–146.
[133] GSG 15, pp. 146–150. [134] GSG 15, p. 131.

and more uncompromising, up to formalism.'[135] On the other hand, this push towards one extreme again leads to an opposite but no less radical result: in the older Goethe, form simply breaks up.[136] Or rather, radical formalism and the destruction of form are one and the same thing. Pursuit of the ultimate form ends up in form reaching the stage where it begins to encompass the entire life. From now onwards, there can be no more forms within life: life as a whole is its own form; or it is both the highest form and no form. For 'that formlessness, that disintegration of synthesis during Goethe's old age is the indication that the great aspiration of his life – the objectivisation of subject – has arrived in his advanced age *near* a new, mysteriously absolute stage of perfection, even if perhaps not *in* it'.[137]

We are thus on the verge of mystical perfection. This perfection would signify the fulfilment of the quest of Goethe's younger years: to live life fully without reservations. Only that the meaning of life has changed in the process. It is no longer a life of inner subjectivity; rather it is a life of objectivity after subjectivity, a life in which there is a 'mystical' connection of personal experience with some primordial living unity. The 'mystical' aspect in Goethe was noticed by Simmel as early as 1906, when he spoke about the poet's vision of the unknowable, of 'the depth of the world we behold losing itself in the mystical realm, one that can be reached without requiring any leap, even though the path to it remains unending'.[138] And later, in *Goethe*, he attributed this mystical outlook specifically to Goethe's old age.[139] Having reached his own old age, Simmel, who then developed interest in mystics such as Meister Eckhart, may have felt a deep affinity with Goethe in this respect, or at least with the image of Goethe he drew for himself.

The mystical disposition, containing, as it were, both awareness of dissonances and yearning for unity, suited Simmel, who was then at pains to keep some hope for unity in the face of the fragmentariness of modern existence. He never let this hope disappear from his thought. Dissonances became more noticeable in his later writings, but they fell short of making him abandon the ideal of *Bildung* altogether. These writings may have had an impact on the disillusioned intellectuals of the next generation, but he himself never crossed the line. Unlike Chamberlain, he remained a believer in unity, committed to the quest for harmonious self-cultivation.[140]

---

[135] GSG 15, p. 250.   [136] GSG 15, p. 256.   [137] GSG 15, p. 261.
[138] 'Kant and Goethe', p. 179. [GSG 10, p. 149.]   [139] *Goethe*, GSG 15, p. 260.
[140] Simmel's contemporaries noticed the difference between Chamberlain's and Simmel's outlooks. Martin Havenstein, e.g., rejected the 'dualism' of the former, while praising Simmel for his

One small example may illustrate the difference between Simmel's attitude to Goethe and that of younger writers, many of whom were his students. Simmel adopted Goethe's own account of his relationship with Frau von Stein. According to this account, she brought him happiness, for her solid and tranquil nature harmoniously reconciled all the varieties and eccentricities of his life.[141] She was the only person with whom Goethe could be fully open. And now consider the interpretation of Emil Ludwig, once an attendee of Simmel's lectures.[142] In his Goethe biography, published just after the end of the First World War, Ludwig suggested that Goethe might not have been sincere when he said to Stein that she was the one to whom he had so much to confess as to no one else: 'and yet we have a witness [his diary] for how much he hides from his friend in that very year'.[143] In Ludwig's account there is no harmony but inner conflict and duplicity.

Not that Simmel was overly sanguine regarding the alleged harmony of Goethe. After speaking about the harmonising influence of Frau von Stein, he also referred to Goethe's sufferings in his relationships with women as a result of his inability to find the point of repose which would enable him to forge a satisfactory relationship. This suffering was the counterpart of his occasional moments of happiness, as darkness is the counterpart of light. And yet Simmel immediately added that both light and darkness arise in Goethe from the same metaphysical unity.[144]

Thus, despite all doubts and discontents, Goethe remained for Simmel what he was for most readers of his and previous generations: the ideal of human integrity. According to him, Goethe was not a professional man, a man of *Beruf*.[145] Rather, as he put it:

---

emphasis on unity. He lashed out at Chamberlain's angry style, errors and anti-Semitism; by contrast, Simmel's work, according to him, 'has absolutely no equal to it, neither in the past nor in the present. I am sure that there is no one in Germany who would be able to write such a book today'. Martin Havenstein, 'Chamberlains und Simmels "Goethe"', *Preußische Jahrbücher* 155, 1914, p. 272 Havenstein overlooked strong dualistic tendencies in Simmel's work that make it closer to Chamberlain's than he allowed, but he was correct in his overall perception of the difference in disposition between the two authors.

[141] GSG 15, p. 203.

[142] For Ludwig's impression of Simmel as a teacher, see Emil Ludwig, 'Erinnerungen an Simmel', in K. Gassen and M. Landmann (eds.), *Buch des Dankes an Georg Simmel* (Berlin: Duncker & Humblot, 1958), pp. 152–157.

[143] Emil Ludwig, *Goethe: Geschichte eines Menschen*, vol. 1 (Stuttgart: J. G. Cotta'sche Buchhandlung Nachfolger, 1922), p. 325. Another example might be the changes in Goethe reception by another student of Simmel, José Ortega y Gasset, who was initially influenced by Simmel's book but then, partly under the influence of Heidegger, departed from it, especially with regard to the image of Goethe as a universal and harmonious person. See Nelson R. Orringer, 'Simmel's *Goethe* in the Thought of Ortega y Gasset', *MLN* 92(2), 1977, pp. 296–311.

[144] *Goethe*, GSG 15, p. 217.   [145] See GSG 15, pp. 218–219.

In the sum and unity of his achievements, in their relation to his life, in that life's rhythm, tone and development in different periods, Goethe, however, not only postulated the universally and absolutely *human* beyond or above all those individual perfections as a value but also lived it as a value: he is the grand justification of the merely human *on its own account*. He once described the meaning of all his writings as 'the triumph of the purely human'; this was the total meaning of his *existence*.[146]

Simmel was aware that neither he himself nor other Germans of his time could commit themselves exclusively to this ideal. The contrasting ideal of *Beruf* was for them no less important. Yet insofar as one remained in the sphere of *Bildung* untouched by *Beruf,* it was Goethe, seen through the prism of life-philosophy, who symbolised for Simmel the highest ideal to aspire to.

4.2   Visual Art and Rembrandt

After finishing *Goethe*, Simmel began working on his Rembrandt mono-graph.[147] As a commentator recently suggested, *Goethe* and *Rembrandt* form a kind of diptych.[148] Indeed, both belonged to Simmel's last period, both were informed by the spirit of his life-philosophy, and in many respects *Rembrandt* was a continuation of the themes explored in *Goethe*.

Yet the two works were not the same; moreover, in some respects *Rembrandt* departed significantly from the preceding work. Although in *Goethe* Simmel found a new theoretical way to solve the problem of the tension between unity and variety, his dilemmas were more than merely theoretical. They touched on the most intimate spheres of his personality and creative energies. And it is not at all clear that in *Goethe* he provided the ultimate answers as to how one could discharge such energies without being consumed by the dissonances of life. For despite Simmel's emphasis on Goethe's harmony, his depiction of the poet's life can be read as a story

---

[146] GSG 15, p. 270.
[147] *Rembrandt: An Essay in the Philosophy of Art* [1916], trans. A. Scott and H. Staubmann (New York: Routledge, 2005). [*Rembrandt: Ein kunstphilosophischer Versuch*, GSG 15, pp. 305–515.] For the most informative research on the subject see Uta Kösser, 'Simmels "Rembrandt"', *Simmel Studies* 13(2), 2003, pp. 439–483. See also Alois Kölbl, *Das Leben der Form: Georg Simmels kunstphilosophischer Versuch über Rembrandt* (Vienna: Böhlau, 1998) and Dominik Brabant, 'Vibrierendes Sehen: Simmels *Rembrandt* und die Kontingenz des kunstwissenschaftlichen Blicks', *KulturPoetik* 17(1), 2017, pp. 21–41.
[148] Meyer, *Georg Simmels Ästhetik*, p. 246.

of the path towards the great divide: between absolute form and the dissolution of all forms.

Furthermore, while interpreting Goethe's life and thought in the life-philosophical manner, Simmel was clearly aware that this world outlook could not be applied to Goethe's art as such. Goethe was clearly too much of a 'Renaissance man', an Italy seeker, a 'universalist'. A different kind of artist was needed to make the language of life-philosophy aesthetically convincing. Simmel found such an artist in Rembrandt.

There was nothing obvious in this turn. Today, it is taken for granted that Simmel was a great lover of Rembrandt's art. What, however, often escapes notice is that for most of his life Simmel displayed rather classicist aesthetic preferences, standing in this respect much closer to Goethe. He was to a great extent a 'Romanist' and 'Renaissancist'.

By using these terms I refer to the cultural divide between two models of identity prominent in Germany at the turn of the twentieth century. Each of the two models proposed a different vector of cultural development, depending on the kind of 'other' in relation to which German identity needed to be negotiated and constructed. On the one hand, there was the 'Romanic' vector that usually involved a strong fascination with Italy. Towards the end of the nineteenth century, this took the form of what came to be known as *Renaissancismus*: scholarly and artistic preoccupation with the culture of the Italian Renaissance.[149] On the other hand, there was the 'Germanic' vector represented by 'National Protestantism'.[150] It usually involved a search for an authentic German tradition, separate from and opposed to 'Roman' influences. This authentic Germanness, however, was usually understood in quite broad terms, as it often incorporated 'Nordic' or 'Teutonic' elements which allowed it to include in itself Dutch, Scandinavian or even English influences.[151] Towards the end of the nineteenth century, the 'Low German' Rembrandt began to be assimilated into this model.

Rembrandt's status became well established in Germany by the early twentieth century as a result of a process that had lasted several decades and transformed him from a source of inspiration for artistic rebels into a central figure in the official cultural pantheon.[152] Its beginnings can be

---

[149] Martin A. Ruehl, *The Italian Renaissance in the German Historical Imagination, 1860–1930* (Cambridge: Cambridge University Press, 2015).

[150] Ibid., pp. 16–17.

[151] On the extreme versions of the 'German Ideology', see Fritz Stern, *The Politics of Cultural Despair: A Study in the Rise of the Germanic Ideology* (Berkeley: University of California Press, 1989).

[152] See Johannes Stückelberger, *Rembrandt und die Moderne: Der Dialog mit Rembrandt in der deutschen Kunst um 1900* (Munich: Wilhelm Fink, 1996).

traced to the France of the 1830s and 1840s and the 'discovery' of
Rembrandt by Romantic painters, such as Eugène Delacroix.[153] Towards
the end of the nineteenth century, Rembrandt became a cult figure for
unorthodox artists in Germany. It is argued that the paintings of German
secessionists, such as Liebermann and Nolde, owed much to Rembrandt's
style and composition.[154] But at the same time Rembrandt was already
being appropriated by the cultural establishment. The main figure responsible for this appropriation was the director of Berlin museums Wilhelm
Bode, who was a great admirer of Rembrandt and who made every effort to
acquire the Dutchman's paintings and drawings for his collection.
Rembrandt's popularity reached its peak by the 1900s with the celebrations
of the three-hundredth anniversary of his birth and with the publication of
a number of detailed studies of his life and art.[155]

As Rembrandt's cultural standing grew, more and more authors tried to
redefine him as a true 'German'. The most extreme example of the
Germanic appropriation of Rembrandt was Langbehn's *Rembrandt as
Educator* (1890). The book's popularity was not an insignificant factor in
sparking a general interest in Rembrandt. It is true that Langbehn was
perceived as a maverick, and experts, such as art historian Carl Neumann,
were quite critical of the quality of his scholarship.[156] Yet even respectable
figures were affected by the Germanic ideas at the heart of Langbehn's
book and prepared to integrate them in moderate form into their own
interpretations. The same Neumann argued, for example: 'Apart from the
painter – the man of a specific art – the German has been revealed to us,
who brings us his special mission and whose vigour should effectively strike
us deeper than the rest of humanity.'[157] And another author – Willy Becker
– was happy to allude to Langbehn in the title of his own, much more
scholarly and coherent book, *Rembrandt as Poet*.[158]

This status, however, was not attained without opposition or reservations. Many art lovers and connoisseurs, especially those committed to the

[153] Ibid., p. 27.
[154] On Rembrandt's reception in France and Germany, see also Annette Wauschkuhn, *Georg Simmels
Rembrandt-Bild: Ein lebensphilosophischer Beitrag zur Rembrandtrezeption im 20. Jahrhundert*
(Worms: Wernersche Verlagsgesellschaft, 2002), pp. 24–48.
[155] E.g. Carl Neumann, *Rembrandt* (Berlin: W. Spemann, 1902); Richard Muther, *Rembrandt: Ein
Künstlerleben* (Berlin: Egon Fleischel & Co., 1904); Richard Muther, *Rembrandt* (Berlin: Bard,
Marquardt, 1906); Wilhelm Bode, *Rembrandt und seine Zeitgenossen* (Leipzig: E. A. Seemann,
1906); Wilhelm Bode and Wilhelm Valentiner, *Rembrandt in Bild und Wort* (Berlin: Rich. Bond,
1906); Richard Hamann, *Rembrandts Radierungen* (Berlin: Bruno Cassirer, 1906).
[156] Neumann, *Rembrandt*, pp. 22–28.   [157] Ibid., p. 28.
[158] Willy Becker, *Rembrandt als Dichter: Eine Untersuchung über das Poetische in den biblischen
Darstellungen Rembrandts* (Leipzig: Klinkhardt & Biermann, 1909).

'Romanic' vector, doubted Rembrandt's greatness. Already in the 1830s, as Rembrandt began to be cultivated by the Romantics, Franz Kugler argued that he failed to represent 'that sublime tranquillity [*Ruhe*] . . . which allows the contemplation of perfect beauty'.[159] From among the Dutch painters Kugler preferred Rubens. This assessment influenced Jacob Burckhardt, who criticised Rembrandt for failing to represent the human body in accordance with classical principles and expressed disdain over the painter's approach to the subject of religion. Burckhardt recognised and respected the peculiarity of Rembrandt's genius but did not recommend that it be emulated.[160]

Herman Grimm, the leading art historian at the University of Berlin and Simmel's teacher, had doubts of his own about Rembrandt and Rembrandt's cult. He was an admirer of the High Renaissance and wrote monographs on Michelangelo and Raphael. In 1891, when a book was published that denied Rembrandt's authorship to several well-known paintings,[161] Grimm was only too happy to dispatch an expert to examine the relevant paintings.[162] Grimm was succeeded in 1901 by Swiss art historian Heinrich Wölfflin. A theorist of the Baroque style, Wölfflin was in a way warmer to Rembrandt, but not to the extent that would lead him to adopt the nationalistic distinction between the Germanic Rembrandt and classical Southern art. To Wölfflin, grand racial extrapolations were of secondary significance. While he admitted that national peculiarities did play a role in the development of style, it was the factor of age that was most fundamental to him. He focused on the division between the age of Renaissance and the age of Baroque, rather than on that between the southern and northern Baroque.[163]

Classicist suspicion of Rembrandt did not characterise only academic scholars. Burckhardt's reservations influenced, for example, Stefan George. In the poetry collection *The Seventh Ring* (1907), of which Simmel wrote a review, he included a short strophe addressed to a 'Nordic master':

---

[159] Franz Kugler, *Handbuch der Geschichte der Malerei in Deutschland, den Niederlanden, Spanien, Frankreich und England* (Berlin: Duncker und Humblot, 1837), vol. 2, p. 176.

[160] Jacob Burckhardt, *Kulturgeschichtliche Vorträge* (Stuttgart: Alfred Kröner, 1959), pp. 109–133. See Joseph Gantner, 'Jacob Burckhardts Urteil über Rembrandt und seine Konzeption des Klassischen', in *Concinnitas: Beiträge zum Problem des Klassischen* (Basel: Schwabe, 1944), pp. 83–114.

[161] Max Lautner, *Wer ist Rembrandt? Grundlagen zu einem Neubau der holländischen Kunstgeschichte* (Breslau: J. U. Kern, 1891).

[162] Catherine B. Scallen, *Rembrandt, Reputation, and the Practice of Connoisseurship* (Amsterdam: Amsterdam University Press, 2004), pp. 116–117.

[163] Heinrich Wölfflin, *Kunstgeschichtliche Grundbegriffe: Das Problem der Stilentwickelung in der neueren Kunst* (Munich: F. Bruckmann, 1915).

Where your secret lay and your affliction
Was the tortuous banishment of our nights:
In your skies you paint the splendorous remains
Around the fallen angel's frame.[164]

According to Ernst Morwitz, these words referred to Rembrandt and his painting *The Abduction of Ganymede*.[165] George criticised Rembrandt's light-darkness technique here, which apparently contradicted his own perception of antiquity influenced by classicist and Renaissance art. George's aesthetic preferences were clearly for the south, and to the northern Romantics he preferred the art of Arnold Böcklin.[166] Böcklin, a Swiss painter who educated himself on the models of Italian art, used contemporary symbolistic techniques to transmit ancient myths in his paintings. His art, being an important reincarnation of the yearning for the unity of the classical and the modern (a yearning that was also often attributed to figures such as Goethe and Nietzsche), became towards the 1880s and 1890s the centre of artistic consensus, appreciated by both adepts of academism and artistic modernists.[167]

Simmel fit in perfectly with this mood, as his tastes combined a veneration for Italy and Renaissance with an interest in the innovative practices of contemporary art. Consider the list of artists and aesthetic images about which Simmel had something to say before 1910. A student of Grimm, friend of George and colleague of Wölfflin, he discussed Italian classical masters such as Dante, Michelangelo and Leonardo da Vinci. He wrote on the beauty of old Italian cities. Among German figures he chose Böcklin, Stefan George and Nietzsche in his third anti-Germanic and anti-Wagnerian period. And he was fascinated with the art of French sculptor Rodin. A Jewish urban intellectual, he seemed to profess no sympathy for any kind of Germanic ideology. As early as 1890 he dismissed the cult of

---

[164] 'Wo dein geheimnis lag und dein gebreste / War unsrer nächte quälender vertreib: / Du malst in deine himmel ein die reste / Von glanz um der gefallnen engel leib'. Stefan George, *Der siebente Ring* (Berlin: Georg Bondi, 1907), p. 200. Michael Landmann speculates that this verse might have been provoked by George's conversations with Simmel, in the course of which Simmel must have defended Rembrandt. Michael Landmann, 'Georg Simmel und Stefan George', in H.-J. Dahme and O. Rammstedt (eds.), *Georg Simmel und die Moderne* (Frankfurt am Main: Suhrkamp, 1984), pp. 152–153.

[165] Ernst Morwitz, *Die Dichtung Stefan Georges* (Berlin: Georg Blondi, 1943), p. 123.

[166] Cf. Jan Aler, 'Zur Deutung von Rembrandts Luminismus (Wie Albert Verwey und Stefan George ihn diskutierten)', *Zeitschrift für Ästhetik und allgemeine Kunstwissenschaft* 12(2), 1967, pp. 220, 230–231.

[167] See Suzanne Marchand, 'Arnold Böcklin und die Krise des Neoklassizismus in Deutschland', in Eva Koczinsky (ed.), *Ruinen in der Moderne: Archäologie und die Künste* (Berlin: Dietrich Reimer, 2011), pp. 161–172.

Rembrandt in *Rembrandt as Educator*. And thereafter Rembrandt appeared in his writings on few occasions and just in passing.

Only in 1907 does one find in Simmel a more 'Germanic' note, as he stated that Rembrandt (together with Dürer) was an 'earlier' Germanic artist who lived according to his own 'individual law', a quality now represented by a French artist: Rodin.[168] But this 'Germanic' motif appears only in Simmel's class transcripts transmitted to us by a student. His published works of that period still seem to display a strong 'Romanic' allegiance.

Therefore it is not surprising that even close acquaintances of Simmel perceived him as a lover of classical balance. Consider Simmel's correspondence with his friend, playwright Paul Ernst, in 1910. At the end of his letter to Ernst, Simmel inserted the following remark:

> and then something personal – that my conception of art must lead to the ideal 'of calm [*Ruhe*] and balance' (Schopenhauer) is a purely factual error of yours. For it is not antiquity and the Renaissance which are for me the deepest and subjectively most valuable in art, but the Gothic and Rembrandt – which are just the opposite of Schopenhauer's ideals.[169]

The reference here is to Schopenhauer's view that aesthetic experience constitutes temporary release from the pains of life and desire. It is supposed to bring 'peace and calm' (*Ruhe*), without which 'true well-being is absolutely impossible'.[170] Simmel cited this phrase in his *Schopenhauer and Nietzsche*.[171] Ernst must have deduced from this that Simmel was expressing his own aesthetic sympathies. Today's reader, who is typically familiar with Simmel as an unabashed modernist or even 'postmodernist', may fully sympathise with Simmel's rebuttal of what appears to be an unforgivable error. But things were not as clear at that time. In fact, many of Simmel's statements before 1910 – personal and public – were in line with Ernst's perception. One may be reminded again of Simmel's love for Florence, his feeling of being at home in its harmonious peacefulness.

Be this as it may, in 1910 Simmel wished to distance himself from Schopenhauer's 'calm' and therefore from the 'unity versus variety' solution to which he had subscribed in the preceding period and which he

[168] 'Philosophie der Kultur' [Winter-Semester 1906/1907, by Hermann Schmalenbach], GSG 21, p. 563.
[169] Letter to Paul Ernst, 14 January 1910, GSG 22, p. 774.
[170] Arthur Schopenhauer, *The Will as World and Representation*, 2 vols., trans. E. F. J. Payne (New York: Dover Publications, 1966), vol. 1, § 38, p. 196.
[171] *Schopenhauer und Nietzsche*, GSG 10, p. 300.

started to see as unsatisfying. Declaring a preference for Rembrandt was one way of doing so. Where all this would lead was not entirely clear to him. At that time, he did not differentiate between Rembrandt and the 'Gothic', as he would do later. And his immediate project would be studying Goethe rather than Rembrandt. However, the Goethe-Rembrandt-Gothic triangle did vaguely indicate Simmel's gradual adoption of the 'Germanic' discourse.

To follow the crystallisation of this discourse in Simmel's mind, one can examine the evolution of his interpretation of the history of the visual and plastic arts. Here too the central question for him was the issue of unity and the ability of art to attain it. His ideas in this sphere evolved more or less according to the familiar pattern. Initially, one finds in him different variations of the notion of unity in variety. Later, the motif of distance comes in, in which unity becomes symbolic and is attained via escape from the chaotic world. But this symbolic unity turns out to be an illusion in the end. Pure aestheticism loses touch with the overall metaphysical unity and is rejected. A more dynamic unity is then regained by means of the conceptual apparatus of life-philosophy.

Simmel's essay on Böcklin (1895) and to some extent his first Rodin text (1902) represent the first approach. Thus Böcklin's unity is fairly unproblematic. In his landscapes he takes us to the realm of timelessness with its mood of youth, as the young have not yet developed an awareness of the significance of time. Böcklin's mood in these landscapes can be described only in terms of the harmonious mixture of two opposites: it is a 'joyful melancholy'.[172] Böcklin is thus too classical, too southern, too close to the Greeks to know the fundamental contradictions of modernity. And Simmel was looking for an artist whose sense of unity would be informed by a more profound grasp of the specific sensibilities of the moderns, 'whose lives, feelings, desires, and senses of worth have fragmented in countless different directions'.[173]

One such artist was, in his view, Auguste Rodin. Simmel was among the first in Germany to appreciate Rodin's greatness. He considered him and Stefan George to be the most important artists of the age, and it has been argued that he was to a great degree responsible for their fame in Germany.[174] In 1902, he expressed his admiration for the French sculptor in an essay entitled 'Rodin's Plastic and the Spiritual Direction of the

---

[172] 'Arnold Böcklin's Landscapes', in Austin Harrington (ed.), *Georg Simmel: Essays on Art and Aesthetics* (Chicago: University of Chicago Press, 2020), p. 209. [GSG 5, p. 101.]
[173] Ibid. [GSG 5, p. 101.]   [174] Cf. Landmann, 'Georg Simmel und Stefan George', pp. 153–154.

Present Age',[175] which had a major impact not only on the general public but also on art critics, such as Julius Meier-Graefe, who quoted it extensively in his own work two years later.[176]

Simmel placed Rodin on a par with Michelangelo. Rodin, according to him, revived the history of plastics which had ended with the Italian master.[177] Having absorbed the technical abilities of older Italian sculptors, Rodin moved beyond them and created a new artistic style suited specifically for the modern man. Modern life creates the most extreme forms of dualism, and the task of specifically modern art is to resolve them:

> To realise the unity of this dualism is the ultimate meaning of all art. But while every great work of art accomplishes this seemingly self-evidently, the hallmark of specifically modern art is that in each case each of these two elements is perfected in sharp and conscious separation from the other. For this is the developmental formula of modern mind: to uproot life's elements from primordial unity, to individualise and to differentiate, and to bring to consciousness of themselves, in order to draw them back again into a new unity.[178]

Rodin's art fulfils this task most perfectly, for example, by overcoming the most extreme form of modern dualism: that between the freedom of the human soul and outward law-like necessity. According to Simmel, Rodin's figures combine the impression of absolute freedom with the complete absence of the accidental. Rodin is therefore the artist of the most daring unity in the conditions of the most extreme variety.

When Simmel published his Rodin essay, Böcklin was quickly going out of fashion. Only five years earlier did Carl Neumann still praise Böcklin for revealing happy harmony to the Germans. In a manner reminiscent of Simmel's 1895 essay on Böcklin's landscapes, he wrote: 'It is as if this man came straight from the primordial splendour of the elements, from paradise, when humans and animals lived together in a brotherly and harmonious way.'[179] But at the turn of the century the mood changed. In 1905, Julius Meier-Graefe launched a vicious attack on Böcklin.[180] Böcklin of the

---

[175] Translated as 'Auguste Rodin: Part I', in Harrington (ed.), *Georg Simmel: Essays on Art and Aesthetics*, pp. 302–308. ['Rodins Plastik und die Geistesrichtung der Gegenwart', GSG 7, pp. 92–100.]

[176] Julius Meier-Graefe, *Entwickelungsgeschichte der modernen Kunst* (Stuttgart: Hoffmann, 1904), vol. I, pp. 277–285. See also J. A. Schmoll gen. Eisenwerth, 'Simmel und Rodin', in H. Böhringer and K. Gründer (eds.), *Ästhetik und Soziologie um die Jahrhundertwende: Georg Simmel* (Frankfurt am Main: Vittorio Klostermann, 1976), pp. 18–38.

[177] 'Auguste Rodin: Part I', p. 302. [GSG 7, p. 92.]   [178] Ibid., p. 306. [GSG 7, p. 98.]

[179] Carl Neumann, 'Zu Arnold Böcklins siebenzigstem Geburtstag', *Die Kunst für Alle* 13(1), 1897, p. 5.

[180] Julius Meier-Graefe, *Der Fall Böcklin und die Lehre von den Einheiten* (Stuttgart: Julius Hoffmann, 1905).

later period, he claimed, was at most a genre painter. The purpose of art is indeed to create unities, but unity can be attained only by those who have reached a high stage of differentiation.[181] Böcklin was too old-fashioned for this task of modernity. He was popular in Germany only because Germany remained old-fashioned: a country of soldiers and officials. The case of Böcklin (his lack of true unity) is therefore the case of Germany.[182] And if Germany wished to progress it had to learn unity from a non-German artist: Rodin. Or it could heed a German artist much worthier of admiration: Hans von Marées. Interestingly, von Marées had been deeply influenced by Rembrandt.

It is not surprising, then, that a year later Simmel praised Rodin and Rembrandt in his class. At the same time, his mind was still preoccupied with Schopenhauer and Italy and with the notion of unity as a release from variety. In respect of visual arts, this approach is exemplified by the ideas outlined in a small piece on Leonardo da Vinci's *The Last Supper*, published in 1905. This essay contains some residues of the unity-in-variety formula. Thus Simmel spoke of Leonardo's ability to create a sense of harmony out of the variety of the individualities of different Apostles and drew a parallel with 'the problem of life in a modern society, the problem of how, from absolutely diverse and at the same time equally justified individual personalities, some kind of organic corporate unity can come to exist'.[183] But he also raised another idea: unity is attained by retreating from the dissonances of reality to the sphere of art, for 'art expresses reality's contents in a completely different language from reality itself'.[184] In art, unity is not made out of the totality of all elements but out of what is significant, whereas actual multiplicity is of no interest to it. For example, 'in *The Last Supper* a completely new concept of time is created. Here time is no all-purpose container for any random elapse of events, but rather that which fuses only those events *most significant and insistent*, irrespective of actual punctual succession'.[185]

But very soon Simmel moved beyond this aestheticism as he explored ways of connecting art with the transcendental. This brought him back to Rodin and to the problem of unity which was now treated as an incomparably more intricate task. In the essay 'Rodin's Art and the Motive of Movement in Plastic' (1909), this problem was no longer described just in terms of specific dualisms, such as the contradiction between freedom and

[181] Ibid., p. 85.   [182] Ibid., p. 270.
[183] 'Leonardo da Vinci's *Last Supper*', in Harrington (ed.), *Georg Simmel: Essays on Art and Aesthetics*, p. 238. [GSG 7, p. 307.]
[184] Ibid. [GSG 7, p. 308.]   [185] Ibid., pp. 238–239. [GSG 7, p. 308.] Italics mine – E. P.

necessity, but rather as the condition of the extreme lability of life that flows without rest or points of departure and destination. Life is conceived as a constant becoming, and it is a sign of Rodin's greatness that his figures convey this movement in its unity. The achievement of Rodin as artist is thus that he 'redeems us ... by creating the most perfect picture of life absorbed into all passion of movement'.[186] But Simmel immediately added a sour note: 'As a Frenchman has said of him, *c'est Michelange avec trois siècles de misère de plus.*'[187] And for Simmel, Michelangelo himself was already a tragic figure.

As early as 1889, in his analysis of Michelangelo's love poetry Simmel presented him as a soul torn by profound dissonances, who incessantly strove to achieve a transcendental peace, which he never attained.[188] And when in 1910 Simmel returned to Michelangelo in an essay later included in *Philosophical Culture*, his attitude remained the same: Michelangelo was an ever-striving tragic figure who failed to attain final redemption, not only in love but also in art and in his personality as a whole.[189]

Michelangelo represented for him a paradoxical coexistence of perfection and failure. On the one hand, Michelangelo's work reveals an absolute unity which, by contrast to the naive unity of the ancients, is achieved by overcoming the body-soul dualism, by bringing these two sides of human existence into a state of perfect equilibrium.[190] Moreover, this unity is not the domain of individuals. Rather, each of Michelangelo's figures reveals humanity as such in its universal unity:

> [T]he deeper and not purely psychological reason for Michelangelo's universalising vision of form, transcending all purely contingent individuality, is that his figures express first of all a felt or metaphysical reality of *life as such* – of life developing in various meanings, stages, and fates but ultimately possessing a verbally indescribable unity in which the antithesis of body and soul has vanished as completely as the antitheses of individual particular existences and attitudes.[191]

But this unity is not a peaceful synthesis. It is rather the moment of equilibrium in the course of struggle, or balance and struggle at the same time. 'Michelangelo's true unity of principles reveals a sense of fulfilment

---

[186] 'Auguste Rodin: Part II', in Harrington (ed.), *Georg Simmel: Essays on Art and Aesthetics*, p. 318. ['Die Kunst Rodins und das Bewegungsmotiv in der Plastik', GSG 12, p. 36.]

[187] 'It is Michelangelo with three more centuries of misery'. Ibid. [GSG 12, p. 36.]

[188] 'Michelangelo als Dichter', GSG 2, pp. 37–48.

[189] 'Michelangelo and the Metaphysics of Culture', in Harrington (ed.), *Georg Simmel: Essays on Art and Aesthetics*, pp. 279–297. [GSG 12, pp. 111–136.]

[190] Ibid., p. 281. [GSG 12, p. 114.]   [191] Ibid., p. 282. [GSG 12, pp. 115–116.]

in nonfulfilment and nonfulfilment in fulfilment.'¹⁹² Artistically considered, Michelangelo's images are embodiments of perfection. Yet their titanic struggles project a yearning towards something which lies beyond their existence, even if that existence is perfect in itself. And this reflects Michelangelo's own yearning for a state of no more struggle and desire; for the absolute, infinite and transcendent. This yearning was religious at its root. It was awakened by Christianity and acquired its form in the Gothic. Simmel would later call Michelangelo 'a Gothic soul'.¹⁹³ Yet Michelangelo was equally a man of the Renaissance with its orientation towards things earthly and human. And the only way open to him in his search for transcendental peaceful infinity was to pursue beauty and perfection in this world. This doomed his task to failure from the beginning, since it is impossible to realise the infinite by means of what earthly beauty is: finite. Therefore, the 'perfection of existence' of his figures, 'freed of all reciprocal limitation of sides, is still in no way a state of bliss'.¹⁹⁴ To supersede the abyss between the earthly and the higher realms required a new unity that would reside beyond the opposition of the two, a unity between immanent existence and the transcendental. Yet, 'as with his creations, so also with Michelangelo's life: it remains the last and most portentous of his tragedies that humanity still has not found any such Third Realm'.¹⁹⁵

It was Rodin who in a way navigated this abyss, as Simmel suggested in yet another essay on the French sculptor, placed in *Philosophical Culture* right after the one on Michelangelo.¹⁹⁶ While drawing on the 1909 essay and some parts of the 1902 text, it also contained significant new additions. In these additions Simmel took Rodin's work to higher metaphysical spheres, claiming that the sculptor's figures possessed a 'cosmic' quality. Their eternal movement did not belong to specifically 'human' life but rather to the cosmos as such. Rodin's figures are dissolved

> by forces mightier than purely personal fates: by a predicament of existence that fills space in general and therefore also their own space and becomes in this way also their predicament. For Rodin, it is love in general, or despair in general or contemplation [*Versenkung*] in general, that become fates of the individual, as cosmic dynamics – and not as universal concepts … but as immediate life, pulsing in the very being of the individual.¹⁹⁷

---

¹⁹² Ibid., p. 287. [GSG 12, p. 123.]   ¹⁹³ *Rembrandt*, p. 157. [GSG 15, p. 509.]
¹⁹⁴ 'Michelangelo and the Metaphysics of Culture', p. 284. [GSG 12, p. 118.]
¹⁹⁵ Ibid., p. 297. [GSG 12, p. 136.]
¹⁹⁶ 'Auguste Rodin: Part II', pp. 309–318. ['Rodin (mit einer Vorbemerkung über *Meunier*)', in *Philosophische Kultur*, GSG 14, pp. 330–348.]
¹⁹⁷ Ibid. [GSG 14, pp. 343–344.]

The unity of the immanent and the transcendent in Rodin therefore took the form of individuals being thrown into and dissolved within the eternal cosmic movement. His third realm gravitated towards the transcendental.

However, there was another way of reaching 'the third realm', and its representative – in both the Michelangelo and Rodin essays – was Rembrandt. Rembrandt retreated into a mood comparable to that of religious piety, in which the infinite enters the immediate experience of the finite that lives in an imperfect world and does not expect any perfection from it. Unlike Michelangelo, Rembrandt did not wage a titanic struggle to unite the two opposite aspects of the universe.[198] Rather, his images display a personal relationship to the transcendent that characterises 'a specifically Germanic concept of ... individuality'.[199] In contrast to Rodin who widened life as such to the full scope of the 'cosmic', Rembrandt approached the realm of the transcendent-immanent via the life of the 'individual'. His third realm gravitated therefore towards the immanent.

Thus by 1911 Simmel's interpretation of visual art already contained all the basic components of his future depiction of Rembrandt: the notion of the third realm as superseding the opposition between the transcendent and the immanent and the view of Rembrandt as a Germanic artist whose perception of individuality takes us into that realm. Nevertheless, these components were still in embryonic form. At that time, Simmel still retained allegiance to the 'Southern' vector and Goethe's universalism. His declared preference for the 'Gothic' indicates this. It is true that in contemporary discourse emphasis on the 'Gothic' had already begun to imply a Germanic, 'Nordic', anti-Italian turn. Moreover, treatments of Italian artists such as Dante and Michelangelo increasingly denied them to Italy and claimed them as embodiments of the northern spirit. Some interpreters went so far as to make outright *völkisch* interpretations of Michelangelo.[200] But this does not appear to have been Simmel's view. For him, the 'Gothic' was never the exclusive property of the Germanic mind. Rather, considered to be a style that the northern and Italian peoples possessed in common,[201] the 'Gothic',

---

[198] 'Michelangelo and the Metaphysics of Culture'. [GSG 12, p. 115.]

[199] 'Auguste Rodin: Part II', p. 315. [GSG 14, p. 343.]

[200] On this see Joseph Imorde, *Michelangelo* Deutsch! (Berlin: Deutscher Kunstverlag, 2009). For a general study of Michelangelo's reception in German culture, see Niklaus Oberholzer, *Das Michelangelo-Bild in der deutschen Literatur: Beitrag zur Geschichte der Künstlerdichtung* (Fribourg, Switzerland: Universitätsverlag, 1969). For an interesting study on the cult of Michelangelo among German Jewish intellectuals of the period, see also Asher D. Biemann, *Dreaming of Michelangelo: Jewish Variations on a Modern Theme* (Stanford: Stanford University Press, 2012).

[201] See, e.g., his Michelangelo essay: *Philosophische Kultur*, GSG 14, p. 305.

like Goethe, served Simmel as a bridge between Germanic and Romanic cultural identities. Later, as will be shown, in order to conceptualise Rembrandt as a Germanic artist, Simmel would have to separate him from the 'Gothic'. But in 1911, as his attention turned to Goethe, he had not yet developed this distinction.

It was in 1913 that Simmel began an intensive study of Rembrandt.[202] In a short time he composed several essays that would become parts of the *Rembrandt* book. Like *Goethe*, *Rembrandt* was not a work of art history in the proper sense. Simmel was of course familiar with scholarly discourse on the history and theory of art, as he occasionally alluded to the conceptual vocabulary that was then prominent in that discipline. Thus, to provide an account of 'movement' in Rembrandt's art he used Konrad Fiedler's term 'expressive movement' (*Ausdrucksbewegung*),[203] and his discussion of the contrast between line and colour in painting was based on the work of Wölfflin.[204] But like in *Goethe*, those observations were of secondary significance. Rather, the artist served here as a medium for reflection on the same set of philosophical issues from yet another angle.

The book consisted of three chapters. The first chapter – 'The Expression of Inner Life [*Seelischen*]' – outlined Simmel's understanding of the essence of Rembrandt's art, especially his portraits and his later period. According to Simmel, Rembrandt's art, more than that of any other artist, transmits the ultimate idea of life. The movements captured in his paintings do not represent isolated moments of life but rather reveal life in its totality as if it were condensed in those moments. Thus:

> Whereas in classical and, in the narrower sense, stylising art, the depiction of a movement is achieved via a sort of abstraction in that the viewing of a certain moment is torn out of its prior and concurrent stream of life and crystallises into a self-sufficient form, with Rembrandt the depicted moment appears to contain the whole living impulse directed toward it; it tells the story of this life course [*Lebensströmung*].[205]

---

[202] The first indication of Simmel working on this subject can be found in his letter from May 1913, in which he reports on his two-day stay in Braunschweig with its 'wonderful Rembrandts and Gothic churches and entire streets where nothing has changed for three centuries' (Letter to Margarete von Bendemann, 4 May 1913, GSG 23, p. 180). The 'Herzogliches Museum' in the town owned a number of Rembrandt's paintings. And in the following month Simmel reported: 'now I am completely immersed in Rembrandt – but my thought that he might be a counterpart to Michelangelo has proven illusory'. (Letter to Margarete von Bendemann, 26 June 1913, GSG 23, p. 190).

[203] Konrad Fiedler, *Schriften über Kunst*, vol. 1 (Munich: R. Piper & Co., 1913). Cf. *Rembrandt*, p. 5. [GSG 15, p. 313.]

[204] Wölfflin, *Kunstgeschichtliche Grundbegriffe*. Cf. *Rembrandt*, p. 47. [GSG 15, p. 371.]

[205] *Rembrandt*, p. 6. [GSG 15, pp. 314–315.]

Life in its totality is therefore a process, and Rembrandt's portraits reveal that life's meaning and value lie in *becoming* rather than pure *being*, such as that displayed in classical paintings where the image is torn out of the stream of life and taken into an abstract timeless sphere.

Rembrandt's portraits reveal the destiny, the peculiar course of life of one person or another. And his inclination to paint a series of portraits of the same person at different phases of that person's life suggests that life is a continuous movement, and no stage should be taken in isolation. Rembrandt's drawings thus

> have something characteristically unfinished about them, as if one follows immediately on from the other, like one breath to the next. And yet, none has the quality of a sketch – of pointing beyond itself. It is at the same time totality and being in a state of flux: a quality that is inherent in our every living act, and only in this.[206]

This brings Simmel to a broader philosophical question. How can the dynamic unity of the life process be transmitted by a painting which merely shows a body, and at only one specific moment? The answer is that life is unity which cannot be divided into body and soul, or into past and present. The two sides of these dualisms in fact constitute a circle, where each side leads to the other. The present moment is deduced from a person's whole past life, and vice versa, a whole life is revealed in the experience of one moment. Similarly, a person's inner life is derived from sight of the body, whereas the appearance of the body can be gleaned from experiencing that person's mind. And the existence of a conceptual circle is a sign that division is illusory, and there is in fact only one unified phenomenon.

Our intuition often provides us with an immediate sense of this unity. But as reflection comes into play, this fundamental experience is divided into categories. However, there is one activity – art – that protects us from this dissociation:

> Only art, whose objectifications preserve the closest relationships to the subjective immediacy of experience, seems to succeed in relatively unre-fracted [*ungebrochene*] reflections of that unity; not a reunification – a synthesis in which the seams never disappear – but rather the reflection of an original inseparability that is presynthetic because it is preanalytic.[207]

Simmel thus begins to bestow a special status on art. It is no longer just a 'symbol'.[208] Rather, it is the nearest possible experience to an immediate

[206] Ibid., pp. 12–13. [GSG 15, p. 323.]   [207] Ibid., p. 18. [GSG 15, p. 331.]

[208] Ibid., p. 21. [GSG 15, p. 335.]

experience of life in its unity. Without being 'metaphysical', art is the custodian at the gate leading to the metaphysical, as it brings us closer to the quintessential reality of life.[209]

Different artists and artistic styles differ between themselves as to the degree of their ability to fulfil this function of bringing us to the unity of life. And Rembrandt, Simmel argued, is the artist who comes closest to this, by depicting the kind of 'individuality' that precedes all categorical distinctions. This individuality is like the germ out of which a person's body and soul both emerge:

> The individuality is either the root or the higher expression that the strangeness or divergence of soul and body does not touch, because individuality gives to each their singular colour. That the corporeal individual and the spiritual individual [*das Individuelle der Körperlichkeit und das Individuelle der Seele*] cannot be highlighted and signified as an identical phenomenon may give intellectual conceptualisation, but certainly not life and art, pause for thought ... [E]ven though the corporeal as such and the spiritual as such may be foreign to each other, the concrete individual is nevertheless a unity. Therefore, only individuality that alone joins that general foreignness can unite body and soul, and – whether conceivable or not – bears the unity of elements. It is clearly a constant experience that the deeper we grasp a person's individuality, the more his exterior and his interior indivisibly merge for us, and the less can we think of him as separate.[210]

Rembrandt's portraits reflect this deep truth. He did not aim at a most exact representation of his models in accordance with 'reality'. Such representations would be no different from photography, and no painting, insofar as it is a work of art, 'represents' reality in this way. Rembrandt painted as if he traced back 'the appearance of the person to a unified transphenomenal intuition of essence that he then entrusted to its concentrated driving forces out of which the forms' spatial extension unfolded in free organic growth'.[211]

Rembrandt's art is thus unsurpassable in its ability to represent the unity of an individual personality. But this ability goes even beyond the depiction of individuals. This can be seen in his group paintings. Not only is each individual figure in them a unity immersed in life, but this life itself is an individual unity. It radiates beyond the figures, filling the entire space with a living wave, so that the lives emanating from each of the highly differentiated personalities interweave with each other. Thus 'it is the space

---

[209] Ibid., pp. 160–161. [GSG 15, pp. 513–514.]   [210] Ibid., p. 32. [GSG 15, pp. 350–351.]
[211] Ibid., p. 29. [GSG 15, p. 347.]

itself and not merely the appearances within the space that has here become living movement'.[212] In the group painting, 'Rembrandt, in a way unknown before, weaves together out of individuals without reaching out to a "higher unity" or abstract form beyond them – and yet . . . inspires the breath of *one* life into the whole'.[213] For life is actually a totality constituted by its inner organic growth rather than extraneous heterogeneous factors.

This expansion of life beyond the figures of specific individuals has radical cultural-philosophical implications examined in the second chapter: 'Individualisation and the General'. There, Simmel distinguished between two conflicting aesthetic and philosophical principles: one oriented towards the universal and the other towards the particular. In the context of this distinction, classical art and that of Rembrandt represent two opposite extremes. The former emphasises the typical and is interested in individual figures only insofar as they represent a type. In Rembrandt, the individual exists as a self-sufficient totality.

At first glance, this appears to be just another expression of the contrast between the general and the individual. This contrast played an important role in Simmel's thought, for example, in his distinction between quantitative individualism, where separate individuals are governed by the same set of general norms, and qualitative individualism, where every individual is peculiar and one is governed by one's own individual law. In his third period, however, Simmel imperceptibly moved beyond this distinction. It was not the contrast between the individual and the general that interested him but the different ways of transcending this contrast.

Already in *Goethe*, Simmel spoke of a certain synthesis of the individual and the general which transcends the distinction between quantitative and qualitative individualism. He implicitly suggested a third notion of individualism, in which the individual is merged within the general while preserving one's own individuality.[214] And what was implied in *Goethe* was stated far more explicitly in *Rembrandt*. Rembrandt's individualities, Simmel argued, transcend the question of individual peculiarity. The existence's

> form and its contents may be comparable, but its process is beyond the alternative of comparability and incomparability. It has the uniqueness of pure becoming that cannot at all be expressed by means of qualities

---

[212] Ibid., p. 44. [GSG 15, pp. 366–367.]   [213] Ibid., p. 49. [GSG 15, p. 373.]
[214] For a detailed exposition of this argument, see Efraim Podoksik, 'Georg Simmel: Three Forms of Individualism and Historical Understanding', *New German Critique* 109(1), 2010, pp. 119–145.

conceived of as static or dynamic [*die sind oder werden*]. It is the meaning of
the 'individuality' of Rembrandt's figures that the life process itself becomes
visible, but not as a qualitative difference or uniqueness of being demonstrable by specific contents, since this is a thoroughly relative and random
individuality.[215]

This radicalisation of individuality brings it to the point of transcending
itself. Especially in Rembrandt's works, there is often an *Aufhebung* of the
connection between individuality and life.[216] Life itself becomes de-par-
ticularised, so to speak, as all the individual features of a person become
irrelevant, and the only thing that matters is the mere stream of life. But
even then it is the life of an individual:

> It is as though the life of this person were admittedly absolutely their own,
> and not detachable from them, yet raised above all the *individual things* that
> one may say about them; as though a stream of life flowed that, although not
> washing over its shores and as though it were as a whole a totality of
> unmistakable unity within itself, nevertheless creates no wave of singular
> characteristic form.[217]

This 'immanent transcendence'[218] of life brings Simmel to the subject of
Rembrandt's religiosity, which he examined in great detail in the book's
third chapter: 'Religious Art'. Simmel began the discussion with his old
distinction between objective and subjective religion, arguing that the
religiosity of Rembrandt's art is entirely of the latter type. It possesses an
aura of piety which is absolutely independent of the specific content of his
religious paintings. For the first time in the history of art, the torrent of
subjective religion 'is brought to complete domination so that, irrespective
of the belief's contents, its metaphysical basis, its dogmatic substance, as
religion it is an act or a specific state of being of the human soul'.[219]

Yet, as in the preceding chapter, in which Simmel went beyond the
distinction between quantitative and qualitative individualism, here too,
while attributing subjective religiosity to Rembrandt, he led this religiosity
away from the merely subjective and towards the metaphysical. He further
qualified the significance of individuality in Rembrandt, relegating it
mainly to the portraits.[220] The figures in the religious paintings, by

---

[215] *Rembrandt*, p. 68. [GSG 15, pp. 397–398.] See also on p. 89 [GSG 15, p. 424]: 'Above all, however,
for Rembrandt's individuality . . . sociological difference vis-à-vis other beings is totally irrelevant.
For him nothing is in this regard socially coloured, neither with respect to the aspect of equality of
type, nor with respect to quantitative or qualitative being.'

[216] Ibid., p. 90. [GSG 15, p. 425.]   [217] Ibid., p. 91. [GSG 15, p. 426.]

[218] Ibid., p. 99. [GSG 15, p. 437.]   [219] Ibid., p. 114. [GSG 15, p. 455.]

[220] Ibid., p. 121. [GSG 15, p. 464–465.]

contrast, 'do not show the lonely uniqueness of the portraits'.[221] There is a 'loosening of the principle of individuality' in them, even if it is no more than a loosening.[222]

This, however, does not mean that Simmel attributed to Rembrandt some kind of universality. His religious paintings also represent the immanent stream of life, only that the role of medium in this stream is filled not by individual human figures but by something else: light.

> It is as though light itself were alive; as though struggle and peace, contrast and relation [*Verwandtschaft*], passion and gentleness immediately bore this play of the struggle between light and darkness not as something existing behind it that finds its first expression in this play, but rather in the same way as we in the statics and dynamics of our individual conceptions and affects think we perceive the deeper rhythm of inner [*seelischen*] life in general.[223]

This immanent flow of life has nothing to do with pure accidental subjectivity. On many occasions, Simmel emphasised the transcendental objectivity of this immanent flow. 'The religious quality [*Beschaffenheit*] of the subject', he said, 'is itself something objective, is an existence that in and of itself has metaphysical meaning'.[224] The religiosity of Rembrandt's representations manifests a certain objectivity, 'something beyond coincidence and ideally solid'.[225] This quality is revealed by light which manifests 'the general atmosphere [*Gesamtstimmung*] ... of a trans-individual soul whose religiosity flows through this portion of the world'.[226] Rembrandt's subjective religiosity thus merges itself in the transcendent without requiring any objective content.

Therefore, if one were to convey the central motif of *Rembrandt* as a whole, one could describe it as an attempt to find the path to metaphysical unity by means of the language of life-philosophy. Taken in this broad sense, *Rembrandt* is a continuation of Simmel's work on Goethe, and this is how Simmel himself understood it. For example, in April 1914 he wrote to Graf von Keyserling: 'I will shortly send you a brief work on Rembrandt that continues some of *Goethe*'s motifs.'[227]

Indeed, both books belong to Simmel's third period and bear its main features. In both, life offers a solution to the problem of modern variety by taking us beyond rational reflection. Both works disavow the significance

---

[221] Ibid., p. 136. [GSG 15, p. 484.] [222] Ibid. [GSG 15, p. 485.]
[223] Ibid., p. 137. [GSG 15, p. 485.] [224] Ibid., p. 126. [GSG 15, p. 471.]
[225] Ibid., p. 132. [GSG 15, p. 479.] [226] Ibid., p. 152. [GSG 15, p. 502.]
[227] Letter to Hermann Graf von Keyserling, 22 April 1914, GSG 23, p. 313. His reference here is to 'Rembrandtstudie' published in *LOGOS*, which later formed the basis of *Rembrandt*'s first chapter.

of form, just that in *Goethe* this disavowal is found only where Simmel discussed Goethe's later period, whereas *Rembrandt* as a whole concentrates on the painter's old age. For even when Rembrandt's earlier paintings are mentioned, they are generally considered in the context of his later period and treated as imperfect premonitions of it. In this sense, Rembrandt's entire artistic personality is regarded as informed by the features that Goethe displays only in his final stage.

Finally, the type of unity embedded in *Rembrandt*'s notion of 'life' is similar to that developed in *Goethe*: it is a unity that transcends variety without cancelling its contradictions. Unsurprisingly, in *Rembrandt* too there are several instances in which the formula of the absolute-versus-relative concept is used. For example, Simmel spoke of absolute life that encompasses relative life and death,[228] or absolute perfection that encompasses both perfection and imperfection.[229]

Nevertheless, in some respects *Rembrandt* departs from *Goethe*. This departure was not apparent to Simmel from the start. Initially, as has been shown, he considered this project as a development of the themes of *Goethe*. Yet, after the First World War broke out, his conception of his work took a somewhat different turn. In May 1915, he reported to Margarete Susman (von Bendemann): 'I am working on a booklet on *Rembrandt* in order to highlight the meaning of Germanic art in contrast to Romanic.'[230]

It is important to note the chronology of the essays included in *Rembrandt*. Whereas some belong to the pre-war period, others were written after the start of the war. The former group includes most of the first and third chapters,[231] whereas the middle chapter, as well as parts of the conclusion, are largely based on essays written between 1914 and 1916.[232] It is thus the middle chapter together with the conclusion that

---

[228] *Rembrandt*, p. 72. [GSG 15, p. 402.] On Simmel's philosophy of old age and death in the context of his *Rembrandt* book, see Thomas Kemple, *Simmel* (Cambridge: Polity Press, 2018), pp. 161–165.

[229] *Rembrandt*, p. 85. [GSG 15, p. 419.]

[230] Letter to Margarete von Bendemann, 27 May 1915, GSG 23, p. 524.

[231] 'Rembrandtstudie' [written around April 1914], GSG 13, pp. 16–52; 'Rembrandts religiöse Kunst' [June–July 1914], GSG 13, pp. 70–89; but also parts of 'Studien zur Philosophie der Kunst, besonders der Rembrandtschen' [1915], GSG 13, pp. 143–164. Simmel's lectures on aesthetics (1913–1914) contain the material included in 'Rembrandtstudie' and 'Rembrandts religiöse Kunst'. See Simmel, 'Philosophie der Kunst' [1913/1914], GSG 21, pp. 200–222; 'Philosophie der Kunst' [Winter-Semester 1913/1914, by Adolf Löwe], GSG 21, pp. 971–978.

[232] 'Rembrandt und die Schönheit' [1914], GSG 13, pp. 105–111; 'Vom Tode in der Kunst: Nach einem Vortrag' [1915], GSG 13, pp. 123–132; parts of 'Studien zur Philosophie der Kunst, besonders der Rembrandtschen'; 'Bruchstücke aus einer Philosophie der Kunst' [1916], GSG 13, pp. 174–183; 'Gestalter und Schöpfer' [1916], GSG 13, pp. 184–189.

should be regarded as Simmel's final word on Rembrandt. And it is there that Simmel drew dividing lines between Goethe and the Germanic mind.

Thus, in the piece 'Creating and Form-Giving' (*Schöpfertum and Gestaltertum*), Simmel distinguished between two types of spiritual and artistic activity.[233] One type is called 'form-giving'. In it the material world already exists, and the artist's task is to mould this original material into some kind of form. It expresses a yearning for 'being', that is, for something solid that lies beyond the artistic will. It is especially characteristic of Greek art. But Goethe and Renaissance artists too, among others, were 'form-givers'. The other type is 'creating'. In it there is no pre-existing matter, and the artist creates, so to speak, out of nothing. Its worldview is one of 'becoming', and it is governed by the principle of life: 'Here life speaks much more in the absolute sense in that it does not stand in any kind of opposition to form, but rather has sprung, as itself [*als Sein selbst*], from a form that is attached to it alone and is inseparable from it.'[234] This is the art of Rembrandt, as well as of Shakespeare and the older Beethoven.

And in the essay 'Human Fate and the Heraclitean Cosmos' at the end of the book's second chapter, Simmel differentiates between Rembrandt on the one hand and Michelangelo and Rodin on the other. We have seen that in his previous texts on Rodin Simmel distinguished him from Michelangelo. Yet here he underlines what is common to both and separates them from Rembrandt: both, each in his own way, transcend individuality. Thus 'the fate of Michelangelo's figures must be of a general, impersonal nature', in which an individual 'can only be something trans-individual, extended into a symbol of humankind'.[235] Rodin's art of course differs from that of Michelangelo. It is all Heraclitean flux, absolute movement. Yet that cosmic movement does not allow for any individual formation to crystallise at any point in time. In a sense, cosmic movement negates individuality no less than the universality of classical forms. Both stand, in fact, beyond time: 'Absolute becoming is just as ahistorical as absolute nonbecoming.'[236] Both Michelangelo and Rodin depict the totality of human fate and even that of the cosmos.[237] And such was also the essence of Dante and Goethe. For Goethe, the meaning of his existence was 'to attain the nature of God in the unity as well as in the separation [*Entzweitheit*] of all appearances'.[238]

---

[233] *Rembrandt*, pp. 155–159. [GSG 15, pp. 506–512.] In the English translation this phrase is rendered somewhat awkwardly as 'the capacity to create and to fashion'. The expressions 'form-giver' and 'to give form' seem to better reflect the meaning and style of *Gestalter* and *gestalten*.

[234] Ibid., p. 158. [GSG 15, p. 510.]   [235] Ibid., p. 103. [GSG 15, p. 442.]

[236] Ibid., p. 106. [GSG 15, p. 446.]   [237] Ibid., p. 107. [GSG 15, p. 448.]

[238] Ibid., p. 108. [GSG 15, p. 449.]

In Rembrandt, however, there is no losing oneself in eternal movement. For as much as Simmel took Rembrandt beyond pure individuality, he nevertheless insisted that his figures remain particular individualities of their own, and that the totality they express is still the totality of their lives with clear contours of time. Rembrandt, as well as Shakespeare, does not devote himself to great human themes. This would be an unnecessary detour from the life lived for its own sake. Rembrandt's work therefore decides in favour of 'the greatness and depth, the miracle of individuality and the beauty of life remaining within itself'.[239] As Simmel put it:

> With Rembrandt, we are not dealing with a total life that dissolves forms and is still in some way exterior to them, but rather with purely individual life. Forms do not disappear in the unity of cosmic life like the particular in the general, but the individual life dissolves form from within. *This* is now the general and disappears as such (in the opposite direction to the former case) in individuality.[240]

This emphasis on the miracle of individuality taken in all its totality and freedom carries with it, however, a certain price: disconnectedness from the universal-human. Rembrandt offers a sense of completeness on the micro level of individual life. But this turns him into a less ecumenical figure than Goethe. Goethe appears in Simmel's interpretation as someone who strives for an all-encompassing experience with all its vibrations, vacillations and inner contradictions, someone who is best described in the language of 'both this . . . and that'. Simmel's interpretation of Rembrandt, by contrast, is better described in the language of 'this rather than that'. He considered Rembrandt's style to be sharply distinguished from any other. In fact, he went as far as to make Rembrandt completely sui generis, utterly disconnected from seemingly related styles and traditions.

For example, Rembrandt would normally be placed within the history of the northern Baroque. Simmel occasionally accepted this classification, for example, when he pointed to certain affinities between the northern Baroque and Rembrandt's *Night Watch*.[241] But on the whole he rejected this interpretation. Instead, he emphasised what was common to the Italian and northern Baroque and distinguished them both from the art of Rembrandt.[242] The German Baroque, he argued, did not have an antirational character imputed to it. He also did not agree that the northern Baroque constituted a revival of the Nordic spirit of Gothic art.

---

[239] Ibid. [GSG 15, p. 449.]   [240] Ibid., p. 70. [GSG 15, p. 399.]
[241] Ibid., pp. 44–45. [GSG 15, pp. 367–368.]   [242] Ibid., pp. 37–38. [GSG 15, pp. 358–359.]

He regarded the Gothic too as cultural property common to Germany and Italy and identified Dante and Michelangelo as Gothic personalities.

A leading proponent of the Germanic Gothic was Wilhelm Worringer. Simmel and Worringer were acquainted, and Worringer even claimed that the central idea of his dissertation *Abstraction and Empathy* (1907) occurred to him as a result of a chance meeting with Simmel in the Trocadero museum. In 1911, Worringer published a detailed study on the cultural-psychological meaning of Gothic art.[243] There he claimed that the Germanic peoples with their peculiar mentality were an indispensable condition for the emergence of the Gothic, even if they were not its only carriers.[244] He perceived the Gothic style as the artistic expression of the world-feeling peculiar to northern European peoples. In this view, the Gothic attitude towards the world was essentially abstract and at the same time dissatisfied with this. Nordic people yearned for an organic living harmony of the kind that characterised the empathic sensibilities of the Greeks and Romans – but were unable to attain it. The path to organic life was closed to them, which made them seek living movement in inanimate material and try to impart life to mechanical constructions. But since these non-organic living entities do not have natural limitations on their growth, the Gothic lines agglomerate into huge structures that strive towards the infinite. The Gothic is thus an intermediate stage in which 'dualism is no longer strong enough to seek artistic liberation in the absolute negation of life, but also not yet weakened enough to derive the meaning of art from the organic regularity of life itself'.[245] Hence the permanent lack of peace in the Gothic soul, 'the unsatisfied urge, constantly hungry for new ascents, in the end losing itself in the infinite'.[246]

Simmel too considered unresolved yearning to be the central moment in the Gothic, and it is on this account that he spoke of Michelangelo as a Gothic soul. But his general understanding of the Gothic in *Rembrandt* sharply contrasted to that of Worringer. Simmel refused to attribute 'life' to the Gothic style. There is indeed a soul in the Gothic, he argued, but it is not an individual soul: 'The essence of the Gothic lies in a straightforward orientation of the soul toward transcendence that has left behind its life, or for which life is merely a bearer irrelevant in itself.'[247] It is rather Rembrandt who imparts life to the soul, and this is precisely because his art is not Gothic: 'Rembrandt's religious paintings are the exact opposite of the innermost principle of the pure Gothic ... The Gothic soul, because

---

[243] Wilhelm Worringer, *Formprobleme der Gotik* (Munich: R. Piper & Co., 1912).
[244] Ibid., p. 29.   [245] Ibid., p. 49.   [246] Ibid., p. 50.   [247] *Rembrandt*, p. 58. [GSG 15, p. 386.]

the transcendental is essential to it, has no individuality. Only life is individual. Only in the form of life is the soul individual.'[248]

Moreover, it is life in its immediate individuality which is really organic. The word 'abstraction' is used by Simmel in the context of Italian art and on the whole bears negative connotations:

> The unity of the well-composed Renaissance painting is external to the content of the picture itself. It should be thought of as abstract form: pyramid, group symmetry, contraposition within and between the individual figures ... Aside from this form, however, which is grounded in an external meaning, the painting often has a very limited unity. It consists, rather, of a series of parts arranged alongside each other which, because they are evenly executed, completely lack an organic relationship.[249]

Not all Italian art is 'abstract' in this sense. In Giotto, an earlier painter, no such inner estrangement between compositional form and the figures' lives is felt. But this is not because his figures are strongly individualised, but because their form is not geometrical but 'architectonic', that is, one that 'does not emerge out of an individual vitality [*Lebendigkeit*] but immediately out of, and identical with, the material extensity and dynamic intensity of its realisation'.[250] In other words, Simmel understood Giotto as a 'Gothic' artist in Worringer's sense, and precisely because of this did he deny him any principle of 'life'. There is no life in the Italian proto-Renaissance Gothic – only pure architectonics, as there is no life in High Renaissance – only abstraction.

Rembrandt is thus not a Gothic artist. Rather, he is a peculiar 'Germanic' spirit. And to be 'Germanic' means to be lacking in style because style is something formally general, whereas the essential Germanic feature is individuality:

> The point at which the Rembrandtian-Germanic sense of individuality is deeply bound to its capacity to create [*Schöpfertum*] lies in the rejection of the generally valid form ... The fact that Shakespeare and Rembrandt often appeared barbaric to classical-oriented times is the artistic metamorphoses of a fundamentally Germanic trait that undeniably appears to the outsider [*Fremden*] to display a particular clumsiness and formlessness ... The solitude and inaccessibility of the German spirit that is demonstrated again and again in its relation to the rest of the cultural world is grounded in the absence of that general form that, to a degree, could serve as a bridge to individual reality.[251]

---

[248] Ibid. [GSG 15, pp. 386–387.]   [249] Ibid., p. 42. [GSG 15, p. 364.]
[250] Ibid. [GSG 15, p. 364.]   [251] Ibid., p. 159. [GSG 15, pp. 511–512.]

Occasionally, it looks as if Simmel's adoption of the 'Germanic' ideology was a bit ironic. It is as if he took the psychological attitude that yearned for organic unity and applied it to Rembrandt, while calling it 'Germanic' along the way. He described the peculiarity of Germans vis-à-vis Romans with the notion of '*Gemütlichkeit*',[252] a notion which imparted a feeling of cosiness rather than of heroism and was certainly not the principal value of hard-core Germanic ideology as it began to crystallise towards the end of the nineteenth century. Goethe would be more at home with this *Gemütlichkeit* than Wagner. One can even spot a sense of ironic disdain when Simmel ignored Wagner while using the expression *Gesamtkunstwerk*, which was then first and foremost associated with the Bayreuth composer, to characterise the vocal music of Bach and Schumann.[253] Or he would suddenly speak about something majestic imparted by Rembrandt through his paintings to petit-bourgeois, intellectually insignificant and 'poorly bred Jewish ... persons [*schlechträssig jüdischen Menschen*]'.[254]

Yet these remarks which at first glance seem ironic may also be interpreted in a very different way. In those years, Simmel often sounded deadly serious on the topic of Germanic identity, as if forcing himself to decide in its favour. The very word 'decision' began to signify for him the condition of existential pre-rational choice and it appeared in *Rembrandt* on several occasions. For example, the work of Shakespeare and of Rembrandt decides ('*entscheidet sich*') for a deeper individuality rather than general human themes.[255] Or, when life dominates form, individuality and life appear to be 'more decisive' (*entschiedenere*).[256] Contrary approaches in philosophical thought require 'ultimate decisions'.[257] And similarly, the existence of antitheses in art demands value decisions (*Wertentscheidung*).[258]

In *Rembrandt*, taken by itself, Simmel did not, in the end, make the ultimate decision for the 'Germanic'. It is as if he stopped half-way between Goethe's all-comprehending irony and the 'Germanic' earnestness of individual decision. He acknowledged the necessity of decision but then took a step back. It is necessary only 'to separate' [*zu scheiden*] between the antithetical values contained in the classical and the Rembrandtian style, he argued, but not to decide ('*zu entscheiden*') 'between them'.[259] Moreover, the very fact of the formlessness of Rembrandtian as well as

---

[252] Ibid., p. 62. [GSG 15, p. 389.]   [253] Ibid., p. 133. [GSG 15, p. 480.]
[254] Ibid., p. 104. [GSG 15, p. 444.]   [255] Ibid., p. 108. [GSG 15, p. 449.]
[256] '[I]f this more definitive [*entschiedenere*] life simultaneously appears as a more definitive [*entschiedenere*] individuality'. Ibid., p. 57. [GSG 15, p. 385.]
[257] Ibid., p. 3. [GSG 15, p. 309.]   [258] Ibid., p. 160. [GSG 15, p. 512.]
[259] Ibid., p. 162. [GSG 15, p. 515.]

Shakespearean art not only emphasises the fundamental opposition between classicist and Germanic art but also 'moderates and reconciles' it.[260]

But the note of dissatisfaction with Goethe's unity is salient. It suddenly becomes apparent that transcending variety does not necessarily lead to the kind of unity which comprehends everything, that the absoluteness of the sphere beyond variety may actually require choosing sides and that the unity which is attained may turn out to be the ultimate unity of fanaticism. It is this motif that began to be voiced in another group of Simmel's texts of that period: his essays related to the First World War.

4.3 War

In my discussion of Simmel's *Rembrandt* in the previous section, I referred to the impact that the First World War seemed to exercise on his thinking. This impact is reflected, for example, in his emphasis on the specifically Germanic form of individualism. Yet when *Rembrandt* and his other philosophical and theoretical works of that period are considered as a whole, the war does not appear to be their predominant subject, and there is no clear break between Simmel's philosophy of the pre-war and war years, as he generally manages to keep an intellectual distance from ongoing events.

At the same time, there is a group of texts where Simmel deals directly with the topic of the war, adopting for the first time since the early 1890s the role of an engaged intellectual. These texts include four essays from 1914–1916 that were collected in the book *The War and the Spiritual Decisions* (1917), as well as a number of other articles and pamphlets that address various war issues. And if one adds to these published works Simmel's letters from the same period, in which he often speaks about the war as a shattering experience on the most personal level,[261] one obtains a significant body of writings which offer a good glimpse into Simmel's philosophical and political attitude to the war and his perception of its role in transforming modern culture and society.[262]

---

[260] Ibid., p. 159. [GSG 15, p. 511.]

[261] E.g.: 'I can indeed say that now, for the first time, I am feeling world history as an immediate experience; that for the first time I not only theoretically know the cruel transitoriness, the disappearance without trace of everything which we lived and thought, created and felt – we always *knew* this – but am also experiencing this from the inside.' Letter to Hugo Liepmann, 22 December 1915, GSG 23, p. 585.

[262] For the most recent accounts of Simmel's stance towards the First World War, see Sven Papcke, 'Jungbrunnen oder Fegefeuer? Georg Simmel und das Kriegserlebnis 1914–1918', in R. Lautmann and H. Wienold (eds.), *Georg Simmel und das Leben in der Gegenwart* (Wiesbaden: Springer, 2018),

The striking aspect of this part of Simmel's oeuvre is the apparent contrast between it and his intellectual personality as we have come to know it.[263] For almost his entire life, Simmel was a progressive liberal and was perceived as an iconoclastic thinker. However one-sided and unprecise this stereotype may be (and in this book I have attempted to challenge it), Simmel's clear-cut commitment to the war cause and his vocal patriotism nevertheless seem to be at odds with his previous attitudes.[264] Moreover, his war essays appear as a deviation not only in respect of their content but also in respect of the degree of passion and intensity with which his patriotic commitment was spelled out. Simmel, known for his love of philosophical paradoxes and his alleged lack of philosophical commitment, took sides in a strongly partisan manner.

This contrast caused uneasiness to many commentators. As one of them noted, 'it is impossible not to be irritated by Georg Simmel'.[265] To explain the peculiarity of Simmel's war writings, various interpretations have been suggested. Patrick Watier, for example, analysed these texts against the background of the general feeling of joy provoked by the declaration of war which 'seems to be an aberration'.[266] He considered them 'an exploration of ... ecstasy ... of which he [Simmel] is simultaneously one of its theoreticians and also one of its ramifications',[267] and he went as far as to find there the anticipation of 'the ideology of totalitarianism'.[268] Others do not see in them any ecstatic aberration, and they stress Simmel's relative moderation and even occasional scepticism regarding the war. Thus Gregor Fitzi argued that Simmel's approval of the war indicated neither aggressive nationalism nor the decadent expectation of recovery from cultural disease, but should rather be interpreted in terms of 'the understanding of citizenship and in the framework of the moral commitment of that intellectual elite of which Simmel considered himself to be part'.[269]

---

pp. 397–421; Wolfgang Knöbl, 'Der Krieg und die geistigen Entscheidungen (1917)', in H.-P. Müller and T. Reitz (eds.), *Simmel-Handbuch: Begriffe, Hauptwerke, Aktualität* (Frankfurt am Main: Suhrkamp, 2018), pp. 734–744.

[263] E.g. Michael Landmann suggested that one can spot here something of a special, *fourth* stage in Simmel's thinking. See Michael Landmann, 'Georg Simmel: Konturen seines Denkens', in Böhringer and Gründer (eds.), *Ästhetik und Soziologie um die Jahrhundertwende*, p. 10.

[264] As Simmel's son Hans later remembered, Simmel was very critical of the policies of Wilhelm II towards England, which he considered dangerous and once (around 1906) even wondered whether there was any Ravaillac around. Hans Simmel, 'Lebenserinnerungen' [1941/1943], *Simmel Studies* 18 (1), 2008, p. 82.

[265] Stefan Breuer, 'Im Grenzenlosen sich zu finden', *Frankfurter Allgemeine Zeitung*, 17 July 1999, p. 47.

[266] Patrick Watier, 'The War Writings of Georg Simmel', *Theory, Culture & Society* 8(3), 1991, p. 222.

[267] Ibid., p. 229.   [268] Ibid., p. 230.

[269] Gregor Fitzi, 'Zwischen Patriotismus und Kulturphilosophie: Zur Deutung der Simmelschen Position im Ersten Weltkrieg', *Simmel Newsletter* 7(2), 1997, p. 121.

My view differs from both approaches. On the one hand, it is true that
Simmel was not a typical war chauvinist. He kept his distance from the
patriotic activities of the German professoriate[270] and even did not sign the
appeal 'To the Cultural World', a petition of 93 German scientists, artists
and writers from 4 October 1914. Furthermore, if one examines his correspondence, one can clearly see that his initial enthusiasm about the war was
actually much less enthusiastic than is commonly believed, and his prevalent state of mind even then was that of anxiety.[271] In any case, a year or two
after the beginning of hostilities, all signs of celebration disappeared from
Simmel's writings, and he began to mourn Europe's senseless self-destruc-
tion which, in his view, served only the purpose of American domination.[272] As the slaughter continued amidst the stalemate, he, like most
Germans, became less confident in the German victory.

Nevertheless, up to the very end Simmel professed a patriotic attachment to the German cause and was opposed to seeking peace at any price.
As he wrote in one of his last letters, 'our enemies should not hear that
Germans are *so* desperate, *so* finished, that they would even accept an
ignominious peace if they could only get it!'[273] This attitude cannot be
explained solely by a sense of duty. Simmel's public and private sayings of
those years are full of genuine hostility towards the enemy countries, of
exalted professions of love towards Germany and of hopes for the regeneration of culture by the young generation. These are not the sentiments of a
detached intellectual who is just performing his civic duty but of someone
who experienced a genuine spiritual attachment to the German cause. This
attachment led to expressions which can be interpreted as instances of
apocalyptic expectation and ecstasy. Thus, at the very beginning of the
essay 'The Inner Transformation of Germany' (1914), Simmel compared
the contemporary atmosphere to the expectations of the end of the world
around the year 1000.[274] And towards the end of the same essay he spoke
about yearning for the 'new man'.[275] These sentiments may have later
receded in his published works, but in his letters Simmel continued to

---

[270] On the position of German intellectuals during the war, see, e.g., Wolfgang J. Mommsen (ed.),
Kultur und Krieg: Die Rolle der Intellektuellen, Künstler, Schriftsteller im Ersten Weltkrieg (Munich:
R. Oldenbourg, 1996).
[271] See letter to Margarete von Bendemann, 22 August 1914, GSG 23, p. 372.
[272] 'Europa und Amerika: Eine weltgeschichtliche Betrachtung' [1915], GSG 13, pp. 138–142.
[273] Letter to Margarete von Bendemann, 17 August 1918, GSG 23, p. 1003.
[274] 'Deutschlands innere Wandlung', in *Der Krieg und die geistigen Entscheidungen: Reden und
Aufsätze*, GSG 16, p. 13.
[275] GSG 16, p. 27. Cf. 'If we survive this war, we will in some, but very radical sense, be different
people.' Letter to Margarete von Bendemann, 9 August 1914, GSG 23, p. 367.

express an intense hope for spiritual renewal out of the ashes of the war, even if he was aware of the danger of inner barbarism embedded in this drive for rejuvenation. In May 1918, for example, he wrote to Graf von Keyserling:

> Our youth of today is consumed with a passionate revolutionary longing for a *Vita Nuova*, a will to fight for a spiritual form of life that takes hold not abstractly, theoretically or aesthetically but practically. This is not an idealistic retreat from the world, instead an engagement with it, but in a by all means idealistic sense. This is a bitter enmity against all bourgeoisie [*Bürgerlichkeit*], against all mechanisation and Americanisation, but which employs the powers that these tendencies nonetheless brought about.[276]

And in a letter to Gertrud Kantorowicz dated the same month he said:

> There is among the youngest but also among the somewhat more mature youth a passionate will for the enlivening of the spirit and the spiritualisation of life, a wonderful stormy penetration through all the old rotten walls within which bourgeoisie [*Bürgerlichkeit*], the satiated privilege, contemporary traditions confine us. Much in it, of course, is thoughtless, merely programmatic, blind as well as superfluous and uncouth bravado. But I am becoming more and more interested in it; here *might* lie something of the future and of real freedom.[277]

Simmel was isolated to some degree from the mainstream German intellectuals. But this isolation was not the consequence of any alleged scepticism towards the war. Other reasons must have intervened, among them his own problematic status within the academic establishment and the idiosyncrasies of his thought that could not appeal to the broad audience[278] – hence the reluctance of the authorities to use his services. Moreover, on a deeper level, his patriotism and war enthusiasm were perhaps more radical than those of many of his colleagues. Simmel understood himself as speaking over the heads of tedious professors to a youth hungry for meaning. Thus in a letter to Paul Natorp (June 1918) he argued:

> Almost everything that is strong-willed, original and promising among the intellectual German youth feels that it is in more or less pronounced opposition to the way the academic humanities operate. This forward-thrusting youth which entered university in good faith and with a sense of reverence now sees it as a rotten remnant of the past which is able to survive

---

[276] Letter to Hermann Graf von Keyserling, 18 May 1918, GSG 23, p. 954.
[277] Letter to Gertrud Kantorowicz, 20 May 1918, GSG 23, p. 961.
[278] Cf. Ernst Morwitz, 'Erinnerungen an Simmel', in Gassen and Landmann (eds.), *Buch des Dankes*, p. 277.

thanks only to the power of the state that stands behind it and the conventions and conspiracies of the learned guild – rigid, encapsulated, deaf to the voices of the times and incapable of assuming the role of spiritual leadership.[279]

These are not the words of a 'moderate' intellectual.

Unlike Watier, however, I do not consider these signs of spiritual commitment occasionally bordering on 'ecstasy' as merely the consequence of Simmel being imbued with the general enthusiasm of the war days. Simmel's war ideas were indeed distinct from other aspects of his work, but they did not appear from nowhere. Their seeds were present in his earlier thought, perhaps only waiting for an occasion to burst forth. Already in the earlier Simmel one can find instances of yearning for a life of passionate commitment, and his philosophy of the pre-war age contains metaphysical possibilities which may justify such a commitment.

As I have shown in the two previous sections, his last decade was marked by the language of life-philosophy that promulgated a peculiar view of encompassing unity, unity which stands above contradictions without eliminating them. And if one reads his wartime writings, the same formulas and motifs can be found there too, on both the practical and philosophical levels. On the practical level, the devotion to unity and totality is salient in Simmel's appraisal of the soldiers' self-sacrifice. The war, he argued in 'The Inner Transformation of Germany', created a new connection 'between the individual and the whole nation'[280] and produced a more profound understanding of individual existence in which 'the most individual and the most general permeate each other at every point up to forming the unity of life'.[281] The war provided an occasion for individuals to obtain true inner unity, and similarly 'our *people* has finally become a unity and totality, and as such it crosses the threshold to the other Germany'.[282]

In 'The Crisis of Culture' (1916), this yearning for unity was applied to the domain of culture. Culture is torn up by contradictions such as the distortion of the relation between ends and means, the growing gap between objective and subjective culture and the growing estrangement between different spheres of culture. The way out of this estrangement, Simmel believed, may be the concept of life that gives 'a more unified rhythm to their [spheres'] heartbeat'.[283] Although Simmel was less

---

[279] Letter to Paul Natorp, 26 June 1918, GSG 23, p. 977.
[280] *Der Krieg und die geistigen Entscheidungen*, GSG 16, p. 14.   [281] GSG 16, p. 14.
[282] GSG 16, p. 29.
[283] 'The Crisis of Culture', trans. D. E. Jenkinson, in D. Frisby and M. Featherstone (eds.), *Simmel on Culture: Selected Writings* (London: Sage, 1997), p. 99. [GSG 16, p. 50.] Cf. Arthur Bueno,

optimistic than he had been at the beginning of the war, arguing that the crisis of culture was chronic, he nevertheless hoped that at least for the time being the progression of this crisis 'will be slowed down, its intensity tempered'.[284]

And on the abstract philosophical level, unity was conceived in accordance with the familiar formula of the absolute concept rising above the conflict between the relative concept and its opposite, such as the absolute good transcending the opposition between the relative good and evil or absolute life transcending the opposition between life and death.[285] With regard to the experience of the war, the absolute/relative formula was used by Simmel to identify the peculiarity of German national identity ever striving to overcome itself and find its own completion in the cultural other:

> Thus, everywhere alongside the German nature there stands its opposite, exclusionary of it and foreign to it; but this sense of the German nature is only relative, and beside it there stands its broadest and unconditional sense which also includes in itself that other, indeed hostile sense, and to which the opposite also belongs as something understood and established, its comprehended and embraced extension and yearning.[286]

So far, we are in the familiar terrain of searching for unity in the condition of conflict and contradictions. Yet, as I already pointed out in respect of Simmel's *Goethe*, this formula of unity that transcends but does not harmonise contradictions is very unstable, and this quest may easily lead to the opposite direction, the result being not a metaphysical harmony but rather a disintegration into formlessness which leads to abandoning the ideal of unity altogether. And if in *Goethe* this possibility was hinted at but never fully adopted, the war essays appear to have crossed the line by choosing conflict and disunity over harmony and unity. For alongside the aforementioned rhetoric of unity, there is in these essays the opposite rhetoric that overshadows the quest for unity, rhetoric that emphasises clear-cut divisions and the partisan choice of one side over the other.

'Rationality – Cultivation – Vitality: Simmel on the Pathologies of Modern Culture', *Dissonância: Critical Theory Journal* 2(2), 2018, pp. 96–135.

[284] Ibid., p. 100. [GSG 16, p. 51.]

[285] 'The Dialectic of the German Spirit', trans. A. Harrington, *Theory, Culture & Society* 24(7–8), 2007, p. 64. [GSG 16, pp. 34–35.]

[286] GSG 16, p. 35. Translation is mine. For a different translation, see 'The Dialectic of the German Spirit', p. 64.

This coexistence of two opposite quests was enabled by a subtle change in the way Simmel spoke of unity in the war essays. Whatever different forms Simmel's approach to the issue of unity and variety might have taken in the preceding years, his understanding of the problem was always dialectical in a broad sense. There was always in his writings a play of affirmations and negations, and the way to the final reconciliation always involved some 'mediator'. And what is striking in Simmel's discussion of unity in the war writings is that he self-consciously abolished mediation, envisioning rather a sort of ecstatic immediate unity.

This move is most salient in 'The Crisis of Culture'. There, Simmel argued that the experience of war might heal the problem of cultural reification, that is, of the situation in which 'things' which are merely mediators of human relationships take preference over those relationships. The solution was simply annulling that mediation:

> For the soldier, the whole system of culture pales into insignificance ... because in wartime the meaning and demands of life are focused on activity of whose value one is conscious without the mediation of any external things. Strength and courage, skill and stamina, prove themselves in direct activity [unmittelbar] as the values of life [seiner Existenz], and the 'war machine' visibly has a quite different, infinitely more vital [lebendigeres] relationship than a factory machine to the men involved in the operation.[287]

And in arts one witnesses a similar yearning, for example, in the pro-gramme of the artistic current of Expressionism which aims to replace concrete images of reality with 'the direct [unmittelbare] expression of psychological process'.[288]

This abolition of mediators is not and cannot be comprehensive. Regarding the sphere of art, at least, Simmel was sceptical about the chances of the Expressionist project, as he understood it. Art, according to him, would always need external forms. Yet in other spheres, especially in those related to ethical life, Simmel began to consider the possibility of rejecting the vision of a dialectical destruction of specific forms to produce more appropriate ones and substituting it with a vision of rebellion against the principle of form as such. Consequently, he described and praised the German spirit as abounding with vitality at the expense of form. And in his lecture 'The Conflict of the Modern Culture' (1918) he theorised the rejection of form as the consummation of the tragedy of culture specifically characteristic of the modern age. 'The repudiation of the principle of

---

[287] 'The Crisis of Culture', p. 93. [GSG 16, p. 40.]   [288] Ibid., pp. 93–94. [GSG 16, p. 41.]

form', he argues, 'culminates … in all those thinkers imbued with a modern sense of life who reject the coherent systems in which an earlier age, dominated by the classical notion of form, saw its entire philosophical salvation'.[289] No period has revealed so clearly as the contemporary one the fundamental opposition of life as life, and because it is life, to form.[290]

This abandoning of the principle of form and envisioning of the possibility of unmediated unity thus signifies a crucial retreat from dialectics. Simmel's yearning for unity is explicitly undialectical here, despite the word 'dialectic' in the title of the essay 'The Dialectic of the German Spirit'. The significance of this step is that this intimates the rejection of the ideal of culture. 'Culture', Margarete Susman once wrote, was 'the central, almost religious concept not only in Simmel's thought but also in his life'.[291] According to her, this was misunderstood by the next generation, for it was centred on 'decision', whereas 'there is no decision in culture'.[292] But in fact the escape from culture to decision, from dialectical comprehensiveness to intense devotion was the central aspect of Simmel's own war essays, and the next generation could hardly be accused of misunderstanding him if it just followed the spirit of those essays.

In them, the quest for unity, deprived from dialectics, quickly transformed itself into a call for singleness, for an intense spark rather than an all-encompassing totality. In both the intellectual and practical spheres Simmel talked about the new demand for spiritual divisions which presupposed the necessity of decision. Occasionally he was uneasy about this new demand, for example, with regard to the field of philosophy. Philosophy, according to him, reached an impasse between its antinomies that could now be solved by only yes or no. It now presented a series of worldview alternatives that were calling for decision (*Entscheidung*).[293] He perceived this situation as a failure and wondered whether philosophy in some future would be capable of finding the 'third' that would solve its antinomies.

But more often Simmel sounded as if he were relieved by the demand for decision. This is especially salient in the field of religion. The war, he suggested, brought about a revival and strengthening of the inner forces of religion, and now everyone was required to make a decision (*Entschluß*) regarding the absolute ground ('*auf welchem absoluten Grunde*'[294]) on which one ultimately stood. Any mature man 'will presumably have long

---

[289] 'The Conflict of Modern Culture', trans. D. E. Jenkinson, in Frisby and Featherstone (eds.), *Simmel on Culture*, p. 85. [GSG 16, pp. 198–199.]
[290] Ibid., p. 90. [GSG 16, p. 206.]
[291] Margarete Susman, *Die geistige Gestalt Georg Simmels* (Tübingen: J. C. B. Mohr, 1959), p. 28.
[292] Ibid.   [293] 'The Crisis of Culture', p. 96. [GSG 16, p. 45.]   [294] GSG 16, p. 43.

since made his decision (*Entscheidung*)' but 'because of the peculiar cultural broadmindedness ... that decision was often intermingled with, or concealed by, its opposite'.[295] The current time, however, in which one's religious depths are agitated, does not allow for such compromises. There is no longer room for the hybrid forms of the past time, and what is required now is an ultimate decision on matters of faith.

The factor of decision was similarly emphasised by Simmel with regard to the war itself. As he put it in 'The Inner Transformation of Germany', 'the war ... confronts all and everything with a ruthless either-or with regard to value and to justice, and leaves room only for true germination and authenticity'.[296] This situation of either/or heralded the time of distinctions. For war rejects compromises, being 'the great separation process between light and darkness, between the noble and the vulgar, for which venial peacetime was able to demarcate far less decided borders'.[297] The question was now one of being or not being, and therefore any pretence of objectivity and holding on to impartial values had to be abandoned.[298] Simmel famously called this condition 'an absolute situation'. It foreboded dangers and required sacrifices, in other words, it demanded 'the absolute decision'.[299]

Denis Thouard justly characterised this stance as 'metaphysical decisionism'.[300] For this decisionism was not a single case of rhetorical exaggeration in an essay written at the beginning of the war. Rather, it became Simmel's *idée fixe*, the constant subject of his reflection during the war years, as he spoke, for example, about 'the tremendous decision of world history',[301] introduced the imperative of decision to various spheres of culture or even included this word as part of the title of the book that appeared as late as 1917. Moreover, the decisionist sentiment was not an entirely new aspect in Simmel's thought. It is true that as an explicit ethical position decisionism belongs to his war period. One can find among his aphorisms, written mostly during those years, sayings like these: 'There is always a certain arrogance in tolerance. Even if you impertinently say "no", you are still on the *same* footing as the one who said "yes". But if you tolerate him, you are his patron.'[302] Or: 'But the one who is against me in

[295] 'The Crisis of Culture', p. 95. [GSG 16, pp. 41–42.]
[296] *Der Krieg und die geistigen Entscheidungen*, GSG 16, p. 21.   [297] GSG 16, p. 19n.
[298] GSG 16, p. 23. Or, as he says in one of his letters right after the outbreak of war: 'a people faces the question: to be or not to be'. Letter to Margarete von Bendemann, 9 August 1914, GSG 23, p. 367.
[299] GSG 16, p. 22.
[300] Denis Thouard, 'Simmel et la guerre: De 14 à 18', *Revue de métaphysique et de morale* 4, 2014, p. 566.
[301] Letter to Ludwig Fulda, 27 July 1915, GSG 23, p. 544.
[302] 'Aus dem nachgelassenen Tagebuche', GSG 20, p. 287.

the positive sense, the one who brings himself to the level where I live and then fights me on it, is in the highest sense *for* me.'[303]

But if one examines his other works closely, one can discover that there was occasionally a hidden motif in them which sailed against the usual stream of tolerance and ambiguity in his writings, as if at times he became tired of this incessant philosophical ping-pong and yearned instead for the certainty of yes or no. Thus as early as 1889, Simmel referred to one of Michelangelo's sonnets where, as he told us, the poet was prepared to take upon himself all the suffering of the world if only he could possess the genius of Dante. Behind the conventional humility of Michelangelo's love poetry lay 'the irrepressible feeling of: all or nothing'.[304] And in another text of that period Simmel used the same formula when he discussed the psychology of women, suggesting that, in contrast to the coquettes with their constant vacillation between granting and non-granting, it is the 'purest women' who were in the acutest danger of seduction by Don Juan or the devil, for their conduct towards men was marked by the alternative of 'all or nothing'.[305]

That this mention of readiness for an existential decision did not reflect sheer intellectual curiosity but rather something deeper on Simmel's part is evident from the fact that he found elements of it in the philosophy of Kant who was the most significant thinker for him in his early period. Thus in the essay 'What is Kant to Us?' (1896), Simmel referred to the Protestant foundations of Kant's thought, arguing that the Protestant emphasis on belief and conscience over action acquired in Kant its 'highest philosophical expression'.[306] This emphasis judged everything in accordance with the inward ethical criterion of the good will, and this concentration on the ethical came at the expense of the renunciation of all other values of existence under the motto: 'all or nothing'.[307]

And in *Kant* (1904) Simmel suggested that the Protestant single-mindedness of Kant showed the modern person the path of moral heroism by which one could overcome one's petit-bourgeois existence. This despite the fact that Simmel considered Kant as being himself guilty of petit-bourgeois moral pettiness, arguing that the rule of categorical imperative might serve as an unambiguous guide for conduct only in the narrow and cosy bourgeois circles.[308] In this respect, Simmel preferred the subtlety of Nietzsche who, as he thought, managed to rise above the narrow bourgeois

[303] GSG 20, p. 296.   [304] 'Michelangelo als Dichter', GSG 2, p. 43.
[305] 'Zur Psychologie der Frauen', GSG 2, p. 96.   [306] 'Was ist uns Kant?', GSG 5, p. 162.
[307] GSG 5, p. 163.   [308] Cf. *Kant*, GSG 9, p. 138.

alternative between egoism and altruism, one's own good and the good of one's neighbour.[309] Nevertheless, in a self-conscious paradox, Simmel assigned to Kant in the context of his moral theory the quality of greatness of soul, underlining this claim with the vocabulary of 'absolute' and 'decision' that would become so significant in his war writings. Simmel put forward the claim that in the final account Kant had been saved from the danger of narrow-mindedness by his 'absolutistic moralism'.[310] This absolutism consisted in considering the good will as the only good in the world, and such an uncompromising position was radical in its grandeur. 'The "dangerous life" that so irresistibly attracts the modern man, has already developed here to full maturity and purity'.[311] Man's moral responsibility becomes here the only card on which everything is gambled: 'existence, directed at the ethical as the only value, faces every moment the *decision*: all or nothing'.[312] And by this gamble a miraculous transformation is achieved. Whereas generally the moralistic attitude to life is philistine through and through, Kant's brave moral thinking brings him to the opposite of all philistinism, 'to abandoning all reserves and to the voluntary danger of *absolute* self-responsibility',[313] even if this devotion deprives life of its richness and precludes it from unfolding in all its variety.

Such passages in Simmel look as if in some rare moments he was awoken by the feeling of the insufficiency of his own dialectics and even perhaps of his own sheltered existence, and wished to combat the fear of degenerating into a *blasé* existence by at least imagining a life of enthusiasm, bordering on fanaticism, that accepts dangers and does away with comfort and ambiguities.

This feeling was, of course, not unique to Simmel. It reflected a sentiment well recognised in European thought and society. In the years leading to the war it accumulated to the point of explosion. But the quest for self-adequacy via action, as well as the emphasis on 'absolute' and 'decision', had long been part of the German cultural vocabulary.

It was a German thinker – Carl von Clausewitz – who coined the expression 'absolute war'. He meant by this a war unencumbered by extraneous considerations, a war waged without respite until a final victory over the enemy is attained.[314] This of course had little to do with the

---

[309] 'Nietzsches Moral', GSG 12, p. 174.   [310] *Kant*, GSG 9, p. 150.
[311] GSG 9, pp. 150–151. Up to the 3rd 1913 edition Simmel explained this attraction to danger as a result of the growing security of external life – cf. GSG 9, p. 448. Naturally this explanation was deleted from the 1918 edition, as the war had made it obsolete.
[312] GSG 9, p. 151. Italics mine – E. P.   [313] GSG 9, p. 151. Italics mine – E. P.
[314] Carl von Clausewitz, *On War*, trans. M. Howard and P. Paret (Oxford: Oxford University Press, 2007), pp. 224–246.

apocalyptic romantic vision of war that would attract many aesthetes at the outbreak of the First World War.[315] And in the history of German culture and philosophy the word 'absolute' could carry a whole array of different connotations, many of them rather pantheistic. But it also formed part of the language reservoir upon which the discourse of absolute *decision* could build.

That other word – 'decision' – could also easily evoke in the mind of an educated German old cultural motifs. Thus a patriotic author chose in August 1914 the first four lines from the following words of Schiller's *Wallenstein* as the motto for his own poem:

> 'Tis decided! 'Tis well! I have received a sudden cure
> From all the pangs of doubt: with steady stream
> Once more my life-blood flows! My soul's secure!
> In the night only Friedland stars can beam.
> Lingering irresolute [*Mit zögerndem Entschluß*], with fitful fears
> I drew the sword – 'twas with an inward strife,
> While yet the choice was mine. The murderous knife
> Is lifted for my heart! Doubt disappears!
> I fight now for my head and for my life.[316]

And the poem itself started as follows:

> It is decided, indeed! and now it is good,
> Now the masks have fallen all around,
> Now the false brood of hypocrites is exposed,
> Now it's on, encircled Germany, war with everyone.
> A deep breath of air – then lift the sword high![317]

Its first line thus repeated Schiller's language of decision, language soon to be used by Simmel in his first war essay. Whereas the title of another essay of Simmel's – 'The Dialectic of the German Spirit' – was also reminiscent

---

[315] Cf. Klaus Vondung, *The Apocalypse in Germany*, trans. S. D. Ricks (Columbia: University of Missouri Press, 2000).

[316] Friedrich Schiller, *The Death of Wallenstein*, trans. S. T. Coleridge (London: Longman and Rees, 1800), III:X, p. 31. 'Es ist entschieden, nun ists gut – und schnell / Bin ich geheilt von allen Zweifelsqualen, / Die Brust ist wieder frei, der Geist ist hell, / Nacht muß es sein, wo Friedlands Sterne strahlen. / Mit zögerndem Entschluß, mit wankendem Gemüt / Zog ich das Schwert, ich tats mit Widerstreben, / Da es in meine Wahl noch war gegeben! / Notwendigkeit ist da, der Zweifel flieht, / Jetzt fecht ich für mein Haupt und für mein Leben'.

[317] Karl Strecker, 'Die Kriegserklärung Englands', in W. E. Windegg (ed.), *Der deutsche Krieg in Dichtungen* (Munich: C. H. Beck, 1915), p. 36. [Es ist entschieden, ja! Und nun ist's gut, / und sind die Masken alle rings gefallen, / nun ist entlarvt die falsche Heuchlerbrut, / nun gilts', umstelltes Deutschland, Kampf mit allen. Ein tiefer Atemzug – dann noch das Schwert!] Translated in Vondung, *The Apocalypse in Germany*, pp. 266–267.

of the same poem, as in its last lines it spoke about the German spirit that would rise as a phoenix from the flames of the conflagration.[318]

This language of decision contained, however, more than merely literary allusions. Today, decisionism is often traced to the intellectual mood between the two world wars with its rejection of the classical *Bildung* ideal of harmony and its adoption of the dualism of struggle, and especially to the writings of Carl Schmitt and his friend-enemy dichotomy. Occasionally, Max Weber is brought as a precursor.[319] But in fact the history of decisionism as an ethical-philosophical stance has a longer history.

The origins of decisionism appear to be theological and are related to the infusion of some strains of Protestantism with the categories of what will later be known as the philosophy of existentialism. A key thinker in this respect was Danish philosopher Søren Kierkegaard. In his *Political Theology*, Schmitt obliquely referred to Kierkegaard in respect of the latter's emphasis on 'exception' that 'thinks the general with intense passion'.[320] Kierkegaard, a fierce critic of Hegelian dialectics, repeatedly spoke about 'decision' in his descriptions of the quality that the contemporary age lacks: the passion to act. The age, he argued, and the individual belonging to it, is imprisoned 'by reflection itself, and it does so by maintaining the flattering and conceited notion that the *possibility* of reflection is far superior to a mere *decision*'.[321]

To what extent Kierkegaard himself may have been on Simmel's mind is unclear. Simmel mentioned the Danish thinker explicitly only once, in the context of his discussion of the 'Germanic' type of individualism exemplified by Rembrandt.[322] He also occasionally used the formula 'either/or', apparently alluding to the title of Kierkegaard's most famous book. In his earlier writings, he considered the condition of 'either/or' as a problem rather than a blessing. In 1895, for example, he envisioned the ideal of overcoming the opposition between 'yes or no', or 'yes and no', by which

---

[318] 'Ein Phönix steigt, so schön wie Morgenrot, / *der deutsche Geist* aus dieses Weltbrands Flammen'.

[319] Cf. Paul Hirst, 'Carl Schmitt's Decisionism', in Chantal Mouffe (ed.), *The Challenge of Carl Schmitt* (London: Verso, 1999), pp. 7–17; Stephen Turner and Regis Factor, 'Decisionism and Politics: Weber as Constitutional Theorist', in Scott Lash and Sam Whimster (eds.), *Max Weber, Rationality and Modernity* (London: Allen & Unwin, 1987), pp. 334–354.

[320] Carl Schmitt, *Political Theology: Four Chapters on the Concept of Sovereignty*, trans. G. Schwab (Chicago: University of Chicago Press, 2005), p. 15. The reference is to Kierkegaard's 'Repetition', see Søren Kierkegaard, *Repetition and Philosophical Crumbs*, trans. M. G. Piety (Oxford: Oxford University Press, 2009), p. 78.

[321] Søren Kierkegaard, 'The Present Age', in *The Present Age and The Difference between a Genius and an Apostle*, trans. A. Dru (New York: Harper & Row, 1962), p. 48.

[322] 'Individualism', trans. A. Harrington, *Theory, Culture & Society* 24(7–8), 2007, p. 68. [GSG 13, p. 301.]

modern man's life is constantly torn, and it was perhaps the function of art to achieve this ideal: '[F]or us, all great art seems to need to unify antitheses and transcend every compulsion of the "either-or".'[323]

As the years went by, he became less sure that this opposition actually needed any overcoming. Perhaps to be torn by opposites was the essence of the human condition, and the function of art was to give it an expression, even if in different ages this could take different forms. In an essay on Rodin (1909), Simmel compared Rodin with Michelangelo, the former representing the modern and the latter Renaissance sensibility. Modern sensibility, he argued, is 'less a switching between "yes" and "no" than the simultaneity of "yes" and "no"'.[324]

Simmel also brought the dilemma of yes and no into his dealing with flirtation. Interestingly, Kierkegaard also used the same topic to illustrate the indecisiveness of the modern age. Flirtation was for Kierkegaard 'the result of doing away with the vital distinction between real love and real debauchery ... A flirtation only toys with the possibility and is therefore a form of indulgence which dares to touch evil and fails to realise the good'.[325] The young Simmel could have accepted this opinion about flirtation.[326] Yet in the 1909 essay on the psychology of flirtation,[327] later included in *Philosophical Culture* (1911), he appeared to have changed his mind, arguing the opposite: flirtation does not contradict that 'unity and resoluteness [*Entschiedenheit*] with which the woman confronts an erotic question as an issue of All or Nothing'; it is rather the symbol of that unity.[328] In the section on women I already referred to these remarks of Simmel to illustrate his emphasis of unity. But if one looks at it from a different angle, one can also spot here yet another sign of Simmel's evolution towards an embrace of the ethics of decision. And if, unlike Kierkegaard, he did not seem to denounce flirtation, it is perhaps because he no longer saw it as a sign of indecisiveness.

Kierkegaard's own position was of course much more complex. As Karl Löwith pointed out, his discussions of the exceptional and the particular, of choice and decision, were themselves part of a more nuanced dialectic.[329]

---

[323] 'Arnold Böcklin's Landscapes'. [GSG, vol. 5, p. 101.]
[324] 'Auguste Rodin: Part II', p. 314. [GSG 12, p. 33.]   [325] Kierkegaard, 'The Present Age', p. 75.
[326] Cf. 'Zur Psychologie der Frauen', GSG 2, pp. 96–98.
[327] Cf. 'Psychologie der Koketterie', GSG 12, p. 45.
[328] 'Flirtation', trans. G. Oakes, in *On Women, Sexuality, and Love* (New Haven: Yale University Press, 1984), p. 147. [*Philosophische Kultur*, GSG 14, p. 272.]
[329] Cf. Søren Kierkegaard, *Either/Or*, vol. 2, trans. W. Lowrie (Princeton: Princeton University Press, 1972), pp. 333–337; Karl Löwith, *Martin Heidegger and European Nihilism*, trans. G. Steiner (New York: Columbia University Press, 1995), pp. 142–143.

Nevertheless, Kierkegaard's catchy formulas provided a path that could be taken by the sentiment of cultural disaffection. In the sphere of theology this led to a turning away from *Bildung* historicism towards existentialism and dialectical theology, represented in the inter-war period by figures such as Friedrich Gogarten, who in his essays sometimes used the Simmelian phraseology of decision and the crisis of culture.[330]

This process, however, was already underway in the early twentieth century when the rise of life-philosophy began to have an impact on theological reflection. One of the thinkers influenced by this trend was Albert Schweitzer: a theologian, physician and musician.[331] In 1906, he published a study on the history of the research of the life of Jesus, in the conclusion to which he launched a critique of the historicist approach to Christianity: 'The historical foundation of Christianity as built up by rationalistic, by liberal, and by modern theology no longer exists.'[332] The true historical Jesus relevant for today is the commanding one:

> He speaks to us the same word: 'Follow thou me!' and sets us to the tasks which He has to fulfil for our time. He commands. And to those who obey Him, whether they be wise or simple, He will reveal Himself in the toils, the conflicts, the sufferings which they shall pass through in His fellowship, and, as an ineffable mystery, they shall learn in their own experience Who He is.[333]

This atmosphere of existential turn also brought about a growing interest in mystical thought, represented, among others, by the mediaeval theologian Meister Eckhart. Eckhart was a complex mind, and for thinkers of different periods he could mean different things. During the nineteenth century, for example, his reception was to a great degree appropriated by the project of German Idealism, especially in respect of his fusion of philosophy with theology and his idea of oneness. Thus scholars point to 'a fundamentally positive' relation between Eckhart and Hegel.[334] By contrast, in the post-Heideggerian deconstructionist twentieth century, Eckhart was appropriated not to heal disintegration but to help 'recognise and embrace disintegration'.[335]

---

[330] Friedrich Gogarten, *Die religiöse Entscheidung* (Jena: Diederichs, 1921).

[331] On Schweitzer's appreciation of Simmel following a brief personal acquaintance in Berlin in 1899, see Albert Schweitzer, 'Erinnerungen an Simmel', in Gassen and Landmann (eds.), *Buch des Dankes*, pp. 292–294.

[332] Albert Schweitzer, *The Quest of the Historical Jesus: A Critical Study of Its Progress from Reimarus to Wrede* (Baltimore: The Johns Hopkins University Press, 1998), p. 399.

[333] Ibid., p. 403.

[334] Cyril O'Regan, 'Eckhart Reception in the 19th Century', in Jeremiah Hackett (ed.), *A Companion to Meister Eckhart* (Leiden: Brill, 2013), p. 639.

[335] Ibid., p. 667. On Eckhart's twentieth-century reception, see also Dermot Moran, 'Meister Eckhart in 20th-Century Philosophy', in ibid., pp. 669–698.

Towards the 1910s, Simmel too developed a strong interest in Meister Eckhart,[336] and one can notice that his attitude to the mediaeval mystic progressed from the older emphasis on unity towards the idea of apartness. Thus, when Simmel in his *Main Problems of Philosophy* (1910) discussed Eckhart's thought for the first time, he seemed to emphasise the pantheistic aspect, the notion of God as encompassing the entirety of creation. As all things are concentrated in God, their concentration at one point allows Eckhart to transfer that point into the human soul. This godly 'spark' (*Fünklein*) in the soul is where the believer is immersed in the unity of all things.[337]

The same spiritual vision can, however, be described not only in relation to the world but also in terms of its negation, as a mystical liberation. And when one examines Simmel's course notes on the history of philosophy dated 1913/14, one can find that it is this aspect of Eckhart's mystical thinking which acquired more prominence in Simmel's account. At the moment of unity with God, 'the soul must extinguish everything it has in itself which is individual, animated and manifold'. And what remains from this is 'nothing'. To attain this nothing is 'the task of the mystics'.[338] This nothing is of course not just nothing. It is a nothing which is at the same time 'all', as Simmel went on to explain. Yet it is worth noticing that he began to pay more attention to that aspect in Eckhart which pointed to mystical detachment from the world and to the divide drawn between God as One and the world as variety.

It is this sentiment of detachment which is prominent in the mystical attitude. Detachment presupposes an act of separation, the decision to place oneself apart from the world. As a contemporary put it, through mysticism the individual is 'taken out of the historical context and made isolated and indifferent towards social, ecclesiastical and political associations'.[339] Interestingly, this was a conclusion to which Simmel arrived on the personal level, having decided to leave the Protestant church. It is *this*

---

[336] In 1911, he reports to Heinrich Rickert: 'Recently I have been dealing with *Meister Eckhart* again and I am completely overwhelmed by the depth and freedom of this mind. Germany has produced broader and more differentiated minds; I doubt, however, whether it ever produced a more profound, concentrated, original one.' Letter to Heinrich Rickert, 29 December 1911, GSG 22, p. 1021. On Simmel's interpretation of Eckhart see, Volkhard Krech, *Georg Simmels Religionstheorie* (Tübingen: Mohr Siebeck, 1998), pp. 211–226; Christopher Adair-Toteff, 'The "Antinomy of God": Simmel on Meister Eckhart and Nietzsche', *Simmel Newsletter* 3(1), 1993, pp. 10–16.

[337] 'On the Nature of Philosophy', trans. R. H. Weingartner, in Wolff (ed.), *Essays on Sociology, Philosophy and Aesthetics*, pp. 286–287. [*Hauptprobleme der Philosophie*, GSG 14, pp. 18–19.]

[338] 'Geschichte der Philosophie' [1913/1914], GSG 21, p. 27.

[339] Gustav Lasch, 'Mystik und Protestantismus', *Religion und Geisteskultur* 5, 1911, p. 41.

decision that he most likely had in mind when he spoke in 'The Crisis of Culture' about the unavoidability of spiritual decisions in the realm of religion. The religious soul of the non-belonging mystic, he argued, does not require any mediation by historically conditioned dogmas. It stands 'naked and alone . . . before its God'.[340]

But religious discourse was not the only sphere in which existential decisionism made itself felt. Similar developments could also be noticed in the spheres of politics and art, where the desperate yearning for action and decision began to be expressed more and more often. Here too this yearning was not something completely new. One can find its traces already among the rebels of the post-Hegelian generation who rejected Hegel's and Goethe's universalism in order to detach Faust's *Tat*, as it were, from the harmony of being and turn it into the ultimate ethical ideal. Kierkegaard was one of them. Yet he did not draw specifically political conclusions from his critique. The decision he called for was that of submission to religious authority. But this was not the only possible conclusion. The critique of the indecisiveness of the modern age could take the form of a critique of political impotence, leading to calls for political action. Thus Kierkergaard's contemporary Karl Marx, another source of inspiration for Schmitt's decisionism,[341] described the events of the 1848 revolution in the following way: 'struggles whose first law is indecision; wild, inane agitation in the name of tranquillity; most solemn preaching of tranquillity in the name of revolution; passions without truth, truths without passion; heroes without heroic deeds, history without events'.[342]

Simmel in his early period stood close to socialists and social democrats, and references to Marx's thought are spread through his writings.[343] Yet his treatment of Marx was on the whole half-ironic, and he never came to espouse any specifically socialist doctrine. Besides, by the late nineteenth century the decisionist Marx was overshadowed by the scientific Marx, as he was domesticated by the German social democrats who adopted in

---

[340] 'The Crisis of Culture', p. 95. [GSG 16, p. 44.]

[341] Löwith, *Martin Heidegger and European Nihilism*, p. 141.

[342] Karl Marx, 'The Eighteenth Brumaire of Louis Bonaparte', in *Marx/Engels Collected Works*, vol. 11 (Moscow: Progress Publishers, 1979), p. 125.

[343] On Simmel's dialogue with Marx, see, e.g., Gregor Fitzi, '"Die Absicht, dem historischen Materialismus ein Stockwerk unterzubauen": Zur Beziehung von Simmel zu Marx', in O. Rammstedt (ed.), *Georg Simmels Philosophie des Geldes* (Frankfurt am Main: Suhrkamp, 2003), pp. 215–242; idem, *The Challenge of Modernity: Simmel's Sociological Theory* (London: Routledge, 2019), pp. 39–44; Mathieu Deflem, 'The Sociology of the Sociology of Money: Simmel and the Contemporary Battle of the Classics', *Journal of Classical Sociology* 3(1), 2003, pp. 80–81.

practice, even if not in theory, revisionist gradualism. Therefore by the 1910s it was not the orthodox Marxist milieu that evoked the imagery of decisive action but the artistic avant-garde, generally of the leftist variety. It could be occasionally inspired by Marx, yet on the whole it was unconcerned with the nuances of this or that political doctrine. In the early 1910s, the most prominent among these artistic trends was the current of Expressionism.[344]

Leftist literary figures associated with it disdained from pursuing compromise with the Wilhelmine establishment and called instead for a complete social and artistic overthrow of the existing order. In this spirit, for example, Carl Einstein distinguished between revolt and dialectical revolution, the latter seen by him as leading merely to meek opposition, whereas revolt 'is the constant principle that the individual carries within himself, a form of disposition and thought'.[345] The title of the weekly magazine that began to appear in 1911 and was most closely associated with the Expressionist movement – *Die Aktion* – fit this sentiment perfectly.

Simmel followed Expressionism closely, regarding it as the most significant cultural development of those years. He claimed that 'of all the hotchpotch [*durcheinanderlaufenden*] of aspirations covered by the general names of futurism, only the movement described as Expressionism seems to stand out with a certain identifiable degree of unity and clarity'.[346] Ralph Leck put forward an argument that it was Simmel himself and his idea of culture that inspired the founders of Expressionism. Simmel, he argued, had been one of the leading thinkers of the cultural avant-garde in Germany already in the 1890s, and suggested that Kurt Hiller, an Expressionist writer and activist, 'was to Simmel what Marx was to Hegel: a political supersession'.[347]

This interpretation appears to me quite exaggerated. Not only were Simmel's cultural tastes not specifically 'Expressionist', but, as I argued earlier, his preferences were much more classicist than is usually believed. I think it is more correct to assume that it was the cultural avant-garde and Expressionism that began to influence Simmel in his last years, which may partly account for the radicalisation of his political and cultural positions during the war. It is then that Simmel seems at times to abandon his

---

[344] For the most comprehensive survey of the ideas of Expressionism and adjacent cultural currents, see Thomas Anz, *Literatur des Expressionismus* (Stuttgart: J. B. Metzler, 2010).

[345] Carl Einstein, 'Anmerkungen', *Die Aktion* 2(35), 28 August 1912, p. 1093.

[346] 'The Conflict of Modern Culture', p. 80. [GSG 16, p. 190.]

[347] Ralph M. Leck, *Georg Simmel and Avant-Garde Sociology: The Birth of Modernity, 1880–1920* (Amherst, NY: Humanity Books, 2000), p. 213.

'dialectical' style of expression, talking instead in terms of an uncompromising rejection of the old world in a manner befitting a man of cultural revolt. Previously, Simmel's essays were a skilful balancing act between the affirmation and negation of modernity. Now, however, he denounces the contemporary 'mammonism', mechanisation and Americanisation, putting his hopes in the younger generation whose task was to lead the world to regeneration and the formation of the new man. His disaffection became reminiscent of his socialist moralism of the 1880s and early 1890s. Thus he castigated immorality and the lack of solidarity of affluent classes, including his fellow academics, reproaching them for their unwillingness to share their material goods with others during the war.[348] This critique was indeed voiced by one who himself remained an affluent bourgeois and academic aesthete. It is as if by means of this self-criticism Simmel tried in his later years to keep pace with the mood of the younger generation of aesthetes, many of them his students. This attempt was hardly a success, as this radicalism never fully drove out his other side, that of an uncommitted intellectual, whereas many younger thinkers to whom he appealed, such as Georg Lukács or Siegfried Kracauer, did not take his newly found devotion seriously, suspecting him of having remained the embodiment of an aloof bourgeois.[349]

A similar ambiguity existed in Simmel's relationship with the right-wing cultural avant-garde. Like its leftist counterpart, the right-wing intellectual scene was moving towards a rejection of the ideal of harmony, looking instead for dividing lines. Action was now preferred to reflection, and if the left-wing activists had *Die Aktion*, their conservative counterparts made *Die Tat* ('the deed'), a journal taken over in 1912 by Eugen Diederichs, their tribune.[350]

Nationalist fringes were busy with developing philosophies in which they rejected monism, unity and harmony, while adopting various forms of esotericism, mysticism and dualism. This turn usually involved anti-Semitism of one kind or another, as the very ideal of unity was increasingly

---

[348] See 'Geld und Nahrung' [1915], GSG 13, pp. 117–122; 'Eine Fastenpredigt: Von dem Opfer der Wohlhabenden' [18 March 1917], GSG 17, pp. 138–142.

[349] As the playwright Paul Ernst wrote to Lukács in 1916, 'Simmel's problem, about which we have indeed often spoken, is the problem of the person who is clever and lacking in instinct. He has no roots; hence in his younger years he developed very unexpectedly and in the years when he should have broadened out he lacked the energy'. Quoted from David Frisby, *Sociological Impressionism: A Reassessment of Georg Simmel's Social Theory* (London: Routledge, 1992), p. 162. See also Siegfried Kracauer, 'Über die Philosophie Georg Simmels und ihren Zusammenhang mit dem geistigen Leben der Zeit', in P. U. Hein (ed.), *Georg Simmel* (Frankfurt am Main: Peter Lang, 1990), pp. 131–158.

[350] Cf. Irmgard Heidler, *Der Verleger Eugen Diederichs und seine Welt (1896–1930)* (Wiesbaden: Harrassowitz, 1998), pp. 834–842.

presented as a 'Jewish' concept that falsified Christian 'Pauline' dualism. This was, for example, the line taken by another nationalist journal – *Der Panther* – and its editor Leonore Ripke-Kühn. On the pages of *Der Panther* she attacked the standard neo-Kantian interpretations of Kant and accused Hermann Cohen of perverting Kant's dualistic German Christian teaching. In the eyes of these nationalists, the striving towards a harmonious *Bildung* was a Jewish business.[351]

In the context of such sentiments, Simmel, who had adopted, as has been shown, Cohen's interpretation of Kant's metaphysics, would easily fit the image of a racially foreign mind who perverted the meaning of 'German' philosophy. No wonder that especially towards the end of his life he increasingly complained about having been an object of anti-Semitic prejudice. And surely, there would be no way for him to ally himself with the overtly nationalistic 'dualistic' trends, as represented by *Der Panther*.

And yet during the same years Simmel drifted significantly towards the dualistic scepticism regarding redemption via harmonious *Kultur*, and at least in respect of the war his position was closer to the nationalist critique of that ideal, than to that of the left-wing aesthetes, many of whom were revolutionary pacifists. And luckily for him, there was on the right wing one artistic group with which he could feel some affinity: the George Circle. It was self-consciously elitist and generally free of anti-Semitism – in fact, many prominent Circle member were themselves Jews. George and his disciples initially professed an apolitical aestheticism but evolved, like many others in the years prior to the war, towards a more activist stance. Some Circle members, including George himself, were old acquaintances of Simmel's, and one – Friedrich Gundolf, a former student of his – remained a good friend.

And yet, like in the case of Expressionism, Simmel could never fully sympathise with the George Circle, despite his personal ties to it and somewhat similar aesthetic inclinations. George's disciples were similarly sceptical about Simmel and did not believe in the seriousness of his decisionism. This is what appears to be the real cause behind the incident between them which took place at the very beginning of the war and which at first glance resembles a comedy of errors.[352]

---

[351] On the quarrel sparked by their criticism of Hermann Cohen's Kant oeuvre and the exchange of opinions between the editor of *Kant-Studien* Bruno Bauch and the *Panther*'s editor Leonore Ripke-Kühn, see *Der Panther* 4(4), 1916, pp. 477–484; 4(6), 1916, pp. 741–746. Cf. Ulrich Sieg, *Geist und Gewalt: Deutsche Philosophen zwischen Kaiserreich und Nationalsozialismus* (Munich: Carl Hanser, 2013), pp. 129–136.

[352] For a detailed description of the conflict, see Otthein Rammstedt and Michael Popp, 'Aufklärung und Propaganda: Zum Konflikt zwischen Georg Simmel und Friedrich Gundolf', *Simmel Newsletter* 5(2), 1995, pp. 139–155.

On 11 October 1914, Friedrich Gundolf published in the *Frankfurter Zeitung* an article entitled 'Deed and Word in the War'. This was a contribution to the polemics between French and German intellectuals, occasioned by the destruction of the university library in Leuven by German troops. Framed as a discussion on the question of 'German barbarism', the exchange turned into a debate on the general issue of the justice of the war. In his attempt to articulate the attitude of the George Circle to the events, Gundolf navigated between their snobbish rejection of everyday concerns and their loyalty to the German cause. The result was a position which still affirmed the seclusion of the artist called upon to create cultural values, a position dismissive of any engagement in the propagandist effort, but which at the same time fully identified with the German aims and conduct, including the event of the library's destruction. As Gundolf wrote,

> Culture is not having or enjoying; it is being, working, becoming, it is creating, destroying, transforming – and Attila has more to do with culture than Shaw, Maeterlinck, d'Annunzio and the like all together … The one who has the strength to create is also allowed to destroy, and if our future could no longer create, it would have no right to enjoy the past.[353]

Five days after the publication of this article, Simmel responded with an article of his own, distancing himself from Gundolf's views.[354] It was not, however, Gundolf's evocation of Attila in his apology for the destruction of cultural artefacts that bothered Simmel. In fact, he himself would later praise the formless drive of vitality characteristic of the German spirit. As he noted in 'The Crisis of Culture', the war bears a positive significance for the form of culture, notwithstanding its destruction of culture's substance.[355] The point on which Simmel differed from Gundolf was rather the latter's disavowal of the propagandist activity, or to use Simmel's expression, the activity of 'enlightening' [*Aufklärung*] foreign public opinion. Simmel was embarking on writing just such enlightening pieces in foreign newspapers, and he must have considered Gundolf's attitude as undermining the value of his own contribution to the war effort. Simmel did not challenge Gundolf's assumption that an attempt at changing hostile public opinion was pointless. However, taking the high moral-intellectual ground, he argued that such enlightening work was nevertheless necessary because the situation in which the lies spread about Germany

---

[353] Cited according to ibid., p. 141.
[354] 'Aufklärung des Auslands' [16 October 1914], GSG 17, pp. 119–120.
[355] 'The Crisis of Culture', p. 99. [GSG 16, p. 51.]

are not rebutted is intolerable for anyone committed to the principle of truth. To buttress his point, Simmel appeared to put the propagandist work on a par with the self-sacrifice of soldiers: 'At a moment when a hundred precious lives put themselves at risk in order perhaps to take a small hill in Argonne which tomorrow might be surrendered again, we will surely not ask whether it is perhaps in vain that we write a hundred pamphlets, explanations and letters.'[356] The 'absolute situation' in which Germans find themselves does not allow one to start weighing the relative prices of action.

This argumentation irritated another member of the Circle, Karl Wolfskehl, who joined the subsequent exchange of letters between Simmel and Gundolf.[357] The gist of all this communication was Wolfskehl's rage at what he took to be Simmel's comparison of his own writing activity to the true sacrifice of soldiers, on the one hand, and Simmel's assurances that he did not intend to make any comparison and that there was no principal disagreement between them, on the other. It did not help matters, however, that Simmel in his letter to Gundolf used the Latin confession formula '*Dixi et salvati animam meum*' to emphasise the absolute value of truth.[358] This provided Wolfskehl with additional ammunition, as he quite unfairly imputed to Simmel a comparison not only with soldiers but also with Jesus standing before Pilate who wonders what the truth is.[359] Despite this formal unfairness, however, there was perhaps a grain of truth in Wolfskehl's accusations. What he was in fact saying was that Simmel's decisionism was fake and that despite all his talk of devotion he would never be able to exercise it even in the spiritual realm, let alone on the battlefield. As Wolfskehl pointed out, 'the *spiritual* parallel to the absolute behaviour of the soldier is ... the mysterious reality of master and community'.[360] Simmel thus stood accused by George's disciples of those qualities from which he himself wished to escape: indecisiveness and philistinism.

Simmel nevertheless continued to voice fascination with heroic decisions. He continued to maintain friendly ties with Gundolf and favourably reviewed his book on Goethe. Although Simmel did not fully accept either

---

[356] 'Aufklärung des Auslands', GSG 17, p. 120.
[357] See Friedrich Gundolf, letter to Georg Simmel, 17 October 1914; Karl Wolfskehl, letter to Georg Simmel, 17 October 1914; Georg Simmel, letter to Friedrich Gundolf, 20 October 1914; Georg Simmel, letter to Margarete von Bendemann, 20 October 1914; Karl Wolfskehl, letter to Georg Simmel, 25 October 1914, GSG 23, pp. 425–426, 427–429, 432–433, 435, 437–438.
[358] Letter to Friedrich Gundolf, 20 October 1914, GSG 23, p. 432.
[359] Karl Wolfskehl, letter to Georg Simmel, 25 October 1914, GSG 23, p. 438. Cf. John 18:38.
[360] Karl Wolfskehl, letter to Georg Simmel, 17 October 1914, GSG 23, p. 428.

Gundolf's method or his interpretation of Goethe, he liked the book's existential motifs. Goethe's demand to live from within, he suggested, was not foreign to many people today, and this 'ought' exists in them in a latent form, even if they lack the depth and courage necessary for its practical realisation. He expressed hope that Gundolf's book would help many to find such courage and strength.[361] But Gundolf also stressed the self-limitations of Goethe's life. Only through those self-limitations did he breathe the air of 'the infinite and absolute'.[362] It is this resignation which explained, according to Gundolf, Goethe's fascination with his antithesis: the daemonic drive of figures such as Napoleon or Lord Byron. On this point Simmel corrected Gundolf: Goethe was a spirit of affirmation too, and 'the renouncing "no" of self-limitations was as much embraced by the great "yes" of his nature as every accomplishment and enjoyment'.[363] Could this correction be an echo of the older discussion between them on the role of thinkers in the age of action?

Existential motifs appear also in Simmel's 1915 essay entitled 'Become What You Are' in an allusion to Nietzsche's appropriation of Pindar's phrase. There, Simmel claimed that the war's most certain success so far had been in causing many people to live 'off what is essential' (*im Wesentlichen*).[364] It enabled them to discover who they are, for in order to know this truly and deeply 'more than any superficial gains, struggle, hardship and danger are required'.[365] The new situation demanded decisions, the choice of 'either-or'. And Simmel focused in this short essay on the decisions to be made in the sphere of religion, since an 'empty peace'[366] was no longer an option. This sounded again like a reference to Simmel's own decision to leave the church.

This decision was apparently a matter of great pride and importance to him. In fact, Simmel's biography consisted to a great extent of a series of landmarks in which he avoided great decisions, choosing instead a cosy bourgeois lifestyle, close to his family, his city and his country. Thus, during his university studies he did not travel to study for a semester at other universities, which was almost a rule for students of his time, and opted instead to stay in Berlin. When in the mid-1890s he received academic offers from America, he declined and again stayed in Berlin where his career failed to advance. As time progressed, he even distanced himself from social activism.

---

[361] 'Das Goethebuch', GSG 13, pp. 236–237.   [362] GSG 13, p. 237.   [363] GSG 13, p. 237.
[364] '"Become What You Are"', trans. U. Teucher and T. M. Kemple, *Theory, Culture & Society* 24(7–8), 2007, p. 58. [GSG 13, p. 134.]
[365] Ibid., p. 60. [GSG 13, p. 137.]   [366] Ibid., p. 59. [GSG 13, p. 135.]

And somewhere deep inside himself he must have felt regret at this pattern of avoiding decisions. Despite being fully immersed in the ideals of German high culture, a culture which was all protest against the *petit-bourgeois* life, he led that kind of life. Occasionally he should have wondered whether it contained resources to overcome its own philistinism. Perhaps Kant could offer hope, as his ostensibly philistine ethical system contained the potential for grandeur. Or perhaps one needed a great artist, such as Rembrandt, who was able to impart something majestic even to 'petit-bourgeois, poorly bred Jewish, intellectually insignificant, persons [*kleinbürgerlichen, schlechtrassig jüdischen, geistig unerheblichen Menschen*]'.[367]

Simmel's letters of the war years are full of unmeasured exaltation. It is this exaltation which was perceptively noticed by his opponents in the George Circle. It is as if Simmel savoured the new situation to which he was driven, even if he was conscious of having very limited physical and spiritual resources to translate it into real heroism. It is to the next generation that he wished to leave the task of spiritual heroism, consoling himself that he might have contributed to the incipient transformation.

Simmel's cultural ideals belonged to the pre-war world. The dialectic of unity and variety was unsuitable to a new heroism. But perhaps Simmel sensed that he had already exhausted the resources of that dialectic. In his *Goethe* book, he brought the idea of absolute unity to such heights that the only way forward was a sharp fall into its opposite. Absolute harmony, all-comprehension and inclusion led to a closer look at absolute decision, an intense concentration on one single point. Goethe's harmony dissolved into the passion for the singular and the partisan.

Let us remember the formula suggested in *Goethe*: the absolute concept includes the positive concept and its opposite without abolishing either. Simmel used this formula everywhere in his writings of these years. Thus the absolute good included the relative good and evil, and the absolute truth included the relative truth and falsehood. This formula may appear to be dialectic, but it was not. Simmel's absolute concepts were not outcomes of a long philosophical process but rather primordial states, instances of *Urphänomen*. There was no Hegelian logic by which the affirmative side of the pair would prevail. There was in fact no affirmation and negation here. The choice was arbitrary. The essay on the differences between the sexes made this clear, as in it Simmel turned both the masculine and the feminine into absolute conceptions, each in its turn

---

[367] *Rembrandt*, p. 104. [GSG 15, p. 444.]

transcending the relativity of the feminine and masculine.[368] There was, then, a simply irreconcilable conflict between two sides, each of which could be made into the absolute. And thus instead of the absoluteness of all-comprehension there was the absoluteness of non-comprehension, the state of absolute struggle. This was almost Schmittian territory. And the signs of this turnabout are already noticeable in the *Goethe* monograph itself, where, as I have shown, the quest for form in Goethe's last period may also be interpreted as leading to formlessness.

Throughout his life, Simmel was preoccupied with the task of integrating the world of culture, and it looked like he was always on the cusp of a solution. But each time he formulated a solution, it immediately proved illusory. Each time a bolder and broader dialectical move was required. But implicitly already in *Goethe* and explicitly in the war essays this dialectic abolished itself, contracting into absolute singleness. Was this the fulfilment of Simmel's quest or its nullification? The methods of intellectual history cannot enter this terrain. Intellectual history tells and interprets what was thought and not what was achieved by thought. To address the question of the measure of success of Simmel's quest for unity requires a different, philosophically oriented study. Meanwhile, it can be remarked that in his last years Simmel himself appeared to vacillate between feelings of satisfaction and despair, feelings energised by the eventful and brutal war.

---

[368] 'The Relative and the Absolute in the Problem of the Sexes', trans. G. Oakes, in *On Women, Sexuality, and Love*, p. 127. [GSG 14, pp. 250–251.]

Conclusion

In his treatise on the epistemological foundations of historical research, Simmel broadened the Kantian understanding of a priori, reformulating it in the neo-Kantian fashion as signifying 'relational forms [*Verbindungsformen*], serviceable to that peculiar capacity of the mind which classifies, defines, and stresses each given mental content in such a way that it can be moulded to fit the most diverse constitutive forms'.[1] Challenging the strict dichotomy between abstract perspective and empirical content, he believed that the notion of a priori could be used in a much more flexible way than had been envisioned by Kant and include contents which are themselves empirically derived and yet function in an a priori fashion, serving as presuppositions for specific branches of knowledge, such as history. Following Simmel in this regard, I will conclude my book with a few remarks on the methodological foundations of the work, or what can be described as the a priori of intellectual history, especially the kind of intellectual history which focuses on the ideas of individual minds.

This type of research draws on two seemingly contrasting presuppositions. The first is that any mental activity revealed in textual artefacts constitutes a series of disparate linguistic interventions on behalf of the historical personality under investigation. These interventions are necessarily fragmentary, or even heterogeneous, incapable of being reduced to one logically consistent idea. Indeed, intellectual historians have already for some time moved away from constructing linear narratives and towards deciphering the fragmentary manifoldness of the inevitably chaotic activities of thinking and making utterances.

This realisation, however, should not overshadow the contrary but equally valid a priori: that the ideas of the thinker who is subject to our inquiry inevitably possess a degree of inner coherence. For a mind's ideas are the outcome of its process of reflection, and any such reflective process

---

[1] *The Problems of the Philosophy of History: An Epistemological Essay*, trans. G. Oakes (New York: The Free Press, 1977), p. 43. [GSG 9, p. 238.]

involves striving towards inner clarity. The a priori postulating coherence on
the subjective side of the inner thought process is thus a necessary counterpart of the a priori postulating incoherence on the objective side of the
outward result of that process. In fact, the more philosophically inclined
a certain mind is, the more manifest its striving for coherence becomes.

Georg Simmel was an exemplary figure in this respect. He lived in
a period of intense intellectual fermentation, which many of his contemporaries felt to be an exciting and at the same time unsettling experience:
exciting because it opened new paths for cultural and intellectual creativity
and experimentation; unsettling because the intellectual anarchy to which
it supposedly led contradicted the highly cherished passion of attaining
inner harmony and integrity via the process of personal cultivation. This
passion, while common to all intense minds, was especially important in
the age of *Bildung*.

Simmel exemplified both sides of this contradiction. An intense and
brilliant mind, he never could become a settled and consistent thinker:
such intellectual tranquillity would mean unwarranted spiritual self-
limitation. But this very intensity turned unity into the *idée fixe* of his
philosophical journey. A random look at almost any of Simmel's texts
immediately brings the motif and vocabulary of unity to one's attention.
The drive for unity governs his thought throughout, and any panoramic
interpretation of his ideas requires that the continuous presence of this
motif be taken seriously when his manifold and often disparate intellectual
pursuits are examined in their particulars.

This is what I have tried to accomplish in this book. By drawing on the
conceptual formula offered by Simmel himself, I have depicted his thought
as a continuous answering of a series of questions that relate to the conflict
between unity and variety, an issue which steadily grew in importance in
Germany during Simmel's lifetime. I have shown that there developed in
Germany in particular a vocabulary of cultivation and *Kultur* that was used
to reflect on the alleged contradiction between the imperative of personal
formation on the one hand and social and intellectual differentiation and
fragmentation on the other, and that Simmel's thought in general, and his
philosophy of culture in particular, can be considered one of the most
important and penetrating accounts of this entire problematic.

Simmel's treatment of this issue began with a generally positive assessment of the modern age, in that it was considered to be moving towards the
integration of its manifold variety in some kind of encompassing unity.
Subsequently, however, as the problem of the reconciliation between unity
and variety revealed itself as far more complex, this optimism turned into

despair and a frantic search for escape from the contradictions of modernity in specifically designated fragments of modern experience. Finally, this despair seemed to be overcome by the development of more radical philosophical means that bordered on the adoption of a mystical attitude to life. Yet, at the same time, this radical solution was perhaps just a more extreme form of the same despair: The poles of unity and variety were driven so far apart that the idea of absolute totality rooted in the primordial pre-reflective unity pushed Simmel's thought towards an apparently contradicting vision of absolute commitment, or absolute singleness. Simmel's writings on Goethe on the one hand and on the war on the other represent these two conflicting attitudes.

To a certain extent, the inner dynamics of Simmel's thought parallel the story of the way this issue developed in European, and especially German, intellectual history in the long nineteenth century. If, at the outset, the essence of the modern age was taken as the progressive movement towards complex unity, this attitude was later challenged by a cultural pessimism which in turn brought about attempts to find a new unity in less 'rational' spheres. Simmel thus represents in the most condensed way the trajectory of the intellectual and cultural life of his time and country and its inward troubles and tragedies.

The question may arise as to the meaning of this issue for other ages. Did this dilemma reflect a fundamental conflict embedded in human aspirations in general? Or did it emerge out of a set of contingent cultural and social circumstances in the European and specifically German cultural life of that period? If the latter is true, then Simmel possesses significance for us mainly as a historical figure who brought the central spiritual obsessions of his time to the fore. If, however, the dilemmas he spoke about are universally valid, then, even if they are not felt with the same degree of intensity at all times, his thought, taken as a whole, can be highly relevant to us and to future generations. The task of tackling this question should be left, however, to philosophers. Whatever the answer, Simmel – one of the leading minds of Imperial Germany – deserves the attention of anyone who is interested in the multi-faceted history of modern ideas.

Bibliography

Simmel's Texts in German

'Das Abendmahl Leonardo da Vincis', GSG 7, pp. 304–309.
'Aesthetik der Schwere', GSG 7, pp. 43–48.
'Aesthetik des Porträts', GSG 7, pp. 321–332.
'Alpenreisen', GSG 5, pp. 91–95.
'Anlage zum Brief Georg Simmels an Stefan George', GSG 22, pp. 449–451.
'Die ästhetische Bedeutung des Gesichts', GSG 7, pp. 36–42.
'"Aufklärung des Auslands"', GSG 17, pp. 119–120.
'Aus dem nachgelassenen Tagebuche', GSG 20, pp. 261–296.
'Die Bauernbefreiung in Preussen', GSG 17, pp. 195–222.
'Der Begriff and die Tragödie der Kultur', GSG 12, pp. 194–223.
'Beiträge zur Erkenntnistheorie der Religion', GSG 7, pp. 9–20.
'Bemerkungen zu socialethischen Problemen', GSG 2, pp. 20–36.
'Berliner Gewerbe-Ausstellung', GSG 17, pp. 33–38.
'Der Bildrahmen: Ein ästhetischer Versuch', GSG 7, pp. 101–108.
'Böcklins Landschaften', GSG 5, pp. 96–104.
'Bruchstücke aus einer Philosophie der Kunst', GSG 13, pp. 174–183.
'Bruchstücke aus einer Psychologie der Frauen', GSG, vol. 7, pp. 289–294.
'Das Christentum und die Kunst', GSG 8, pp. 264–275.
'Dantes Psychologie', GSG 1, pp. 91–177.
'Die Dialektik des deutschen Geistes', GSG 13, pp. 224–230.
'Einige Bemerkungen über Goethes Verhältnis zur Ethik', GSG 1, pp. 215–220.
'Einiges über die Prostitution in Gegenwart und Zukunft', GSG 17, pp. 261–273.
Einleitung in die Moralwissenschaft: Eine Kritik der ethischen Grundbegriffe, GSG 3–4.
'Elizabeth Försters Nietzsche-Biographie', GSG 1, pp. 338–346.
'Etwas vom Spiritismus', GSG 17, pp. 274–283.
'Europa und Amerika: Eine weltgeschichtliche Betrachtung', GSG 13, pp. 138–142.
Ex malis minima! Reflexionen zur Prostitutionsfrage, GSG 17, pp. 251–260.
'Eine Fastenpredigt: Von dem Opfer der Wohlhabenden', GSG 17, pp. 138–142.

'Der Frauenkongreß und die Sozialdemokratie', GSG 17, pp. 39–45.

'Frauenstudium an der Berlin Universität . . . ' [Lesebrief vom 21 December 1899], GSG 17, pp. 326–327.

'Friedrich Nietzsche: Eine moralphilosophische Silhouette', GSG 5, pp. 115–129.

'Die Gegensätze des Lebens und die Religion', GSG 7, pp. 295–303.

'Geld und Nahrung', GSG 13, pp. 117–122.

'Geschichte der Philosophie' [1913/1914], GSG 21, pp. 11–139.

'Gestalter und Schöpfer', GSG 13, pp. 184–189.

Goethe, GSG 15, pp. 7–270.

'Goethe und die Jugend', GSG 13, pp. 98–104.

'Das Goethebuch', GSG 13, pp. 231–243.

'Goethes Gerechtigkeit', GSG 13, pp. 90–97.

Grundfragen der Soziologie (Individuum und Gesellschaft), GSG 16, pp. 59–149.

[Gutachten über die Petition zur >Gestattung bzw. Errichtung vollständiger Mädchengymnasien<, 27 March 1903], GSG 17, p. 64.

Hauptprobleme der Philosophie, GSG 14, pp. 7–157.

'Individualismus', GSG 13, pp. 299–306.

'Infelices Possidentes!', GSG 17, pp. 293–297.

'Ein Jubiläum der Frauenbewegung', GSG 1, pp. 284–294.

Kant: Sechzehn Vorlesungen gehalten an der Berliner Universität, GSG 9, pp. 7–226.

'Kant und Goethe', GSG 5, pp. 445–478.

Kant und Goethe: Zur Geschichte der modernen Weltanschauung, GSG 10, pp. 119–166.

Der Konflikt der modernen Kultur: Ein Vortrag, GSG 16, pp. 181–207.

Der Krieg und die geistigen Entscheidungen: Reden und Aufsätze, GSG 16, pp. 7–58.

'Die Kunst Rodins und das Bewegungsmotiv in der Plastik', GSG 12, pp. 28–36.

Lebensanschauung: Vier metaphysische Kapitel, GSG 16, pp. 209–425.

Letter to Célestin Bouglé, 13 December 1899, GSG 22, pp. 342–343.

Letter to Friedrich Gundolf, 20 October 1914, GSG 23, pp. 432–433.

Letter to Gertrud Kantorowicz, 20 May 1918, GSG 23, pp. 960–962.

Letter to Hermann Graf von Keyserling, 22 April 1914, GSG 23, pp. 312–313.

Letter to Hermann Graf von Keyserling, 18 May 1918, GSG 23, pp. 952–955.

Letter to Heinrich Rickert, 15 August 1898, GSG 22, pp. 304–305.

Letter to Heinrich Rickert, 29 December 1911, GSG 22, pp. 1020–1021.

Letter to Heinrich Rickert, 13 December 1915, GSG 23, pp. 578–579.

Letter to Hugo Liepmann, 22 December 1915, GSG 23, pp. 585–586.

Letter to Lou Andreas-Salomé, 10 May 1896, GSG 22, p. 203.

Letter to Ludwig Fulda, 27 July 1915, GSG 23, pp. 543–544.

Letter to Margarete von Bendemann, 4 August 1912, GSG 23, pp. 93–94.

Letter to Margarete von Bendemann, 4 May 1913, GSG 23, pp. 180–181.

Letter to Margarete von Bendemann, 26 June 1913, GSG 23, pp. 189–190.

Letter to Margarete von Bendemann, 9 August 1914, GSG 23, pp. 367–368.

Letter to Margarete von Bendemann, 22 August 1914, GSG 23, p. 372.

Letter to Margarete von Bendemann, 20 October 1914, GSG 23, p. 435.

Letter to Margarete von Bendemann, 27 May 1915, GSG 23, p. 524.

Letter to Margarete von Bendemann, 23 October 1917, GSG 23, pp. 851–853.

Letter to Margarete von Bendemann, 17 August 1918, GSG 23, pp. 1003–1004.

Letter to Paul Ernst, 14 January 1910, GSG 22, pp. 773–774.

Letter to Paul Natorp, 26 June 1918, GSG 23, pp. 976–978.

Letter to Rainer Maria Rilke, 20 January 1898, GSG 22, p. 280.

Letter to Ricarda Huch, 5 March 1903, GSG 22, pp. 455–456.

Letter to Stefan George, 24 February 1903, GSG 22, pp. 445–447.

Letter to Vorstand der DGS, 10 June 1912, GSG 23, pp. 69–70.

'Michelangelo als Dichter', GSG 2, pp. 37–48.

'Michelangelo: Ein Kapitel zur Metaphysik der Kunst', GSG 12, pp. 111–136.

Der Militarismus und die Stellung der Frauen', GSG 5, pp. 37–51.

'Moltke als Stilist', GSG 2, pp. 103–107.

'Eine neue Popularisirung Kants', GSG 1, pp. 181–184.

'Nietzsches Moral', GSG 12, pp. 170–176.

'Persönliche und sachliche Kultur', GSG 5, pp. 560–582.

'Die Persönlichkeit Gottes: Ein philosophischer Versuch', GSG 12, pp. 290–307.

'Philosophie der Geschlechter: Fragmente', GSG 8, pp. 74–81.

'Philosophie der Kultur' [Winter-Semester 1906/07, by Hermann Schmalenbach], GSG 21, pp. 557–571.

'Philosophie der Kunst' [1913/1914], GSG 21, pp. 141–222.

'Philosophie der Kunst' [Winter-Semester 1913/14, by Adolf Löwe], GSG 21, pp. 940–987.

Philosophie des Geldes, GSG 6.

Philosophische Kultur GSG 14, pp. 159–459.

'Das Problem der religiösen Lage', GSG 12, pp. 148–161.

'Das Problem der Sociologie', GSG 5, pp. 52–61.

'Das Problem des Stiles', GSG 8, pp. 374–384.

Die Probleme der Geschichtsphilosophie: Eine erkenntnistheoretische Studie, GSG 2, pp. 297–421.

Die Probleme der Geschichtsphilosophie: Eine erkenntnistheoretische Studie, GSG 9, pp. 227–419.

'Psychologie der Koketterie', GSG 12, pp. 37–50.

'Das Relative und das Absolute im Geschlechter-Problem', GSG 12, pp. 224–250.

Die Religion, GSG 10, pp. 39–118.

Rembrandt: Ein kunstphilosophischer Versuch, GSG 15, pp. 305–515.

'Rembrandt und die Schönheit', GSG 13, pp. 105–111.

'Rembrandts religiöse Kunst', GSG 13, pp. 70–89.

'Rembrandtstudie', GSG 13, pp. 16–52.

Review of F. Tönnies, *Der Nietzsche-Kultus*, GSG 1, pp. 400–408.

Review of H. Steinthal, *Allgemeine Ethik*, GSG 1, pp. 192–210.

Review of Machetes, *Das Unrecht des Stärkeren in der Frauenfrage*, GSG 1, p. 283.

Review of *Rembrandt als Erzieher*, GSG 1, pp. 232–243.

'Rodins Plastik und die Geistesrichtung der Gegenwart', GSG 7, pp. 92–100.

'Rom: Eine ästhetische Analyse', GSG 5, pp. 301–310.

Schopenhauer und Nietzsche: Ein Vortragszyklus, GSG 10, pp. 167–408.

'Sociale Medicin', GSG 1, pp. 381–388.

'Socialismus und Pessimismus', GSG 5, pp. 552–559.

Soziologie: Untersuchungen über die Formen der Vergesellschaftung, GSG 11.

'Soziologische Aesthetik', GSG 5, pp. 197–214.

'Studien zur Philosophie der Kunst, besonders der Rembrandtschen', GSG 13, pp. 143–164.

Ueber den Unterschied der Wahrnehmungs- und der Erfahrungsurteile: Ein Deutungsversuch', GSG 5, pp. 235–245.

'Über die Grundfrage des Pessimismus in methodischer Hinsicht', GSG 2, pp. 9–20.

'Ueber eine Beziehung der Selectionstheorie zur Erkenntnistheorie', GSG 5, pp. 62–74.

Über Goethes und Kants moralische Weltanschauung: Aus einem Vorlesungszyklus', GSG 8, pp. 416–423.

'[Über:] *Karl Joël*, Professor in Basel: *Philosophenwege*. Ausblicke und Rückblicke. Berlin, Heyfelder, 1901' [27 April 1901], GSG 17, pp. 328–329.

'Ueber Kunstausstellungen', GSG 17, pp. 242–250.

Über soziale Differenzierung: Sociologische und psychologische Untersuchungen, GSG 2, pp. 109–295.

'Venedig', GSG 8, pp. 258–263.

'Vom Tode in der Kunst: Nach einem Vortrag', GSG 13, pp. 123–132.

'Vom Wesen der Kultur', GSG 8, pp. 363–373.

'Was ist uns Kant?', GSG 5, pp. 145–177.

'Weibliche Kultur' [1902], GSG 7, pp. 64–83.

'Weibliche Kultur' [1911], GSG 12, pp. 251–289.

'"Werde, was du bist"', GSG 13, pp. 133–137.

'Werte des Goetheschen Lebens', GSG 20, pp. 11–79.

Das Wesen der Materie nach Kant's Physischer Monadologie, GSG 1, pp. 9–41.

'Ein Wort über soziale Freiheit', GSG 17, pp. 21–25.

'Zu einer Theorie des Pessimismus', GSG 5, pp. 543–551.

'Die Zukunft unserer Kultur: Stimmen über Kulturtendenzen und Kulturpolitik' [Beitrag zu:], GSG 17, pp. 79–83.

'Zum Problem der Naturalismus', GSG 20, pp. 220–248.

'Zum Verständnis Nietzsches', GSG 7, pp. 57–63.

'Zur Ästhetik der Alpen', GSG 12, pp. 162–169.

'Zur Philosophie des Schauspielers', GSG 8, pp. 424–432.

'Zur Psychologie des Pessimismus', GSG 17, pp. 223–233.

'Zur Psychologie der Frauen', GSG 2, pp. 66–102.

'Zur Soziologie der Religion', GSG 5, pp. 266–286.

Simmel's Translated Texts in English

'The Aesthetic Significance of the Face', trans. L. Ferguson, in Kurt H. Wolff (ed.), *Essays on Sociology, Philosophy and Aesthetics*. New York: Harper & Row, 1959, pp. 276–281.

'Aesthetics of Gravity', in Austin Harrington (ed.), *Georg Simmel: Essays on Art and Aesthetics*. Chicago: University of Chicago Press, 2020, pp. 143–147.

'Aesthetics of the Portrait: Part I', in Austin Harrington (ed.), *Georg Simmel: Essays on Art and Aesthetics*. Chicago: University of Chicago Press, 2020, pp. 240–248.

'The Alpine Journey', trans. S. Whimster, in D. Frisby and M. Featherstone (eds.), *Simmel on Culture: Selected Writings*. London: Sage, 1997, pp. 219–221.

'Arnold Böcklin's Landscapes', in Austin Harrington (ed.), *Georg Simmel: Essays on Art and Aesthetics*. Chicago: University of Chicago Press, 2020, pp. 205–211.

'Auguste Rodin: Part I', in Austin Harrington (ed.), *Georg Simmel: Essays on Art and Aesthetics*. Chicago: University of Chicago Press, 2020, pp. 302–308.

'Auguste Rodin: Part II', in Austin Harrington (ed.), *Georg Simmel: Essays on Art and Aesthetics*. Chicago: University of Chicago Press, 2020, pp. 309–318.

'"Become What You Are"', trans. U. Teucher and T. M. Kemple, *Theory, Culture & Society* 24(7–8), 2007, pp. 57–60.

'The Berlin Trade Exhibition', in D. Frisby and M. Featherstone (eds.), *Simmel on Culture: Selected Writings*. London: Sage, 1997, pp. 255–258.

'Christianity and Art', trans. H. J. Helle, in G. Simmel, *Essays on Religion*. New Haven: Yale University Press, 1997, pp. 65–77.

'The Concept and Tragedy of Culture', trans. M. Ritter and D. Frisby, in D. Frisby and M. Featherstone (eds.), *Simmel on Culture: Selected Writings*. London: Sage, 1997, pp. 55–75.

'The Conflict of Modern Culture', in D. Frisby and M. Featherstone (eds.), *Simmel on Culture: Selected Writings*. London: Sage, 1997, pp. 87–99.

'A Contribution to the Sociology of Religion' [1898], trans. H. J. Helle, in G. Simmel, *Essays on Religion*. New Haven: Yale University Press, 1997, pp. 101–120.

'A Contribution to the Sociology of Religion' [1905], trans. W. W. Ewlang, in *Georg Simmel Gesamtausgabe*. Frankfurt am Main: Suhrkamp, 1989–2015, vol. 10, pp. 387–404.

'Contributions to the Epistemology of Religion', trans. H. J. Helle, in G. Simmel, *Essays on Religion*. New Haven: Yale University Press, 1997, pp. 121–133.

'The Crisis of Culture', trans. D. E. Jenkinson, in D. Frisby and M. Featherstone (eds.), *Simmel on Culture: Selected Writings*. London: Sage, 1997, pp. 90–101.

'The Dialectic of the German Spirit', trans. A. Harrington, *Theory, Culture & Society* 24(7–8), 2007, pp. 61–65.

'Differentiation and the Principle of Saving Energy', trans. D. E. Jenkinson, in P. A. Lawrence (ed.), *Georg Simmel: Sociologist and European*. Sunbury-on-Thames: Thomas Nelson and Sons, 1976, pp. 111–138.

'Female Culture', trans. G. Oakes, in *On Women, Sexuality, and Love*. New Haven: Yale University Press, 1984, pp. 65–101.

'Flirtation', trans. G. Oakes, in *On Women, Sexuality, and Love*. New Haven: Yale University Press, 1984, pp. 133–152.

'Florence', trans. U. Teucher and T. M. Kemple, *Theory, Culture & Society* 24 (7–8), 2007, pp. 38–41.

'Fundamental Problems of Sociology: Individual and Society', trans. K. H. Wolff, in Kurt H. Wolff (ed.), *The Sociology of Georg Simmel*. New York: The Free Press, 1950, pp. 1–84.

'The Future of Our Culture', trans. D. E. Jenkinson, in D. Frisby and M. Featherstone (eds.), *Simmel on Culture: Selected Writings*. London: Sage, 1997, pp. 101–102.

'The Handle', trans. R. H. Weingartner, in Kurt H. Wolff (ed.), *Essays on Sociology, Philosophy and Aesthetics*. New York: Harper & Row, 1959, pp. 267–275.

'How Is Society Possible?', trans. K. H. Wolff, in Kurt H. Wolff (ed.), *Essays on Sociology, Philosophy and Aesthetics*. New York: Harper & Row, 1959, pp. 337–356.

'Individualism', trans. A. Harrington, *Theory, Culture & Society* 24(7–8), 2007, pp. 66–71.

'*Infelices Possidentes!* (Unhappy Dwellers)', trans. M. Ritter and D. Frisby, in D. Frisby and M. Featherstone (eds.), *Simmel on Culture: Selected Writings*. London: Sage, 1997, pp. 259–262.

'The Intersection of Social Spheres', trans. D. E. Jenkinson, in P. A. Lawrence (ed.), *Georg Simmel: Sociologist and European*. Sunbury-on-Thames: Thomas Nelson and Sons, 1976, pp. 95–110.

'"Introduction" to *Philosophical Culture*', trans. M. Ritter and D. Frisby, in D. Frisby and M. Featherstone (eds.), *Simmel on Culture: Selected Writings*. London: Sage, 1997, pp. 33–36.

'Kant and Goethe: On the History of the Modern *Weltanschauung*', trans. J. Bleicher, *Theory, Culture & Society* 24(6), 2007, pp. 159–191.

'Leonardo da Vinci's *Last Supper*', in Austin Harrington (ed.), *Georg Simmel: Essays on Art and Aesthetics*. Chicago: University of Chicago Press, 2020, pp. 236–239.

'Michelangelo and the Metaphysics of Culture', in Austin Harrington (ed.), *Georg Simmel: Essays on Art and Aesthetics*. Chicago: University of Chicago Press, 2020, pp. 279–297.

'On Art Exhibitions', in Austin Harrington (ed.), *Georg Simmel: Essays on Art and Aesthetics*. Chicago: University of Chicago Press, 2020, pp. 137–142.

'On the Aesthetics of the Alps', in Austin Harrington (ed.), *Georg Simmel: Essays on Art and Aesthetics*. Chicago: University of Chicago Press, 2020, pp. 212–217.

'On the Essence of Culture', trans. D. E. Jenkinson, in D. Frisby and M. Featherstone (eds.), *Simmel on Culture: Selected Writings*. London: Sage, 1997, pp. 40–45.

'On the Nature of Philosophy', trans. R. H. Weingartner, in Kurt H. Wolff (ed.), *Essays on Sociology, Philosophy and Aesthetics*. New York: Harper & Row, 1959, pp. 276–309.

'The Personality of God', trans. H. J. Helle, in G. Simmel, *Essays on Religion*. New Haven: Yale University Press, 1997, pp. 45–62.

The Philosophy of Money, trans. T. Bottomore and D. Frisby. London: Routledge, 2004.

'The Picture Frame: An Aesthetic Study', in Austin Harrington (ed.), *Georg Simmel: Essays on Art and Aesthetics*. Chicago: University of Chicago Press, 2020, pp. 148–153.

'The Problem of Religion Today', trans. H. J. Helle, in G. Simmel, *Essays on Religion*. New Haven: Yale University Press, 1997, pp. 7–19.

'The Problem of Style', trans. M. Ritter, in D. Frisby and M. Featherstone (eds.), *Simmel on Culture: Selected Writings*. London: Sage, 1997, pp. 211–217.

The Problems of the Philosophy of History: An Epistemological Essay, trans. G. Oakes. New York: The Free Press, 1977.

'The Relative and the Absolute in the Problem of the Sexes', trans. G. Oakes, in *On Women, Sexuality, and Love*. New Haven: Yale University Press, 1984, pp. 102–132.

'Religion', trans. H. J. Helle, in G. Simmel, *Essays on Religion*. New Haven: Yale University Press, 1997, pp. 137–214.

'Religion and the Contradictions of Life', trans. H. J. Helle, in G. Simmel, *Essays on Religion*. New Haven: Yale University Press, 1997, pp. 36–44.

Rembrandt: An Essay in the Philosophy of Art, trans. A. Scott and H. Staubmann. New York: Routledge, 2005.

'A Review of *Social Medicine*', trans. J. Casparis and A. C. Higgins, *Social Forces* 47 (3), 1969, pp. 331–334.

'Rome', trans. U. Teucher and T. M. Kemple, *Theory, Culture & Society* 24(7–8), 2007, pp. 30–37.

Schopenhauer and Nietzsche, trans. H. Loiskandl, D. Weinstein and M. Weinstein. Urbana: University of Illinois Press, 1986.

'Sociological Aesthetics', trans. K. P. Etzkorn, in *The Conflict in Modern Culture and Other Essays*. New York: Teachers College Press, 1968, pp. 68–80.

'Some Remarks on Prostitution in the Present and in Future', trans. M. Ritter and D. Frisby, in D. Frisby and M. Featherstone (eds.), *Simmel on Culture: Selected Writings*. London: Sage, 1997, pp. 262–270.

'Theatre and the Dramatic Actor: Part I', in Austin Harrington (ed.), *Georg Simmel: Essays on Art and Aesthetics*. Chicago: University of Chicago Press, 2020, pp. 261–266.

'Venice', trans. U. Teucher and T. M. Kemple, *Theory, Culture & Society* 24(7–8), 2007, pp. 42–46.

The View of Life: Four Metaphysical Essays with Journal Aphorisms, trans. J. A. Y. Andrews and D. N. Levine. Chicago: University of Chicago Press, 2010.

'The Women's Congress and Social Democracy', trans. M. Ritter and D. Frisby, in D. Frisby and M. Featherstone (eds.), *Simmel on Culture: Selected Writings*. London: Sage, 1997, pp. 270–274.

Secondary Literature

Adair-Toteff, Christopher. 'The "Antinomy of God": Simmel on Meister Eckhart and Nietzsche', *Simmel Newsletter* 3(1), 1993, pp. 10–16.

Adolf, Heinrich. *Erkenntnistheorie auf dem Weg zur Metaphysik: Interpretation, Modifikation und Überschreitung des Kantischen Apriorikonzepts bei Georg Simmel*. Munich: Herbert Utz, 2002.

Adolf, Heinrich. 'Kultur ohne Tragik: Cassirers Entschärfung von Simmels tragischer Konzeption von Kultur', *Dialektik* (2), 2003, pp. 75–103.

Aler, Jan. 'Zur Deutung von Rembrandts Luminismus (Wie Albert Verwey und Stefan George ihn diskutierten)', *Zeitschrift für Ästhetik und allgemeine Kunstwissenschaft* 12(2), 1967, pp. 204–242.

Amat, Matthieu. *Le relationisme philosophique de Georg Simmel: Une idée de la culture*. Paris: Honoré Champion, 2018.

Andreas-Salomé, Lou. 'Jesus der Jude', *Neue Deutsche Rundschau* 7, 1896, pp. 342–351.

Andreas-Salomé, Lou. 'Der Mensch als Weib: Ein Bild im Umriß' [1899], in *Die Erotik: Vier Aufsätze*. Frankfurt am Main: Ullstein, 1992, pp. 7–44.

Andreas-Salomé, Lou. 'Religion und Cultur: Religionspsychologische Studie', *Die Zeit* 183, 2 April 1898, pp. 5–7.

Anz, Thomas. *Literatur des Expressionismus*. Stuttgart: J. B. Metzler, 2010.

Arendt, Hannah. *The Human Condition* [1958]. Chicago: University of Chicago Press, 1998.

Arendt, Hannah. 'On Humanity in Dark Times: Thoughts about Lessing' [1959], in *Men in Dark Times*. New York: Harcourt, Brace & World, 1968, pp. 3–31.

Arnold, Matthew. *Culture and Anarchy: An Essay in Political and Social Criticism*, in *Culture and Anarchy and Other Writings*. Cambridge: Cambridge University Press, 1993, pp. 53–211.

Aschheim, Steven. *The Nietzsche Legacy in Germany 1890–1990*. Berkeley: University of California Press, 1992.

Assmann, Aleida. *Arbeit am nationalen Gedächtnis: Eine kurze Geschichte der deutschen Bildungsidee*. Frankfurt am Main: Campus, 1993.

Avenarius, Ferdinand. 'Kultur und Zivilisation', *Kunstwart* 14(2), 1901, pp. 81–83.

Bachofen, Johann Jakob. *Das Mutterrecht: Eine Untersuchung über die Gynaikokratie der alten Welt nach ihrer religiösen und rechtlichen Natur*. Stuttgart: Krais und Hoffmann, 1861.

Bachofen, Johann Jakob. *Myth, Religion and Mother Right: Selected Writings of J.J. Bachofen*, trans. R. Manheim. Princeton: Princeton University Press, 1967.

Barnard, Frederick M. *Herder's Social and Political Thought: From Enlightenment to Nationalism*. Oxford: Clarendon Press, 1965.

Barth, Paul. *Die Philosophie der Geschichte als Soziologie*. Leipzig: O. R. Reisland, 1897.

Bauch, Bruno. 'Nochmals "Ein Briefwechsel"', *Der Panther* 4(6), 1916, pp. 741–746.

Bauch, Bruno. 'Ueber Goethes philosophische Weltanschauung', *Preußische Jahrbücher* 115(3), 1904, pp. 518–529.

Becker, Willy. *Rembrandt als Dichter: Eine Untersuchung über das Poetische in den biblischen Darstellungen Rembrandts*. Leipzig: Klinkhardt & Biermann, 1909.

Behr, Michael, Volkhard Krech and Gert Schmidt. 'Editorischer Bericht', in *Georg Simmel Gesamtausgabe*. Frankfurt am Main: Suhrkamp, 1989–2015, vol. 10, pp. 409–421.

Beiser, Frederick C. *The Genesis of Neo-Kantianism 1796–1880*. Oxford: Oxford University Press, 2014.

Beiser, Frederick C. *Weltschmerz: Pessimism in German Philosophy, 1860–1900*. Oxford: Oxford University Press, 2016.

Ben-David, Joseph. *The Scientist's Role in Society*. Chicago: University of Chicago Press, 1984.

Bielschowsky, Albert. *The Life of Goethe*, 3 vols., trans. W. A. Cooper. New York: G. P. Putnam's Sons, 1905–1908.

Biemann, Asher D. *Dreaming of Michelangelo: Jewish Variations on a Modern Theme*. Stanford: Stanford University Press, 2012.

Blankertz, Herwig. *Bildung im Zeitalter der großen Industrie: Pädagogik, Schule und Berufsbildung im 19. Jahrhundert*. Hannover: Hermann Schroedel, 1969.

Bleicher, Josef. 'From Kant to Goethe: Georg Simmel on the Way to *Leben*', *Theory, Culture & Society* 24(6), 2007, pp. 139–158.

Blumenfeld, David. 'Perfection and Happiness in the Best Possible World', in N. Jolley (ed.), *The Cambridge Companion to Leibniz*. Cambridge: Cambridge University Press, 1995, pp. 383–393.

Bode, Wilhelm. *Rembrandt und seine Zeitgenossen*. Leipzig: E. A. Seemann, 1906.

Bode, Wilhelm and Wilhelm Valentiner. *Rembrandt in Bild und Wort*. Berlin: Rich. Bond, 1906.

Boeckh, August. 'Von der Philologie, besonders der klassischen in Beziehung zur morgenländischen, zum Unterricht und zur Gegenwart' [1850], in *Gesammelte kleine Schriften II: Reden gehalten auf der Universität und in der Akademie der Wissenschaften zu Berlin*. Leipzig: B. G. Teubner, 1859, pp. 183–199.

Böhringer, Hannes. 'Spuren von spekulativem Atomismus in Simmels formaler Soziologie', in H. Böhringer and K. Gründer (eds.), *Ästhetik und Soziologie um die Jahrhundertwende: Georg Simmel*. Frankfurt am Main: Vittorio Klostermann, 1976, pp. 105–114.

Bollenbeck, Georg. *Bildung und Kultur: Glanz und Elend eines deutschen Deutungsmusters*. Frankfurt am Main: Insel, 1994.

Bölsche, W. *Das Liebesleben in der Natur: Eine Entwickelungsgeschichte der Liebe*, vol. 3. Leipzig: Eugen Diederichs, 1903.

Botz-Bornstein, Torsten. 'What Is the Difference between Culture and Civilization? Two Hundred Years of Confusion', *Comparative Civilizations Review* 66, 2012, pp. 10–28.

Boyle, Nicholas. 'General Introduction: The Eighteenth and Nineteenth Centuries', in Nicholas Boyle and Liz Disley (eds.), *The Impact of Idealism: The Legacy of Post-Kantian German Thought, vol. I: Philosophy and Natural Sciences*, ed. Karl Ameriks. Cambridge: Cambridge University Press, 2013, pp. 1–40.

Brabant, Dominik. 'Vibrierendes Sehen: Simmels *Rembrandt* und die Kontingenz des kunstwissenschaftlichen Blicks', *KulturPoetik* 17(1), 2017, pp. 21–41.

Brasch, Moritz. 'Goethes Beziehungen zur Philosophie', *Die Gegenwart* 48(36), 1895, pp. 152–155; 48(37), 1895, pp. 168–172.

Braun, Otto. 'Review of M. Kronenberg, *Geschichte des deutschen Idealismus*', *Kant-Studien* 22, 1918, pp. 149–151.

Brausch, Ernst. 'Das psychologische Wesen der Religion', *Zeitschrift für wissenschaftliche Theologie* 37(2), 1894, pp. 161–174.

Breuer, Stefan. 'Im Grenzlosen sich zu finden', *Frankfurter Allgemeine Zeitung* 17, July 1999, p. 47.

Breysig, Kurt. *Von Gegenwart und von Zukunft des deutschen Menschen*. Berlin: Georg Bondi, 1912.

Bruch, Rüdiger vom. 'Einleitung: Kulturbegriff, Kulturkritik und Kulturwissenschaften um 1900', in Rüdiger vom Bruch, Friedrich Wilhelm Graf and Gangolf Hübinger (eds.), *Kultur und Kulturwissenschaften um 1900: Krise der Moderne und Glaube an die Wissenschaft*. Stuttgart: Franz Steiner, 1989, pp. 9–24.

Bruford, W. H. *Culture and Society in Classical Weimar 1775–1806*. Cambridge: University Press, 1962.

Bruford, W. H. *The German Tradition of Self-Cultivation: Bildung from Humboldt to Thomas Mann*. London: Cambridge University Press, 1975.

Bueno, Arthur. 'Economic Pathologies of Life', in G. Fitzi (ed.), *The Routledge International Handbook of Simmel Studies*. London: Routledge, 2021, pp. 336–349.

Bueno, Arthur. 'Rationality – Cultivation – Vitality: Simmel on the Pathologies of Modern Culture', *Dissonância: Critical Theory Journal* 2(2), 2018, pp. 96–135.

Burckhardt, Jacob. *The Civilization of the Renaissance in Italy*, trans. S. G. C. Middlemore. New York: Albert & Charles Boni, 1935.

Burckhardt, Jacob. *Kulturgeschichtliche Vorträge*. Stuttgart: Alfred Kröner, 1959.

Burckhardt, Jacob. *Weltgeschichtliche Betrachtungen*. Hamburg: Heinrich Ellermann, 1948.

Burdach, Konrad. 'Einleitung', in F. Schultz (ed.), *Goethes sämtliche Werke: Jubiläums-Ausgabe in 40 Bänden*. Stuttgart: J. G. Cotta, 1902–1912, vol. 5 [*West-östlicher Divan*], pp. v–l.

Busche, Hubertus. 'Georg Simmels "Tragödie der Kultur": 90 Jahre danach', *JABLIS: Jahrbuch für europäische Prozesse* 3, 2004, pp. 211–239.

Busche, Hubertus. '"Kultur": Ein Wort, viele Begriffe', in H. Busche et al. (eds.), *Kultur – Interdisziplinäre Zugänge*. Wiesbaden: Springer, 2018, pp. 3–41.

Busche, Hubertus. 'Was ist Kultur? Zweiter Teil: Die dramatisierende Verknüpfung verschiedener Kulturbegriffe in Georg Simmels "Tragödie der Kultur"', *Dialektik: Zeitschrift für Kuturphilosophie* (2), 2000, pp. 5–16.

Butler, E. M. *The Tyranny of Greece over Germany.* Boston: Beacon Press, 1955.

Carus, Carl Gustav. *Goethe: Zu dessen näheren Verständnis* [1842]. Dresden: Wolfgang Jess, 1955.

Cassirer, Ernst. *The Logic of the Cultural Science*, trans. S. G. Lofts. New Haven: Yale University Press, 2000.

Chamberlain, Houston Stewart. *Goethe.* Munich: F. Bruckmann, 1912.

Chapman, Mark D. *Religion and Cultural Synthesis in Wilhelmine Germany.* Oxford: Oxford University Press, 2001.

Clausewitz, Carl von. *On War*, trans. M. Howard and P. Paret. Oxford: Oxford University Press, 2007.

Cohen, Hermann. *Ästhetik des reinen Gefühls*, 2 vols. Berlin: Bruno Cassirer, 1912.

Cohen, Hermann. *Kants Begründung der Ethik.* Berlin: Ferd. Dümmler, 1877.

Cohen, Hermann. *Kants Theorie der Erfahrung*, 2nd ed. Berlin: Ferd. Dümmler, 1885.

Coser, Lewis A. 'Georg Simmel's Neglected Contributions to the Sociology of Women', *Signs: Journal of Women in Culture and Society* 2(4), 1977, pp. 869–876.

Coser, Lewis A. *Masters of Sociological Thought: Ideas in Historical and Social Context.* Long Grove, IL: Waveland Press, 1977.

Dahme, Heinz-Jürgen. *Soziologie als exakte Wissenschaft: Georg Simmels Ansatz und seine Bedeutung in der gegenwärtigen Soziologie.* Stuttgart: Ferdinand Enke, 1981, pp. 274–275.

D'Andrea, Fabio. 'Simmel: Bildung as the Form of Subjectivity', *Simmel Studies* 23 (1), 2019, pp. 43–66.

Davies, Peter. *Myth, Matriarchy and Modernity: Johann Jakob Bachofen in German Culture 1860–1945.* Berlin: Walter de Gruyter, 2010.

Deflem, Mathieu. 'The Sociology of the Sociology of Money: Simmel and the Contemporary Battle of the Classics', *Journal of Classical Sociology* 3(1), 2003, pp. 67–96.

Dewey, John. *Democracy and Education.* New York: The Free Press, 1944.

Dewey, John. *German Philosophy and Politics.* New York: Henry Holt and Company, 1915.

Dilthey, Wilhelm. *Einleitung in die Geisteswissenschaften: Versuch einer Grundlegung für das Studium der Gesellschaft und der Geschichte.* Berlin: Duncker & Humblot, 1883.

Dilthey, Wilhelm. *Das Erlebnis und die Dichtung.* Leipzig: B. G. Teubner, 1916.

Diner, Dan. *America in the Eyes of the Germans: An Essay on Anti-Americanism.* Princeton: Markus Wiener Publishers, 1996.

Doerry, Martin. *Übergangsmenschen: Die Mentalität der Wilhelminer und die Krise des Kaiserreichs.* Weinheim: Juventa, 1986.

Dohm, Hedwig. *Der Frauen Natur und Recht.* Berlin: Wedekind & Schwieger, 1876.

Dohmen, Günther. *Bildung und Schule: Die Entstehung des deutschen Bildungsbegriffs und die Entwicklung seines Verhältnisses zur Schule, vol. 1, Der religiöse und der organologische Bildungsbegriff.* Weinheim: Julius Beltz, 1964.

Dorner, A. 'Über das Wesen der Religion', *Theologische Studien und Kritiken* 56(1), 1883, pp. 217–277.

Douglas, Richard M. 'Talent and Vocation in Humanist and Protestant Thought', in T. K. Rabb and J. E. Seigel (eds.), *Action and Conviction in Early Modern Europe.* Princeton: Princeton University Press, 1969, pp. 261–298.

Düntzer, Heinrich. *Goethes Leben.* Leipzig: Fues's Verlag (R. Reisland), 1880.

Durkheim, Émile. *The Division of Labour in Society* [1893], trans. W. D. Halls. New York: The Free Press, 1997.

Durkheim, Émile. *The Elementary Forms of Religious Life* [1912], trans. C. Cosman. Oxford: Oxford University Press, 2008.

Eckhardt, Katja. *Die Auseinandersetzung zwischen Marianne Weber und Georg Simmel über die 'Frauenfrage'.* Stuttgart: ibidem, 2000.

Einstein, Carl. 'Anmerkungen', *Die Aktion* 2(35), 28 August 1912, pp. 1093–1094.

Eller, Cynthia. *Gentlemen and Amazons: The Myth of Matriarchal Prehistory, 1861–1900.* Berkeley: University of California Press, 2011.

Eucken, Rudolph. 'Goethe und die Philosophie', *Goethe-Jahrbuch* 21, 1900, pp. 3*–22*.

Eucken, Rudolph. *Zur Sammlung der Geister.* Leipzig: Quelle & Meyer, 1913.

Evans, Richard J. *The Feminist Movement in Germany, 1894–1933.* London: Sage, 1976.

Faath, Ute. *Mehr-als-Kunst: Zur Kunstphilosophie Georg Simmels.* Würzburg: Königshausen und Neumann, 1998.

Felski, Rita. *The Gender of Modernity.* Cambridge, MA: Harvard University Press, 1995.

Fichte, Johann Gottlieb. *Addresses to the German Nation*, trans. G. Moore. Cambridge: Cambridge University Press, 2008.

Fichte, Johann Gottlieb. *Beitrag zur Berechtigung der Urtheile des Publicums über die französische Revolution* [1793]. Berlin: Contumax, 2014.

Fiedler, Konrad. *Schriften über Kunst,* vol. 1. Munich: R. Piper & Co., 1913.

Firsching, Horst. 'Émile Durkheims Religionssoziologie – Made in Germany? Zu einer These vom Simon Deploige', in V. Krech and H. Tyrell (eds.), *Religionssoziologie um 1900.* Würzburg: Ergon, 1995, pp. 351–363.

Fischer, Aloys. 'Berufsbildung und Allgemeinbildung', *Zeitschrift für pädagogische Psychologie und experimentelle Pädagogik* 12(3), 1911, pp. 165–175.

Fischer, Kuno. *Arthur Schopenhauer.* Heidelberg: C. Winter, 1893.

Fischer, Kuno. *Geschichte der neuen Philosophie,* vols. 3–4, 2nd ed. Heidelberg: Friedrich Bassermann, 1869.

Fitzi, Gregor. '"Die Absicht, dem historischen Materialismus ein Stockwerk unterzubauen": Zur Beziehung von Simmel zu Marx', in O. Rammstedt (ed.), *Georg Simmels Philosophie des Geldes.* Frankfurt am Main: Suhrkamp, 2003, pp. 215–242.

Fitzi, Gregor. *The Challenge of Modernity: Simmel's Sociological Theory*. London: Routledge, 2019.

Fitzi, Gregor. *Soziale Erfahrung und Lebensphilosophie: Georg Simmels Beziehung zu Henri Bergson*. Constance: UVK, 2002.

Fitzi, Gregor. 'Zwischen Patriotismus und Kulturphilosophie: Zur Deutung der Simmelschen Position im Ersten Weltkrieg', *Simmel Newsletter* 7(2), 1997, pp. 115–130.

Fleischmann, Eugène. 'De Weber à Nietzsche', *Archives Européennes de Sociologie* 5 (2), 1964, pp. 190–238.

Forster, Michael N. *Herder's Philosophy*. Oxford: Oxford University Press, 2018.

Freudenthal, Gideon. '"Substanzbegriff und Funktionsbegriff" als Zivilisationstheorie bei Georg Simmel und Ernst Cassirer', in L. Bauer and K. Hamberger (eds.), *Gesellschaft denken: Eine erkenntnistheoretische Standortbestimmung der Sozialwissenschaften*. Vienna: Springer, 2002, pp. 251–276.

Frevert, Ute. *Women in German History: From Bourgeois Emancipation to Sexual Liberation*. Oxford: Berg Publishers, 1989.

Freyer, Hans. *Revolution von rechts*. Jena: Eugen Diederichs, 1931.

Freyer, Hans. *Über das Dominantwerden technischer Kategorien in der Lebenswelt der industriellen Gesellschaft*. Mainz: Akademie der Wissenschaften und der Literatur, 1960.

Freyer, Hans. 'Zur Bildungskrise der Gegenwart', *Die Erziehung* 6(10/11), 1931, pp. 597–626.

Frisby, David. *Fragments of Modernity: Theories of Modernity in the Work of Simmel, Kracauer and Benjamin*. Cambridge, MA: The MIT Press, 1986.

Frisby, David. *Georg Simmel*. London: Routledge, 2002.

Frisby, David. *Simmel and Since: Essays on Georg Simmel's Social Theory*. London: Routledge, 1992.

Frisby, David. *Sociological Impressionism: A Reassessment of Georg Simmel's Social Theory*. London: Routledge, 1992.

Frisby, David (ed.). *Georg Simmel in Wien: Texte und Kontexte aus dem Wien der Jahrhundertwende*. Vienna: WUV, 2000.

Fuente, Eduardo de la. 'The Art of Social Forms and the Social Forms of Art: The Sociology-Aesthetics Nexus in Georg Simmel's Thought', *Sociological Theory* 26 (4), 2008, pp. 344–362.

Gadamer, Hans-Georg. *Truth and Method* [1960], trans. J. Weinsheimer and D. G. Marshall. New York: Crossroad, 1989.

Gantner, Joseph. 'Jacob Burckhardts Urteil über Rembrandt und seine Konzeption des Klassischen', in *Concinnitas: Beiträge zum Problem des Klassischen*. Basel: Schwabe, 1944, pp. 83–114.

Gassen, Kurt. 'Erinnerungen an Simmel', in K. Gassen and M. Landmann (eds.), *Buch des Dankes an Georg Simmel*. Berlin: Duncker & Humblot, 1958, pp. 298–308.

Gassen, Kurt and Michael Landmann (eds.). *Buch des Dankes an Georg Simmel*. Berlin: Duncker & Humblot, 1958.

George, Stefan. 'Goethe-Tag', in Karl Robert Mandelkow (ed.), *Goethe im Urteil seiner Kritiker: Dokumente zur Wirkungsgeschichte Goethes in Deutschland*, part III: 1870–1918. Munich: C. H. Beck, 1979, pp. 308–309.

George, Stefan. *Der siebente Ring*. Berlin: Georg Bondi, 1907.

Gerhardt, Uta. 'The Two Faces of Modernity in Georg Simmel's Social Thought', *Simmel Studies* 16(1), 2006, pp. 49–74.

Geßner, Willfried. 'Geld als symbolische Form: Simmel, Cassirer, und die Objektivität der Kultur', *Simmel Newsletter* 6(1), 1996, pp. 1–30.

Geßner, Willfried. *Der Schatz im Acker: Georg Simmels Philosophie der Kultur*. Weilerswist: Velbrück Wissenschaft, 2003.

Geßner, Willfried. 'Tragödie oder Schauspiel? Cassirers Kritik an Simmels Kulturkritik', *Simmel Newsletter* 6(1), 1996, pp. 57–72.

Geuss, Raymond. 'Kultur, Bildung, Geist', *History & Theory* 35(2), 1996, pp. 151–164.

Giacomoni, Paola. *Classicità e frammento: Georg Simmel Goethiano*. Naples: Guida, 1995.

Gilcher-Holtey, Ingrid. 'Modelle "moderner" Weiblichkeit: Diskussionen im akademischen Milieu Heidelbergs um 1900', in R. M. Lepsius (ed.), *Bildungsbürgertum im 19. Jahrhundert, III: Lebensführung und ständische Vergesellschaftung*. Stuttgart: Klett-Cota, 1992, pp. 176–205.

Gilpin, Robert. *France in the Age of the Scientific State*. Princeton: Princeton University Press, 1968.

Goethe, J. W. von. *Wilhelm Meister's Apprenticeship*, trans. E. A. Blackall, in *Goethe's Collected Works*, vol. 9. New York: Suhrkamp Publishers, 1989.

Goethe, J. W. von. *Wilhelm Meister's Journeyman Years or The Renunciants*, trans. K. Winston, in *Goethe's Collected Works*, vol. 10. New York: Suhrkamp Publishers, 1989, pp. 93–440.

Goetz, Walter. *Geschichte der Deutschen Dante-Gesellschaft und der deutschen Dante-Forschung*. Weimar: Hermann Böhlaus, 1940.

Gogarten, Friedrich. *Die religiöse Entscheidung*. Jena: Diederichs, 1921.

Good, James A. *A Search for Unity in Diversity: The 'Permanent Hegelian Deposit' in the Philosophy of John Dewey*. London: Lexington Books, 2006.

Goodstein, Elizabeth S. *Georg Simmel and the Disciplinary Imaginary*. Stanford: Stanford University Press, 2017.

Goodstein, Elizabeth S. 'Sociology as a Sideline: Does It Matter That Georg Simmel (Thought He) Was a Philosopher?', in T. Kemple and O. Pyyhtinen (eds.), *The Anthem Companion to Georg Simmel*. London: Anthem Press, 2016, pp. 29–57.

Gordin, Jakob. *Untersuchungen zur Theorie des unendlichen Urteils*. Berlin: Akademie Verlag, 1929.

Graf, Friedrich Wilhelm. 'Why Theology? Strategies of Legitimation: Protestant Theology in German Protestantism', in Efraim Podoksik (ed.), *Doing Humanities in Nineteenth-Century Germany*. Leiden: Brill, 2019, pp. 40–58.

Grafton, Anthony. 'Polyhistor into *Philolog*: Notes on the Transformation of German Classical Scholarship, 1870–1850', *History of Universities* 3, 1983, pp. 159–192.

Grimm, Herman. 'Fiorenza: Anmerkungen zu einigen Gedichten Dante's und Michelangelo's', in *Fünfzehn Essays*. Gütersloh: C. Bertelsmann, 1822, pp. 1–61.

Grimm, Herman. *Goethe: Vorlesungen gehalten an der Kgl. Universität zu Berlin*, 2 vols. Stuttgart: J. G. Cotta, 1903.

Gundolf, Friedrich. Letter to Georg Simmel, 17.10.1914, in *Georg Simmel Gesamtausgabe*. Frankfurt am Main: Suhrkamp, 1989–2015, vol. 23, pp. 425–426.

Hagen, Karl. *Der Geist der Reformation und seine Gegensätze*, vol. 1. Erlangen: Palm, 1841.

Hamann, Richard. *Rembrandts Radierungen*. Berlin: Bruno Cassirer, 1906.

Harnack, Adolf. *Geschichte der Königlich Preussischen Akademie der Wissenschaften zu Berlin*, vol. 1. Berlin: Reichsdruckerei, 1900.

Harnack, Adolf. *Lehrbuch der Dogmengeschichte, vol. 1: Die Entstehung des kirchlichen Dogmas*, 3rd ed. Freiburg im Breisgau: J.C.B. Mohr, 1894.

Harnack, Adolf. 'Vom Großbetrieb der Wissenschaft' [1905], in *Aus Wissenschaft und Leben I*. Gießen: Alfred Töpelmann, 1911, pp. 10–20.

Harnack, Adolf. *Das Wesen des Christentums*. Leipzig: J.C. Hinrichs, 1900.

Harnack, Otto. 'Goethes Kunstanschauung in ihrer Bedeutung für die Gegenwart', *Goethe-Jahrbuch* 15, 1894, pp. 187–205.

Härpfer, Claudius. *Georg Simmel und die Entstehung der Soziologie in Deutschland: Eine netzwerksoziologische Studie*. Wiesbaden: Springer, 2014.

Harrington, Austin. 'Simmel und die Religionssoziologie', in H. Tyrell, O. Rammstedt and I. Meyer (eds.), *Georg Simmels große 'Soziologie': Eine kritische Sichtung nach hundert Jahren*. Bielefeld: transcript, 2011, pp. 275–299.

Hartmann, Alois. *Sinn und Wert des Geldes in der Philosophie von Georg Simmel und Adam (von) Müller: Untersuchungen zur anthropologisch sinn- und werttheoretischen und soziopolitisch-kulturellen Bedeutung des Geldes in der Lebenswelt und der Staatskunst*. Berlin: WiKu, 2002.

Hartmann, Eduard von. *Philosophie des Unbewussten: Versuch einer Weltanschauung*. Berlin: Carl Duncker, 1869.

Hartmann, Eduard von. *Zur Geschichte und Begründung des Pessimismus*. Berlin: Carl Duncker, 1880.

Hartmann, Eduard von. *Zur Geschichte und Begründung des Pessimismus*, 2nd ed. Leipzig: Wilhelm Friedrich, 1891.

Hausen, Karin. 'Family and Role-Division: The Polarisation of Sexual Stereotypes in the Nineteenth Century: An Aspect of the Dissociation of Work and Family Life', in Richard J. Evans and W. R. Lee (eds.), *German Family: Essays on the Social History of the Family in Nineteenth- and Twentieth-Century Germany*. London: Croom Helm, 1981, pp. 51–83.

Häußling, Roger. 'Nietzsche, Friedrich', in H.-P. Müller and T. Reitz (eds.), *Simmel-Handbuch: Begriffe, Hauptwerke, Aktualität*. Frankfurt am Main: Suhrkamp, 2018, pp. 398–405.

Havenstein, Martin. 'Chamberlains und Simmels "Goethe"', *Preußische Jahrbücher* 155, 1914, pp. 27–70, 271–291.

Heath, Arthur George. *The Moral and Social Significance of the Conception of Personality*. Oxford: Clarendon Press, 1921.

Heesen-Cremer, Gabriele von. 'Zum Problem des Kulturpessimismus: Schopenhauer-Rezeption bei Künstlern und Intellektuellen von 1871 bis 1918', in E. Mai, S. Waetzoldt and G. Wolandt (eds.), *Ideengeschichte und Kunstwissenschaft: Philosophie und bildende Kunst im Kaiserreich*. Berlin: Gebr. Mann, 1983, pp. 45–70.

Hegar, Alfred. *Spezialismus und allgemeine Bildung*. Freiburg: J.C.B. Mohr, 1882.

Hegel, G. W. F. *Hegel's Logic* (Part I of the Encyclopaedia of the Philosophical Sciences [1830]), trans. W. Wallace. Oxford: Clarendon Press, 1975.

Hegel, G. W. F. *Hegel's Science of Logic*, 2 vols., trans. W. H. Johnston and L. G. Struthers. London: Georg Allen & Unwin, 1929.

Hegel, G. W. F. *Phenomenology of Spirit* [1807], trans. A. V. Miller. Oxford: Oxford University Press, 1977.

Heidler, Irmgard. *Der Verleger Eugen Diederichs und seine Welt (1896–1930)*. Wiesbaden: Harrassowitz, 1998.

Heine, Heinrich. 'Ideas: Book Le Grand', trans. Ch. G. Leland, in *Pictures of Travel*. New York: D. Appleton and Company, 1904, pp. 121–178.

Helle, Horst-Jürgen. 'Introduction', in G. Simmel, *Essays on Religion*. New Haven: Yale University Press, 1997, pp. xi–xx.

Heyfelder, Erich. 'Die Ausdrücke "Renaissance" und "Humanismus"', *Deutsche Literaturzeitung* 34, 6 September 1913, pp. 2245–2250.

Hillebrand, Karl. 'Halbbildung und Gymnasialreform: Ein Appell an die Unzufriedenen', *Deutsche Rundschau* 18, 1879, pp. 422–451.

Hillebrand, Karl. 'On Half-Culture in Germany: Its Causes and Remedies', *Contemporary Review* 38, 1880, pp. 199–220.

Hillebrand, Karl. 'On the Sources of German Discontent', *Contemporary Review* 38, 1880, pp. 40–54.

Hippel, Theodor Gottlieb von. *Über die bürgerliche Verbesserung der Weiber*. Berlin: Vossische Buchhandlung, 1792.

Hirst, Paul. 'Carl Schmitt's Decisionism', in Chantal Mouffe (ed.), *The Challenge of Carl Schmitt*. London: Verso, 1999, pp. 7–17.

Holl, Karl. 'Die Geschichte des Worts Beruf', in *Gesammelte Aufsätze zur Kirchengeschichte, vol. 3: Der Westen*. Tübingen: J. C. B. Mohr, 1928, pp. 189–219.

Hölter, Eva. *'Der Dichter der Hölle und des Exils': Historische und systematische Profil der deutschsprachigen Dante-Rezeption*. Würzburg: Königshausen & Neumann, 2002.

Holzhey, Helmut. 'Der Neukantianismus', in H. Holzhey and W. Röd (eds.), *Die Philosophie des ausgehenden 19. und des 20. Jahrhunderts 2: Neukantianismus, Idealismus, Realismus, Phänomenologie*. Munich: C.H. Beck, 2004, pp. 11–129.

Holzhey, Helmut. 'Neukantianismus', in J. Ritter and K. Gründer (eds.), *Historisches Wörterbuch der Philosophie*. Darmstadt: Wissenschaftliche Buchgesellschaft, 1984, pp. 747–754.

Horlacher, Rebekka. '*Bildung* – A Construction of a History of Philosophy of Education', *Studies in Philosophy and Education* 23(5/6), 2004, pp. 409–426.

Hornig, Gottfried. *Johann Salomo Semler: Studien zu Leben und Werk des Hallenser Aufklärungstheologen*. Tübingen: Niemeyer, 1996.

Hotam, Yotam. 'Gnosis and Modernity: A Postwar German Intellectual Debate on Secularisation, Religion and "Overcoming" the Past', *Totalitarian Movements and Political Religions* 8(3), 2007, pp. 591–608.

Howard, T. A. *Protestant Theology and the Making of the Modern German University*. Oxford: Oxford University Press, 2006.

Huerkamp, Claudia. 'Die preußisch-deutsche Ärtzeschaft als Teil des Bildungsbürgertums: Wandel in Lage und Selbstverständnis vom ausgehenden 18. Jahrhundert bis zum Kaiserreich', in Werner Conze and Jürgen Kocka (eds.), *Bildungsbürgertum im 19. Jahrhundert, vol. 1: Bildungssystem und Professionalisierung in internationalen Vergleichen*. Stuttgart: Klett-Cotta, 1985, pp. 358–387.

Hughes, H. Stuart. *Consciousness and Society: The Reorientation of European Social Thought 1890–1930*. New York: Alfred A. Knopff, 1961.

Humboldt, Wilhelm von. *The Limits of State Action*, trans. J. W. Burrow. Indianapolis: Liberty Fund, 1993.

Hurwicz, Elias. 'Georg Simmel als jüdischer Denker', *Neue jüdische Monatshefte* 3, 1918/19, pp. 196–198.

Imorde, Joseph. *Michelangelo Deutsch!* Berlin: Deutscher Kunstverlag, 2009.

Jaeger, Werner. 'Philologie und Historie' [1914], in *Humanistische Reden und Vorträge*. Berlin: Walter de Gruyter, 1937, pp. 1–17.

Jaume, Lucien. *Tocqueville: The Aristocratic Sources of Liberty*, trans. A. Goldhammer. Princeton: Princeton University Press, 2013.

Jefferies, Matthew. *Imperial Culture in Germany, 1871–1918*. Basingstoke: Palgrave Macmillan, 2003.

Joas, Hans. *The Genesis of Values*. Chicago: University of Chicago Press, 2000.

Joël, Karl. 'Erinnerungen an Simmel', in K. Gassen and M. Landmann (eds.), *Buch des Dankes an Georg Simmel*. Berlin: Duncker & Humblot, 1958, pp. 166–169.

Joël, Karl. 'Das Zeitalter der Ethik. II: Das Herz der Wissenschaft', *Neue Deutsche Rundschau* 6(1), 1895, pp. 470–481.

Jones, Robert Alun. *The Development of Durkheim's Social Realism*. Cambridge: Cambridge University Press, 1999.

Kaftan, Julius. *Das Wesen der christlichen Religion*. Basel: C. Detloff, 1888.

Kandal, Terry R. *The Woman Question in Classical Sociological Theory*. Miami: Florida International University Press, 1988.

Kant, Immanuel. *Critique of Practical Reason, in Practical Philosophy*, trans. M. J. Gregor. Cambridge: Cambridge University Press, 1996, pp. 137–271.

Kant, Immanuel. 'Idea for a Universal History with a Cosmopolitan Purpose', in *Political Writings*, trans. H. B. Nisbet. Cambridge: Cambridge University Press, 1991, pp. 41–53.

Kemple, Thomas. *Simmel*. Cambridge: Polity Press, 2018.

Kerschensteiner, Georg. *Grundfragen der Schulorganisation.* Leipzig: B. G. Teubner, 1912.

Kierkegaard, Søren. *Either/Or*, vol. II, trans. W. Lowrie. Princeton: Princeton University Press, 1972.

Kierkegaard, Søren. 'The Present Age', in *The Present Age and The Difference between a Genius and an Apostle*, trans. A. Dru. New York: Harper & Row, 1962, pp. 31–86.

Kierkegaard, Søren. 'Repetition', in *Repetition and Philosophical Crumbs*, trans. M. G. Piety. Oxford: Oxford University Press, 2009, pp. 1–81.

Kindermann, Heinz. *Das Goethebild des 20. Jahrhundert.* Darmstadt: Wissenschaftliche Buchgesellschaft, 1966.

Klautke, Egbert. 'The French Reception of *Völkerpsychologie* and the Origins of the Social Sciences', *Modern Intellectual History* 10(2), 2013, pp. 293–316.

Klautke, Egbert. *The Mind of the Nation: Völkerpsychologie in Germany, 1851–1955.* New York: Berghahn Books, 2016.

Klautke, Egbert. '*Völkerpsychologie* in Nineteenth-Century Germany: Lazarus, Steinthal, Wundt', in Efraim Podoksik (ed.), *Doing Humanities in Nineteenth-Century Germany.* Leiden: Brill, 2019, pp. 243–263.

Klein, André. Simmel und Lazarus: Kulturwissenschaft und Völkerpsychologie in ihren Beziehungen, PhD dissertation, University of Leipzig, 2004.

Klemm, Gustav. *Allgemeine Cultur-Geschichte der Menschheit.* Leipzig: B. G. Teubner, 1843.

Klinger, Cornelia. 'Geschlecht', in H.-P. Müller and T. Reitz (eds.), *Simmel-Handbuch: Begriffe, Hauptwerke, Aktualität.* Frankfurt am Main: Suhrkamp, 2018, pp. 241–246.

Klinger, Cornelia. 'Simmels Geschlechtertheorie zwischen kritischer Beobachtung und Metaphysik', in H.-P. Müller and T. Reitz (eds.), *Simmel-Handbuch: Begriffe, Hauptwerke, Aktualität.* Frankfurt am Main: Suhrkamp, 2018, pp. 828–843.

Knöbl, Wolfgang. 'Der Krieg und die geistigen Entscheidungen (1917)', in H.-P. Müller and T. Reitz (eds.), *Simmel-Handbuch: Begriffe, Hauptwerke, Aktualität.* Frankfurt am Main: Suhrkamp, 2018, pp. 734–744.

Koenig, Heike. 'Enabling the Individual: Simmel, Dewey and "The Need for a Philosophy of Education"', *Simmel Studies* 23(1), 2019, pp. 109–146.

Kölbl, Alois. *Das Leben der Form: Georg Simmels kunstphilosophischer Versuch über Rembrandt.* Vienna: Böhlau, 1998.

Köhnke, Klaus Christian. 'Georg Simmel als Jude', *Simmel Newsletter* 5(1), 1995, pp. 53–72.

Köhnke, Klaus Christian. *Der junge Simmel: in Theoriebeziehungen und sozialen Bewegungen.* Frankfurt am Main: Suhrkamp, 1996.

Köhnke, Klaus Christian. *The Rise of Neo-Kantianism: German Academic Philosophy between Idealism and Positivism.* Cambridge: Cambridge University Press, 1991.

Kösser, Uta. 'Simmels "Rembrandt"', *Simmel Studies* 13(2), 2003, pp. 439–483.

Kracauer, Siegfried. 'Über die Philosophie Georg Simmels und ihren Zusammenhang mit dem geistigen Leben der Zeit', in P. U. Hein (ed.), *Georg Simmel*. Frankfurt am Main: Peter Lang, 1990, pp. 131–158.

Kramme, Rüdiger. 'Brücke und Trost? Zu Georg Simmels Engagement für den "Logos"', *Simmel Newsletter* 3(1), 1993, pp. 64–73.

Kramme, Rüdiger and Otthein Rammstedt, 'Editorischer Bericht', in *Georg Simmel Gesamtausgabe*. Frankfurt am Main: Suhrkamp, 1989–2015, vol. 14, pp. 461–480.

Krech, Volkhard. *Georg Simmels Religionstheorie*. Tübingen: Mohr Siebeck, 1998.

Krech, Volkhard. 'Die "Soziologie der Religion": Neu gestehen', in R. Lautmann and H. Wienold (eds.), *Georg Simmel und das Leben in der Gegenwart*. Wiesbaden: Springer, 2018, pp. 325–346.

Kroeber, A. L. and Clyde Kluckhohn. *Culture: A Critical Review of Concepts and Definitions*. New York: Vintage Books, 1952.

Krois, John Michael. 'Ten Theses on Cassirer's Late Reception of Simmel's Thought', *Simmel Newsletter* 6(1), 1996, pp. 73–78.

Kruckis, Hans-Martin. *'Ein potenziertes Abbild der Menschheit': Biographischer Diskurs und Etablierung der Neugermanistik in der Goethe-Biographik bis Gundolf*. Heidelberg: Universitätsverlag C. Winter, 1995.

Kugler, Franz. *Handbuch der Geschichte der Malerei in Deutschland, den Niederlanden, Spanien, Frankreich und England*. Berlin: Duncker und Humblot, 1837.

Lamprecht, Karl. *Americana: Reiseeindrücke, Betrachtungen, Geschichtliche Gesamtansicht*. Freiburg im Breisgau: Hermann Heyfelder, 1906.

Landmann, Edith. 'Erinnerungen an Simmel', in K. Gassen and M. Landmann (eds.), *Buch des Dankes an Georg Simmel*. Berlin: Duncker & Humblot, 1958, pp. 208–211.

Landmann, Michael. 'Bausteine zur Biographie', in K. Gassen and M. Landmann (eds.), *Buch des Dankes an Georg Simmel*. Berlin: Duncker & Humblot, 1958, pp. 11–33.

Landmann, Michael. 'Georg Simmel: Konturen seines Denkens', in H. Böhringer and K. Gründer (eds.), *Ästhetik und Soziologie um die Jahrhundertwende: Georg Simmel*. Frankfurt am Main: Vittorio Klostermann, 1976, pp. 3–11.

Landmann, Michael. 'Georg Simmel und Stefan George', in H.-J. Dahme and O. Rammstedt (eds.), *Georg Simmel und die Moderne*. Frankfurt am Main: Suhrkamp, 1984, pp. 147–173.

Langbehn, Julius. *Rembrandt als Erzieher: Von einem Deutschen*. Leipzig: C. L. Hirschfeld, 1890.

Lange, Friedrich Albert. *Geschichte des Materialismus und Kritik seiner Bedeutungen in der Gegenwart*, 1st ed. Iserlohn: J. Baedeker, 1866.

Lange, Friedrich Albert. *Geschichte des Materialismus und Kritik seiner Bedeutungen in der Gegenwart*, vol. 2, 2nd ed. Iserlohn: J. Baedeker, 1875.

Langguth, Adolf. *Die Bilanz der akademischen Bildung*. Berlin: Carl Heymann, 1901.

Lasch, Gustav. 'Mystik und Protestantismus', *Religion und Geisteskultur* 5, 1911, pp. 34–52.

Lasker, Eduard. 'Ueber Halbbildung' [1878], in *Wege und Ziele der Culturentwickelung*. Leipzig: Brockhaus, 1881, pp. 141–205.

Lautner, Max. *Wer ist Rembrandt? Grundlagen zu einem Neubau der holländischen Kunstgeschichte*. Breslau, J. U. Kern, 1891.

LaVopa, Anthony J. *Grace, Talent, and Merit: Poor Students, Clerical Careers, and Professional Ideology in Eighteenth-Century Germany*. Cambridge: Cambridge University Press, 1988.

Lazarus, M. 'Bildung und Wissenschaft [1856]', in *Leben der Seele: in Monographien über seine Erscheinungen und Gesetze*, 2nd ed. Berlin: Ferd. Dümmler, 1876, vol. 1, pp. 3–123.

Lazarus, M. 'Einige synthetische Gedanken zur Völkerpsychologie', *Zeitschrift für Völkerpsychologie und Sprachwissenschaft* 3(1), 1865, pp. 1–94.

Lazarus, M. 'Ueber das Verhältnis des Einzelnen zur Gesammtheit', in *Leben der Seele: in Monographien über seine Erscheinungen und Gesetze*, 2nd ed. Berlin: Ferd. Dümmler, 1876, vol. 1, pp. 321–411.

Lazarus, M. *Was heißt national?* Berlin: Ferd. Dümmler, 1880.

Lazarus, M. 'Zum Ursprung der Sitte [1860]' in *Leben der Seele: in Monographien über seine Erscheinungen und Gesetze*, 2nd ed. Berlin: Ferd. Dümmler, 1876, vol. 3, pp. 349–420.

Lechner, Frank J. 'Social Differentiation and Modernity: On Simmel's Macrosociology', in M. Kaern, B. S. Phillips and R. S. Cohen (eds.), *Georg Simmel and Contemporary Sociology*. Dordrecht: Kluwert Academic Publishers, 1990, pp. 155–179.

Leck, Ralph M. *Georg Simmel and Avant-Garde Sociology: The Birth of Modernity, 1880–1920*. Amherst, NY: Humanity Books, 2000.

Léger, François. *La Pensée de Georg Simmel: Contribution à l'histoire des idées en Allemagne au début du XXe siècle*. Paris: Kime, 1989.

Leibniz, Gottfried Wilhelm. 'Correspondence with Arnauld [1686]', in *Philosophical Writings*, trans. M. Morris. London: J. M. Dent, 1934, pp. 52–87.

Leibniz, Gottfried Wilhelm. 'Monadology [1714]', in *Philosophical Writings*, trans. M. Morris. London: J. M. Dent, 1934, pp. 3–20.

Leppmann, Wolfgang. *The German Image of Goethe*. Oxford: Clarendon Press, 1969.

Levine, Donald N. '*Soziologie* and *Lebensanschauung*: Two Approaches to Synthesizing "Kant" and "Goethe" in Simmel's Work', *Theory, Culture & Society* 29(7–8), 2012, pp. 26–52.

Levine, Donald N. *Visions of the Sociological Tradition*. Chicago: University of Chicago Press, 1995.

Lexis, Wilhelm et al. *Die allgemeinen Grundlagen der Kultur der Gegenwart*. Berlin: B. G. Teubner, 1906.

Lexis, Wilhelm. 'Das Wesen der Kultur', in W. Lexis et al., *Die allgemeinen Grundlagen der Kultur der Gegenwart*. Berlin: B. G. Teubner, 1906, pp. 11–53.

Lichtblau, Klaus. 'Ästhetische Konzeptionen im Werk Georg Simmels', *Simmel Newsletter* 1(1), 1991, pp. 22–35.

Lichtblau, Klaus. *Georg Simmel*. Frankfurt am Main: Campus, 1997.

Lichtblau, Klaus. 'Das "Pathos der Distanz": Präliminarien zur Nietzsche-Rezeption bei Georg Simmel', in H.-J. Dahme and O. Rammstedt (eds.), *Georg Simmel und die Moderne*. Frankfurt am Main: Suhrkamp, 1984, pp. 231–281.

Lichtenstein, Ernst. 'Bildung', in J. Ritter (ed.), *Historisches Wörterbuch der Philosophie*. Basel: Schwabe & Co., 1971, vol. i, pp. 921–937.

Lichtenstein, Ernst. *Zur Entwicklung des Bildungsbegriffs von Meister Eckhart bis Hegel*. Heidelberg: Quelle & Mayer, 1966.

Liebersohn, Harry. 'The American Academic Community before the First World War: A Comparison with the German "Bildungsbürgertum"', in Werner Conze and Jürgen Kocka (eds.), *Bildungsbürgertum im 19. Jahrhundert, vol. 1: Bildungssystem und Professionalisierung in internationalen Vergleichen*. Stuttgart: Klett-Cotta, 1985, pp. 163–185.

Liebeschütz, Hans. *Von Georg Simmel zu Franz Rosenzweig: Studien zum Jüdischen Denken im deutschen Kulturbereich*. Tübingen: J. C. B. Mohr, 1970.

Liebig, Hans v. 'Nietzsches Religion', *Die Umschau* 4(42), 1900, pp. 821–826.

Liebmann, Otto. *Kant und die Epigonen: Eine kritische Abhandlung*. Stuttgart: Carl Schober, 1865.

Lilienfeld, Paul v. *Die Religion betrachtet vom Standpunkte der real-genetischen Socialwissenschaft, oder Versuch einer natürlichen Theologie*. Hamburg: Gebr. Behre, 1881.

Litt, Theodor. *Berufsbildung und Allgemeinbildung*. Wiesbaden: Eberhard Brockhaus, 1947.

Litt, Theodor. *Das Bildungsideal der deutschen Klassik und die moderne Arbeitswelt*. Bonn: Bundeszentrale für Heimatdienst, 1958.

Loader, Colin. *Alfred Weber and the Crisis of Culture, 1890–1933*. New York: Palgrave Macmillan, 2012.

Loiskandl, Helmut, Deena Weinstein and Michael Weinstein. 'Introduction', in G. Simmel, *Schopenhauer and Nietzsche*. Amherst, NY: University of Chicago Press, 1986, pp. xi–lii.

Lovejoy, Arthur O. *The Great Chain of Being: A Study in the History of Ideas*. Cambridge, MA: Harvard University Press, 1936.

Löwith, Karl. *From Hegel to Nietzsche: The Revolution in Nineteenth-Century Thought*, trans. D. E. Green. New York: Columbia University Press, 1964.

Löwith, Karl. *Martin Heidegger and European Nihilism*, trans. G. Steiner. New York: Columbia University Press, 1995.

Ludwig, Emil. 'Erinnerungen an Simmel', in K. Gassen and M. Landmann (eds.), *Buch des Dankes an Georg Simmel*. Berlin: Duncker & Humblot, 1958, pp. 152–157.

Ludwig, Emil. *Goethe: Geschichte eines Menschen*, vol. 1. Stuttgart: J.G. Cotta'sche Buchhandlung Nachfolger, 1922.

McClelland, Charles E. *State, Society, and University in Germany 1700–1914*. Cambridge: Cambridge University Press, 1980.

Mamelet, A. *Le relativisme philosophique chez Georg Simmel*. Paris: Félix Aclan, 1914.

Mandelkow, Karl Robert. *Goethe in Deutschland: Rezeptionsgeschichte eines Klassikers*, 2 vols. Munich: C. H. Beck, 1980–1989.

Mann, Heinrich. 'Zum Verständnisse Nietzsches', *Das Zwanzigste Jahrhundert* 6 (9), 1896, pp. 245–251.

Mann, Thomas. *Reflections of a Nonpolitical Man*, trans. W. D. Morris. New York: Frederick Ungar, 1983.

Marchand, Suzanne. 'Arnold Böcklin und die Krise des Neoklassizismus in Deutschland', in Eva Koczinsky (ed.), *Ruinen in der Moderne: Archäologie und die Künste*. Berlin: Dietrich Reimer, 2011, pp. 161–172.

Marx, Karl. 'The Eighteenth Brumaire of Louis Bonaparte', in *Marx/Engels Collected Works*, vol. 11. Moscow: Progress Publishers, 1979, pp. 99–197.

Meier-Graefe, Julius. *Entwickelungsgeschichte der modernen Kunst*. Stuttgart: Hoffmann, 1904.

Meier-Graefe, Julius. *Der Fall Böcklin und die Lehre von den Einheiten*. Stuttgart: Julius Hoffmann, 1905.

Menze, Clemens. *Die philosophische Idee der Universität und ihre Krise im Zeitalter der Wissenschaften*. Krefeld: Scherpe, 1975.

Meschiari, Alberto. 'Moritz Lazarus and Georg Simmel', *Simmel Newsletter* 7(1), 1997, pp. 11–16.

Mestrovic, Stjepan G. 'Simmel's Sociology in Relation to Schopenhauer's Philosophy', in M. Kaern, B. S. Phillips and R. S. Cohen (eds.), *Georg Simmel and Contemporary Sociology*. Dordrecht: Kluwert Academic Publishers, 1990, pp. 181–197.

Meyer, Ingo. *Georg Simmels Ästhetik: Autonomiepostulat und soziologische Referenz*. Weilerswist: Velbrück, 2017.

Meyer-Erlach, Wolf. *Dante: Der Prophet der nordischen Sehnsucht*. Munich: J. F. Lehmann, 1927.

Midgley, David. 'After Materialism – Reflections of Idealism in *Lebensphilosophie*: Dilthey, Bergson and Simmel', in Nicholas Boyle and Liz Disley (eds.), *The Impact of Idealism: The Legacy of Post-Kantian German Thought, vol. 2: Historical, Social and Political Thought*, ed. John Walker. Cambridge: Cambridge University Press, 2013, pp. 161–185.

Mirandola, Giovanni Pico della. *Oration on the Dignity of Man*, trans. A. R. Caponigri. Washington: Regnery Publishing, 1956.

Mitzman, Arthur. *Sociology and Estrangement: Three Sociologists in Imperial Germany*. New York: Alfred A. Knopf, 1973.

Mommsen, Theodor. 'Das Verhältnis der Wissenschaft zum Staat' [1895], in *Reden und Aufsätze*. Berlin: Weidmannsche Buchhandlung, 1905, pp. 196–199.

Mommsen, Wolfgang J. (ed.). *Kultur und Krieg: Die Rolle der Intellektuellen, Künstler, Schriftsteller im Ersten Weltkrieg*. Munich: R. Oldenbourg, 1996.

Montemaggi, Francesca E. S. *Authenticity and Religion in the Pluralistic Age: A Simmelian Study of Christian Evangelicals and New Monastics*. Lanham: Lexington Books, 2019.

Moran, Dermot. 'Meister Eckhart in 20th-Century Philosophy', in Jeremiah Hackett (ed.), *A Companion to Meister Eckhart*. Leiden: Brill, 2013, pp. 669–698.

Morris-Reich, Amos. 'The Beautiful Jew is a Moneylender: Money and Individuality in Simmel's Rehabilitation of the "Jew"', *Theory, Culture & Society* 20(4), 2003, pp. 127–142.

Morris-Reich, Amos. 'Georg Simmel's Logic of the Future: "The Stranger," Zionism, and "Bounded Contingency"', *Theory, Culture & Society* 36(5), 2019, pp. 71–94.

Morris-Reich, Amos. 'Three Paradigms of "The Negative Jew": Identity from Simmel to Žižek', *Jewish Social Studies* 10(2), 2004, pp. 179–214.

Morwitz, Ernst. *Die Dichtung Stefan Georges*. Berlin: Georg Blondi, 1943.

Morwitz, Ernst. 'Erinnerungen an Simmel', in K. Gassen and M. Landmann (eds.), *Buch des Dankes an Georg Simmel*. Berlin: Duncker & Humblot, 1958, pp. 276–277.

Müller, Hans-Peter. 'Wie ist Individualität möglich? Strukturelle und kulturellen Bedingungen eines modernen Kulturideals', *Zeitschrift für Theoretische Soziologie* 4(1), 2015, pp. 89–111.

Müller-Lyer, Franz. *The History of Social Development*, trans. E. Coote Lake and H. A. Lake. London: George Allen & Unwin, 1920.

Müller-Lyer, Franz. *Phasen der Kultur und Richtungen des Fortschritts: Soziologische Überblicke*. Munich: J.F. Lehmann, 1908.

Münch, Wilhelm. 'Kulturfortschritt und Gegenwart', in *Zum deutschen Kultur- und Bildungsleben*. Berlin: Weidmannsche Buchhandlung, 1912, pp. 26–71.

Muther, Richard. *Rembrandt*. Berlin: Bard, Marquardt, 1906.

Muther, Richard. *Rembrandt: Ein Künstlerleben*. Berlin: Egon Fleischel & Co., 1904.

Nachtsheim, Stephan. 'The Concept and Philosophy of Culture in Neo-Kantianism', in Nicholas Boyle and Liz Disley (eds.), *The Impact of Idealism: The Legacy of Post-Kantian German Thought, vol. II: Historical, Social and Political Thought*, ed. John Walker. Cambridge: Cambridge University Press, 2013, pp. 136–160.

Natorp, Paul. 'Kant und die Marburger Schule', *Kant-Studien* 17, 1912, pp. 193–221.

Neumann, Carl. *Rembrandt*. Berlin: W. Spemann, 1902.

Neumann, Carl. 'Zu Arnold Böcklins siebenzigstem Geburtstag', *Die Kunst für Alle* 13(1), 1897, pp. 1–6.

Niethammer, Friedrich Immanuel. *Der Streit des Philanthropinismus und Humanismus in der Theorie des Erziehungs-Unterrichts unsrer Zeit*. Jena: Friedrich Frommann, 1808.

Nietzsche, Friedrich. 'Aus dem Nachlaß', in Karl Robert Mandelkow (ed.), *Goethe im Urteil seiner Kritiker: Dokumente zur Wirkungsgeschichte Goethes in Deutschland, part III: 1870–1918*. Munich: C. H. Beck, 1979, p.137.

Nietzsche, Friedrich. *On the Future of Our Educational Institutions*, trans. M. W. Grenke. South Bend: St. Augustine's Press, 2004.

Nietzsche, Friedrich. *On the Genealogy of Morality*, trans. C. Diethe. Cambridge: Cambridge University Press, 1994.

Nietzsche, Friedrich. 'Twilight of the Idols or How to Philosophize with a Hammer', trans. Judith Norman, in *The Anti-Christ, Ecce Homo, Twilight of the Idols, and Other Writings*. Cambridge: Cambridge University Press, 2005, pp. 153–229.

Nietzsche, Friedrich. *Untimely Meditations*, trans. R. J. Hollingdale. Cambridge: Cambridge University Press, 1997.

Nipkow, Karl Ernst. '"Ganzheitliche Bildung" zwischen dem Ich und dem anderen: Eine anthropologisch-ethische und bildungsphilosophische Skizze', in V. Drehsen (ed.), *Der 'ganze' Mensch: Perspektiven lebensgeschichtlicher Individualität*. Berlin: Walter de Gruyter, 1997, pp. 407–430.

Oakes, Guy. 'Introduction: The Problem of Women in Simmel's Theory of Culture', in G. Oakes (ed.), *Georg Simmel: On Women, Sexuality, and Love*. New Haven: Yale University Press, 1984, pp. 3–62.

Oakes, Guy. 'Metaphysik des Geldes: Die *Philosophie des Geldes* als Philosophie', in W. Geßner and R. Kramme (eds.), *Aspekte der Geldkultur: Neue Beiträge zu Georg Simmels*. Philosophie des Geldes. Magdeburg: Scriptum, 2002, pp. 63–76.

Oberholzer, Niklaus. *Das Michelangelo-Bild in der deutschen Literatur: Beitrag zur Geschichte der Künstlerdichtung*. Fribourg, Switzerland: Universitätsverlag, 1969.

O'Boyle, Leonore. 'Learning for Its Own Sake: The German University as Nineteenth-Century Model', *Comparative Studies in Society and History* 25(1), 1983, pp. 3–25.

Oppenheimer, Franz. 'Werdende Wissenschaften', *Neue Rundschau* 15, 1904, pp. 823–828.

O'Regan, Cyril. 'Eckhart Reception in the 19th Century', in Jeremiah Hackett (ed.), *A Companion to Meister Eckhart*. Leiden: Brill, 2013, pp. 629–667.

Orringer, Nelson R. 'Simmel's *Goethe* in the Thought of Ortega y Gasset', *MLN* 92(2), 1977, pp. 296–311.

Oz-Salzberger, Fania. *Translating the Enlightenment: Scottish Civic Discourse in Eighteenth-Century Germany*. Oxford: Clarendon Press, 1995.

Papcke, Sven. 'Jungbrunnen oder Fegefeuer? Georg Simmel und das Kriegserlebnis 1914–1918', in R. Lautmann and H. Wienold (eds.), *Georg Simmel und das Leben in der Gegenwart*. Wiesbaden: Springer, 2018, pp. 397–421.

Parkins, Ilya. 'Fashion, Femininity and the Ambiguities of the Modern: A Feminist Theoretical Approach to Simmel', in D. D. Kim (ed.), *Georg Simmel in Translation: Interdisciplinary Border-Crossings in Culture and Modernity*. Newcastle: Cambridge Scholars Press, 2006, pp. 28–49.

Partyga, Dominika. 'Simmel's Reading of Nietzsche: The Promise of "Philosophical Sociology"', *Journal of Classical Sociology* 16(4), 2016, pp. 414–437.

Pascher, Manfred. *Einführung in den Neukantianismus: Kontext – Grundpositionen – Praktische Philosophie*. Munich: Wilhelm Fink, 1997.

Passmore, John. *A Hundred Years of Philosophy*. London: Penguin Books, 1994.

Pauen, Michael. *Pessimismus: Geschichtsphilosophie, Metaphysik und Moderne von Nietzsche bis Spengler*. Berlin: Akademie, 1997.

Paulsen, Friedrich. 'Arthur Schopenhauer' [1882], in *Schopenhauer, Hamlet, Mephistopheles: Drei Aufsätze zur Naturgeschichte des Pessimismus*. Stuttgart: J. G. Cotta, 1911, pp. 13–111.

Paulsen, Friedrich. *Geschichte des gelehrten Unterrichts: Auf den deutschen Schulen und Universitäten vom Ausgang des Mittelalters bis zur Gegenwart.* Leipzig: Veit, 1885.

Paulsen, Friedrich. 'Goethes ethische Anschauungen', *Goethe-Jahrbuch* 23, 1902, pp.3*–32*.

Paulsen, Friedrich. 'Das moderne Bildungswesen', in W. Lexis et al. (eds), *Die allgemeinen Grundlagen der Kultur der Gegenwart.* Berlin: B. G. Teubner, 1906, pp. 54–86.

Paulsen, Friedrich. 'Was uns Kant sein kann?', *Vierteljahrsschrift für wissenschaftliche Philosophie* 5(1), 1881, pp. 1–96.

Peacock, Sandra J. 'Struggling with the Daimon: Eliza M. Butler on Germany and Germans', *History of European Ideas* 32(1), 2006, pp. 99–115.

Pestalozzi, Johann Heinrich. 'An die Unschuld, den Ernst und den Edelmuth meines Zeitalters und meines Vaterlandes: Aufzeichnungen zu einer zweiten Auflage' [1815–1816], in *Sämtliche Werke. Zurich: Orell Füssli*, 1978, vol. 24B, pp. 1–27.

Pettenkofer, Max v. *Rerum cognoscere causas.* Munich: K. B. Akademie der Wissenschaften, 1890.

Pflaum, Michael. 'Die Kultur-Zivilisations-Antithese im Deutschen', in Johann Knobloch et al. (eds.), *Kultur und Zivilisation.* Munich: Max Hueber, 1967, pp. 288–427.

Pflüger, Christine. *Georg Simmels Religionstheorie in ihren werk- und theologiegeschichtlichen Bezügen.* Frankfurt am Main: Peter Lang, 2007.

Phillipson, Nicholas. 'The Scottish Enlightenment', in R. Porter and M. Teich (eds.), *The Enlightenment in National Context.* Cambridge: Cambridge University Press, 1981, pp. 19–40.

Pickering, Mary. *Auguste Comte: An Intellectual Biography*, 3 vols. Cambridge: Cambridge University Press, 1993–2009.

Pinkard, Terry. *Hegel: A Biography.* Cambridge: Cambridge University Press, 2000.

Pleßner, Helmuth. 'Zur Soziologie der modernen Forschung und ihrer Organisation in der deutschen Universität', in Max Scheler (ed.), *Versuche zu einer Soziologie des Wissens.* Munich: Duncker & Humblot, 1924, pp. 407–425.

Pocock, J. G. A. 'Languages and Their Implications: The Transformation of the Study of Political Thought', in *Politics, Language & Time: Essays on Political Thought and History.* Chicago: University of Chicago Press, 1989, pp. 3–41.

Pocock, J. G. A. 'Virtues, Rights, and Manners: A Model for Historians of Political Thought', in *Virtue, Commerce, and History: Essays on Political Thought and History, Chiefly in the Eighteenth Century.* Cambridge: Cambridge University Press, 1985, pp. 37–50.

Podoksik, Efraim. 'Georg Simmel: Three Forms of Individualism and Historical Understanding', *New German Critique* 109(1), 2010, pp. 119–145.

Podoksik, Efraim. 'How Is Modern Intellectual History Possible?', *European Political Science* 9(3), 2010, pp. 304–315.

Podoksik, Efraim. 'In Search of Unity: Georg Simmel on Italian Cities as Works of Art', *Theory, Culture & Society* 29(7–8), 2012, pp. 101–123.

Poggi, Gianfranco. *Money and the Modern Mind: Georg Simmel's Philosophy of Money*. Berkeley: University of California Press, 1993.

Portioli, Claudia. 'Alpen', in H.-P. Müller and T. Reitz (eds.), *Simmel-Handbuch: Begriffe, Hauptwerke, Aktualität*. Frankfurt am Main: Suhrkamp, 2018, pp. 105–110.

Preuße, Ute. *Humanismus und Gesellschaft: Zur Geschichte des altsprachlichen Unterrichts in Deutschland von 1890 bis 1933*. Frankfurt am Main: Peter Lang, 1988.

Pyyhtinen, Olli. 'Life, Death and Individuation: Simmel on the Problem of Life Itself', *Theory, Culture & Society* 29(7–8), 2012, pp. 78–100.

Pyyhtinen, Olli. *Simmel and 'the Social'*. New York: Palgrave Macmillan, 2010.

Pyyhtinen, Olli and Thomas Kemple (eds.). *The Anthem Companion to Georg Simmel*. London: Anthem Press, 2016.

Rammstedt, Otthein. 'Editorischer Bericht', in *Georg Simmel Gesamtausgabe*. Frankfurt am Main: Suhrkamp, 1989–2015, vol. 11, pp. 877–905.

Rammstedt, Otthein (ed.). *Georg Simmels Philosophie des Geldes*. Frankfurt am Main: Suhrkamp, 2003.

Rammstedt, Otthein. 'On Simmel's Aesthetics: Argumentation in the Journal *Jugend*, 1897–1906', *Theory, Culture & Society* 8(3), 1991, pp. 125–144.

Rammstedt, Otthein and Michael Popp. 'Aufklärung und Propaganda: Zum Konflikt zwischen Georg Simmel und Friedrich Gundolf', *Simmel Newsletter* 5(2), 1995, pp. 139–155.

Rehberg, Karl-Siegbert. 'Kultur, subjektive und objektive', in H.-P. Müller and T. Reitz (eds.), *Simmel-Handbuch: Begriffe, Hauptwerke, Aktualität*. Frankfurt am Main: Suhrkamp, 2018, pp. 328–334.

Rickert, Heinrich. *Der Gegenstand der Erkenntnis: Ein Beitrag zum Problem der philosophischen Transcendenz*. Freiburg im Breisgau: J. C. B. Mohr, 1892.

Rickert, Heinrich. *Kant als Philosoph der modernen Kultur*. Tübingen: J.C.B. Mohr, 1924.

Rickert, Heinrich. *Die Philosophie des Lebens: Darstellung und Kritik der philosophischen Modeströmungen unserer Zeit*. Tübingen: J. C. B. Mohr, 1920.

Riehl, Alois. *Friedrich Nietzsche: Der Künstler und der Denker*. Stuttgart: Fr. Frommann, 1897.

Ringer, Fritz K. *The Decline of the German Mandarins: The German Academic Community, 1890–1933*. Hanover: Wesleyan University Press, 1990.

Ringer, Fritz K. *Fields of Knowledge: French Academic Culture in Comparative Perspective, 1890–1920*. Cambridge: Cambridge University Press, 1992.

Ringer, Fritz K. *Max Weber: An Intellectual Biography*. Princeton: Princeton University Press, 2004.

Ripke-Kühn, Leonore. 'Ein Briefwechsel', *Der Panther* 4(4), 1916, pp. 477–484.

Ritschl, Albrecht. *Die christliche Lehre von der Rechtfertigung und Versöhnung, vol. 3: Die positive Entwickelung der Lehre*, 3rd ed. Bonn: Adolph Marcus, 1888.

Roeck, Bernd. *Florence 1900: The Quest for Arcadia*, trans. S. Spencer. New Haven: Yale University Press, 2009.

Röttgers, Kurt. 'Die "große" Soziologie und die "große" Philosophie', in H. Tyrell, O. Rammstedt and I. Meyer (eds.), *Georg Simmels große 'Soziologie': Eine kritische Sichtung nach hundert Jahren*. Bielefeld: transcript, 2011, pp. 69–81.

Rowe, Dorothy. 'Georg Simmel and the Berlin Trade Exhibition of 1896', *Urban History* 22(2), 1995, pp. 216–228.

Rüegg, Walter. *Cicero und der Humanismus: Formale Untersuchungen über Petrarcha und Erasmus*. Zurich: Rhein, 1946.

Ruehl, Martin A. *The Italian Renaissance in the German Historical Imagination, 1860–1930*. Cambridge: Cambridge University Press, 2015.

Ruggieri, Davide. 'Georg Simmel and the Question of Pessimism: A Sociophilosophical Analysis between "Wertfrage" and "Lebensphilosophie"', *Simmel Studies* 16(2), 2006, pp. 161–181.

Ruggieri, Davide. *Il conflitto della società moderna: la ricezione del pensiero di Arthur Schopenhauer nell'opera di Georg Simmel (1887–1918)*. Lecce: Pensa Multimedia, 2010.

Scallen, Catherine B. *Rembrandt, Reputation, and the Practice of Connoisseurship*. Amsterdam: Amsterdam University Press, 2004.

Schaarschmidt, Ilse. *Der Bedeutungswandel der Worte 'bilden' und 'Bildung' in der Literatur-Epoche von Gottsched bis Herder*. Elbing: Seiffert, 1931.

Schäffle, Albert. *Bau und Leben des socialen Körpers*, 4 vols. Tübingen: H. Laupp, 1876–1878.

Scheler, Max. *Bildung und Wissen* [1925]. Frankfurt am Main: G. Schulte-Blumke, 1947.

Schemer, Henry and David Jary. *Form and Dialectic in Georg Simmel's Sociology: A New Interpretation*. New York: Palgrave Macmillan, 2013.

Scherer, Wilhelm. 'Goethe-Philologie', in *Aufsätze über Goethe*. Berlin: Weidmannsche Buchhandlung, 1900, pp. 3–27.

Schermer, Henry and David Jary. *Form and Dialectic in Georg Simmel's Sociology: A New Interpretation*. New York: Palgrave Macmillan, 2013.

Schiller, Friedrich. *The Death of Wallenstein*, trans. S. T. Coleridge. London: Longman and Rees, 1800.

Schiller, Friedrich. 'On Grace and Dignity', trans. J. V. Curran, in J. V. Curran and Ch. Fricker (eds.), *Schiller's 'On Grace and Dignity' in Its Cultural Contexts: Essays and a New Translation*. Rochester, NY: Camden House, 2005, pp. 123–170.

Schiller, Friedrich. *On the Aesthetic Education of Man*, trans. E. M. Wilkinson and L. A. Willoughby. Oxford: Clarendon Press, 1967.

Schilling, Hans. *Bildung als Gottesbildlichkeit*. Freiburg: Lambertus, 1961.

Schleiermacher, Friedrich. *The Christian Faith* [1830–1831]. London: Bloomsbury, 2016.

Schleiermacher, Friedrich. *On Religion: Speeches to Its Cultural Despisers* [1799], trans. John Oman. London: Kegan Paul, 1893.

Schleiermacher, Friedrich. *Soliloquies*, trans. H. L. Friess. Chicago: The Open Court Publishing Company, 1957.

Schlitte, Annika. *Die Macht des Geldes und die Symbolik der Kultur: Georg Simmels Philosophie des Geldes*. Munich: Wilhelm Funk, 2012.

Schluchter, Wolfgang. 'Zeitgemäße Unzeitgemäße: Von Friedrich Nietzsche über Georg Simmel zu Max Weber', *Revue Internationale de Philosophie* 192(2), 1995, pp. 107–126.

Schmitt, Carl. *Political Theology: Four Chapters on the Concept of Sovereignty*, trans. G. Schwab. Chicago: University of Chicago Press, 2005.

Schmoll gen. Eisenwerth, J.A. 'Simmel und Rodin', in H. Böhringer and K. Gründer (eds.), *Ästhetik und Soziologie um die Jahrhundertwende: Georg Simmel*. Frankfurt am Main: Vittorio Klostermann, 1976, pp.18–38.

Schnädelbach, Herbert. *Philosophy in Germany 1831–1933*, trans. E. Matthews. Cambridge: Cambridge University Press, 1984.

Schneiderreit, Georg. 'Die individualistische Grundzug in Goethes Weltanschauung', *Goethe-Jahrbuch* 33, 1912, pp. 31–42.

Scholz, Hannelore. *Widersprüche im bürgerlichen Frauenbild: Zur ästhetischen Reflexion und poetischen Praxis bei Lessing, Friedrich Schlegel und Schiller*. Weinheim: Deutscher Studien, 1992.

Schopenhauer, Arthur. 'On Women', trans. E. F. J. Payne, in *Parerga and Paralipomena*. Oxford: Clarendon Press, 1974, vol. 2, pp. 614–626.

Schopenhauer, Arthur. *The Will as World and Representation*, 2 vols., trans. E. F. J. Payne. New York: Dover Publications, 1966.

Schulze, Rudolf. 'Religion: Eine philosophische Skizze', *Zeitschrift für Missionskunde und Religionswissenschaft* 16(9–12), 1901, pp. 257–261, 289–305, 335–338, 358–365.

Schweitzer, Albert. 'Erinnerungen an Simmel', in K. Gassen and M. Landmann (eds.), *Buch des Dankes an Georg Simmel*. Berlin: Duncker & Humblot, 1958, pp. 292–294.

Schweitzer, Albert. *The Quest of the Historical Jesus: A Critical Study of Its Progress from Reimarus to Wrede*. Baltimore: The Johns Hopkins University Press, 1998.

Siebeck, Hermann. *Goethe als Denker*. Stuttgart: Fr. Frommann, 1902.

Siebeck, Hermann. *Lehrbuch der Religionsphilosophie*. Freiburg im Breisgau: J.C.B. Mohr, 1893.

Sieg, Ulrich. *Geist und Gewalt: Deutsche Philosophen zwischen Kaiserreich und Nationalsozialismus*. Munich: Carl Hanser, 2013.

Simmel, Hans. 'Lebenserinnerungen' [1941/43], *Simmel Studies* 18(1), 2008, pp. 9–136.

Skinner, Quentin. *The Foundations of Modern Political Thought, vol. 1: The Renaissance*. Cambridge: Cambridge University Press, 1978.

Skinner, Quentin. 'Meaning and Understanding in the History of Ideas', in *Visions of Politics, vol. 1: Regarding Method*. Cambridge: Cambridge University Press, 2002, pp. 57–89.

Smitmans-Vajda, Barbara. *Die Bedeutung der Bildenden Kunst in der Philosophie Georg Simmels*. Aachen: Shaker, 1997.

Solies, Dirk. 'Ist Simmel ein Schopenhauerianer?', in F. Ciracì, D. M. Fazio and M. Koßler (eds.), *Schopenhauer und Schopenhauer-Schule*. Würzburg: Königshausen & Neumann, 2009, pp. 327–333.

Solies, Dirk. *Natur in der Distanz: Zur Bedeutung von Georg Simmels Kulturphilosophie für die Landschaftsästhetik*. St. Augustin: Gardez, 1998.

Sorkin, David. 'Wilhelm von Humboldt: The Theory and Practice of Self-Formation (*Bildung*), 1791–1810', *Journal of the History of Ideas* 44(1), 1983, pp. 55–73.

Spencer, Herbert. *The Principles of Sociology*, 3 vols. New Brunswick: Transaction Publishers, 2002.

Spranger, Eduard. *Wandlungen im Wesen der Universität seit 100 Jahren*. Leipzig: Ernst Wiegandt, 1913.

Spranger, Eduard. *Wilhelm von Humboldt und die Humanitätsidee*. Berlin: Reuther & Reichard, 1909.

Stage, W. T. *The Philosophy of Hegel: A Systematic Exposition*. New York: Dover Publications, 1955.

Stahl, E. L. *Die religiöse und die humanitätsphilosophische Bildungsidee und die Entstehung des deutschen Bildungsromans im 18. Jahrhundert*. Bern: Paul Haupt, 1934.

Stauth, Georg and Bryan S. Turner, 'Nietzsche in Weber oder die Geburt des modernen Genius' im professionellen Menschen', *Zeitschrift für Soziologie* 15(2), 1986, pp. 81–94.

Steiner, Rudolf. *Goethes naturwissenschaftliche Schriften*. Dornach: Philosophisch-Anthroposophischer Verlag, 1926.

Steinthal, H. *Allgemeine Ethik*. Berlin: Georg Reimer, 1885.

Stern, Fritz. *The Politics of Cultural Despair: A Study in the Rise of the Germanic Ideology*. Berkeley: University of California Press, 1989.

Stoetzler, Marcel. 'Intersectional Individuality: Georg Simmel's Concept of "The Intersection of Social Circles" and the Emancipation of Women', *Sociological Inquiry* 86(2), 2016, pp. 216–240.

Strecker, Karl. 'Die Kriegserklärung Englands', in W. E. Windegg (ed.), *Der deutsche Krieg in Dichtungen*. Munich: C. H. Beck, 1915, p.36.

Stückelberger, Johannes. *Rembrandt und die Moderne: Der Dialog mit Rembrandt in der deutschen Kunst um 1900*. Munich: Wilhelm Fink, 1996.

Susman, Margarete. *Die geistige Gestalt Georg Simmels*. Tübingen: J. C. B. Mohr, 1959.

Swart, Koenraad W. *The Sense of Decadence in Nineteenth-Century France*. The Hague: Martin Nijhoff, 1964.

Sybel, Heinrich von. 'Die deutschen und die auswärtigen Universitäten' [1868], in *Die deutschen Universitäten, ihre Leistungen und Bedürfnisse*. Bonn: Max Cohen & Sohn, 1874, pp. 3–32.

Taubert, A. *Der Pessimismus und seine Gegner*. Berlin: Carl Duncker, 1873.

Taylor, Charles. *Hegel and Modern Society*. Cambridge: Cambridge University Press, 1979.

Taylor, Irmgard. *Kultur, Aufklärung, Bildung, Humanität und verwandte Begriffe bei Herder*. Gießen: von Münchow, 1938.

Thouard, Denis. 'Schopenhauer, Arthur', in H.-P. Müller and T. Reitz (eds.), *Simmel-Handbuch: Begriffe, Hauptwerke, Aktualität*. Frankfurt am Main: Suhrkamp, 2018, pp. 503–508.

Thouard, Denis. 'Simmel et la guerre: De 14 à 18', *Revue de métaphysique et de morale* 4, 2014, pp. 561–575.

Tönnies, Ferdinand. *Community and Civil Society*, trans. J. Harris and M. Hollis. Cambridge: Cambridge University Press, 2001.

Tönnies, Ferdinand. *Der Nietzsche-Kultus: Eine Kritik* [1897]. Berlin: Akademie, 1990.

Townsend, Dabney. 'From Shaftesbury to Kant: The Development of the Concept of Aesthetic Experience', in P. Kivy (ed.), *Essays on the History of Aesthetics*. Rochester: University of Rochester Press, 1992, pp. 205–223.

Treitschke, Heinrich von. 'Einige Bemerkungen über unser Gymnasialwesen', *Preußische Jahrbücher* 51(2), 1883, pp. 158–190.

Troeltsch, Ernst. 'Der Begriff des Glaubens', *Religion und Geisteskultur* 1(3), 1907, pp. 191–201.

Troeltsch, Ernst. *Der Berg der Läuterung*. Berlin: E. S. Mittler & Sohn, 1921.

Troeltsch, Ernst. 'Zur modernen Religionsphilosophie', *Deutsche Literaturzeitung* 28(14), 6 April 1907, pp. 836–841.

Turner, R. Steven. 'The Prussian Universities and the Concept of Research', *Internationales Archiv für Sozialgeschichte der deutschen Literatur* 5, 1980, pp. 68–93.

Turner, Stephen and Regis Factor. 'Decisionism and Politics: Weber as Constitutional Theorist', in Scott Lash and Sam Whimster (eds.), *Max Weber, Rationality and Modernity*. London: Allen & Unwin, 1987, pp. 334–354.

Tylor, Edward B. *Primitive Culture*, 2 vols. London: John Murray, 1871.

Tyrell, Hartmann. 'Pessimismus: Eine begriffsgeschichtliche Notiz', *Simmel Newsletter* 2(2), 1992, pp. 138–145.

Tyrell, Hartmann. 'Das *Religioide* und der *Glaube*: Drei Überlegungen zu einer Religionssoziologie der Zeit um 1900', in R. Lautmann and H. Wienold (eds.), *Georg Simmel und das Leben in der Gegenwart*. Wiesbaden: Springer, 2018, pp. 347–362.

Tyrell, Hartmann, Otthein Rammstedt and Ingo Meyer (eds.). *Georg Simmels große 'Soziologie': Eine kritische Sichtung nach hundert Jahren*. Bielefeld: transcript, 2011.

Ueberweg, Friedrich. *Grundriß der Geschichte der Philosophie, part 4: vom Beginn des neunzehnten Jahrhunderts bis auf die Gegenwart*, 11th ed., ed. K. Oesterreich. Berlin: Ernst Siegfried und Sohn, 1916.

Ullrich, Volker. *Die nervöse Großmacht: Aufstieg und Untergang des deutschen Kaiserreichs 1871–1918*. Frankfurt am Main: Fischer, 2007.

Ulmi, Marianne. *Frauenfragen, Männergedanken: Zu Georg Simmels Philosophie und Soziologie der Geschlechter*. Zurich: Efef, 1989.

Utitz, Emil. 'Georg Simmel und die Philosophie der Kunst', in P. U. Hein (ed.), *Georg Simmel*. Frankfurt am Main: Peter Lang, 1990, pp. 85–124.

Vaihinger, Hans. *Die Philosophie des Als Ob: System der theoretischen, praktischen und religiösen Fiktionen der Menschheit auf Grund eines idealistischen Positivismus*. Berlin: Reuther & Reichard, 1911.

Velkley, Richard. 'The Tension in the Beautiful: On Culture and Civilization in Rousseau and German Philosophy', in C. Orwin and N. Tarcov (eds.), *The Legacy of Rousseau*. Chicago: University of Chicago Press, 1997, pp. 65–86.

Die Verhandlungen des achtzehnten Evangelisch-sozialen Kongresses. Göttingen: Vandenhoeck & Ruprecht, 1907.

Voigt, Friedemann. *'Die Tragödie des Reiches Gottes'? Ernst Troeltsch als Leser Georg Simmels*. Gütersloh: Gütersloher Verlagshaus, 1998.

Voigt, Georg. *Die Wiederbelebung des classischen Alterthums, oder das erste Jahrhundert des Humanismus*. Berlin: G. Reimer, 1859.

Volkelt, Johannes. *Arthur Schopenhauer: Seine Persönlichkeit, seine Lehre, sein Glaube*. Stuttgart: Fr. Frommann, 1900.

Vondung, Klaus. *The Apocalypse in Germany*, trans. S. D. Ricks. Columbia: University of Missouri Press, 2000.

Vorländer, Karl. 'Goethe und Kant', *Goethe-Jahrbuch* 19, 1898, pp. 167–185.

Vorländer, Karl. 'Goethes Verhältnis zu Kant in seiner historischen Entwicklung', *Kant-Studien* 1(1–3), 1897, pp. 60–99, 315–351.

Voßkamp, Wilhelm. '"Diese Rastlosigkeit von Selbstentwicklung und Produktivität": Georg Simmels *Goethe*-Buch', *Simmel Studies* 19(1), 2009, pp. 5–19.

Vromen, Suzanne. 'Georg Simmel and the Cultural Dilemma of Women', *History of European Ideas* 8(4/5), 1987, pp. 563–579.

Vucht Tijssen, Lieteke van. 'Women and Objective Culture: Georg Simmel and Marianne Weber', *Theory, Culture & Society* 8(3), 1991, pp. 203–218.

Wagner, Richard. 'Art and Revolution' [1849], in *Richard Wagner's Prose Works*, vol. 1, trans. W. A. Ellis. London: Kegan Paul, Trench, Trübner & Co., 1895, pp. 21–65.

Wagner, Richard. 'Religion and Art' [1880], in *Richard Wagner's Prose Works*, vol. 6, trans. W. A. Ellis. London: Kegan Paul, Trench, Trübner & Co., 1897, pp. 211–284.

Watier, Patrick. 'The War Writings of Georg Simmel', *Theory, Culture & Society* 8(3), 1991, pp. 219–233.

Wauschkuhn, Annette. *Georg Simmels Rembrandt-Bild: Ein lebensphilosophischer Beitrag zur Rembrandtrezeption im 20. Jahrhundert*. Worms: Wernersche Verlagsgesellschaft, 2002.

Weber, Alfred. 'Die Bedeutung der geistigen Führer in Deutschland', *Die neue Rundschau* 29(10), 1918, pp. 1249–1268.

Weber, Alfred. 'Prinzipielles zur Kultursoziologie: Gesellschaftsprozess, Zivilisationsprozess und Kulturbewegung', *Archiv für Sozialwissenschaft und Sozialpolitik* 47, 1920, pp. 1–49.

Weber, Alfred. 'Der soziologische Kulturbegriff', in *Verhandlungen des Zweiten Deutschen Soziologentages*. Tübingen: J.C.B. Mohr, 1913, pp. 1–20.

Weber, Marianne. 'Die Frau und die objektive Kultur' [1913], in *Frauenfragen und Frauengedanken: Gesammelte Aufsätze*. Tübingen: J.C.B. Mohr, 1919, pp. 95–133.

Weber, Max. 'Politics as a Vocation' [1919], in *Essays in Sociology*, trans. H. H. Gerth and C. Wright Mills. London: Routledge, 1991, pp. 77–128.

Weber, Max. *The Protestant Ethics and the Spirit of Capitalism* [1904–1905], trans. T. Parsons. New York: Charles Scribner's Sons, 1958.

Weber, Max. *Die protestantische Ethik und der Geist des Kapitalismus* [1904–1905]. Tübingen: J. C. B. Mohr, 1934.

Weber, Max. 'Religious Dimensions of the World and Their Directions' [1915], in *Essays in Sociology*, trans. H. H. Gerth and C. Wright Mills. London: Routledge, 1991, pp. 323–359.

Wehlte-Höschele, Martina. Der Deutsche Künstlerbund im Spektrum von Kunst und Kulturpolitik des Wilhelminischen Kaiserreichs, PhD dissertation, University of Heidelberg, 1993.

Weil, Hans. *Die Entstehung des deutschen Bildungsprinzips*. Bonn: Friedrich Cohen, 1930.

Weingartner, Rudolph H. *Experience and Culture: The Philosophy of Georg Simmel*. Middletown, CO: Wesleyan University Press, 1962.

Weinstein, David. *Equal Freedom and Utility: Herbert Spencer's Liberal Utilitarianism*. Cambridge: Cambridge University Press, 1998.

Weiser, Christian Friedrich. *Shaftesbury und das deutsche Geistesleben*. Leipzig: B.G. Teubner, 1916.

Wenzel, Uwe Justus. 'Unter Null: Simmel, Nietzsche, Schopenhauer, Kant und die "ewige Wiederkehr"', *Neue Rundschau* 111(1), 2000, pp. 43–46.

Willey, Thomas E. *Back to Kant: The Revival of Kantianism in German Social and Historical Thought, 1860–1914*. Detroit: Wayne State University Press, 1978.

Willmann, Otto. *Didaktik als Bildungslehre: nach ihren Beziehungen zur Socialforschung und zur Geschichte der Bildung*, vol. 1. Braunschweig: Friedrich Vieweg und Sohn, 1882.

Windelband, Wilhelm. 'Immanuel Kant: Zur Säkularfeier seiner Philosophie', in *Präludien: Aufsätze und Reden zur Einführung in die Philosophie*, Tübingen: J. C. B. Mohr, 1911, vol. 1, pp. 112–146.

Windelband, Wilhelm. 'Kulturphilosophie und transzendentaler Idealismus', *Logos* 1, 1910/1911, pp. 186–196.

Windelband, Wilhelm. 'Nach hundert Jahren', *Kant-Studien* 9, 1904, pp. 5–20.

Windelband, Wilhelm. 'Pessimismus und Wissenschaft', in *Präludien: Aufsätze und Reden zur Einführung in die Philosophie*. Tübingen: J. C. B. Mohr, 1911, vol. 2, pp. 195–220.

Windelband, Wilhelm. *Präludien: Aufsätze und Reden zur Einführung in die Philosophie*, 2 vols. Tübingen: J. C. B. Mohr, 1911.

Windelband, Wilhelm. 'Ueber Friedrich Hölderlin und sein Geschick', in *Präludien*. Freiburg, J. C. B. Mohr, 1884, pp. 146–175.

Winkler, Heinrich August. *Germany: The Long Road West, vol. 1: 1789–1933*. Oxford: Oxford University Press, 2006.

Witz, Anne. 'Georg Simmel and the Masculinity of Modernity', *Journal of Classical Sociology* 1(3), 2001, pp. 353–370.

Wolff, Janet. 'The Feminine in Modern Art: Benjamin, Simmel and the Gender of Modernity', *Theory, Culture & Society* 17(6), 2000, pp. 33–53.

Wölfflin, Heinrich. *Kunstgeschichtliche Grundbegriffe: Das Problem der Stilentwickelung in der neueren Kunst.* Munich: F. Bruckmann, 1915.

Wolfskehl, Karl. Letter to Georg Simmel, 17.10.1914, in *Georg Simmel Gesamtausgabe.* Frankfurt am Main: Suhrkamp, 1989–2015, vol. 23, pp. 427–429.

Wolfskehl, Karl. Letter to Georg Simmel, 25.10.1914, in *Georg Simmel Gesamtausgabe.* Frankfurt am Main: Suhrkamp, 1989–2015, vol. 23, pp. 437–438.

Worringer, Wilhelm. *Formprobleme der Gotik.* Munich: R. Piper & Co., 1911.

Wundt, Max. *Goethes Wilhelm Meister und die Entwicklung des modernen Lebensideals.* Berlin: Walter de Gruyter, 1932 [1913].

Young, Julian. 'Nietzsche and Women', in Ken Gemes and John Richardson (eds.), *The Oxford Handbook of Nietzsche.* Oxford: Oxford University Press, 2013, pp. 46–62.

Yourgrau, Wolfgang. 'Reflections on the Natural Philosophy of Goethe', *Philosophy* 26(96), 1951, pp. 69–84.

Zeldin, Theodore. *France 1848–1945, vol. 2: Intellect, Taste and Anxiety.* Oxford: Clarendon Press, 1977.

Ziegler, Leopold. *Das Wesen der Kultur.* Leipzig: E. R. Weiss, 1903.

Index

a priori, 17, 120, 125–126, 129, 130–131, 132, 133, 189, 293, 294
absolute, 11, 51, 61, 92, 158, 186, 187, 240, 254, 263, 275, 276, 278–279, 289–290, 291–292
absolute spirit. *See* spirit
absolute versus relative, 210, 212–213, 237–238, 262, 268, 273, 291
aestheticism, 81, 85, 169, 172, 173, 177, 208, 209, 219, 238, 240, 250, 252, 287, *See also* aesthetics
aesthetics, 10, 17, 25, 44, 47, 53, 55, 60, 61, 75, 101, 118, 141–142, 158, 161–173, 184, 190, 209, 214, 220, 222–223, 233, 234–236, 245, 248, 249, 259, 271, 287, *See also* aestheticism; art; beauty
alienation, 13, 82, 85, 86, 120, 147, 156, 168, 208, 266, 272
Alps, 95–96
America, 28, 29–31, 73, 270, 290
Americanisation, 271, 286
Andreas-Salomé, Lou, 180, 181, 182, 205
anthropology, 69, 70, 102, 110, 111, 199, 204
Anti-Semitism, 8, 22, 243, 287
Arendt, Hannah, 61
Aristotle, 57, 58, 125, 225
Arnim, Bettina von, 216
Arnim, Gisela von, 216
Arnold, Matthew, 28–29, 56
art, 18, 20, 22, 23, 25, 37, 45, 50, 58, 69, 72, 80, 82, 83, 91, 99, 100, 101, 141, 145, 153, 161–173, 175, 177–178, 181, 189, 190, 191, 200, 208, 211, 216, 219, 222, 223, 224, 226, 229, 231, 233, 234–235, 239–240, 245–268, 274, 281, 284, 285, 288, *See also* aesthetics; beauty
Attila, 288
Aufklärung. See Enlightenment
avant-garde, 153, 168, 191, 194, 285, 286
Avenarius, Ferdinand, 72
Avenarius, Richard, 128

Bach, Johann Sebastian, 267
Bachofen, Johann Jakob, 204
Baroque, 97, 247, 264
Barth, Paul, 73, 74
beauty, 47, 54, 55, 56, 111, 141, 142, 150, 161–162, 165–166, 168, 170, 171–173, 177, 189, 196, 208, 209, 210, 219, 222, 226, 237, 239, 240, 247, 254, *See also* art; aesthetics
Becker, Willy, 246
Beethoven, Ludwig van, 223, 263
Bergson, Henri, 148
Berlin Trade Exhibition, 163
Berlin Women's Congress, 194
Bernstein, Eduard, 136
Beruf, 17, 18, 21, 26, 33–34, 35, 37, 42–45, 50, 57, 61, 62, 63, 64–65, 66, 67, 111, 121, 152, 243–244, *See also* vocation; professionalisation
Bielschowsky, Albert, 216
Bildung, 21, 22, 33–67, 70–71, 72, 74–75, 78, 79, 95–96, 98, 110–111, 113, 115, 121, 135, 145, 152, 156, 165, 167, 168, 179, 186, 195, 203, 215, 216–217, 218, 220, 242, 244, 280, 282, 287, 294, *See also* cultivation
Bildungsbürgertum, 220
Bismarck, Otto von, 21, 26, 153
Blütezeit, 36, 115
Böcklin, Arnold, 163–164, 248, 250, 251–252
Bode, Wilhelm, 246
Boeckh, August, 51
Bölsche, Wilhelm, 203
Bonald, Louis de, 104
Bosanquet, Bernard, 54
Bradley, F.H., 54
Brasch, Moritz, 224
Breysig, Kurt, 26
Britain, 5, 27–29, 54, 56, 65, 103, 104, 196, 269
British Idealism. *See* Idealism
Buber, Martin, 8, 174, 187
Burckhardt, Jacob, 20, 201, 247
Burdach, Konrad, 236

329

Busche, Hubertus, 68–69, 82
Byron, Lord, 290

Calvinism, 59
capitalism, 193
Carlyle, Thomas, 28, 220
Carus, Carl Gustav, 216, 229
Cassirer, Ernst, 81–82, 136
Catholicism, 104, 183, 218
Cellini, Benvenuto, 19
Chamberlain, Houston Stewart, 242, 243
character, 17, 55, 56, 94, 171
  national character, 92, 109
Cicero, Marcus Tullius, 60, 61
civilisation – concept of, 22, 69–77, 79–80, *See
  also Zivilisation*
Clausewitz, Carl von, 278
Cohen, Hermann, 124–126, 129, 132–137, 142, 287
coincidentia oppositorum, 164, 186, 189
Coleridge, Samuel Taylor, 28
collectivism, 106
communism, 187
Comte, Auguste, 102–103, 104, 106
conservatism, 21, 22, 25, 153, 207, 219, 286
conservative revolution. *See* revolution
Cosmic Circle, 205
cultivation, 5, 11, 27, 36, 40, 41, 43, 44, 45, 50, 55,
  56, 57, 58, 63, 64, 66–70, 75, 78–81, 83, 95,
  98, 114, 115, 116, 179, 218, 220, 294, *See also
  Bildung*
  self-cultivation, 33, 35, 36, 37, 38, 45, 54, 55, 57,
  62, 63, 65, 67, 75, 78, 110–112, 114, 116, 145,
  172, 173, 218, 242
Cultur. See Kultur
cultural spheres, 53, 64, 67, 69, 79, 80, 83, 84, 118,
  135–137, 138–139, 158, 161, 181, 272, 276, *See
  also* forms of experience
culture, 6, 10, 21, 23, 28, 52–53, 62, 63, 67–89, 91,
  135, 136, 144, 168, 181, 201, 203, 208, 210, 224,
  270, 272–273, 274, 275, 276, 282, 285, 288,
  292, 294, *See also Kultur*
  inward culture, 25
  objective culture, 77, 79, 80, 81, 82–84, 85, 86,
  210, 211, 272
  personal culture, 85, 146
  subjective culture, 79, 80, 81, 82, 83, 84, 85, 86,
  208, 272

d'Annunzio, Gabriele, 288
Dante Alighieri, 91–97, 98, 248, 255, 263, 265, 277
Darwin, Charles, 148
Darwinism, 193, 203
decision, 11, 267, 275–280, 281–282, 283–284, 287,
  289, 290–291
Delacroix, Eugène, 246

dependence, 184–185
Deutscher Künstlerbund, 168
Deutungsmuster, 68
Dewey, John, 30–31
Diederichs, Eugen, 286
differentiation, 13, 17, 18, 21, 25, 34, 51, 63,
  67, 83, 88, 97, 103, 105, 107, 108, 111, 112–115,
  117, 165, 166, 173, 179, 181, 187–188, 189,
  199–204, 205, 206, 208, 210, 219, 224, 239,
  252, 258, 294
dignity, 170
Dilthey, Wilhelm, 3, 12, 144, 227, 228–229, 231
diversity. *See* variety; unity in [versus, above]
  variety
division of labour, 25, 30, 32, 73, 85, 86, 100, 105,
  106, 162, 163, 168, 169, 179, 187, 188, 196, 203,
  See also specialisation
Don Juan, 277
Douglas, Richard, 59
Droysen, Johann Gustav, 116
dualism, 66, 84, 88, 90, 94, 124, 126, 128, 130, 132,
  133, 135, 138, 141, 156, 160, 164, 167, 171, 186,
  190, 206, 212, 221, 233, 235, 237, 242, 243, 251,
  252, 253, 257, 280, 286–287, *See also* variety;
  monism
Dürer, Albrecht, 216, 249
Durkheim, Émile, 31–32, 176

Einstein, Carl, 285
empiricism, 93, 104, 128–129, 137
empirio-criticism, 128
Engels, Friedrich, 105, 204
England. *See* Britain
Enlightenment, 18, 38, 42, 196, 202
  Aufklärung, 42, 59
  Scottish Enlightenment, 58
epigones, 22, 24
equality, 117, 154, 188, 192, 193, 195, 202
Erlebnis, 144, 228, 231
Ernst, Paul, 249, 286
essentialism, 106, 116, 199, 206
estrangement. *See* alienation
Eucken, Rudolf, 25, 225, 227–229
evolution, 76, 102, 104, 112, 125, 131–132, 133, 143,
  200, 202, 203, 204
existentialism, 280, 282
Expressionism, 274, 285, 287

Faust, 284
feeling, 77, 79, 161, 179–180, 200, 218, 241
Felski, Rita, 209
femininity. *See* women
feminism, 191–192, 194–195, 196, 202, 203, 207
Feuerbach, Ludwig, 76
Fichte, Johann Gottlieb, 6, 26, 72, 197

Fiedler, Konrad, 256
First World War, 26, 35, 85, 124, 235, 243, 262,
  268–277, 278–280, 285–292, 295
Fischer, Kuno, 123, 136
Fitzi, Gregor, 269
Fleischmann, Eugène, 155, 156
flirtation, 201, 206–207, 281
Florence, 91, 167, 168, 169, 171, 172, 189, 209, 249
form, 42, 44, 87, 91, 97, 112, 114, 120, 129, 130, 157,
  160, 167, 172, 189, 211, 219, 233, 234, 236, 237,
  240, 241–242, 245, 253, 256, 259, 262,
  263–264, 266, 267, 274–275, 288, 292, 293,
  See also life
formalism, 242
formlessness, 97, 230, 242, 245, 266, 267, 273,
  288, 292
forms of experience, 53, 91, 124, 125, 126, 127, 131,
  135, 136, 143, 155, 156, 158, 159, 160, 174, 176,
  177, 178, 184, 185, 186, 189, 190, 210, 211–212,
  222, 234, 235, *See also* cultural spheres
Förster-Nietzsche, Elisabeth, 153
fragmentation, 9, 13, 20, 25, 26, 27, 28, 36, 47, 54,
  63, 64, 67, 73, 90, 99, 121, 146, 172, 182, 214,
  242, 250, 293, 294
France, 5, 6, 28, 31–32, 60, 73, 103, 104, 105, 108,
  110, 196, 246
free action, 61, 138
free choice, 42, 76
freedom, 30, 72, 93, 94, 98, 105, 106, 112, 118, 134,
  138, 140, 154, 170, 177, 183, 190, 198, 251, 252,
  264, 271
  freedom of women, 193
French Revolution. *See* revolution
Freyer, Hans, 35, 65
function, 128, 129, 211, 231, *See also* substance
Fundamental Problems of Sociology, 16
futurism, 285

Gadamer, Hans-Georg, 61–62
Gassen, Kurt, 3
Geiger, Abraham, 217
Geiger, Ludwig, 217, 219, 223
Geist, 40, 45, 68, 81, *See also* spirit: objective spirit:
  subjective spirit; *Kultur*
George Circle. *See* George, Stefan
George, Stefan, 2, 168, 219, 223, 247, 248, 250, 287
  George Circle, 287–289, 291
Gerhardt, Uta, 120
German Idealism. *See* Idealism
German Society for Ethical Culture, 102
German spirit. *See* spirit
Germanism, 153, 245, 246, 247, 248, 249, 250, 255,
  256, 262, 263, 265, 266–268, 280, *See also*
  Romanism
Gesamtkunstwerk, 267

Giotto di Bondone, 266
Goethe, 12, 161, 223–224, 228–231, 232, 233–235,
  237–242, 244–245, 256, 259, 261, 262, 273,
  291–292
Goethe, Johann Wolfgang von, 11, 12, 14, 20, 22,
  23, 25, 27, 35, 36, 37–38, 40, 46, 72, 94, 96,
  97, 123, 144, 145, 148, 164, 165, 172, 198,
  214–245, 248, 250, 255, 256, 261–264, 267,
  268, 284, 289–290, 291, 292, 295
Goethe Society, 217, 220, 225
Gogarten, Friedrich, 282
Gothic, 249, 250, 254, 255, 256, 264–266
grace, 165–167, 173
graciousness, 169–170
Grafton, Anthony, 55
gravity, 169, 170, 171
Greeks, ancient, 17, 19, 20, 21, 22, 36, 44, 53, 57,
  60–61, 63, 142, 168, 239, 250, 263, 265
Grimm, Herman, 91, 116, 216, 217, 219, 223,
  247, 248
Grimm, Jacob, 216
Grimm, Wilhelm, 216
Gumplowicz, Ludwig, 110
Gundolf, Friedrich, 228, 287–290

harmony, 13, 17, 19, 20, 24, 50, 60, 67, 80, 82, 83,
  88, 90, 95, 96, 116, 146, 166–170, 172, 173,
  205, 208, 209, 220, 232, 233, 235, 238, 251,
  265, 273, 280, 284, 286, 291
Harnack, Adolf von, 24–25, 33, 183, 187
Harnack, Otto, 226
Hartmann, Eduard von, 149–151
Havenstein, Martin, 242, 243
Heath, Arthur George, 29
Hegar, Alfred, 23
Hegel, G.W.F., 20, 26, 27, 30, 35–36, 40, 46,
  47–49, 50, 51–52, 61, 62, 68, 150, 193, 280,
  282, 284, 285, 291
Hegelianism, 29, 30, 54
Heidegger, Martin, 243
Heine, Heinrich, 95
Helmholtz, Hermann von, 61, 129
Heraclitus, 263
Herder, Johann Gottfried, 40, 105
Hillebrand, Karl, 27–28, 63
Hiller, Kurt, 285
Hippel, Theodor Gottlieb von, 193–194, 202
Hobbes, Thomas, 225
Hofmannsthal, Hugo von, 236
Hölderlin, Friedrich, 20–21, 38
Homer, 55
Huch, Ricarda, 168
humanism, 29, 39, 40, 57, 58, 59–60, 64, *See also*
  neo-humanism
  Third Humanism, 63

Humboldt, Alexander von, 27
Humboldt, Wilhelm von, 26, 27, 41, 46, 47, 49, 50, 54, 55, 73, 145, 197, 198–199, 216
Hume, David, 144
Hurwicz, Elias, 8

Idealism, 57, 129, 204
  British Idealism, 54
  German Idealism, 18, 45, 47, 49, 51–52, 57, 75, 124, 145, 282
immanent transcendence, 254, 255, 260
impressionism, 209
individualisation, 18, 93, 94, 105–108, 121, 138, 206, 251, 259, 266
individualism, 81, 95, 104, 105, 106, 107, 112, 116, 120, 138, 154, 179, 198, 204, 229, 230, 232, 259, 260, 268, 280
individuality, 24, 32, 37–38, 39, 47, 49, 82, 93, 94, 99, 100, 103–112, 114, 115, 138, 154, 156, 158, 188, 202, 223, 230, 253, 255, 258, 259–260, 261, 263–264, 266, 267
intellectualism, 129, 139, 141, 142, 143, 144, 231
interaction, 10, 17, 106, 112, 118, 120, 121, 165, 227
Introduction to Moral Sciences, 6, 16, 139, 151, 175
inward culture. *See* culture
Italy, 5, 91, 92, 239, 240, 245, 248, 252, 255, 265

Jacobi, Friedrich Heinrich, 224
Jaeger, Werner, 63–64, 67
Jesus, 43, 150, 183, 282, 289
Jews, 7–8, 115–116, 136, 188, 195, 217, 255, 267, 287, 291
Joël, Karl, 83
Judaism. *See* Jews

Kaiser Wilhelm Society, 24
Kandal, Terry, 194
Kant, 121, 122, 123, 128, 129, 130, 132, 133, 139–142, 143, 144, 146, 147, 277
Kant and Goethe, 70, 220, 221, 225, 231, 232
Kant, Immanuel, 14, 25, 30, 52, 53–54, 72, 73, 85, 94, 98, 99, 121–144, 145, 146, 154, 155, 156, 161, 165, 197, 214, 218, 220, 221–222, 224, 225, 235, 277–278, 287, 291, 293
Kant Society, 122, 123
Kantorowicz, Gertrud, 173, 271
Kautsky, Karl, 192
Keyserling, Hermann Graf von, 261, 271
Kierkegaard, Søren, 282, 284
Klages, Ludwig, 205
Klemm, Gustav, 69
Kluckhohn, Clyde, 74
Köhnke, Klaus Christian, 7, 109
Kracauer, Siegfried, 286
Kroeber, A.L., 74

Kugler, Franz, 247
Kultur, 67–75, 83, 94, 287, 294, *See also* culture
Kulturprotestantismus. *See* Protestantism

Lamprecht, Karl, 73
Langbehn, Julius, 23–24, 99, 246
Lange, F.A., 123, 124, 125
Lasker, Eduard, 21–22
Lassalle, Ferdinand, 26
Lazarus, Moritz, 7, 91, 92, 109–112, 115, 116, 135, 179, 199
Leck, Ralph, 285
Leibniz, Gottfried Wilhelm, 24–25, 27, 46–47, 49, 226, 227, 230, 231, 236
Leonardo da Vinci, 27, 248, 252
Lessing, Gotthold Ephraim, 61
liberal theology, 24, 178, 179, 183, 282
liberalism, 22, 28, 33, 76, 103, 104, 152, 154, 194, 196, 202, 203, 232, 233, 269
Lichtblau, Klaus, 155
Lichtenberg, Georg Christoph, 149
Liebermann, Max, 246
Liebmann, Otto, 123, 124, 125
Liesegang, Paul [Simmel's pseudonym], 101
life, 10, 17, 90–91, 133, 143, 144, 148, 149, 152, 154, 155, 156, 161, 167, 169, 172, 177, 181, 186, 190, 209, 212, 226, 227–231, 237, 241–242, 244, 251, 253, 254, 255, 256–267, 272, 273, 275, 295, *See also* form; more-life; more-than-life
life experience. *See Erlebnis*
life-philosophy, 3, 6, 25, 85, 148, 149, 211, 225, 227, 228, 229, 230, 231, 244, 245, 250, 261, 272, 282
life process, 177, 230, 231, 233, 241, 257, 260
life stream, 91, 209, 227, 229, 231, 241, 256, 257, 260, 261
Lippert, Julius, 73, 74
Litt, Theodor, 36
Locke, John, 144
love, 94, 95–96, 159, 161, 186, 196, 201, 203, 230, 253, 254, 277, 281
Lovejoy, Arthur, 49–50, 66
Löwith, Karl, 35, 36, 281
Ludwig, Emil, 243
Lukács, Georg, 286
Luther, Martin, 43
Lutheranism, 41, 59, 105, 179, 183

Mach, Ernst, 128
macrocosm, 49, 66, 146
Maeterlinck, Maurice, 154, 288
Main Problems of Philosophy, 6, 211, 283
Maistre, Joseph de, 104
mammonism, 286
Mann, Heinrich, 153

Mann, Thomas, 218
Marburg School. *See* neo-Kantianism
Marées, Hans von, 252
Marr, Wilhelm, 26
Marx, Karl, 105, 284–285
Marxism, 101, 105, 136, 193, 285
masculinity. *See* men
matriarchy, 204–205
mechanisation, 26, 65, 69, 114, 271, 286
mediaeval. *See* Middle Ages
Meier-Graefe, Julius, 251
Meister Eckhart, 41, 188, 242, 282–283
men, 190, 192, 193, 194, 196–208, 210–213, 277,
    291, 292, *See also* women
Meunier, Constantin, 154
Michelangelo Buonarroti, 91, 208, 247, 248, 251,
    253–255, 263, 265, 277, 281
microcosm, 49, 66, 146, 229, 241
Middle Ages, 18, 39, 63, 91, 92, 93, 114, 178, 283
modernism, 209, 248, 249
Moltke, Helmuth von, 97–98
Mommsen, Theodor, 24, 33, 60
monism, 30, 90, 155, 156, 286, *See also* dualism
more-life, 148, 155, *See also* life
more-than-life, 79, 155, 156, *See also* life
Morris-Reich, Amos, 7
Morwitz, Ernst, 248
Müller-Lyer, Franz, 203
mysticism, 41–43, 82, 92–93, 154, 157, 188, 226,
    235, 242, 282, 283–284, 286, 295

Napoleon Bonaparte, 290
national character. *See* character
National Liberals, 21
National Protestantism. *See* Protestantism
National Socialism, 4, 62
national spirit. *See* spirit
nationalism, 152, 247, 269, 286, 287
Natorp, Paul, 129, 131, 134, 136, 271
neo-humanism, 39–41, 44–45, 47, 50, 51, 54–55,
    57, 59, 60–61, 145, *See also* humanism
neo-Kantianism, 6, 52–54, 85, 122–139, 142,
    143–144, 145, 221, 234, 287, 293
    Marburg School, 122, 129, 130, 134–136, 142
    Southwest School, 20, 52, 64, 122, 134–137, 142
neo-Platonism, 41, 44
Neumann, Carl, 246, 251
Newton, Isaac, 125, 126
Nicholas of Cusa, 186
Niethammer, Friedrich Immanuel, 39
Nietzsche, Friedrich, 3, 19–20, 21, 23, 26, 45, 56,
    62, 63, 64, 67, 83, 85, 94, 116, 119, 146–150,
    152–156, 159–160, 167, 180, 182, 197, 198, 215,
    218, 219, 221, 223, 248, 277, 290
nihilism, 137, 150, 151, 152, 154

Nolde, Emil, 246
nominalism, 106
Nordic spirit. *See* spirit: northern spirit
northern spirit. *See* spirit

objectification, 60, 85, 157, 158, 170, 206, 210, 211,
    229, 241–242, 257
objective culture. *See* culture
objective religion. *See* religion
objective spirit. *See* spirit
objectivity, 16, 17, 25, 55, 60, 61, 80, 127, 128–132,
    150, 151, 155, 180, 200, 205, 207, 208, 210, 213,
    229, 230, 239, 240, 242, 261, 276
Oesterreich, Konstantin, 122
On Social Differentiation, 103, 106–109, 112–115,
    116, 117, 120, 138
Oppenheimer, Franz, 33
optimism, 22, 27, 30, 33, 38, 89, 115, 116, 117, 135,
    148, 150, 159, 186, 205, 273, 294
Ortega y Gasset, José, 243

pantheism, 40, 45, 66, 175, 227, 231, 279, 283
part. *See* whole and part
patriarchy, 196, 204
Paulsen, Friedrich, 33, 39, 134, 137, 150, 151,
    152, 221
personal culture. *See* culture
personality, 16, 17, 19, 29, 30, 32, 33, 37–41, 46–49,
    51, 60, 63, 66, 68, 69, 75, 77, 80, 81, 82, 84,
    86, 96, 106, 108, 111, 112, 113, 121, 138, 167,
    200, 206, 233, 258
    personality of God, 66, 175
pessimism, 31, 33, 38, 51, 86, 87, 116, 136, 148,
    149–152, 156, 157, 159, 163, 187, 295
Pestalozzi, Johann Heinrich, 73
Pettenkofer, Max von, 32
philistinism, 21, 28, 62, 64, 168, 218, 219, 238, 278,
    289, 291
Philosophical Culture, 85, 175, 176, 210, 213, 237,
    253, 254, 281
Philosophy of Money, 6, 17, 85, 86, 88, 209
Pico della Mirandola, Giovanni, 58
pietism, 37, 41, 42
piety, 184–185, 222, 255, 260
Pilate, Pontius, 289
Pindar, 290
Plato, 24, 49, 159, 225
Plessner, Helmuth, 65, 67
pluralism, 135, 136, 137, 158, *See also* plurality
plurality, 53, 64, 69, 135, 137, 149, 155, 156, 158–160,
    177, 190, 211, 231, *See also* pluralism
Pocock, J.G.A., 10
positivism, 23, 25, 52, 102, 103, 108, 109, 128, 145,
    219, 220
post-modernism, 249

pragmatism, 30, 85, 131, 143

professionalisation, 5, 6, 21, 25, 27, 29, 31, 32, 55, 58, 64, 67, 111, 218, *See also Beruf;* vocation

progress, 22, 24, 27, 32, 71, 77, 90, 93, 103, 105, 111, 114, 126, 165, 178, 203

prostitution, 117, 193, 194, 195

Protestantism, 5, 43, 59, 105, 187, 277, 280, 283
   Kulturprotestantismus, 7, 179
   National Protestantism, 245

proto-Romantic, 198, 218, *See also* Romantics

Prussian Academy of Sciences, 24, 25

psychology of peoples. *See Völkerpsychologie*

Pufendorf, Samuel, 68

Rammstedt, Otthein, 1, 120

Raphael Santi, 216, 247

rationalism, 23, 42, 93, 133, 138, 144, 282

Ravaillac, François, 269

reactionaries, 26, 65, 104, 198

Reformation, 41, 183

reification, 86, 87, 274

relationism, 106, 212

relative. *See* absolute versus relative

religion, 16, 18, 20, 25, 76, 82, 118, 141, 145, 161, 173–190, 247, 260–261, 275, 284, 290, *See also* religiosity
   objective religion, 181, 182, 260
   subjective religion, 182, 183, 184, 260, 261

Religion, 7, 141, 173–178

religiosity, 179–186, 189, 190, 214, 234, 260, 261, *See also* religion

Rembrandt, 90, 161, 182, 244, 256–268

Rembrandt as Educator, 23, 98, 99–100, 102, 246, 249

Rembrandt Harmenszoon van Rijn, 14, 94, 148, 175, 223, 244–250, 252, 255–268, 280, 291

Renaissance, 18, 19, 21, 24, 39, 59, 221, 245, 247–249, 254, 263, 266, 281

Renaissancism, 245

republicanism, 32, 65

revisionism, 136, 285

revolution, 154, 204, 271, 284, 285, 287
   conservative revolution, 65, 75
   French Revolution, 193
   Revolution of 1848, 284

Revolution of 1848. *See* revolution

Rickert, Heinrich, 3, 52, 53–54, 134, 136, 195

Riehl, Alois, 129, 153

Rilke, Rainer Maria, 180

Ripke-Kühn, Leonore, 287

Ritschl, Albrecht, 179–180, 183, 186, 188

Rodin, Auguste, 18, 208, 209, 248, 249, 250–253, 254–255, 263, 281

Romanism, 245–249, 255, 256, 262, 267, 268, *See also* Germanism

Romans, ancient, 19, 24, 53, 60, 265

Romanticism. *See* Romantics

Romantics, 25, 197, 198, 204, 230, 246, 247, 248, *See also* proto-Romantic
   Romanticism, 50, 105, 196

Rome, 164, 167, 171

Rousseau, Jean-Jacques, 36, 193

Royal Bavarian Academy of Sciences, 33

Rubens, Peter Paul, 247

Rüegg, Walter, 60–61

Ruskin, John, 28

Russia, 5, 196

Saint-Simonians, 232

scepticism, 97, 127, 133, 137

Schäffle, Albert, 32, 73, 105–106, 108, 110, 115, 179

Scherer, Wilhelm, 217

Schiller, Friedrich, 25, 36, 47, 57, 61, 75, 76, 170, 228, 279

Schlegel, August Wilhelm, 96

Schleiermacher, Friedrich, 37–38, 46, 57, 161, 179–180, 184, 185

Schluchter, Wolfgang, 155, 156

Schmitt, Carl, 280, 284, 292

Schmoller, Gustav, 76, 199

scholastics, 43, 92

Schopenhauer and Nietzsche, 70, 147–148, 155, 157–160, 249

Schopenhauer, Arthur, 6, 26, 72, 75, 94, 146–151, 152, 156–161, 170, 171, 172, 197, 198, 234, 249–250, 252

Schumann, Robert, 267

Schweitzer, Albert, 282

Scottish Enlightenment. *See* Enlightenment

Second World War, 61, 280

self-cultivation. *See* cultivation

Semler, Johann Salomo, 178

sensualism, 133, 138, 144

Shaftesbury, Third Earl of, Anthony Ashley Cooper, 44

Shakespeare, William, 96, 223, 228, 263, 264, 266, 267, 268

Shaw, George Bernard, 288

Siebeck, Hermann, 225

social democracy, 101, 136, 192, 194, 284

socialism, 33, 116, 117, 136, 152, 192–193, 194, 220, 284, 286

sociologism, 118, 119, 176, 177

sociology, 14, 16, 70, 76, 78, 85, 99, 100, 102, 104–121, 138, 145, 163, 174

Sociology, 175–177, 179, 199, 217

Solzhenitsyn, Alexandr, 92

soul, 23, 26, 41, 42, 68, 72, 81, 82, 86, 87, 88, 93, 94, 129, 139, 147, 154, 158, 160, 163, 164, 166, 167,

169, 175, 182, 184, 186, 187, 188, 198, 241, 251, 253, 257, 258, 260, 261, 265, 266, 283, 284
beautiful soul, 170, 206, 212
feminine soul, 206, 210
Southwest School. *See* neo-Kantianism
specialisation, 6, 18, 20, 21, 23–25, 28, 30–34, 39, 51, 56, 63, 64, 77, 86, 98, 99, 100, 113, 162, 163, 168, 169, 181, 200, 201, 205, *See also* division of labour
Spencer, Herbert, 85, 104, 106, 109, 199
Spinoza, Benedict de, 224, 227, 231
spirit, 23, 53, 68, 76, 88, 214, 229, *See also* Geist
  absolute spirit, 40, 76
  German spirit, 266, 274, 275, 280, 288
  national spirit, 92
  northern spirit, 255, 264
  objective spirit, 87, 112, 155
  subjective spirit, 81, 87, 112
Spranger, Eduard, 25, 47
St.-Simonians, 104
Stein, Charlotte von, 243
Steiner, Rudolf, 219
Steinthal, Heymann, 71, 91, 109, 110, 115, 199
Strauss, David, 62
subjective culture. *See* culture
subjective religion. *See* religion; *see* also religiosity
subjective spirit. *See* spirit
subjectivity, 78, 81, 86, 127, 129, 130, 132, 146, 171, 179, 180, 184, 187, 206, 210, 229, 239, 240, 242, 261
substance, 47, 128, 161, *See also* function
Susman [von Bendemann], Margarete, 121, 173, 262, 275
Sybel, Heinrich von, 51
symbol, 82, 146, 160, 168, 172, 178, 190, 208, 209, 214, 233–234, 240, 241, 250, 257, 281
symbolism, 248

Taubert, Agnes, 150
thing-in-itself, 124, 126–128, 132, 135, 157
Third Humanism. *See* humanism
third realm, 78, 130, 254, 255, 275
Thouard, Denis, 276
Tocqueville, Alexis de, 104
Tönnies, Ferdinand, 72, 149, 154, 197, 198
totalitarianism, 269
totality, 24, 26, 31, 37, 40, 47, 49, 54, 57, 93, 106, 110, 135, 149, 169, 205, 211–212, 218, 230, 235, 236, 238, 241, 257, 259, 264, 272, 275, 295, *See also* whole and part; unity
tragedy, 20, 28, 29, 57, 79, 82, 85–87, 97, 160, 161, 163, 170, 171, 205, 218, 228, 253, 254, 274, 295
Treitschke, Heinrich von, 22, 24, 26, 63, 116
Troeltsch, Ernst, 97, 178, 183
Tylor, E.B., 69

Übermensch, 153, 154, 182
Ueberweg, Friedrich, 122
Ulmi, Marianne, 210
United States. *See* America
unity, 11, 13, 17, 18, 19, 21, 25, 27, 40, 51, 53–54, 57, 73, 75, 80, 81, 90, 92, 93, 106, 112, 113, 124, 126, 130, 135, 136, 138, 139, 142, 144, 145, 147, 155, 177, 181, 184, 186, 188, 190–191, 200, 204, 209, 210, 219, 220–223, 226, 227, 229–232, 236, 239, 243, 250, 251–252, 253–255, 257–259, 260, 261, 263, 264, 266, 267, 281, 283, 286, 292, 294, *See also* totality; variety
  unity above variety, 88, 89, 190, 209, 211–212, 213, 215, 233–235, 237–242, 250, 262, 268, 274, 275, 291, 295
  unity and variety, 14, 16–89, 149, 162, 165–166, 228, 232, 239, 244, 291, 294
  unity in variety, 46, 49, 80, 88, 89, 90–91, 94, 98, 115–117, 121, 133, 134, 135, 143, 145, 156, 162, 164–165, 169, 173, 186–187, 188, 190, 201, 202, 209, 219, 233, 250, 252, 295
  unity versus variety, 88, 89, 145–146, 156, 157–158, 159–161, 162, 165–168, 169, 171–173, 186–190, 201–202, 206, 207, 208, 209, 211, 214–215, 219, 222, 233, 234, 249, 250, 252, 294
Urphänomen, 172, 173, 224, 227, 230, 235, 236, 241, 291
utilitarianism, 104, 150

Vaihinger, Hans, 123, 130
variety, 11, 31, 37, 38, 41, 46, 90, 124, 168, 214, *See also* plurality; dualism; unity
Venice, 171–172, 189, 209
View of Life, 6, 148
vocation, 21, 58, 59, 83, *See also* Beruf; professionalisation
Völkerpsychologie, 92, 109–111, 112, 115
völkism, 255
Vorländer, Karl, 221

Wagner, Adolph, 25, 32
Wagner, Richard, 71, 72, 248, 267
Watier, Patrick, 269, 272
Weber, Alfred, 26, 28, 76–77, 78–79
Weber, Marianne, 207
Weber, Max, 43, 64, 65, 67, 155–156, 280
Weil, Hans, 41
Weimar Republic, 35
whole and part, 16, 18, 19, 23, 24, 27–29, 31, 33, 48, 49, 57, 66, 100, 108, 113, 115, 160, 185, 186, 200, 236, 241
Wilhelm II, 269
Willmann, Otto, 74
Winckelmann, Johann Joachim, 44

Windelband, Wilhelm, 20–22, 33, 38, 52–54, 116, 125, 134–137, 142, 151
Wölfflin, Heinrich, 247, 248, 256
Wolfskehl, Karl, 205, 289
women, 161, 177, 190–213, 214, 243, 277, 281, 291, 292, *See also* men
worlds of experience. *See* forms of experience
Worringer, Wilhelm, 265–266

Wundt, Max, 37
Wundt, Wilhelm, 32

Young Germany, 218

Zeller, Eduard, 116
Ziegler, Leopold, 75–77
Zionism, 7
Zivilisation, 70–71, 74, *See also* civilisation